ENEMY IN THE EAST

HITLER'S SECRET PLANS TO INVADE THE SOVIET UNION

ROLF-DIETER MÜLLER

Translated by ALEXANDER STARRITT

Published in 2015 by I.B.Tauris & Co. Ltd
6 Salem Road, London W2 4BU
175 Fifth Avenue, New York NY 10010
www.ibtauris.com

Distributed in the United States and Canada Exclusively by Palgrave Macmillan
175 Fifth Avenue, New York NY 10010

ISBN: 978 1 78076 829 8
eISBN: 978 0 85773 537 9

A full CIP record for this book is available from the British Library
A full CIP record is available from the Library of Congress

Library of Congress Catalog Card Number: available

Printed and bound in Sweden by ScandBook AB
Text design, typesetting and eBook by Tetragon, London

The translation of this work was funded by Geisteswissenschaften International – Translation Funding for Humanities and Social Sciences from Germany, a joint initiative of the Fritz Thyssen Foundation, the German Federal Foreign Office, the collecting society VG WORT and the Börsenverein des Deutschen Buchhandels (German Publishers & Booksellers Association).

Contents

List of Illustrations

List of Maps

Introduction

On 22 June 1941, the German Wehrmacht and its allies began their assault on the USSR. The operation was code named 'Barbarossa'. It was the opening move in the largest and bloodiest war in world history. In its first weeks, Hitler's armies marched east, confident of victory despite high losses and a gradual slowing of their advance. But Stalin's empire did not, as expected, collapse under the initial onslaught. The Russian resistance stiffened amid monstrous sacrifices by the Red Army. Although the Germans succeeded in reaching the outskirts of Moscow within a mere five months, Stalin then struck back and knocked the whole German eastern front off balance. It took, however, another forty months for the Soviet armed forces to fight their way down the long road into the west, at which point Hitler killed himself in his bunker and so opened the door to capitulation.

The German–Soviet conflict stands at the centre of World War II history. It was more than a duel between dictators. Hitler conceived of it as an ethnically ideological war of annihilation. He made sure from the German side that the campaign was fought with the utmost intensity and viciousness, and that the occupation of the conquered territories was a criminal one. It was undoubtedly the most extensive war of plunder and obliteration ever seen, one beside whose powers of destruction even the terrors of a Genghis Khan were attenuated. The defeat of Germany destroyed not only the German Reich, but also all the states of Eastern Europe, which were annexed by the Soviet imperium for the next forty years. This division of Europe and the ensuing Cold War between East and West defined an era's politics worldwide.

All this began with the German invasion on 22 June 1941. It is therefore no surprise that this war still stands out in our collective memory and prompts our historians to ask new questions of the past.[1] Many contemporaries even during World War II saw the decision to invade the USSR as Hitler's greatest strategic mistake. The victorious powers considered the planning of this war of aggression one of the Nazi regime's gravest crimes, especially because the German Reich had signed a non-aggression pact with the Soviet Union as recently as August 1939. The invasion that took place perfidiously, treacherously, deceitfully, less than two years later, was entirely unprovoked.

In the explanation he gave the German populace and the soldiers of the Wehrmacht, Hitler claimed that he had been forced to counter Soviet expansionism with a preventive strike.[2] Proponents of this absurd justification can still be found today, a few even among historians and retired generals.[3] To the judges in the Nuremberg War Crimes Tribunal, on the other hand, it was beyond doubt that Barbarossa was a rapacious act of aggression. They did, however, largely accept the interpretation put forward by the accused and their lawyers, namely that Hitler had made the decision himself and, on 31 July 1940, given the military leadership the task of carrying it out. Whether he had been acting more from a strategic or an ideological standpoint remained an open question. While Wilhelm Keitel, as head of the Supreme Command of the Armed Forces (*Oberkommando der Wehrmacht*, OKW), and Alfred Jodl, as head of the OKW's operations staff, were sentenced to death, the High Command of the Army itself (*Oberkommando des Heeres*, OKH) went unpunished. After 1945, Hitler's generals were able to disseminate the uncontested impression that they, after receiving the dictator's decision, had drawn up and implemented an ingenious plan which had failed only because of Hitler's constant meddling. Their worst enemy had not been the Red Army, but rather their own Führer. To the myth of the 'guiltless Wehrmacht' was thus added the myth of its leaders' unimpeachable professionalism.

The theory that Hitler alone was responsible for the attack on the USSR and that he let himself be guided in it by the ideological obsessions whose origins can be read in his early political manifesto, *Mein Kampf*, has become an important pillar in the historical edifice. For decades it has been the mainstay of a far-reaching interpretation of Hitler's foreign policy. This assumes that, with the taking of power, the internal consolidation of his regime and the gigantic policy of rearmament, Hitler was consistently and purposefully moving step by step closer to his actual goal, the war for Lebensraum ('living space') in the east. After Austria and Czechoslovakia, the next victim of German expansionism had to be Poland. These moves were necessary preliminaries for the overthrow of France, which would secure Hitler's rear and so allow him to turn his attention to his real target. The conquest of the USSR would then provide the basis for a 'war of the continents', that is, the war for world domination.

Was Hitler really in possession of this kind of step-by-step plan, or of the ability to carry it out consistently and with tactical nous? Could the USSR really only be the penultimate stage in such a plan? Was Hitler then a brilliant strategist throughout the first years of the war, one who succeeded almost wherever he turned, and who had at his command a Wehrmacht made almost invincible by the tactic of blitzkrieg? An older generation of historians were convinced. It was guided by a series of ground-breaking studies written by historians who were junior officers during the war. They garnered the highest acclaim in the 1960s and 1970s, and to this day they still shape our understanding of what caused or led up to Barbarossa. Andreas Hillgruber and Hans-Adolf Jacobsen are the most prominent proponents of this view. Particularly significant for the interpretation of Hitler's 'step-by-step plan' was Klaus Hildebrand's systematic depiction of the Third Reich's foreign policy. Many German and international historians have followed this line. Even the multi-volume work produced by the Bundeswehr's Military History Research Office, *The German Reich and the Second World War* (*Das Deutsche Reich und der Zweite Weltkrieg*), oriented its comprehensive examination of Operation Barbarossa in its fourth volume (1983) on the same points. Hardly mentioned in that account was an important discovery of Ernst Klink's, who had established that the first military plans and preparations for a war against the USSR were made by the Army High Command (OKH) without any instructions from Hitler. This finding was explained away with the assertion that the OKH had naturally been familiar with Hitler's eastern programme and had, as it were, geared up to meet the dictator's wishes with pre-emptive obedience.[4]

In the past three decades, historical research, public debate and the media in Germany have concerned themselves almost exclusively with Operation Barbarossa's criminal aspects. The Hamburg Institute's disputed Wehrmacht exhibition in 1995 provided a further important impetus to that trend. Today there is hardly any doubt that the Wehrmacht's leadership carries a large proportion of the responsibility for the breakdown of law during the war in the east. Nor is it questioned that this 'war of ideologies' had already been built into the plans and preparations for the campaign, and that this had been expressed in a set of now-notorious instructions.

But was this in any way connected to the audacity of the OKH's operational planning, and is it possible that the top brass allowed themselves to be led by their own anti-Bolshevik, anti-Slavic prejudices? Was the plan for Operation Barbarossa a masterpiece by the German General Staff, in which a few assumptions turned out to be erroneous, a result perhaps of the image of the USSR as a 'clay colossus'? Does the phase of military planning begun in summer 1940 really represent a wholly new approach, one marked by a cockiness born of the intoxicatingly unexpected victory over France – a set of ideas sketched out, 'while, as it were, still in the saddle', as Andreas Hillgruber thought[5] – or were the planners drawing on previous designs? And, between 1933 and 1940, was the notion of war against the Soviet Union no more than a vision of the future propagated by fanatical Nazis, one outside the realm of sober military calculation? Did Hitler, believing himself to be the 'Greatest Field Commander of All Time', have his own ideas for how an eastern war was to be waged?

These are questions that lead onto the field of traditional military history, into the world of the Wehrmacht's operations staffs and decision-makers. Given the widespread dominance of cultural perspectives in today's history-writing, this may seem an old-fashioned approach to the subject, especially as the questions of operational planning and preparation for Barbarossa are considered to have been answered three decades ago. Of course, the new route that this book takes through an old story will have to touch upon political, ideological, social and – above all – economic considerations as and where necessary. But the focus is on military planning.

That is why this investigation does not begin with an analysis of *Mein Kampf*, but with the question of when a war against Russia, or, more precisely, a war to capture Russian territory, became conceivable for politicians and the top brass in Germany, along with an analysis of what axioms were developed and what misgivings were raised in the discussion. The effortfully gained yet ultimately futile victory over the Russian Army in 1917–18 deeply marked the generation of officers who later, as Hitler's generals, planned and led the second war in the east. That these experiences, which Hitler used in developing his Lebensraum ideology, did not lead the German Army down a one-way street to Stalingrad can be demonstrated with a brief overview of the Weimar Republic. Although the military elite did command significant political influence in the first half of the twentieth century, particularly in Germany, they were nevertheless still subordinate to the politicians.

How did the military's leaders adjust after 1933 when, instead of having to plan for a campaign against Poland with the help of the USSR, Hitler's pact with the Poles in 1934 made it conceivable that there would be a war against the Red Army in alliance with Poland and Japan? By drawing in these two countries, each of which had already managed to defeat the Russian Army (in 1920 and 1905 respectively), this investigation has chosen an entirely new perspective. It counters, above all, any attempt to conduct the analysis of the prelude to Barbarossa as a form of German navel-gazing. This kind of insularity marginalises important aspects of German foreign policy and war-planning that – as will be shown – influenced not only how the leading German generals imagined war with Russia before 1939, but how Hitler did, too.

An overview of the operational thinking in the German Army brings to our attention the geographical area between Riga, Minsk and Kiev, which was where the fate of the Russian Army had supposedly been decided in World War I and in the Soviet–Polish War, and where it was to be decided again in the war to come. This book therefore examines the prelude to Barbarossa as a German–Polish–Russian triangle, while always keeping an eye on Japan as the possible Far Eastern partner in a pincer movement to shatter the Red empire. This will bring in a discussion of just how serious the proposals were for an anti-Russian military alliance under the aegis of the Hitler–Piłsudski pact of 1934, and how Hitler's eventual turn against Poland developed into the pact with Stalin. Relations between the German and Polish militaries in the 1930s are still a largely unknown area of historical research. Here we will have to cut our own path.

So the questions to be addressed are: When did plans for a war against the USSR emerge and become a part of the Third Reich's military deliberations? What role was played by the relationship with Poland, the 'anti-Russian trench'? Was Hitler's turn against Poland in spring 1939 intended to create the basis for a subsequent war in the west or in the east? These questions lead to the core of this investigation. And the following arguments are based on the hypothesis that until October 1939 there were a number of different roads that the Germans could have taken into World War II, among them a collision with the Red Army. Contrary to a widespread supposition in history-writing, a German war against the USSR was already both conceivable and possible in 1939.

To illustrate that, this investigation will examine new, little-known and forgotten sources, and recall historical episodes and contexts that, in counterfactual analysis, call the accepted interpretation of Germany's expansionist politics into question. One fundamental caveat to be observed is that a number of things to do with German military planning in 1939 are obscure, because files from the run-up to World War II have been lost, and because some central sources begin somewhat late, such as the war diaries of the OKW (August 1940) and of the Chief of the Army's General Staff, Franz Halder (14 August 1939).[6] Moreover, the accounts of some key sources are questionable and there are a number of out-and-out forgeries.

What is not disputed is that in 1939 Hitler was firmly resolved to unleash a war in Europe as quickly as possible. He wanted finally to command his campaigns and to have 'a free hand in the east'. He had had enough of participating in discussions and accepting compromises. 'Blows' were what he wanted to dispense. To the sequence of those blows he was ultimately indifferent. The evaluation of risk and opportunity was the only discussion he could still stomach. But he was not afraid, if necessary, to lead the feared total war on multiple fronts. For him, the overall course had been set for the last two decades: to Russia!

Hitler was deeply convinced in 1939 that conquering the USSR would be a piece of cake and that it would make his Third Reich unassailable for all time. A Barbarossa in 1939 probably would have led to the collapse of the Soviet Union and the destruction of Russia. Stalin's cooperation was useful only as a bluff against the western powers. When these refused to come to an understanding with Hitler, it cost him a great deal of effort to compel the General Staff to mount a campaign in the west.

The last section of this book will analyse Hitler's decision to again turn his attention eastward in summer 1940. Did the dictator really provide the impetus for it? What role was played by ideology and what ideas did he develop for how to conduct the war? It will have to be taken into account that the generals later charged at the Nuremberg trials had good reason to conceal their early plans against the USSR. How was it that the 1939 model of a small-scale war of intervention became the Operation Barbarossa of conquest and annihilation, which in 1941 operationally failed within a few short weeks? The answer to that question reveals the army's leaders to have borne more responsibility than has hitherto been discussed.

1

GERMANY AND ITS NEIGHBOURS TO THE EAST

Germany's Foreign and Alliance Politics in the Nineteenth Century

A 'Holy Alliance' in the first half of the nineteenth century secured the longest ever period of peaceful and constructive German–Russian cooperation. It was based essentially on a confederation of the three great powers in Central and Eastern Europe – Austria, Prussia and Russia – which had come about as a result of the Napoleonic Wars. Their common interest was in keeping down both France and the revolutionary and nationalist movements that seemed to be spreading from there to threaten the conservative, multinational empires. In the middle of this European triangle of Vienna, Berlin and Moscow lay the Kingdom of Poland, which, after being partitioned three times at the end of the eighteenth century, had now disappeared from the map. Napoleon's reconstructed 'Grand Duchy of Warsaw' had not lasted long and had cost around 100,000 Polish soldiers their lives when the Corsican led them and his Grande Armée into the expanses of Russia. Of the three powers, Russia had annexed the greatest part of Poland.

The postwar order instituted by the Congress of Vienna in 1815 gave Prussia and the subsequent German Empire a long border with Russia for almost exactly a hundred years. For the Polish subjects on either side of this border, however, the dream of their nation's rebirth did not fade away. 'Poland has not yet perished': this was the slogan the intellectuals implanted in the people's hearts. And this was an idea for which Polish people were ready to fight and die. During the nineteenth century, Poland became the biggest source of unrest on the Continent, giving birth to insurrection after insurrection. Most of these were directed against the harsh government of the tsar and concentrated on the capital, Warsaw. But Krakow (Austria) and Poznań (Prussia) also became focal points of Polish discontent, albeit one that remained militarily fruitless.

The Prussian–Russian alliance managed to endure in this stormy century of new departures and radical changes. It was maintained by the powers of monarchy and shaped generations of officers. Among the liberal bourgeoisie in Germany, however, there long prevailed an enthusiasm for Poland, which was bound up with their own democratic and nationalist ambitions.

The stability of these relations with their eastern neighbour changed after the German victory over France in 1870–1. As Prussian prime minister, Otto von Bismarck had placed a high value on the concord with Russia, not least because it was a prerequisite for the unification of the Reich. As chancellor of that Reich, he then attempted to sustain a balance of self-assertion and self-denial. The other great powers had to be convinced that Germany was 'saturated' and would stake no more territorial claims in Europe. Bismarck succeeded in 1873 in establishing the League of the Three Emperors with Austria and Russia, which aligned their political interests in Central Europe and again emphasised that the three great conservative powers would cooperate against dangerous revolutionaries.[1]

This consensus in security policy, however, proved to be fragile and required constant German efforts to shore it up. Austria-Hungary and Russia pursued rival ambitions in the Balkans, where the weakness of the Ottoman Empire had created a power vacuum. As early as 1878, Bismarck had to play the 'honest broker' to defuse the conflict at the Congress of Berlin, something he managed only in part, as Russia felt it had been mishandled. This led to tensions between Germany and Russia, which were heightened when Berlin, to protect domestic agriculture, imposed high tariffs on Russian imports and in 1887 even excluded the Russians from the German capital market. The tsar's empire was urgently reliant on foreign capital for the modernisation of its economy. It was also vital that Russia extend its railway network, but the tracks being laid in the west of the country were seen in Berlin as a strategic menace, because they would make a Russian advance easier in the event of war.[2]

France, on the other hand, would be able to fulfil its striving for revenge only if it broke up the German–Russian alliance. Paris worked to make that happen, with some success. And Berlin made insufficient efforts to stem this portentous development. Above all, Berlin was not prepared to leave

Austria-Hungary in the lurch as Vienna and Moscow became increasingly opposed to each other.

So the Prussian–German General Staff had to take into account the possibility that a future Franco–Russian alliance would expose Germany to the dangers of a war on two fronts. This prospect triggered a number of planning exercises and analyses. Experience of fighting the Russians had been gathered in the Seven Years War (1756–63), but on their own territory and with erratic success. The death of Empress Elizabeth of Russia in 1762 and the coming to power of her Prussophile son had led Russia to withdraw from the encirclement – the later much-invoked Miracle of the House of Brandenburg, a repeat of which Hitler was still vainly hoping for in April 1945.

The memory of the German–Russian brotherhood-in-arms that secured the victory over Napoleon in 1813–14 had faded within two generations. The German image of Russia was now increasingly influenced by anti-Slavic prejudice. For the Social Democrats, the tsar ruled over an empire of evil, the incarnation of reactionary despotism.[3] In 1849, Friedrich Engels had already demanded 'an implacable struggle to the death against the Slavdom that has betrayed the revolution; a war of annihilation and ruthless terrorism'.[4]

The reverse side of the bourgeois liberal enthusiasm for Poland was a pronounced Russophobia. The Prussian conservatives, who had hitherto been the 'Russian party', complained after the founding of the Reich about increasing competition from cheap eastern grain, which threatened the economic foundations of the Junker society east of the Elbe. The still insignificant but growing number of ultra-nationalists even saw that as a disadvantage in a supposed racial struggle between the Germanic and Slavic peoples, thinking it weakened the German rampart in the east.[5]

The Polish population, in any case, was exposed to pressure on both sides. The pan-Slavism pursued by Russia did not protect the tsar's Polish subjects from the duress of Russification, while, on the Prussian side, as the nineteenth century came to a close, cultural warfare and increased settlement were used to strengthen the German element in the eastern provinces and forcibly integrate the Polish populace.

As Chancellor, Bismarck encouraged this pressure, but simultaneously made sure to maintain the Russian treaty that was covering his back. He viewed military eagerness for conquest with the greatest scepticism. When in 1887 Bernhard von Bülow, the German chargé d'affaires in St Petersburg, demanded a pre-emptive war against Russia, Bismarck was severe in dismissing the idea. Bülow who, when he became chancellor himself, again put his faith in a German–Russian alliance, became at that time the first politician in German history to develop further-reaching ideas for a war against Russia.

Bülow in a letter of 1887:

We will have to drain the Russian of so much blood that [...] he is unable to stand on his own two feet for the next 25 years. [Margin note from Bismarck: That is not so easily done.] We will have to bury the wellsprings of Russia's economy by devastating its agricultural territories, bombarding its coastal cities and achieving the maximum possible destruction of its industry and trade. We will have to force Russia back from the two seas, the Baltic and the Pontus Euxinus [the Black Sea], on which its global position is based. I believe Russia will be truly and lastingly weakened, however, only by removal of those regions lying to the west of a line Onega Bay–Valdai Hills–Dnieper. A peace of this sort [...] could be dictated only if we were standing on the banks of the Volga...[6]

This was a case of radical fantasy, fed by fear of war on two fronts. Bülow's strategy may remind us of Hitler, but for him it was about weakening Russia rather than destroying it. And of course Bülow was aware that the gigantic empire in the east would defend itself with all its might. In the Reichstag, Bismarck gave these kinds of ideas a clear rebuff: 'Russia does not wish to conquer any German territory, and we wish no Russian. It could only be Polish provinces, and of those we already have more than we are comfortable with.'[7]

For the purposes of this book, it is important to note that even the German leadership's first discussions of a war against Russia apparently bore in mind the Napoleonic experience and did not assume that it would be possible to completely defeat and occupy the enormous empire in the east. What could, however, be imagined were military victories against the Russian Army on the Polish battlefields. Officers of the Austrian General Staff, who sometimes also had the ear of Crown Prince Wilhelm, the future kaiser, argued for a pre-emptive war to counter the supposedly mounting Russian menace. A glance at the map immediately suggested cutting off the tsar's Polish 'balcony'; German troops could advance from East Prussia, and Austrian troops from Galicia to encircle and annihilate Russia's western armies. But would that induce far-off Moscow to accept a subjugating peace? And what would be won if the tsar, as Bismarck might easily assume, simply relinquished his Polish provinces?

If the tsar instead mobilised the inexhaustible forces of his empire, the next steps in such a war would be offensives against the Baltic states and towards the Ukraine, with the aim of destroying Russia's most important regions of production. But would that kind of operation force Russia permanently to its knees? Bismarck and the Reich's chiefs of staff doubted it. Field Marshal Helmuth Moltke (the Elder) did, however, think it would be possible to defend the Baltic states – once they had been annexed as Prussian provinces – against Russian attack by constructing a front by Lake Peipus and the swamps of the western Dvina.[8] Nonetheless, from the perspective of the Reich's leaders at the end of the nineteenth century, war against Russia would be a 'misfortune' from which Germany would gain nothing and not even cover its own costs.[9]

The idea of not destroying Russia's supposed 'life sources', but instead capturing them and using them to lift Germany to the status of a global power, was to become influential in German planning only a generation later, during World War I. Although some of the conceptual roots of Hitler's war in the East can undoubtedly be found here, it would be excesssive to imply there was any continuity of thought. The alternatives and contradictions in the Reich's Russian policy – and in the policies of its successors – remained all too distinct.[10]

While Bismarck would probably have been willing, if it came to it, even to abandon the Habsburg empire if that meant avoiding a war on two fronts, his opponents in the Foreign Ministry and the General Staff insisted after 1890 on unconditional adherence to the alliance with Vienna. The former general Leo von Caprivi, who replaced Bismarck as chancellor that year, steered his 'new course' towards this Central European bloc, hoping for support from the great naval power, Britain. He believed that that could counter the threatened Franco–Russian alliance.

As kaiser, however, Wilhelm II accelerated the building of a fleet to rival Great Britain's, while Bülow, named chancellor in 1900, tried to pursue 'global politics' by returning to the traditional alliance with Russia. Bülow failed and in 1907 Great Britain and Russia came to an understanding about their interests in Asia. With that, the 'Entente Cordiale' between Paris and London extended into an encirclement of the Reich. What must be underlined, though, is that the growing ideological enmity towards Russia in Germany at the beginning of the twentieth century did not yet overlay the power-political and strategic considerations of the Reich's leadership. The recognition that their forces might be overmatched, however, nourished a need among politicians and the military to draw on ideological justifications and reassurances.

The image of Russia became two-faced: on one side, an insistence on the dangers of Russia's expansionist politics and, on the other, the assessment of Russia as a 'clay colossus'. During Wilhelm's reign, the militant propaganda of Baltic-German journalists transformed this image into the idea of a German 'drive eastward'. After 1905, this attained a dominant position in public opinion. If all that was needed to make the Russian Empire collapse was one solid blow, the strategic and economic gains could be sufficiently tempting to make the Germans consider an eastward expansion. Ideological justifications could be easily found.

At the height of the Balkan crisis in 1912, Moltke (the Younger), in his role as chief of the General Staff, advocated a pre-emptive war against both Continental powers: that is, against France and Russia. In 1913, he declared in Vienna, 'that a European war must come sooner or later, which at heart will be a war between the Germanic peoples and the Slavs. Preparing for that is the duty of all the states that are standard bearers of Germanic culture. The attack, however, must by made by the Slavs.' Although it can be seen here that some of the slogans of racial ideology have been adopted, they are still being used as political instruments. Moreover, Moltke was arguing in view of a threat that was supposed to originate not solely from the east and whose full military significance lay in the prospect of a war on two fronts.

War on the eastern border was evidently unpopular, so Wilhelm II called for a publicity campaign to 'better prepare the popularity of a war against Russia', and with considerable success; in spring 1914, there was an anti-Russian wave of downright hatred. Leaving aside the often rambling fantasies in journalism and some of the stated aims among political radicals, which ran to the subjugation and colonisation of Russia, this was no more than part of a 'nervous perception of reality' (Joachim Radkau) at the end of the 'long nineteenth century'. The image of the east was subject to drastic changes in tone.[11]

The military, in any case, stuck to their plans for a battle on Polish soil, which would be waged defensively in East Prussia and Galicia so as to free up the bulk of their forces for the defeat of their main enemy, France, in the west. That was where, the General Staff was convinced, the war would be decided. A subsequent turn to the east could then become a battle for the Polish balcony. The destruction of Russia's western armies would presumably induce Moscow to back down. In that case, however, the Germans would demand more than the mere relinquishing of Polish provinces.

World War I and the Rebirth of Poland

The First World War began differently from how the German side had planned. Unexpectedly quick and massive Russian advances brought the Central Powers' eastern front into difficulties. Austria-Hungary was even forced to beat a hasty retreat from Galicia. At the improvised encirclement at Tannenberg in East Prussia, however, the Germans managed to destroy the attacking Russian 2nd Army. For this propagandistically inflated victory they paid a high price: the Battle of the Marne was broken off in the west, and with it went the hope of a swift end to the war. The feared war of attrition began. For the next four years, the main part of the German armed forces fought in the trenches of the western front.

The forces stationed in the east were insufficient for the Germans to defeat the Russian Army in the following years, despite the victory at Tannenberg. The notion of a decisive battle near their own border proved impossible to realise in view of the Russians' tenacious resistance and their huge offensives in 1915–16, as well as, and not least because of, the weakness of the Austro-Hungarian 'wing' in the south-east. In three years of arduous combat, the Central Powers succeeded merely in pushing their Russian opponent back to the line drawn from Riga to the mouth of the Danube.

It was only the internal collapse of the tsarist empire at the end of 1917 that again breathed life into German hopes for a victory in the east. To achieve that collapse, the Army High Command had played a trump card in the form of a certain Mr Lenin. Driven through Germany and into the east on a sealed train of the Reichsbahn from his exile in Zurich, the leader of the Bolsheviks, equipped with several million goldmarks, succeeded in carrying out the revolutionary machinations that caved in the Russian front and allowed him to conduct peace talks with the Germans. As chaos and civil war broke out, the Central Powers were able at the onset of 1918 to make an advance deep into the east, despite the fact that they were simultaneously deploying all available strength on the western front to wrest a victory before the overwhelming arrival of the US Army.

In retrospect, most Germans' memory of the hard three-year struggle for the Polish territories quickly faded. The military, in particular, preferred to remember the victorious second phase (1917–18) on the eastern front. For Corporal Adolf Hitler, a dispatch runner in the emplacement network on the western front who had been forced into the trenches by enemy bombardment, the long advance into Russian territory in 1918 provided the starting point for his visions of global power. All of them suppressed the memory that this 'railroad advance' had not been the result of German military proficiency, nor of work by the General Staff. The Germans attained the greatest success of their military history, the defeat of Russia, by means of their *political* warfare. That victory made it possible for them to dictate the peace treaty signed in Brest-Litovsk in March 1918, in which Lenin agreed that the Baltic provinces would become German duchies and that the Ukraine would be a protectorate of the Central Powers.

It was, as is well known, an exceedingly fragile victory, and not enough to prevent the downfall of the German Reich. The outcome of World War I was decided in the fight against the western powers. Victory in the east could not outweigh it. That, too, was very rapidly forgotten in Germany. What remained distinct, though contradictory, was the memory that they had been supported by the various nationalities striving for independence on the periphery of the Russian Empire.

One great success, which became the keystone of a 'loyal' friendship in both world wars, was the creation of a Finnish rifle battalion from Russian prisoners of war. In 1916–17, the unit fought on the German side against the Russians at Riga. In 1918, it formed the basis of the Finnish Army under Carl Gustaf Emil Mannerheim, a former tsarist general. In the Baltic provinces and the Ukraine, too, there were nationalist forces agitating for independence. The Germans succeeded only partially in using them for their own ends. After the Germans' withdrawal in autumn 1918, a number of newly established indigenous regimes had to seek military backing from the victorious western powers. The Baltic states succeeded: the Ukraine did not. The Ukrainians, divided among themselves, had to ward off attacks not only from the east by Lenin's Red Army, which followed the departing Germans, Austrians and Hungarians, but also from Polish units west of the Dnieper.

During World War I, the German Reich had particularly high expectations of the Poles.[12] The tsar and the kaiser in Vienna, too, had assumed that a few vague promises would be enough to motivate their Polish recruits to fight, as well as to persuade their countrymen on the other side of the front to defect. After all, 1.5 million Polish soldiers served in the armies of the three partitioning powers, and the Polish provinces were their battlefield.

The Austrians had made the best preparations for this in the time before the war. The Polish Socialist Party was represented at the state council in Vienna and played a conspicuous role under Józef Piłsudski. The former revolutionary, terrorist and Russian convict had hoped, in the event of war, to be able to provoke an uprising in the part of Poland annexed by Russia, the former Congress Poland, and so use a 'great war' as a means of winning back a Polish state. The double monarchy (Austria-Hungary) would perhaps become a triple monarchy. As early as 1908, Vienna allowed him to form the Association of Active Struggle, in which Piłsudski gathered followers and gave them military training. This paramilitary organisation of volunteer riflemen (Strzelec) was able to field three battalions upon the outbreak of war. And although the advance of these poorly armed legionaries on Kielce in August 1914 proved a failure, because the wider military situation demanded a precipitous withdrawal, volunteers for his legion continued to arrive. Piłsudski had been able to set down a marker, to show that there were Polish soldiers in Polish uniforms again. In 1915, he had three brigades totalling 20,000 men at his command as the Central Powers' summer offensive forced the Russians backwards out of the Polish balcony.

But Piłsudski did not want to deploy his volunteers as cannon fodder for other nations and insisted on receiving unambiguous political commitments. With the occupation of Warsaw, the Germans came more strongly into play. They, however, disagreed among themselves about Poland's future. From the perspective of the governor general, Hans von Beseler, an autonomous Kingdom of Poland could be an ally against the Russians in the future. After all, in the former Congress Poland alone there were more than 800,000 militarily eligible men who hadn't been conscripted by the tsar's army and who could be rallied under the Polish flag. A pretender to the throne, however, quickly turned the offer down. After the costly experiences of his forefather Augustus II the Strong in the eighteenth century, the king of Saxony did not want to again reach for the Polish crown.

The opposite political opinion was held by the Army High Command, which was at this point advocating a conciliatory peace with Russia, including the restoration of prewar borders. Interest in an even partly autonomous Poland was scant among Prussian conservatives. The great landowners east of the Elbe were reliant on a cheap Polish workforce. Strengthening the Poles' national consciousness would only heighten existing problems of integration. On the other hand, the conservatives did discover that they had an interest in liberating the Ukraine from the Russian Empire.

1. Józef Piłsudski as commander of the Polish Legions during World War I.

Hardly had the Russian summer offensive in 1916 been beaten back in heavy fighting when the military urged that the losses be partly replaced with Polish volunteers. Thus, on 5 November 1916, the German kaiser, Wilhelm II, and the Austrian kaiser, Franz Joseph, proclaimed that they had founded a Kingdom of Poland, which was to encompass only territories that had belonged to Russia and remain heavily reliant on the Central Powers. Tsar Nicholas II's own promise of an autonomous Poland, issued six weeks later with the prospect of territorial gains at the expense of the Central Powers, was equally unattractive from the Polish point of view.

As yet, the Polish territories were still in German and Austrian hands. The act of state on 5 November also announced the formation of a Polish Army. Its core would be made up of those legions already fighting on the eastern front under Austro-Hungarian command. They were now transferred to German command. Some of the troops refused, however, to take an oath of loyalty to either an imaginary Polish king or the German and Austrian kaisers. These soldiers were disarmed and some were drafted directly into German units; 'ringleaders' were arrested and Piłsudski was imprisoned in the fortress of Magdeburg. Imprisoned at the same time in the fortress of Ingolstadt was a tsarist Guards officer called Mikhail Tukhachevsky. After several futile escapes, leading to recapture, he was able to join the Bolshevik uprising in Russia in 1917. Three years later, he and Piłsudski were facing each other on the battlefield outside Warsaw.

With the disintegration of the Russian front in 1917, a Polish contribution no longer seemed of urgent interest. So, in 1918 the Germans ignored Polish dismay as they promoted independence for Lithuania and the Ukraine, both of which bore heavily on historical Polish ambitions. All political camps in Poland breathed easier when, in autumn, the German western front began to totter. Now the Poles could count on western help in setting up a far larger independent state. In France, General Józef Haller was standing ready with his 'Blue Army' of 70,000 Polish volunteers and former prisoners of war.

Meanwhile, the German Army was concentrating on creating a paramilitary protection force for the eastern border and on having to vacate all the outposts it had been trying to cling to, particularly in the Baltic states. Polish units, some of which had fought for the Germans on the Russian front, took over the eastern provinces of the collapsed Austro-Hungarian monarchy, the former Habsburg Kingdom of Galicia and Lodomeria. In its capital, Lviv, however, the Ukrainian nationalists had declared their own independence. Their military proved to be too weak and too divided to halt the Polish advance. These were territories with a Polish minority, which itself took part in the fighting. In this Polish–Ukrainian War, there was heavy fighting around Lviv at the end of 1918 before Polish volunteers and regular troops succeeded in occupying the city.

Since then there has been a cemetery in Lviv for Polish soldiers, where the graves of numerous child soldiers are to be found. Among the 'Orlęta Lwowskie', the 'Lviv Eaglets' was 14-year-old Jurek Bitschan. A lugubrious ballad from 1919 tells the story of his death. Two Ukrainian shells tore him apart on 21 November 1918 as his mother commanded a women's battalion on another section of the front.

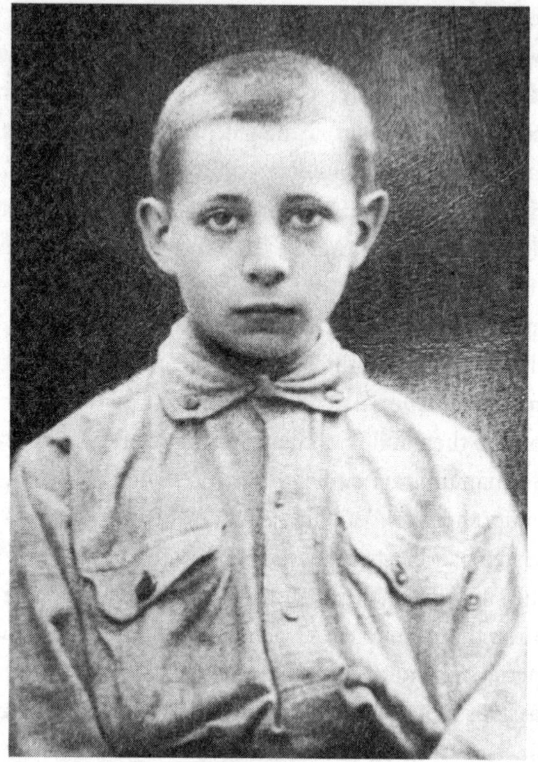

2. Jurek Bitschan, member of the 'Lviv Eaglets', killed in November 1918.

A treaty with the nationalist Ukrainian People's Republic under Symon Petlyura in April 1919 halted the fighting only temporarily, because now the Soviet-Russian troops entered the arena. Polish forces secured old historical claims along the Dnieper. At times, as in the seventeenth century, they even controlled Kiev, until a breakthrough by the Bolshevik General Budyonny's legendary cavalry army forced them to retreat, although the Poles managed to hold onto Lviv. After 1920, Galicia was part of 'eastern Poland', something never recognised by western Ukrainians.

The Poles, for their part, did not recognise the border with the new Soviet republic of Byelorussia, which had been drawn along the linguistic border by the British foreign secretary, George Curzon. The Polish claim to the Kresy Wschodnie, the 'Borderlands', was based on the eighteenth-century borders and on the existence of a Polish minority in this heterogeneous territory of various nationalities, religions and cultures. The former western poorhouse of the tsar's empire eventually became the eastern poorhouse of the Second

Polish Republic. Polish advances on Vilnius as well as towards Minsk and Kiev finally made the Red Army their main opponent. Leon Trotsky forged remnants of the Russian Army and Bolshevik supporters into large troop formations that had to fight at every turn: against the White armies of the Civil War, against intervening allied troops and against various nationalist uprisings. At the beginning of 1920, the Red Army also advanced westward to restore the former border of the tsarist empire and, if possible, to spread the world revolution to Western Europe, from which, according to Marxist dogma, its impulse should have come in the first place.

This was the high point of the Polish–Soviet War[13] that Piłsudski and his armies had to contest from 1919 to 1921. Fought between the Vistula and the Dnieper on the then still fresh German battlefields, it elicited very close attention in German military circles of the 1930s. The Army High Command compiled a comprehensive study in 1939–40,[14] as the Germans considered fighting a decisive battle against the Soviet Army on that same terrain. An overview of the situation at the beginning of April 1919, in the initial phase of the war, shows that the Polish armies had positioned themselves behind the natural barriers of the Polesia region, the swamps and forests along the Pripet Marshes. North of them, Germans and Lithuanians held the front along the Neman. In the south, Ukrainian nationalists were fighting their war on two fronts against the Poles and the Red Army.

At the start of 1920, the Poles made a preventive strike to anticipate the imminent Soviet offensive. They captured Daugavpils and handed the city over to Latvia. Their offensive in Byelorussia took them beyond Minsk. The main thrust was made in the Ukraine, crossing the Dnieper near Kiev. The Russians largely avoided them until, on 15 May, Army Group Yegorov began a counter-offensive that forced the Poles to withdraw from Kiev and led to the siege of Lviv. The army group under General Tukhachevsky, to the north of the Pripet Marshes, broke though the passive and flat-footed Polish front, then advanced in a breathtaking forced march to the banks of the Vistula just north of Warsaw.

The Germans oscillated between fear of the Bolsheviks and the faint hope of a joint war against the Entente. To the south of the broad swamp barrier of the Pripet, it took great Polish exertions to delay the advance of the cavalry army under General Budyonny. Nonetheless, they did manage to prevent the two Soviet offensives from joining up. As Warsaw was directly threatened and the morale of the Polish forces seemed to be dwindling,

Piłsudski pulled troops off from the south, organised the resistance and prepared a counter-attack.

Tukhachevsky's vanguard reached the Narew estuary – a situation that was to repeat itself at the beginning of 1944 and allow the Wehrmacht, in the tank battle outside Warsaw, to gain one last operational success against the Red Army.[15] Stalin himself had experienced the 1920 disaster as a political commissar. Twenty-four years later, he was again unable to prevent it. The geography and an operational idea derived from it saved Poland in 1920. This was the 'miracle on the Vistula'. In 1944 the successful German defence of the same spot made it possible for them to crush the Polish nationalist uprising in Warsaw. Poland then fell like a ripe fruit into Stalin's hands – and the country lost its independence for more than four decades.

If we delve into the military particulars of the war in 1920, two factors come to the fore. Firstly, the significance of the area's geography, which gave tactical importance to certain rivers, towns and routes of advance, which is why the same towns and rivers come up in the accounts of operations in the two world wars. Secondly, rapid, long-range advances and surprising concentrations of force, when firmly and decisively led, allowed even numerically inferior armies to defeat their opponents. The cavalry was again able to demonstrate, at least in this region, its importance as a means of making quick and wide-ranging movements with large numbers of troops.

In August 1920, in any case, Piłsudski mounted a far-ranging counter-attack from the area around Brest towards Białystok and managed to transform the Russian offensive, already halted outside Warsaw, into a hasty retreat. In the end, large parts of the three Soviet armies were destroyed. Piłsudski's vanguard was formed of the legionary divisions trained under German command during the Great War. Tukhachevsky's elite unit, the 4th Army, was pressed back towards the East Prussian border. To elude capture, they needed German help. So the remnants of that army crossed the border on 25 August. 'A day later, their example was followed by Gai's cavalry corps, which, with red flags flying and singing the Internationale, crossed the border to be disarmed in Germany.'[16] The soldiers of the Red Army could go home.

The appearance of French military advisers in Warsaw strengthened the German military's inclination to bet on the Russians, Bolshevism or no Bolshevism. At that point, the Germans played down both the political and technical significance of Piłsudski's success. That would change in 1934, when Hitler made his pact with the first marshal of Poland. The victory over the

Russian Army in 1920 was certainly equal to the Germans' at Tannenberg in 1914. Tukhachevsky later compared his operation to the German advance on Paris in 1914. His attempt, after the defeat, to organise a new defence on the Neman was smashed by the Poles. They also managed to throw back Budyonny's cavalry army in the south. The war finally ended in March 1921 with the signing of the Peace of Riga. Both sides were exhausted and Poland was, as it were, saturated, because Piłsudski had also managed to secure, if not the borders of 1772, then at least territory to a depth of 120 miles east of the Curzon Line.

A few years after the war, there was a remarkable literary duel between the two commanders. Tukhachevsky analysed his advance on the Vistula in a brief essay – an extract from which was appended in August 1940 to the Wehrmacht's first operational study for an invasion of the USSR[17] – and Piłsudski answered with his own memoirs, in which he engaged with his opposite number fairly, one might even say in comradely fashion. The German translation of both works, united in one volume, appeared in 1935 with an introduction from the Third Reich's defence minister, Werner von Blomberg. This was plainly a teaching text for Hitler's General Staff. More on this later.

Piłsudski, the former revolutionary and military autodidact, had shown himself to be more skilled and more successful in the defence of Poland in 1920 than the formally trained German career officer Erich Ludendorff on the same terrain in 1914–15. Piłsudski won fame fighting for the Germans against the Russians, and then as Europe's saviour from Bolshevism, while a former German corporal was only just beginning his career as a politician and self-proclaimed 'Greatest Field Commander of All Time' in the beer cellars of Munich.

The German–Polish brotherhood-in-arms could have lasted beyond the year 1918. That history took another direction was not due solely to Polish territorial claims on the Reich and to the role that Warsaw took in the 1920s as a bulwark of the French 'encirclement' of Germany. In Berlin, the points had already been set. They prioritised the alliance between the German Army and the Russian revolutionaries that had brought the tsarist empire to collapse in 1917, and they maintained their cooperation with the Red Army of Lenin and Trotsky. Despite Germany's catastrophic defeat, this cooperation enabled them to pursue a secret policy of revision and rearmament that brought the two armies together again in 1939 and led to the outbreak of World War II.

One of the vital players in this game is General Hans von Seeckt.[18] In 1920 he became head of the Army High Command in Berlin and he was one of the men who even in 1918 had been fascinated by the supposed prospect of making Germany a global political force on the foundation of a German–Russian bloc. Together with his then commander-in-chief, August von Mackensen, he was regarded as the architect of the strategically important German victory of Gorlice–Tarnów, which succeeded in 1915 in forcing back the Russians on Polish soil. So Seeckt knew the terrain on which Piłsudski won his fame in 1920. But as the head of the German Army in the Weimar Republic he nonetheless held fast to cooperation with Trotsky's Red Army for reasons of strategy. That this was not just a question of national defence, and that he was also working with ideas of global political power, is demonstrated by the

3. The future chief of the Soviet Union's General Staff, Mikhail Tukhachevsky, as a Red Army officer in 1918.

assignment of Captain Oskar Ritter von Niedermayer to the military's Moscow bureau. Niedermayer had led an expedition to Kabul in World War I and prepared an advance of German and Afghan troops into the heart of the British Empire. As Seeckt's representative in Moscow in the 1920s, he tried to bring about a German–Soviet alliance with the same geopolitical focus. In 1939–40, the time of the Hitler–Stalin pact, he, now an influential professor of geopolitics at Berlin University, found much support for this idea in the military and the Foreign Ministry. In 1942, Stauffenberg, the future would-be assassin of Hitler, arranged for Niedermayer – reactivated as a major-general – to set up a Turkoman infantry division in the occupied Ukraine, which, after a successful German summer offensive, was supposed to march via the Caucasus to India.[19]

But back to the early years of the Weimar Republic, in which the military, as a 'state within the state', chose to dream of better times and work by all legal and illegal means towards 'rising again'. There was complete consensus in this between the military and the Foreign Ministry. The leaders of the Reichswehr, just like the republic's prevailing political circles, rejected the conditions of the 'Versailles Diktat' and strove to restore both the 1914 borders and Germany's position as a great power.[20] On an ideological level, however, there was a broad spectrum of opinion, as there was on precisely what steps and objectives were necessary in revising the outcome of World War I.

Rapallo and the German–Soviet Alliance of Convenience

In the early 1920s, the military's leaders proved, despite their avowed realpolitik, to be subject to certain illusions. Because they saw the association of Paris and Warsaw as a vice-like grip on Germany, they could not imagine so much as successfully defending their own territory. With their small 100,000-man army, no heavy or modern weapons and unstable domestic politics, any opposition to foreign intervention would be doomed to failure.

It is against this background that we must assess the Treaty of Rapallo, made between the German Reich and Soviet Russia in April 1922. Behind the diplomatic smokescreen of normalising relations between the two states was hidden a range of far-reaching military and rearmament agreements, with which Seeckt and Trotsky placed the secret cooperation of the Reichswehr and the Red Army on a new footing.[21] In terms of political ideology, each viewed the other as the very incarnation of evil, but those emotions were put as far aside as possible, because the abyssal hatred of Poland outweighed everything else. The Reichswehr and the Red Army both saw themselves as humiliated by supposed Polish arrogance and keenly sought revenge. Erich von Manstein, the Wehrmacht's greatest operational talent in World War II, later remembered: 'Poland could not be other than a source of bitter feelings for us.'[22] The Poles were regarded as traitors undeservedly demanding the status of a great power.

> **Seeckt in September 1922:**
> Poland's existence is unendurable, incommensurable with Germany's vital needs. It must disappear and will disappear, thanks to its own internal weakness and thanks to Russia – with our help. […] Poland will never offer Germany any kind of advantage, neither economic, because it is not capable of development, nor political, because it is a vassal of France.[23]

The Reichswehr and the Red Army needed each other in the short term. Soviet Russia offered terrain on which the Germans could test and produce banned weapons. In the event of war, it was hoped that great quantities of weapons and munitions could be brought over the Baltic Sea from jointly run Russian factories. It would then also be possible to catch Poland in a pincer movement, although the Red Army would have to provide the main offensive because the bulk of the Reichswehr, in its two-front dilemma, would be tied up against France in the west. Regardless of the fact that the forces available to either partner were still wholly inadequate, many in the German military daydreamed, as in 1813–14, of a battle on the Rhine with the Russian Cossacks by their side.

The leaders of the Red Army, for their part, were in the process of a thorough reorganisation and professionalisation and hoped to receive a significant boost to their development from German military expertise and armaments. The USSR was still by and large internationally isolated. Invasions and uprisings threatened from all sides. Cooperation with the Reichswehr provided some leverage against Poland, which was seen as Soviet Russia's main military opponent.

In Berlin and Moscow, this secret collaboration was seen in no way as a love match, but as an alliance of convenience. The leaders of the German Army were fervent anti-communists and their readiness to embark on such a risky liaison was bound up with the presumption that there would be further revolution in Soviet Russia. Just as it was long assumed in Moscow that Germany would sooner or later fall victim to the Revolution, more than a few politicians, economists and military men in Berlin believed that Russian communism was fated to fail. It was therefore all the more important to prevent a post-revolutionary Russia from again establishing relations with France. They believed their strong economic and military presence in the east would create staging posts of German influence, which would ensure a close relationship between Berlin and Moscow after communism had collapsed. Their expectations were directed in particular at the higher officer corps of the Red Army, much of which, like Tukhachevsky, consisted of the tsarist army's former military elite.

That expectation, as is well known, proved illusory, but it was still very common in the 1930s. In the daily reality of German military and foreign politics, however, far soberer calculation was required. German–Polish relations in the 1920s developed into a cold war.[24] The 'national struggle' in the disputed border areas was encouraged by both sides. Every democratic government of the German Republic saw itself as duty-bound to financially support the German element in Poland. Gustav Stresemann, who won the Nobel Peace Prize as foreign minister and who took Germany into the League of Nations in 1926 and sought a settlement with France, shared with most German politicians the opinion that the border with Poland was unacceptable.

Economic warfare was waged and support was given to the German minority in the expectation that the Polish state would disintegrate economically and politically, and that that would allow the Germans to make border corrections. German revisionist politics in regard to Poland aimed at Danzig, the Polish Corridor and East Upper Silesia.[25]

Warsaw meanwhile could still claim to be Europe's strongest bulwark against Soviet communism, despite being surrounded by hostile neighbours. And in Berlin, opinion on relations with Russia was in no way homogeneous. From the extremists of the right-wing periphery through to the mainstream conservative camp, there were anti-Russian attitudes – some of them aggressive and founded on racial ideology – which, under the aegis of anti-communism and anti-Semitism, were a continuation of ideas that had already been formulated in the nineteenth century and whose most extreme forms had been promoted by pan-German propagandists during World War I. Alongside these, there were also pragmatic and even Russophile elements, which we can group together as the Rapallo faction. What they had in common – but for a few exceptions – was a clearly marked animosity towards Poland, resulting mainly from the contemporary confrontation.

In the Reichswehr's war games and national security discussions in the 1920s, a war with Poland was seen as possible at any time, indeed as ultimately inevitable. But with the sacking of Seeckt in 1926 and the long-term plans for the systematic rearmament of the Reichswehr, defensive strategies took priority. The first concealed efforts were made to modernise and extend the eastern border defences. An 'eastern wall' – though not yet a line of fortifications, which the Treaty of Versailles had banned – took shape. It was intended, if Germany was attacked, to allow the Reichswehr's scant forces to halt a surprise Polish advance on Berlin at the Oder until more troops could be mobilised. Defending East Prussia, isolated as it was by the Polish Corridor and the neutrality of Danzig, presented a particularly important problem.

The most potentially dangerous opponent was still France, which, since the mid 1920s had, however, been concentrating on defending its own territory. It dug in, building the gigantic Maginot Line opposite the German border. Stresemann's policy of appeasement towards Paris bore fruit. This allowed the Foreign Ministry to keep the dispute over the eastern borders under discussion. No rapid solutions were to be expected. At the start of 1926, the Troop Office formulated the aims of a long-term revisionist policy to be underpinned by military means: restoration of German sovereignty, liberation of the Rhineland

and the Saarland, Anschluss of German Austria, removal of the Corridor and recovery of Polish Upper Silesia. In the embryonic disarmament negotiations at the League of Nations, the Germans' priority was therefore to demand that France and Poland forfeit their military dominance.[26] This could hardly be hoped for, but a collapse of the negotiations could boost the German 'right to equal status' and so support their own rearmament.

Domestically and militarily, Poland had not consolidated itself in the way Marshal Piłsudski had hoped. In 1923, he had resentfully withdrawn from politics. For him, as for many of his contemporaries, parliamentary democracy was a deep disappointment. His socialist and soldierly mentality desired other forms of state and society. In Italy, people had just begun to talk about a certain Benito Mussolini, on whose example the political adventurer Adolf Hitler was also orienting himself. But it would be wrong to draw any equivalence between them, because Piłsudski dreamed differently from his opponents – Poland's nationalist right wing. He wanted not an ethnically homogeneous state, but a Poland that would be 'the home of many nations, a community of many cultures', including the Jewish one.[27]

In May 1926, he used the support of his many followers in the army and the leftist parties to stage a *coup d'état* and seize power, which he held until his death in 1935, albeit that Piłsudski in fact only seldom occupied important official posts and even then only for a short time. He was never president, but left this office to his loyal devotee, Ignacy Mościcki. Piłsudski served mainly as defence minister. Nonetheless, he was recognised as the state's highest authority. Until the end of the 1920s, there was also a more or less functioning opposition represented in parliament, though it was consistently prevented from coming to power. The regime is often described by historians as a 'reasonable dictatorship' and itself called its political concept 'Sanacja' (restoration to health). Piłsudski's political writings and speeches nevertheless made their way into the spectacular National Socialist edition of his works that appeared in 1935 and of which there will be much more to say below. In the same year, shortly after his death, a constitution came into effect that had been tailored to suit him.

The Polish Army, again personally commanded by Piłsudski after 1926, was in anything but excellent shape. Władysław Sikorski (chief of the General Staff, 1921–2; prime minister, 1922–3; defence minister, 1924–5), a close confidant of the marshal's, published his memoirs of the 1920 war in Paris in 1928.[28] In his analysis of the strengths and weaknesses of the Polish Army, his main criticisms were: inadequate planning by the army's leaders, passivity and fearfulness among the middle and lower commanders, mistakes in tactical and operational leadership, inadequate construction of defensive fortifications and the sometimes low quality of the officer corps. Many had lacked both the urge to advance and the ability to react quickly and vigorously when under fire.

In the Defence Ministry in Berlin, these developments were noted with great interest. They confirmed the impression that had already been gained of the Polish Army, and that it had made only scant progress since 1920, a conclusion that was to remain essentially unchanged until 1939. The Reichswehr undertook a secret comprehensive appraisal of the Polish Army.[29] What impressed the Germans above all was its strong political position – understandable given the comparison with their own stabilised governmental system, in which the Reichswehr had lost some of its political clout.

Although Poland was France's favoured ally, it could command only outdated weapons and a weak armaments industry. With around 28 million inhabitants, it was numerically far smaller than Germany, but could lead a far larger army onto the field. Its peacetime strength of 320,000 was three times that of the Reichswehr. If, however, that figure was divided across two fronts, it didn't present all that great a threat to German security.

Moreover, Berlin recognised the qualitative weakness of the Polish officer corps and took the nationalities question into account. Only 58 per cent of the populace were classed as 'pure Poles'. Those from the formerly German territories were regarded as the most culturally advanced and, when well led in the Great War and the war of 1920, 'had in general made rather good soldiers'. By contrast, those from Congress Poland were the most backward and had often given way under Russian leadership. In the event of war, so said the appraisal, the nationalities question could 'become decisive for the reliability and combat effectiveness of the Polish military' – a prognosis that played an important role in 1938–9. The most important minorities to consider were the Ukrainians (17.9 per cent), the Jews (10.7 per cent) and the Germans (5.7 per cent). 'Hatred for the Poles is most strongly pronounced in the East Galician Ukrainians [...] The Jews, too, are bitterly repressed by the Poles.'[30]

Strategically, the study found that the Polish troops were insufficient to comprehensively defend their expanded borders. For that reason, Warsaw – in contrast to France's expectations – would seek to concentrate its forces into a few quick, manoeuvrable formations. This closely approached German military thinking. The Polish Army at the end of the 1920s possessed a hotchpotch of mainly outdated armoured vehicles, most of them lightly shielded and unsuitable for off-road use – though the Reichswehr's secret prototypes looked no better – but would nonetheless be able to put together two mechanised divisions in the event of war. In view of the poor road conditions, Poland still put more faith in cavalry than mechanised forces[31] – something which actually did not imply that the Poles had plans ever to go on the offensive on their western border, into Germany.

And if it was correct that the Polish defensive arrangements were not set up for a war on two fronts, because they trusted that their western border would be protected against Germany by a French relief invasion, then they were obviously preparing for a repeat of the war against Soviet Russia. But how were the abilities and intentions of the Red Army to be assessed?

To answer that question, the German Army in 1926 commissioned a seminal, secret study, which clear-headedly and objectively acknowledged several weaknesses in the possible Russian ally, but also found considerable potential for development.[32] Though the campaign in 1920 was said to have brought notable initial successes, the Red Army had succumbed utterly to the 'powerful, coherently led counter-attack'. This was not the fault of the Russian High Command – Tukhachevsky, who had risen into the General Staff, was not to be blamed – but of the junior officers, who had been chosen for their political attitude, and of the 'substandard discipline' of the ordinary soldiers, who had fought only for fear of both informers and their officers. Even convinced communists, after their period of active duty ended and they returned to the countryside, had soon gone back to being 'anti-communist' farmers. Nevertheless, the Red Army would 'willingly and self-sacrificingly take to the field at any time to protect the fatherland against any foreign enemy, especially as the Soviet regime understands how to play on Russian patriotic feeling in those cases'.

Since the Red Army had been reduced and restructured into a professional standing army of around 400,000 men, considerable progress could be recorded in every area. That was why Seeckt thought it proper, before the signing of the German–Soviet 'Treaty of Berlin', to receive the acting people's commissar for war, Józef Unszlicht, and his delegation. With the treaty, Germany promised the USSR that it would remain neutral in the event that the Soviets had to fight a defensive war. That meant that in a conflict with Poland, which is ultimately what the treaty was about, Moscow was guaranteed

German cover. That would make it well-nigh impossible for France to provide its Polish ally with support. That there could be no talk of true neutrality on the part of the Germans was shown by an intensification of the secret military relations; among other projects, they agreed to construct a tank academy in Kazan and to expand the flying academy in Lipetsk, as well as to participate jointly in manoeuvres, General Staff exercises and war games.[33]

In the following years these relations developed satisfactorily, despite some difficulties and even though the increasing assertiveness of the Soviet side meant the Germans could not but get the impression that their investments in the Soviet Union were highly insecure. But there were always more encouraging signals. The head of the Army Organisation Section (T3), Colonel Ritter von Mittelberger, reported after an inspection tour of the Soviet Union that the – emphatically singled out – former tsarist Guards lieutenant and present chief of the Red Army's General Staff, Mikhail Tukhachevsky, was a man of extraordinary brilliance and ambition. 'It is generally known that he is a communist only on opportunistic grounds. He is seen as possessing the personal courage to dare to break with communism if it seems advisable in the further development of things.' In the event of an 'upheaval', the decisive role would be played by the Red Army. Even now it was distancing itself more and more from the party's ideology.[34]

The Troop Office, that is, the German General Staff in disguise, involved the Foreign Ministry in its training exercises from winter 1927–8 onwards. Wartime planning structures and decision-making processes were played through as realistically as possible. The political groupings they assumed to exist were only fiction, but it can be presumed that the conjectures of these diplomats and officers were probable or at least feasible scenarios.

The war game in 1927–8 started from the following position. It had become apparent that Poland was intending to undertake a surprise occupation of East Prussia without even mobilising. As cover, the Poles would make some attacks on the main German territory, using irregular units in their vanguard. This would result in a German–Polish duel, because German relations with France had been consolidated and Russia was so occupied with internal conflicts that it could pose no danger to Poland. The background to this last assumption was the power struggle between Stalin and Trotsky, who had lost his post as war commissar in 1925 and was being officially exiled just at the time of the German war game.

The military men had, by their own account, given themselves an 'extraordinarily favourable' starting position, which led the Foreign Ministry's representative to write a malicious note, saying: 'It also appears to be assumed that Britain has fallen victim to an undersea earthquake and that America has tumbled into ruin as a result partly of tornados, partly of misguided speculation, while Czechoslovakia is entirely preoccupied with the conclusion of certain concordat-negotiations.'[35]

Nevertheless, the head of the Troop Office, Werner von Blomberg, had to concede that the war game showed Germany's chances, with the current level of armament, to be as adverse as could be imagined. Even if Germany was facing only Poland, and Poland wasn't otherwise allied, it would be able to maintain 'a resistance with any prospects of success only for a short time and with the loss of more German territories'. The defence of isolated East Prussia and the necessity of supply by sea caused the greatest concern.

Blomberg must have been all the more satisfied when he went on an inspection trip to the USSR a few months later and found the joint undertakings there 'in the best condition'. For him, this confirmed his judgement that '[t]here is no doubt about their great value to our armaments programme. To make full use of them is, from an armaments perspective, of existential importance.'[36] In many areas, the Reichswehr, he said, could even learn from the Soviet Army. As regards the officer corps, there were obvious defects, but the tactical and operational fundamentals corresponded to the German example. And the Red Army was more skilled in defence and retreat than it was in attack. In any case, it was desirable that the Red Army strengthen its capabilities in those areas. It was already a force to be reckoned with. 'Having it as a friend can only be an advantage.' Accompanied by Oskar Ritter von Niedermayer, the head of the Moscow bureau, Blomberg met the Red Army's leaders. Kliment Voroshilov, Trotsky's successor, assured him 'that in the event of a Polish attack on Germany, Russia would be ready to offer every kind of assistance'. In response to the question of whether the Red Army, for its part, could count on the support of Germany, Blomberg stayed tight-lipped and told his counterparts that that was the politicians' responsibility.[37]

In retrospect, he wrote: 'Seen from the outside, the Red Army was already a strong protector of its country. It relied upon the inexhaustible numbers and the enormous expanses of its inaccessible landscape. It seemed then that an invading enemy whose warfare was predicated on technology would soon be bogged down. So much so that I at that time judged an incursion into Russia [...] to be unlikely.'[38]

It seems that Blomberg retained this realistic assessment as Hitler's defence minister until 1938, even if he did then play down the extent of the previous relations with the Red Army and their importance for German rearmament.[39]

The war games of 1928–9 then demonstrated the weaknesses of the Reichswehr with utmost clarity. This time, the Troop Office assumed that secret rearmament had been successfully carried out until 1933, and posited that there was a war between Poland and Russia in which France wanted to force its way through Germany to support its ally. The results showed that the Reichswehr would not be able to risk fighting any kind of decisive battle and would be able only to delay the enemy's advance. For the foreseeable future, then, any military conflict was doomed to end in catastrophe.[40]

This bitter realisation doubtless contributed to the decision of the Reichswehr's leaders in 1932–3 to favour the political movement that loudly proclaimed such aims as 'making Germany again able to defend itself' and 'fighting against Versailles'. At this point, however, it must be emphasised that for more than a decade after the end of World War I, war with Russia was not under discussion, neither in the prevailing political circles nor in the military. Rather, the new neighbour in the east, the resurrected Polish Republic, was seen as a potential enemy – even if the chief enemy was still, of course, France. Subject to the terms of the Treaty of Versailles and under the control – albeit not always the full control – of the Reichstag and democratic opinion, the military could not consider solving 'the Polish problem', even if an opportunity presented itself, 'on the offensive'. A battle in the area between Warsaw, Minsk and Kiev was conceivable only as one between Poland and Russia. Whether the Red Army would be able, unlike in 1920, to cross the Vistula into the west seemed more than doubtful at the start of the 1930s. And who in Germany except the communists would look forward to a joint 'war of liberation'?

'Lebensraum in the East'? Hitler and Eastern Politics

In 1933, when the National Socialists came to power and effected a dramatic caesura in German history, a war with Russia was not within the realm of what either the new government or the populace thought likely. 'Hitler means war': this insight, derived from reading the new chancellor's previous statements and writings, was certainly widespread, but it indicated neither that Germany would soon take up arms nor that it would embark on a particular war of aggression. In the cabinet of the 'National Revolution', the responsibility for foreign and military policy still lay in seasoned conservative hands. And there was still the venerable president, Paul von Hindenburg, to whom the military considered themselves honour-bound. Hitler's pronouncements about energetically pursuing German rearmament and overturning Versailles created a consensus. But this in no way resulted in a definite schedule for war, nor in any predetermined sequence of steps leading up to it.

When invited by the defence minister to give a now well-known speech to the military's leaders on 2 February 1933, Hitler left it at a few hints and general phrases. He retained a variety of options for expanding the Reich's power, but said he would prioritise the conquest of 'Lebensraum in the East' and its 'uncompromising Germanisation'.[41] This part of his speech dealing with foreign policy met with general agreement, even if there was no clarification of what the next steps were to be. His first priorities, however, were to consolidate his new regime domestically, and to accelerate secret rearmament. Regaining 'military sovereignty' remained the most important objective at present, something the military of course unreservedly supported. But they were also aware that for a transition period of as yet undeterminable length, there was a danger of intervention by the victorious powers, above all by France, perhaps with the assistance of its Polish ally.

That would actually be a reason for not breaking off the secret relationship with Moscow. The willingness to maintain it remained unaltered on the Russian side, although the military contact did also induce some ideological pangs in the Russians. Tukhachevsky, as chief of the Red Army's weapons ministry, along with a group of other Soviet commanders, attended the autumn manoeuvres in East Prussia as a guest of the German Army. He confirmed Moscow's readiness to continue the mutually beneficial military relationship. Colonel Herbert Fischer, a long-time liaison officer with the Red Army, noted in his assessment that Tukhachevsky would probably be the commander-in-chief of the anti-Polish front in a future war.[42]

Shortly after Hitler came to power, Seeckt again, in a kind of political testament, laid out the motives for the direction he had chosen in eastern politics. The former head of the Army High Command warned forcefully against an appetite for premature expansion, which would be condemned to failure given the present balance of power in Europe. If Germany wanted to become a great power, it must pursue realpolitik, and this pointed towards cooperation with Moscow.[43] But it could be assumed that the new chancellor, given the vehemently anti-Bolshevik propaganda of his NSDAP, would get into difficulties if he made himself dependent to any degree upon the Russians. Kurt Freiherr von Hammerstein-Equord, the current head of the Army High Command, advocated a clear position: 'Relationship with M[oscow] is pact with Beelzebub. But we have no choice. To forgo it for fear of effect on dom. politics would be wrong. "Fear is not a philosophy" (Seeckt).'[44]

As the freshly appointed chancellor, Hitler encountered very varied opinions on the Russian option among the military, diplomats and other representatives of the conservative elite. The escalating situation within Russia had, for example, led thousands of Russian Germans to leave their homes and emigrate, as a consequence of which they ceased to represent a potential influence on the USSR's development. German economic 'staging posts' had also come under pressure in the course of Stalinisation, and the brutal collectivisation ultimately meant that the agricultural population, in whom the Germans had placed their political faith in the event of the regime's collapse, was plunged into poverty and catastrophic famine. Although German industry did profit significantly from the orders Moscow placed as part of the country's forced industrialisation (the five-year plans), the USSR in return delivered mainly agricultural goods, which in times of world economic crisis again riled the German agrarians.

In military circles there was also a growing sympathy for National Socialism and its creed of 'making Germany again able to defend itself'. Despite all the foreign political risk bound up with that, many thought it seemed more sensible than making Germany lastingly dependent on the goodwill of the Soviet Union.[45] In the right circumstances, the raw materials Germany would need in a war could be captured by a quick, manoeuvrable attacking army. War, after all, was no more than 'the continuation of economics by other means'.[46] That could, as in World War I, be taken as far as overthrowing the Russian government and creating a pact along the lines of Brest-Litovsk and/or establishing a ring of satellite states from the Baltic via the Ukraine to the Caucasus. How these, as it were, 'limited' expansionist aims were to correspond to Hitler's slogans of 'Lebensraum in the East' and its 'uncompromising Germanisation' remained unclear. It is probable that Hitler himself, well into the 1930s, did not have any distinct notion of under what circumstances and at what point such visions could be realised.

The highest economic circles thought it would also be possible to use 'peaceful' means to establish a German 'greater economic area', which would then exert an influence on the global balance of power. In the early 1930s, these expectations were animated in particular by the allure of South-East Europe, though they weren't limited to it. In the striving for 'autarky' – the period's magic word, which seemed to promise a solution to every problem – one of the most pressing tasks was to rapidly solve the 'eastern problem'.[47] The Germans may have rhapsodised about the Baltic states, the Ukraine and the Caucasus, and even assumed that there was no future for the Soviet regime, but the geographical and military key for the 'Gateway to the East' still lay in Poland.

What role did Poland play in the political ideas of the greenhorn chancellor Adolf Hitler, and how can we explain his sensational leap to an understanding with the ancient Marshal Piłsudski at the start of 1934? This must be prefaced by saying that the ominous conversations between Hitler and Hermann Rauschning, which were regarded after 1945 as a key source on the dictator's attitude to Poland, are now considered to be a forgery dating from 1939 – not the only one encountered in researching the outbreak of World War II.[48] Rauschning was the National Socialist senate president in Danzig in 1933–4, but fell out with the Gauleiter, Albert Forster, then left the party and fled abroad in 1936. He wrote his supposed 'conversations with Hitler' for a sizeable fee in the summer of 1939. The book was published in French at the end of that year. It became a bestseller in many languages and was extensively quoted by historians for decades.[49]

In fact, no specific animosity towards the Poles can be determined in Hitler's political thinking at the start of the 1920s.[50] There was a certain antipathy to bustling Polish nationalism left over from his time in Vienna, but his distaste in this regard was directed more strongly against the Czechs and Hungarians. In line with his slogans of a 'fight against Versailles', his revisionist policies naturally aimed in part at the Polish state, though he also admired Piłsudski both as a victor over the Red Army and for his soldierly nationalism.[51] Hitler engaged in a retroactive polemic against the Prussian conservatives. It had been wrong to annex parts of Poland in the eighteenth century in order to turn Poles into good Germans, that is, Prussians. Instead – and here his racial thinking comes to the fore – they should have contained or removed the foreign blood and settled the newly gained provinces with their own fellow Germans.

Even before it was written down in his manifesto, *Mein Kampf*, the centrepoint of Hitler's political thinking was the relationship with Russia. In his ideas were combined anti-Semitism, racial ideology, anti-communism and a war of conquest that would secure areas of settlement, Lebensraum and economic autarky. Though Hitler had initially identified himself with the aims of a pan-German programme, this was soon outweighed by an extreme anti-Semitism that equated Bolshevism with Jewishness and so ruled out any cooperation with the Soviet regime. He was the only party leader among the right-wing opposition to consider the Rapallo treaty a complete mistake and spoke out during the 1923 Ruhr crisis against the suggestions made from various sides for a German–Russian alliance.[52] His increasing fixation on racial ideology eventually precluded even the possibility of an alliance with a post-revolutionary Russia, which was the hope of such leading men as Seeckt and the 'compliance politicians' whom Hitler berated.

Among the numerous ideological and political ideas out of which he constructed his programme, what stands out as regards Russia is the influence of the Baltic German Alfred Rosenberg. The future party ideologue and, from 1941, minister for the Occupied Eastern Territories, did not in the mid 1920s yet have a clear picture of the war for Lebensraum. Like many others at that time, he believed that 'Jewish Bolshevism' would soon collapse and that the nationalist movements in the east, especially in the Baltic and the Ukraine, would win the upper hand. The disintegration of the Russian empire into 'ethnically purified' nation states would give Germany the opportunity to exert a dominant influence on them. Moreover, Rosenberg, in reference to the 1926 Treaty of Berlin, did not fundamentally rule out a tactical alliance with the Soviet regime.[53] His preferred option was, as in the 1918 model, to have an independent Ukraine, something that would necessarily be at the expense of Poland.

Hitler had to vehemently stamp out this pro-Russian tendency within his own party. The NSDAP's internal opposition, the so-called Strasser group, advocated a shift to the left and a 'National Bolshevism' that would make Soviet Russia a natural ally in a war of liberation against the western powers. At the Bamberg party conference in 1926, there was a collision with the socialist faction, one of whose adherents was Joseph Goebbels.

Note in Goebbels's diary, 15 February 1926:

I feel defeated. What Hitler was this? A reactionary? Phenomenally clumsy and uncertain. Russian question: totally wrong, Italy and Britain our natural alliance partners. Horrendous! Our task is to smash Bolshevism. Bolshevism is a Jewish front! We must inherit Russia! 180 million people!!! [...] One of the greatest disappointments of my life. I no longer believe unreservedly in Hitler. That is what's terrible: I've lost my inner handhold. I feel only half myself.[54]

It didn't take long for Goebbels to defect to Hitler and let himself be convinced by his line. His beloved Führer made the effort in the second volume of *Mein Kampf* (1926–7) to comprehensively elucidate his unusual doctrine. Russia was 'perhaps the most momentous concern of German foreign policy, bar none' and 'a touchstone for the political ability of the young National Socialist movement to think clearly and act rightly'.[55] Exerting the Reich's influence in the east, whether politically or economically, would not be enough. The 'territorial politics of the future' would have to be taken by storm. Only 'territorial acquisition' would make Germany a global power. 'But if in Europe today we speak of new ground and new territory, we can be thinking only of Russia and the subservient states on its periphery.' The ability to think clearly? Which peripheral states does he suppose are subservient to Russia? The anti-communist bulwark of Poland? Not a word in explanation. And later on in his clear thinking, territorial acquisition is to be achieved on the offensive with a new network of alliances. 'In Europe there is only a single ally: Britain. Only with Britain covering our backs could we set out on the new Teutonic migration. [...] No sacrifice is too large in winning Britain's goodwill.' Germany would have to do without colonies and naval prestige and refrain from competing with British industries.[56]

The criticism that the Reich's largest mistake under the kaiser was to turn against both Russia and Britain – that is, not to have decided on one side or the other – reveals the power-political core of Hitler's thinking as well as the dilemma from which he, as the Führer of the Greater German Reich, proved unable to free himself in World War II. It was only on the basis of the dangerous assumption that Britain would not stand in the way of Germany's push to the east that Hitler could coherently formulate his foreign political doctrine and then pursue it in the 1930s. But his route was doomed to failure from the outset, because he was consistently wrong in his assessment not only of British politics, but also of internal German contradictions. To come to power he had had to bring extremely diverse political tendencies under the roof of the NSDAP, including colonial enthusiasts, anti-British naval strategists and the global market interests of the industrialists.

What is certain is that in January 1933 Hitler did not yet have any conclusive opinion on the role of Poland in his political programme.[57] Many of his followers, however, demanded immediately after Hitler's accession to power that he begin the loudly trumpeted 'fight against Versailles' on Polish soil. Walther Darré, the new 'Reich Farmers' Leader', proposed that Poland relinquish its previously German territories, pull back to its 'ethnic territory' and, in doing so, take its rightful place among the middling states of the east. This extremist position was supported by Goebbels and Forster, the Gauleiter of Danzig. Their goal was a rapid and, if necessary, violent annexation of the former eastern territories and of the Memel Territory, regardless of the Reich's precarious international situation. But how was this to be achieved? Military pressure was ruled out by the current weakness of the Reichswehr, especially if an alliance with Russia did not come into consideration.

Hitler, in a letter to Colonel Walter von Reichenau, chief of staff of Military District I, East Prussia, 4 December 1932:

> Russia is not a state, but an ideology which is presently limited to that territory, i.e. controls it, and which maintains departments in all other countries, which not only strive towards the same revolutionary ends, but are also organisationally subordinate to the Moscow headquarters. A victory for these principles in Germany would have unimaginable consequences. A war against these poisonous tendencies becomes all the harder when considerations of foreign policy lead to political and military cooperation with the headquarters of that poison.[58]

Werner Daitz, National Socialist expert for the projected greater German economic zone, looked to the 'economic activation of the whole belt of states from Latvia to the Black Sea', none of which would be able to remain independently stable in the long term. 'These people, and this can never be forgotten, form a protective wall from behind which the Central European area will one day observe the inevitable disintegration of Soviet Russia.'[59] The 'measured' milieux around Hermann Göring, Rudolf Heß and Hermann Rauschning were regarded as adherents of a longer-term 'greater solution'. They were said to have advocated compensation for Poland at the expense of the Ukraine.[60] But did the Poles want that? And, for that matter, did the Ukrainians, of whom the party's chief ideologue, Rosenberg, had such a high opinion?

Danzig was the trouble spot around which it quickly came to clashes with Poland. Terrorist activity flared up at the border. The 'German Eastern Union' loudly demanded border revisions. Poland reacted with a military demonstration on the Westerplatte peninsula opposite Danzig. In Poland, there were anti-German demonstrations against the Nazi governments in Danzig and Berlin, as well as a protest against the Reich's boycott of Jewish businesses. Piłsudski's government felt out their French ally as to whether a pre-emptive war might become necessary against the apparently crazed Nazi regime. It might be worth trying to take control of certain bargaining chips, such as Danzig, and using them to force Hitler to relinquish his plans for rearmament. But Paris opted for conciliation and attempted to use diplomatic means to keep Germany's revisionist politics on a peaceful track.[61]

Now Hitler's opportunities for a change of course in foreign or military policy were actually very limited, because in his cabinet these policy areas seemed to be firmly in the hands of conservatives. The leaders of the Reichswehr, along with the foreign minister, Konstantin Freiherr von Neurath, and his junior minister, Bernhard Wilhelm von Bülow, saw no need for a change of course. They regarded the growing power of the USSR as something that could be used, by continuing the existing cooperation between the countries, as both a counterweight to France and a means of exerting pressure on Poland. They wanted to avoid international confrontation – at least until Germany was militarily strengthened – and direct the first phase of revisionist policies against Poland. A certain degree of tension with Poland would, from their point of view, be advantageous, because it would keep the 'Polish question' under international discussion. An agreement with Poland was 'neither possible nor desirable'.[62]

In this they distanced themselves from the brief attempt in summer 1932 by the next-to-last chancellor, Franz von Papen, to forge a German–French–Polish bloc with an anti-Soviet bias, an idea that derived from French economic circles.[63] For Neurath, recognising Poland's western border was as far from coming into consideration as a German–French guarantee of its eastern one. Papen, now vice-chancellor in Hitler's cabinet, proved to be a political lightweight, but nevertheless brought a little flexibility into previously rigid German revisionist policy.

Hitler recognised that he had the rudiments of a strategy for loosening up the status quo. From his point of view, it was a matter of breaking up the French encirclement and arranging European politics in such a way that it would be possible for him to make rapid progress in his revisionist programme without binding himself too strongly to anyone. Above all, he needed to find some wiggle room so that he could rearm without fear of intervention and move as fast as possible towards his ultimate goal: victory over Russia. Only days after taking power, he began an agile, undogmatic manoeuvring over foreign policy. Within a year there had been a complete change of course: the Soviet Union had been renounced and a friendly overture had been made to Poland. It was a sensational reversal, often underestimated in its importance.

The 'ABC of German eastern policy'[64] was overthrown and Hitler gained six years in which to prepare for his war. To put it bluntly, the repercussions of the Hitler–Piłsudski pact in 1934 were no less significant than those of the Hitler–Stalin pact in 1939.

In 1933 the leaders of the Reichswehr and the Foreign Ministry opposed the change of course by attempting to play for time. To their surprise, the military learned from their new chancellor that he intended to break off the secret cooperation with the Red Army at any cost. This when the most recent visits of Reichswehr officers to the USSR showed that the construction of a modern armaments industry there was making great progress, and that Germany would be able to benefit from it.[65] The head of the army's Weapons Agency wrote on 13 June 1933 after the end of his visit: 'Given the scale of the Russian plans and the energy demonstrated in implementing them, cooperation with the Red Army and the Soviet armaments industry is urgently desirable not only for reasons of national defence, but also for those of weapons technology.'[66]

On the same grounds, Soviet military espionage came to the conclusion that, in summer 1933, the Reichswehr's leaders were still counting on Russian support in the event of a German war against Poland. But the Reichswehr's 'Moscow bureau' was permanently dissolved in September 1933. Individual attempts to maintain secret contact on a military level were all in vain. Only after the Hitler–Stalin pact in 1939 could they be taken up again.

The head of the Army High Command, Hammerstein-Equord, totally rejected the change of course. At the send-off for the Red Army officers who had taken part in the exchange programme, he declared on 1 July 1933 that the two 'friendly armies' could hold tight to the 'proven bond of cooperation.'[67] He was forced out at the end of the year. The Reichswehr's leaders adapted to the new political orientation, though some of those in high office retained good memories of working with the Russians. Adjusting to the idea of making preparations for a war against the USSR took some time. As late as November 1934, the defence minister, Werner von Blomberg, is said to have raised his glass of champagne during a reception at the Soviet embassy in Berlin and made the following toast: it would never be forgotten what the Soviet Army had done for Germany; to the future of the great and glorious Soviet Army, and to a trusting brotherhood-in-arms, now and for the future.[68]

Resistance to this change of course was palpable also in the Foreign Ministry. But Chancellor Hitler did not think much of his diplomats as it was. At a meeting of the Council of Ministers on 28 September 1933, he insisted that there was a 'keen antagonism' between the USSR and the new Reich, which, diplomatic conventions aside, precluded any earnestly meant restoration of good relations.[69] In his speech at the opening of the Reichstag on 23 March 1933, he had publicly declared that the Reich's government sought to cultivate friendly and mutually beneficial relations with Russia, although the fight against German communists was a domestic matter in which he would not tolerate any interference. On 5 May 1933, the Reichstag again extended the Treaty of Berlin with the USSR. By the end of that year, however, German–Russian relations had sunk to a nadir from which they would not recover until summer 1939. The diplomats' efforts to preserve at least the economic links were ignored by Hitler.

Instead, Hitler sought contact with Poland ever more eagerly and made efforts to relax the tensions over Danzig.[70] In April, he indicated to the German ambassador in Moscow, Herbert von Dirksen, that he was thinking of a treaty with Poland. The objection that this would necessitate giving up on the Corridor was passed over by the chancellor.[71] On 2 May 1933, he received the Polish ambassador, Alfred Wysocki, and personally dictated the draft of a communiqué in which both sides promised to keep their activities strictly within the bounds of existing treaties.[72] Wysocki's successor, Józef Lipski, was also presented with Hitler's readiness for cooperation. He proposed that the contentious border questions be peaceably resolved at a later date. He also indicated his sympathy with Poland's territorial ambitions vis-à-vis Lithuania (the Vilnius region), Czechoslovakia (the Cieszyn area) and the Ukraine. Finally, he emphasised their common defensive position in the face of the USSR and offered to sign a non-aggression pact. Warsaw recognised that Hitler was personally effecting this departure from the Prussian tradition that in the past had sought friendship with Russia at the expense of Poland. 'Hitler is, rather, an Austrian; in any case, not a Prussian.' With this assessment, Foreign Minister Józef Beck was not far wide of the mark.[73]

To confirm the change of course in foreign policy, a bilateral trade agreement was signed by the two countries. In September 1933, Beck and Goebbels agreed to discontinue the mutual antagonism in the press and expand their cultural relations. According to new research, this should not be interpreted as mere deception on Hitler's part. Both sides sincerely tried to implement the agreement and to significantly improve their relationship.[74] The signing of the non-aggression pact on 26 January 1934 represented the crowning moment of the German–Polish rapprochement.

German–Polish Non-Aggression Pact, 26 January 1934:

Declaration

The Polish government and the German government consider the time to have come in which to inaugurate a new phase in political relations between Poland and Germany by means of a direct understanding between state and state. They have therefore decided to lay down in this declaration the foundations for the form these relations will take in future.

Both governments recognise the fact that maintaining and securing a lasting peace between their countries is an essential prerequisite for general peace in Europe. They are therefore determined to base their relations on the principles contained in the Paris Treaty of 27 August 1928 and want to more precisely define the application of those principles in regard of the relationship between Poland and Germany.

In doing so, each of the two governments affirms that the international obligations it has already entered into with other parties do not impede the peaceful development of their mutual relations, do not contradict this declaration and are not impinged upon by it. Moreover, they affirm that this declaration has no bearing on such questions as are regarded in international law as the domestic matters of either of the two states.

Both governments affirm their intention to reach agreement without delay on questions pertaining to their relations, of whatever type they may be. Should any issues arise and should it not prove possible to settle them though direct negotiation, they will in each case search for a solution by other peaceful means on the basis of mutual agreement, notwithstanding the possibility of, if necessary, bringing to bear the other kinds of process provided for such cases in the other treaties already in force between them. Under no circumstances will they, in dealing with such issues, move on to the use of violence.

The guarantee of peace created on these foundations will make it easier for both governments to carry out the great task of finding solutions for their political, economic and cultural problems that will rest on a just and condign settlement of the two sides' interests.

Both governments are convinced that in this way the relations between their countries will develop productively and lead to the establishment of a good neighbourly relationship that will be a blessing not only to their two countries, but to the other peoples of Europe.

This declaration will be ratified and the ratification documents will be exchanged in Warsaw as soon as possible. This declaration is valid for a period of ten years, calculated from the day the ratification documents are exchanged. Should it not be terminated by either of the governments six months before this period comes to an end, it will remain in force with the proviso that it can then be terminated by either government with a notice period of six months.

Made out in a double original in Polish and German.

Berlin, 26 January 1934

For the Polish government: Józef Lipski

For the German government: K. Freiherr von Neurath [...][75]

The Polish interests are easily parsed. Their French ally would not countenance a pre-emptive war against Germany and had embarked on discussions of a four-way pact suggested by Mussolini. The prospect of Europe's disagreements being settled by a tetrarchy of Britain, Italy, France and Germany, perhaps at the expense of Poland and, above all, without respecting Poland's ambitions as a great power, made Warsaw extremely nervous. The offer from Berlin came at just the right time, especially as Berlin was losing interest in Mussolini's suggestion due to ever louder rumours about a Franco–Soviet pact.

In the hectic diplomatic game that preceded the finalising of the Hitler–Piłsudski pact, it can be clearly seen how the German chancellor, having taken Germany out of the League of Nations in October 1933, tried to organise his foreign politics on bilateral lines and so secure his room to manoeuvre. Of course, his priority was to protect his long-term policy of rearmament. His approach of small steps and great tactical flexibility did not preclude the search for a first revisionist success. A hasty annexation of Austria, for example, was entirely imaginable. The National Socialists there were already putting on so much pressure in summer 1933 that the Austrian chancellor, Dollfuß, imposed a ban on NSDAP activity. After that, a National Socialist 'legion' was set up in Bavaria, in which 6,000 Austrians were given training for a possible military invasion of their own country.[76]

It cost the Foreign Ministry considerable effort to hold Hitler back from such reckless undertakings. Only a year later, his party comrades in Vienna attempted a putsch after the murder of Dollfuß. It failed but the option of a putsch was brought up again and again until the Anschluss in 1938. To achieve that goal, Hitler in 1933–4 risked conflict with Mussolini, even though the hope of an alliance with Italy and Britain was the founding principle of his foreign-policy ideas. That alliance was supposed to guard his back against France while he went on the attack in the east. So it made sense to think of

Poland as a well-suited potential ally. It quietly condoned Germany's ambitions in Austria as well as, in 1936, the spectacular reoccupation and militarisation of the Rhineland.[77] And this agreement with Piłsudski didn't just ease the tensions at the German–Polish border, but it also created a possible starting point for a war of eastern conquest in the not-too-distant future.

But wasn't the pact with Piłsudski, after all, merely a tactical manoeuvre, one intended to gain time at the expense of an 'arch-enemy who did not lose this stigma in the coming years'?[78] 'Any treaties with Poland are only temporary. I would never even think of making a sincere agreement with Poland': this is what Hitler is reported to have said on 18 October 1934 in front of party officials. Such and similar reported declarations originate, however, in the extremely dubious memoirs of Hermann Rauschning – and are therefore worthless.[79]

Hitler's speech in the Reichstag on relations with Poland, 30 January 1934:

When I assumed government on 30 January, relations between the two countries seemed less than satisfactory. There was a danger that the differences that undoubtedly existed, whose causes lay partly in the territorial provisions of the Treaty of Versailles and partly in the resulting anger on both sides, would harden into an enmity that, if it continued, would all too easily take on the character of an inherited political burden for both sides.

A development of this kind, quite apart from the looming dangers it latently contained, would have been an impediment to the whole future of beneficial cooperation between the two countries.

Germans and Poles will have to come to terms with the fact of the others' existence. It is therefore expedient to organise this situation, which the last thousand years have not done away with and that the thousand after us will not do away with either, in such a way that both sides can derive the greatest possible use from it.[80]

Of course, one cannot always take Hitler's public statements at face value. But the announcement of a thousand-year friendship was certainly unusual. The German–Polish pact was more soberly concluded for an initial period of ten years. That corresponded to the limit of Hitler's plans, the end of the rearmament project, which, when finished, would give him permanent freedom to act as he chose. So were both sides merely trying to gain time? In answer to that question, history-writing often quotes a secret speech Hitler is said to have given to the heads of the Reichswehr, the SA and the SS on 28 February

1934, that is, a month after the pact with Piłsudski. In it he is reported to have explained that the 'new army must be fit for any manner of defence within five years, and for attack in eight'. Germany would have to take the Lebensraum that the western powers would not grant it. 'So it may become necessary to make short, decisive blows to the west and then to the east.'[81]

What is meant here by the term 'east'? And does this mean the sequence had already been decided? Not at all. At root, the dictator was merely drawing on the fundamental strategic model that had been part of German operational thinking since Schlieffen. There will be much more to say about this below.

It would be an equal misunderstanding to totally dismiss Hitler's public slogans of peace and his understandable hope that there would be several years in which to rearm systematically. The risk of invasion from abroad remained high in this transitional phase. For that reason alone, the Reichswehr had to prepare for war at any time – even if only in the form of defence for the time being. So they placed great value on being able to factor 2 million militarily trained members of the SA into their calculations. Nonetheless, it cannot be overlooked that Hitler, even on coming to power in 1933, counted on being able to attack the USSR should favourable circumstances emerge, and not just in the 1940s at the end of a long rise to continental dominance that included the neutralisation of the western powers. It must be constantly borne in mind what a pivotal position the desired alliance with Great Britain took in his political programme. He may, as we know today, have been fundamentally mistaken about British politics, but he was plainly convinced until 1940 that it would be possible for him to come to an understanding with Britain and exchange a renunciation of claims to Germany's former colonies for a free hand in the east.

In the 1930s, London seemed entirely sympathetic to German revisionism and willing to make concessions. The British were familiar with Germany's intentions towards the USSR. The then head of the RAF's intelligence service, Fred Winterbotham, reports in his memoirs that on a visit to Germany in 1934 he met with Hitler, Rosenberg, Heß and Koch, as well as with military leaders. He says Hitler explained that he was going to annihilate communism and do so by conquering Russia.[82] The Führer also complained that his generals were still in too powerful a position. The one Hitler valued most highly was then Major-General Walther von Reichenau, who gave Winterbotham details of the German plans against Russia and of the blitzkrieg strategy. Reichenau had been chief of staff in the East Prussian Military District I since 1930 and was naturally fully acquainted with the military plans being made there.

Winterbotham's account is neither very precise nor verifiable. One would also like to know more about the effect reports of this kind had inside the British governmental apparatus. Western historians' discussions of Britain's 'appeasement politics' are always concerned with the British intention to contain Hitler's expansionist impulses. Soviet or Russian history, on the other hand, accuses the British of intending to *direct* those impulses, namely, towards the east.[83]

In contrast to France's efforts to bring the USSR into the European security system, the British government remained extremely mistrustful of the Soviet regime, not least because of the traditional British–Russian rivalry in Asia. In 1932, Poland, under pressure from France, had relieved the pressure on its eastern border by entering into a non-aggression pact with Moscow, but in doing so had also relieved the pressure on the Soviet Union from the west, leading to an escalation of tensions in the Far East. Joachim von Ribbentrop, whom Hitler had sent to London as his personal emissary in summer 1933, found that his proposals were met with interest and goodwill. Hitler offered a series of non-aggression treaties and guarantees in an attempt to secure more freedom for a rearmament programme directed against the USSR.[84]

Was Hitler's presentation of himself as a bulwark against communism only a propagandist trick to fool the western powers and allow him to secretly arm for a war against them? Or was the German–Polish bulwark, after all, underpinned by the real possibility that, at its 'greatest possible usefulness', it would become a jumping-off point for a joint war against the USSR? The theory that 'Poland was immune to the thought of any kind of complicity against the Soviet Union'[85] is not at all compelling upon closer inspection. This is something on which the reappraisal of Polish foreign policy in the 1930s may well shed new light.[86] But back to the German perspective.

Hitler's dramatic break with the pro-Soviet policies of the Weimar Republic and his no less dramatic shift towards friendliness with Poland are better understood against the background of developments in the Far East. Since staging the Mukden Incident in 1931, Japan had controlled the rich natural resources of Manchuria and in 1932 had proclaimed the founding of the Chinese satellite state Manchukuo. It was the beginning of Japan's policy of conquest towards China. This was a challenge also to the Soviet regime, which worried about its own interests in the Far East. Memories of defeat by Japan in 1905 were as fresh in Moscow as the scars of Japan's incursions into Siberia in 1918. Escalating tensions led to worldwide speculation that, if it came to blows in Manchuria, the Red Army would be given another drubbing, which would prompt the disintegration of the USSR and a return to civil war.

Not only Berlin but Warsaw, too, was forced to consider the consequences of the Soviet Union's collapse for their eastern borders. In a conference with the leaders of his military on 12 April 1934, Piłsudski declared that the danger of a war with the Soviet Union was greater than that of war with Germany, and that he was convinced Poland's future lay in the east, in Lithuania, Byelorussia and the Ukraine. The majority of the officers in his General Staff regarded Germany as the potentially more dangerous opponent, something that could, however, also be an argument in favour of reaching an understanding with the Reich.[87]

Piłsudski may well have been safe from the lure of military adventure. His country was already suffering because of the global economic crisis and would not have been able to afford a large war. But a German–Polish bloc would be able to provide backing for counter-revolutionary forces that could orchestrate upheaval on Soviet soil, particularly in the Ukraine, which was being ravaged by a terrible famine. This was the result of the forced collectivisation ordered by Stalin and directed primarily against the so-called kulaks, the agricultural middle class. Let it be remembered here that the Reichswehr's Rapallo politics had been consistently based on the assumption that the country people, with their anti-communist mindset, would be the agents of possible 'evolution' in the USSR. They would be able to overcome Bolshevism if aligned with the higher-ranking officers of the Red Army.

For Hitler, a restoration of the Russian Empire with German support was out of the question. Should Bolshevism collapse – as the world expected – then Germany might be able, as in 1918, to make easy gains by supporting various nationalist movements without having to directly commit significant military resources. For this kind of policy of indirect intervention, it was enough that Poland remain neutral. That would, however, necessitate an agreement on the complicated question of Ukrainian independence, because the Poles regarded Galicia and Lviv as belonging indisputably to Poland. But that was precisely the area that might be the launch pad for the independence of a greater Ukraine.

That was where the Organisation of Ukrainian Nationalists (OUN) was carrying out a campaign of separatist terrorism to mobilise the large Ukrainian minority within the Polish state.[88] On 15 June 1934, they murdered the Polish

4. Reich Propaganda Minister Joseph Goebbels (second from right) visits Poland's Marshal Józef Piłsudski in Warsaw on 15 June 1934. On the left is the German ambassador, Hans von Moltke; on the right is Polish Foreign Minister Józef Beck.

Minister of the Interior, Bronisław Pieracki, in broad daylight on a street in Warsaw.[89] Pieracki had just waved off Joseph Goebbels, whom another Ukrainian tried to assassinate during an evening reception at the German embassy.[90] These individual strikes attracted worldwide attention and were designed to stoke up the declining willingness of Ukrainian exiles in America to make donations.[91] The OUN feared, probably quite correctly, that German–Polish agreement on the Ukrainian question would be at the expense of an independent greater Ukraine.

The government in Warsaw, in any case, left no doubt that it would fight this separatism just as it would all the other, similar aspirations within its country. In the hastily erected concentration camp at Bereza Kartuska were collected Ukrainian, Byelorussian and ethnic German activists. The German and Polish governments consulted each other on how to further their joint resistance to Ukrainian terrorism. Berlin even delivered a leading member of the OUN – who had previously worked for the German side – to Poland, where the arrest of several more of its high officials practically sidelined the organisation for a number of years.

The assassination of Pieracki had been ordered by the OUN leadership inside the Ukraine; those trying to cultivate contacts in Germany were horrified. They had, after all, managed to interest Alfred Rosenberg, Hitler's adviser on the east, in their cause.

In Warsaw, just as in Berlin, there was no unified view of the strategic questions and the next steps in their bilateral relations, especially where these concerned the partners' stance on the USSR. On the occasion of a speech in Warsaw in mid June 1934, Goebbels became the first member of the German government to meet the Polish leadership. He appeared to be deeply impressed, particularly after his reception by the head of state: 'The marshal is our friend. He is a very imposing man.'[92] His deep-lying prejudices and anti-Polish stereotypes naturally remained untouched.

Goebbels on his visit to the Polish capital:

A drive through Warsaw. Jewish quarter. Stinking and dirty. Eastern Jews. That's them. Talk with Beck. About cultural exchange. He is friendly and devious. Like all Poles. Says everything, pledges nothing. That is an art we'll have to learn. The Poles are ahead of us there. And we mustn't delude ourselves. [...] Then to Piłsudski. The French want to undermine that. But no success. The marshal really is ill. But he speaks to me for almost an hour. Very jovial and charming. Half-Asiatic. Full of sickness. Old revolutionary. Even older than Hindenburg. But the clarity of a soldier. Army is good in any case. Piłsudski holds Poland together. A great man and a fanatic Pole. Hatred of people and the big city. A despot, I imagine. Very anecdotal in the discussion. We are photographed together at his request.[93]

The propaganda minister supported pro-Polish publishing in the Reich. Academic research into Eastern Europe produced a new series under the title *Reports on the Eastern Zone* (Ostraum), in which problems of economic geography and settlement politics were discussed. In the first issue, which appeared at the start of 1935, the Eastern Zone was defined as the area between the Rhine and the Urals, between Finland and Persia, which Germany would take the decisive role in shaping.[94] There was always to be room for Poland. So they spoke about a 'German–Polish territorial community in the whole Eastern Zone', the pressure of which might lead to overthrow in Moscow, which would in turn lead to the Ukraine's being detached from Russia and incorporated into a German economic area.[95]

For his part and despite all rebuffs, Piłsudski clung to his idea of an eastern federation stretching from the Baltic over the Ukraine to the Caucasus. It would push Russia back and give Poland, as the strongest element in the federation, the status of an independently great power. So he fostered the efforts of the governor Henryk Józewski towards 'Ukrainianisation' in the former Russian province of Volhynia. This, unlike in Galicia, was not directed against the Polish Republic, but created a refuge for adherents of Symon Petlyura, the last head of the Ukrainian government, murdered in 1926, who had worked together with the Poles in 1920. This kind of Ukrainian policy was thus directed at Kiev and the Soviet Ukraine.[96]

The possible dismemberment of the USSR was a topic of discussion not only in the circles of Ukrainian and Russian emigrants in Berlin, as well as presumably among those Georgian officers who had gambled on the German advance into the Caucasus in 1918 and had, after the Civil War and their subsequent flight into the west, been taken on by the Polish Army. The Soviet government, too, proved to be seriously concerned, as was discovered by the German ambassador to Moscow. Nadolny, who had been routinely appointed to the post in 1933, took the dramatic about-face in German eastern policy as an opportunity to issue a minatory political report.[97] In it he said that the commissar for foreign affairs, Maxim Litvinov, had emphasised the Soviet government's support for Germany's revisionist policy, but added that it rejected Hitler's recognisable intention of using force to achieve it. The completely and utterly banned *Mein Kampf* even expressed the opinion that the restoration of Germany would come at the expense of Russia.

Commissar for Foreign Affairs Maxim Litvinov to the German ambassador in Moscow:

Alfred Rosenberg, the head of the NSDAP's foreign-policy department, was said to have repeatedly 'spoken about an intended German–Polish deal in which Poland would acquire the Ukraine in exchange for returning the Corridor to Germany, or some other severing of the Ukraine from Soviet Russia, and was said to be in contact with Ukrainian separatists. Hitler himself had dedicated the entire fourteenth chapter of his book *Mein Kampf* to considering the collapse of Soviet Russia and how to use that collapse for the purposes of German colonialism. There was a legitimate fear that Germany would use a Russo-Japanese conflict to realise those plans and the pro-Japanese sympathies recently expressed in Germany indicated that that was in fact intended.'[98]

Nadolny was convinced that a war in the Far East was probably inevitable, but was doubtful about whether that would seriously shake the USSR, something that he did not even consider to be in the German interest. He advocated a return to the Rapallo policies, which he described as follows: 'German policy in its effects on the west and east has always been guided by the principle: stasis in the west, dynamism in the east. In the west, it is limited to achieving national unification and bringing about stable relations with the traditional European states; in the east, by contrast, dynamism in the sense of extending our influence into the vastnesses of the East European and Asian territory.'

This had so far been thoroughly successful in concord with Russia. Hitler and Rosenberg, however, were assuming there would be a rapid collapse of the Soviet regime, something that had been taken on by a 'strong element' in Germany. Germany's national aims, however, could not be achieved with, but only against, Poland. 'Cooperating with Poland to realise our national territorial claims in the east at the expense of Russia is thus a chimera.'

The German ambassador to Moscow, Rudolf Nadolny, 9 January 1934:

Furthermore, the other possibility for realising these claims at the expense of the Soviet Union, i.e. the idea of precipitating Poland into a war against the Union and then taking the opportunity to recover the Corridor against Poland's will, cannot be the main thrust of a policy undertaken with that objective, to say nothing of its being openly declared. These kinds of opportunity may perhaps arise out of an existing situation and it will then be up to us to use the moment in our own interest. But in the present situation, Poland is the object of our demands and Russia is not.[99]

So Nadolny could easily imagine using the opportunity of a German–Polish war against the Soviet Union simply to simply take the Corridor away from the Poles. Warsaw could presumably imagine the same thing and kept its cards close to its chest on the question of military cooperation.

Nadolny did not share the contemporary sympathy for Japan. 'What can Japan be to us? Nothing other than a very uncomfortable rival on the global market, who will undercut us everywhere. The blessings that our military and cultural education has given them were poorly rewarded in the Great War.' Should the Soviet Union indeed tumble into a catastrophe, 'our political task will be to draw the best consequences for ourselves from the situation'. Nadolny's pro-Russian argument, with which he could expect agreement among the conservative leaders of the Foreign Ministry, plainly did not completely contradict the line of the chancellor and his National Socialists, in that it entailed developing 'dynamism' in the east and using any opportunity offered to take action against the USSR.

Nadolny did not believe that a Japanese attack in the Far East would fundamentally destabilise the Soviet Union. The German military attachés in Tokyo and Moscow proved equally convinced that the Red Army's western group would remain unaffected.[100] In the Troop Office, which was, as mentioned, the General Staff in disguise, the prospects were similarly assessed. A study in April 1934 found that an escalation of the conflict in the Far East was not to be expected. Should there nonetheless be a military collision between the Russians and the Japanese, the study predicted good odds for the Red Army.[101]

Hitler heedlessly brushed aside the military's prognoses and Nadolny, grumblingly, had to vacate his post in Moscow. The chancellor had now become convinced, despite the fact that rearmament had only just begun and the Reich was still militarily weak, that an opportunity might arise for him to activate the eagerly desired 'dynamism' in the east even now, in the first years of his rule. A policy of placation towards the western powers, particularly if it comprised British neutrality and an alliance with Poland, seemed to offer favourable prospects. Rosenberg, who had taken up a position opposing conservative Foreign Minister Neurath, circulated a memorandum in May 1934 about German–British relations. In it he proposed a German–British–Polish intervention in Soviet Russia. Poland would receive the Ukraine; the British were said to have interests in southern Russian oil.[102] Rosenberg had made the appropriate contact with British economic circles and Mussolini's adviser on eastern politics had told him that, based on his impression of discussions in Warsaw, there existed a desire in Poland to gather 'all the peripheral peoples from Finland to Turkey' for a crusade against the USSR under Piłsudski's leadership.[103] Rosenberg's Führer gave him the task of keeping the 'centrifugal' forces in Russia under observation, so as to be ready 'when things have developed sufficiently'.[104] Military conflict with the Soviet Union seemed to be moving into the realm of the possible and, according to the impression gained not just by Nadolny, into the realm of the probable. That would naturally not have been the 'greater' solution of Operation Barbarossa in 1941, not a march on Moscow, but a 'lesser', improvised German–Polish intervention to remove the Ukraine, possibly also including a march on Kiev. The trigger would have been a Japanese attack in the Far East. In the NSDAP's foreign-policy department, it was assumed that a Japanese 'liberation' of Soviet Russia's Mongolian peoples would instigate the disintegration of the Soviet imperium in the Ukraine and the Caucasus, and that Germany would have to 'carefully observe' this process.[105]

The Soviet leadership, in any case, did not understand the programme outlined in *Mein Kampf* to mean that the fascist dictator first wanted to defeat all of Europe, including Poland, in order to then use amassed German military force to overthrow the USSR. In Moscow, too, memories of the years 1918–20 still seem to have been very fresh and to have shaped their perception of the threat.

1935: Is There an Opportunity for a Campaign against the USSR?

The Soviet military's intelligence services supposedly possessed a dossier in which a departmental leader in the Polish General Staff, a former Russian officer, reported a discussion in Warsaw's Ministry of Defence.[106] Piłsudski was said to believe that the main task of Polish foreign policy was not to prevent the German armies from advancing eastward, but to prevent them at all costs from ever setting foot on Polish soil again, because they would never leave the territories they claimed. If Poland limited itself to benevolent neutrality, the Germans would proceed to the north and south of them, that is, via the Baltic states and the countries along the Danube. Its flank covered by the Poles, the northern thrust would probably aim at the industrial regions of Leningrad, the southern at the grain fields of the Ukraine, the lower Volga and the oilfields of the Caucasus. But this southern offensive could begin only once Hitler had taken Austria and Czechoslovakia in hand and established control over Hungary and Romania. Because these conditions were not yet met, Poland still had time to build up its own forces. If the Germans were to defeat the Red Army – which would have to leave considerable forces in the centre to guard against Poland – in a pincer movement and reach the Volga, but then be weakened by losses and overextended supply lines, Poland and its hitherto unused armed forces would be able to dictate their own terms. This kind of German–Soviet war could then lead to the creation of the desired Polish–Byelorussian–Ukrainian union, which would lastingly secure Poland against Russia and Germany.

It cannot be ruled out that both sides – as seen in the case of Nadolny – thought that, if it came to a German and Polish war against the USSR, they might be able to outsmart their alliance partner and assert their own national interests. What is telling is that – as is shown by a number of incidents – this kind of war was not only discussed, but the decision-makers were convinced of its likelihood and made the corresponding preparations, which were continued even though the international situation then evolved in a way that again reduced the risk of war on the USSR's borders.

That Hitler was in complete earnest in 1934–5 about this Polish variation is demonstrated by an almost forgotten event. Still unregarded by historians, Piłsudski's memoirs and papers appeared in Germany in 1935. The four-volume work was authorised by the old marshal shortly before his death and selected, edited and translated by the Polish Army's Office of Military History. The presence of a comprehensive self-presentation by the Polish head of state on the German book market was in itself highly unusual. Joseph Stalin, for one, was not given a similar opportunity between 1939 and 1941 to introduce himself to the German public. The memoirs of an old soldier and field

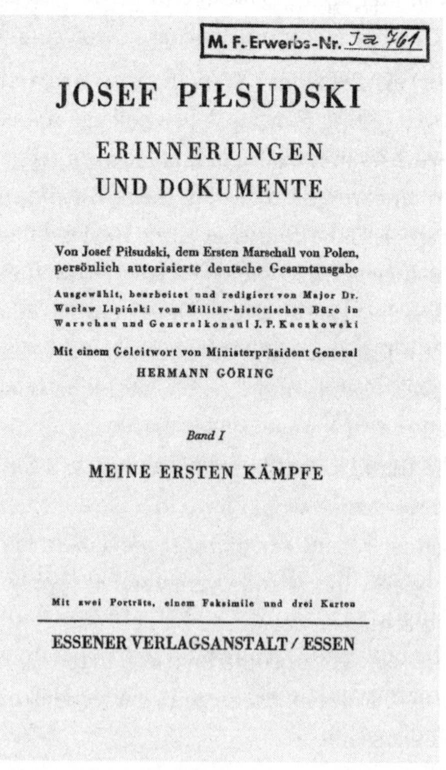

JOSEF PIŁSUDSKI

ERINNERUNGEN
UND DOKUMENTE

Von Josef Piłsudski, dem Ersten Marschall von Polen, persönlich autorisierte deutsche Gesamtausgabe

Ausgewählt, bearbeitet und redigiert von Major Dr. Wacław Lipiński vom Militär-historischen Büro in Warschau und Generalkonsul J. P. Kaczkowski

Mit einem Geleitwort von Ministerpräsident General
HERMANN GÖRING

Band I

MEINE ERSTEN KÄMPFE

Mit zwei Porträts, einem Faksimile und drei Karten

ESSENER VERLAGSANSTALT / ESSEN

5. Title page of the limited 'Marshal Edition' of 1937.

commander, a patriot and a statesman, who did not shy away from publicising his authoritarian attitudes and his keen criticism of democratic and corrupt politicians, were perfectly suited to eliciting great sympathy not just among National Socialist readers. Even convinced Nazis could temporarily become admirers of the Polish leader.

There is no doubt that the old marshal in Warsaw, the nationalist and former socialist, must have been a more sympathetic figure for the Führer in Berlin than the Prussian field marshal and Reich president who was fading away on the Neudeck estate in East Prussia and who at least nominally restricted Hitler's exercise of power until his death on 2 August 1934. Piłsudski died a few months after Hindenburg, on 2 May 1935, but the two marshals would presumably have had little to say to each other even after the non-aggression pact. The Pole's memoirs appeared shortly after his death, and the first three volumes each received a foreword from the German side, which, as befitted the topic, came from the most prominent of officials. The introduction to the first volume, the memoirs, was signed by the Prussian prime minister, General Hermann Göring. The second man in the Third Reich found some very personal words:

Hermann Göring, 8 August 1935:

Marshal Piłsudski was a man. I knew him personally and was deeply impressed by the force of his personality. Marshal Piłsudski worked in selfless and total devotion to his fatherland. Even in his lifetime he entered the annals of his fatherland in mythical stature. Today's Poland would not exist without Piłsudski.

We Germans have had our feeling for heroism and the iron footstep given back to us by Adolf Hitler. That is why we revere the world's great men. That is why the flags were lowered in Germany, too, when, surrounded by a mourning nation, the Polish Army paraded for a final time past the coffin of their country's first marshal.[107]

Göring went on to say that Hitler and Piłsudski had created the basis 'on which, as a blessing to our nations and others beyond them, a permanent world peace can be built and is being built'. He hoped that the appearance of this work in Germany would deepen understanding of its neighbour. It was 'more than a friendly gesture'!

These phrases can certainly be taken with a pinch of salt. For the third volume, consisting of Piłsudski's military lectures, which appeared in 1936, the foreword was written by Major-General Friedrich von Rabenau. The head of the army's new archive in Potsdam praised the Pole's sense of honour and his leadership: 'He was the only one for a long time to unite in himself the commander and the statesman. The last such man known to us is Frederick the Great.' For the Germans, there was no higher honour than that.

Volume four contained speeches and orders. More on the second volume later. As a whole, the work was lent formidable significance because the publishing house, apparently at the instigation of the highest circles in Germany, produced a limited luxury edition. The subscription list for this particularly lavish 'Marshal Edition' was closed on 23 November 1936. At the start of 1937, the four volumes were sent to the most prominent people in both states. The list was headed by Reich Chancellor Hitler and the president of the Polish Republic, Ignacy Mościcki, as well as the marshal's widow. These were followed by the captains of German industry, the cabinet and the top brass, first among them the defence minister, Werner von Blomberg, and the commander-in-chief of the army, Werner Freiherr von Fritsch. Heinrich Himmler and Reinhard Heydrich were also on the list.[108] 'More than friendly': so said Göring in his foreword, still entirely under the influence of his visit to Piłsudski in January 1935. This spectacular state occasion on the first anniversary of the non-aggression pact evidently served both sides as a means of finding out how far they could go together. At that point, Hitler regarded Russia as a 'gigantic military force' against which the Reich would be able to move only with Polish support. To Rosenberg he spoke about how German–Polish cooperation should not end when the pact expired after ten years, but should be put into place permanently.[109]

This was how Göring ended up participating in some unusual discussions in Poland in 1935, which are presented differently in German and Polish accounts. It is not disputed that Göring and his Polish interlocutors discussed transforming the existing defensive pact into an aggressive one with anti-Soviet intent. It is usually said that the initiative came from Göring on Hitler's orders and that he received an unmistakeable rebuff from the Poles.[110] It was all said to have been a 'great tactical game' played to deceive Germany's Polish partners.[111] A reconstruction of the discussions, however, gives a rather different picture.

First of all, it was the Polish government that invited Göring to visit the former royal hunting estate of Białowieża. According to the report made by the German ambassador to Warsaw, the Poles were unusually attentive to their guest and, as well as ensuring the hunting went well, arranged a special train to Warsaw, a series of receptions and accompaniment by the Polish foreign secretary to make sure that Göring would regard the visit as a 'great personal success'. In particular, the two-hour audience with Marshal Piłsudski and his closest military advisers was seen as sensational by Polish public opinion.[112]

As for the political content of the discussions and, especially, the military element, the German military attaché in Warsaw, General Max Joseph Schindler, made his report three weeks later to the defence minister and the head of the Troop Office. In the meantime, it had trickled out that very far-ranging ambitions had been on the table. Schindler, who had participated in Göring's discussions, subsequently learned that Chancellor Hitler did not think they had gone too far. According to him, Hitler had not given Göring full power to negotiate, but had accepted Göring's report after his return. To his adviser on eastern policy, Rosenberg, Hitler said merely: 'Any intentions Poland has further east are of no interest to us.'[113]

According to Schindler's report, it was the Poles – presumably their military representatives – who in discussing 'possible military cooperation to defend against a Russian advance' made the far-ranging suggestions on their own initiative.[114] If Poland were given 'a free hand in the Ukraine', Germany would receive 'influence in the Baltic states' in exchange. There were suggestions for how to solve the problem of the Corridor. Looking at it calmly, the Polish side evidently had to recognise that any military cooperation against Russia would be possible only if Germany controlled a secure overland link to East Prussia and so to an area near the Russian border. Hitler was apprised of this situation, just like Defence Minister Werner von Blomberg and Chief of Staff Ludwig Beck, and must have been satisfied. He could not have guessed that the group that came to power after Piłsudski would adopt an uncompromising stance on the questions of Danzig and the Corridor soon after the marshal's death, and again seek to strengthen ties with France.

On his hunting trip, Göring initially spoke to General Kazimierz Sosnkowski, the army inspector responsible for the eastern border area Polesia. It seems evident that they discussed options for defence against the Soviet Union. Sosnkowski, who was standing, as it were, directly opposite the Red Army, had explained a few days beforehand to the French ambassador and his military attaché that any kind of cooperation between France and the USSR was undesirable from a Polish perspective. It would be insane to imagine that, in the event of a Franco–German war, thousands of Soviet bombers would attack Berlin to help the French citizenry. In the case of a Polish–Soviet war, which Sosnkowski expected within two or three years, German military assistance would be extremely desirable – and how would France be able to help Poland in that case? The Polish general was thinking above all of a defensive battle, because a joint assault on the USSR would entail enormous dangers and, even if it were to succeed, it might well be that the Ukrainians would 'prefer to work for the king of Prussia'.[115]

This is where the Polish ambassador to Berlin, Józef Lipski, who also accompanied Göring, comes into play. Lipski immediately relayed to Deputy Foreign Minister Jan Szembek in Warsaw that Göring had suggested 'almost an anti-Russian alliance and a joint march on Russia' and had held out the prospect of 'great opportunities in the Ukraine' for Poland.[116] Given the well-known grandiloquence of the 'Reich Huntmaster', it is easy to envision Göring having a drink with Sosnkowski and letting himself be carried away by his political imagination. And he was of course familiar with his Führer's intentions and ideas in this area. These vague intimations of Göring's were apparently enough to electrify the Poles.[117] They quickly took steps to extend Göring's visit and drove him to Warsaw in an official train.

The Polish foreign minister, Colonel Beck, accompanied the Prussian prime minister and was presumably responsible for Göring's being accorded great honours and much friendly attention in the capital, contrary to initial Polish statements that the visit would not be political in character.[118] Here, too, sources from the later milieu of the Polish government-in-exile describe a course of events different from that reported by the German military attaché. At a reception in the German embassy, Göring met Prime Minister Leon Kozłowski. Then came the sensational audience with the marshal and his military advisers. While there, Göring was said to have proposed that Piłsudski be commander-in-chief of a joint German–Polish invasion force. The Polish generals, it seems, were not convinced by Göring's eagerness and perhaps feared that the marshal would accept the offer. According to the legends surrounding the old warhorse, Piłsudski would sometimes in his sleep order the advance on Minsk.[119]

But the marshal is said to have reacted cautiously and emphasised that Poland could do nothing that would lead to tensions with the Soviet Union.[120] Despite the contradictions between sources, it is certain that military cooperation was discussed during Göring's visit and that a division of spheres of interest in Russian territory was brought up. And Göring in no way took his

6. Polish Foreign Minister Józef Beck (right) on a visit to Hermann Göring at Carinhall, July 1935.

conversation with Piłsudski as an outright rejection. On the contrary.[121] His foreword to the marshal's memoirs, which appeared that same year, conveyed the deep impression that the conversation had made on him, which he had carried back to Berlin. The Führer's reaction was correspondingly positive.

According to information from the Soviet secret service, there was considerable internal criticism of Beck's pro-German foreign policy. One of those against it was General Józef Haller, a close comrade of Piłsudski's in World War I, commander on the Russian front and, by the end of the war, creator of the Blue Army of Polish volunteers in France. He had become a political opponent of Piłsudski's in the mid 1920s and been sacked by him from the army. Haller accused him in 1935 of wanting to agree an anti-Soviet treaty with the Germans, which in the event of war with the USSR would allow Germany to make military use of the Corridor for its supply lines. He said Piłsudski was obviously prepared to surrender the Corridor to realise his fantastical plans for the Ukraine and Lithuania.[122] After hearing about this, Stalin might easily assume that there was a secret additional protocol in the German–Polish Non-Aggression Pact of 1934. Indeed, the German–Polish discussions did continue to circle around that subject until the start of 1939.

The marshal died shortly afterwards and his successors seemed open to further negotiations about the partnership's anti-Soviet stance. So in the following years, Hitler repeatedly tried to pull Warsaw onto his side by pitching the idea of a German–Polish campaign against the Soviet Union. Göring was the most prominent intermediary and he held talks with the Poles on the occasion of Piłsudski's funeral in May 1935, on hunting trips in February 1936 and 1937, and then again in 1938.[123]

Colonel Beck, who, as foreign minister, toed Piłsudski's line until 1935, indicated the new government's priorities in a talk with Göring on 19 May, when the German came to Warsaw after attending the marshal's funeral in Krakow.[124] Their main concern was to undermine negotiations for an 'Eastern Locarno' with which France was attempting to create a collective security system in Eastern and Central Europe by bringing in the USSR. The Franco–Soviet mutual-assistance pact, signed a few days earlier, had unsettled Warsaw. Piłsudski had seen that the mechanisms of the pact could, in the event of a conflict in Central Europe, make his country an avenue of advance or a battleground for the Red Army. Moreover, Poland was not prepared to agree to Czechoslovakia's involvement, because the border guarantee that came with it would have meant relinquishing Poland's claims to the province of Cieszyn.

7. German–Polish military relations: Polish officers visit the Infantry Academy in Dresden in August 1935 on the invitation of the Wehrmacht's commander-in-chief, Werner von Blomberg.

So Beck emphasised German–Polish togetherness without committing himself to anything more concrete.

Summer 1935 brought the possibility of closer cooperation on a military level. Today this is a forgotten episode in a largely unknown chapter of German–Polish relations. The director of the Polish military academy, Major-General Tadeusz Kutrzeba, was invited to Dresden by the commander-in-chief of the Wehrmacht, Werner von Blomberg. Kutrzeba commanded the Poznań Army in September 1939 and fought a bitter battle on the Bzura, the only occasion on which the Wehrmacht, for a short while at least, found itself in serious difficulties. On 24 August 1935, he was received in Dresden by the commanding general of the II Army Corps, Lieutenant General Wilhelm List (who in September 1939 commanded the 14th Army and carried out the advance on Lviv). Together with the Polish military attaché, Staff Lieutenant Colonel Antoni Szymański, Kutrzeba viewed troop exercises and visited the famous infantry academy where Erwin Rommel had taught.

From today's standpoint, the idea that Germany and Poland could have organised a joint campaign in the Soviet Union may seem absurd. At the time, the peacetime strength of the Red Army, at 1.3 million men, outnumbered the German and Polish armies by two to one. But those in command saw things differently. The conflict in the Far East might have simmered down in the meantime, but it continued to bubble. Were the Red Army to find itself fighting a war on two fronts, it would be able to deploy only a part of its forces in the west. That could in theory reduce it to level pegging with a German–Polish alliance, and Moscow would fall short even of that if it also had to factor in Finland, the Baltic states and Romania as potential enemies. Moreover, Piłsudski had built up a close relationship with Turkey, which was giving support to the nationalist movements of the USSR's Asian peoples.

The idea of breaking up Soviet Russia with a pincer movement continued to fascinate, especially as it was believed that there might be willingness among the leaders of the Red Army to turn against Stalin and the Soviet system. Although the dying Piłsudski and his slick foreign minister were clinging to the status quo and currently indisposed to adventure, there also appeared to be – and this was the impression the Germans took from Warsaw – other opinions in circulation among Poland's leaders. Ultimately, everything depended on whether and when a Japanese–Soviet war broke out in the Far East, and on whether the USSR would survive its domestic unrest.

On 16 March 1935, Hitler announced that the Reich's 'military sovereignty' had been restored. That signified a clear break with the limits imposed by the Treaty of Versailles and initiated unrestrained rearmament of the new 'Wehrmacht' (the Armed Forces), including the reintroduction of compulsory military service and an increase in troop numbers to a peacetime strength of 800,000 men.

France reacted by concluding its mutual-assistance pact with the USSR on 2 May 1935. The pact, signed into force for five years, obliged both sides to offer immediate aid in the event of an unprovoked attack on the other by a third country. Two weeks later, a Czechoslovak–Soviet treaty completed the security system which Paris hoped would contain Hitler's aggressive revisionism.[125] France's previous efforts towards an 'eastern pact' had failed because the Poles, the Baltic states and Romania declined to cooperate with the USSR, because they feared that in a war Soviet troops would march through their territory and take away their independence.

Hitler countered the French initiative on 18 June with the Anglo–German Naval Agreement. Concluding that agreement encouraged his belief that London would let him have his free hand in the East. Two months later, the prospect of an Italian war in Abyssinia gave him hope that, despite the current lull in the Far East, his march on Russia would soon be able to begin.

Goebbels's diary, 19 August 1935:

The Führer is happy. Gives us an outline of his plans for foreign policy: eternal partnership with Britain. [...] But expansion to the east. [...] The conflicts Italy–Abyssinia–Britain and Japan–Russia are imminent. Then our great and historic hour will have struck. We must be ready. Wonderful moment. We are all deeply moved.[126]

Its cooperation with Moscow made Czechoslovakia a potential enemy that had to be neutralised at the next opportunity. The question of French intervention seemed to resolve itself because in 1936 a Popular Front government paralysed the country and, in the same year, a civil war broke out south of the Pyrenees. A German expeditionary force helped Francisco Franco's fascist regime take power in Spain. Finally, Italy's invasion of Abyssinia brought it into international difficulties that made it dependent on Hitler's support. Il Duce was forced to put aside his distrust of the Führer and relinquish his patronage of Austria.

In 1935–6, the Third Reich gained both room to manoeuvre and considerable prestige on the international stage. The USSR's entry into the League of Nations and Stalin's pacts with Paris and Prague seemed feeble gestures in comparison. So the Soviet dictator moved to an emergency footing. He employed brutal domestic policies to stabilise his empire and secure it against the threat of international intervention. The Holodomor, as the famine of 1932–3 is called today, had already destroyed the social basis of the anti-communist agricultural population, especially in the Ukraine. According to the most recent calculations, at least 3.5 million people lost their lives there.[127] And Stalin began a witch-hunt aimed at supposed internal enemies and potential traitors. Although these 'purges' strengthened his personal rule, they led by the end of the 1930s to a fateful weakening of the USSR in general and of the Red Army in particular. The most eminent victim was, in 1937, Chief of the General Staff Mikhail Tukhachevsky, who only two years earlier, on summer manoeuvres in the Ukraine, had displayed the Red Army at the height of its powers. The decision to stage the exercises near Kiev, and the nature of the battles practised, were a clear warning to the foreign powers discussing intervention in the Ukraine or even speculating about a pincer movement that would crush the USSR from the west and the Far East.

On those manoeuvres, paratroopers were included in an operation for the first time in military history. They assisted the rest of the forces in breaking through an entrenched line of defence, in rapidly broadening the attack and in encircling and destroying the opponent with the aid of mechanised forces. Even river-crossings with heavy artillery were practised. Overall, the principles of the Soviet theory of deep operations were substantiated. It earned Tukhachevsky a promotion to the youngest marshal of the Red Army. He was 42 and had every reason to believe that he would never again experience a debacle like the one in 1920 at the hands of the recently deceased Marshal Piłsudski. In those late-summer days of 1935, his analysis of the 1920 campaign appeared in the Berlin edition of Piłsudski's writing and was passed on to the German General Staff for study – but more on that below.

In Berlin, tangible measures were put in place to improve Germany's ability to resist a westward advance by the visibly strengthened Red Army. The shortest route via Warsaw to Berlin led through the Oder–Warta region, where all the Germans had so far done in terms of fortification was to develop the natural obstacles. This previous work was now upgraded on the model of the French Maginot Line, becoming an 'eastern wall' complete with bunkers

8. Soviet paratroopers conduct airborne exercises, around 1935.

and miles of underground tunnels. Moreover, the Luftwaffe developed a long-range bomber under the designation 'Uralbomber' and the Army Weapons Agency, when designing rail-mounted artillery, took into account the problem of switching onto the Russian gauge.[128]

The USSR in the Wehrmacht's Operational Planning

Whether Hitler already had definite ideas about how to wage the war he was proposing in the east is impossible to say. We can, however, proceed on the assumption that it was only after Hindenburg had died, the Reichswehr had sworn an oath of allegiance to him personally and, in March 1935, he had become supreme commander of the new Wehrmacht, that he was able to exert a significant influence on processes and plans internal to the military. Even so, he treated the General Staff with the greatest respect until well into World War II. It was only during Operation Barbarossa that Hitler began to intervene more strongly in operational planning and decision-making – because he recognised that the war was not taking the course he had imagined.

In the 1930s, he generally restricted himself to the macro-level political and strategic issues of foreign and military policy. That dovetailed with the expectations of the military, which had advocated a division of responsibilities since the mid-nineteenth century. According to Moltke, it was the politicians' task before a war to secure a favourable starting position for the military, in particular by gathering allies. The military was responsible for fielding, arming and training its forces, for analysing potential enemies and their capabilities and intentions, for careful reconnaissance of routes of advance and possible battlefields, and, finally, for the meticulous planning of the advance at – preferably before – the outbreak of war. When war began, the politicians were to step back and give the military the support it needed to achieve victory. It was only after that had been done that the responsibility again lay with the politicians, who had to take care of the peace treaty and postwar relations.

This was of course only an ideal. There had been friction even between Moltke and Bismarck during the wars to unify the Reich, and although the military had succeeded in World War I in reducing the significance of the Reich's civilian leadership ever further – until the Supreme Command was exercising what was almost a military dictatorship – the Great War had been lost partly because the military had not been capable of solving the problems of domestic and alliance politics, nor those of overall strategy. In the Reichswehr under Seeckt, that experience had intensified the tendency to stay largely out of politics and concentrate on the tasks originally considered military.

From an organisational or a tactical-operational perspective, there was no doubt that the Prussian–German officer corps could look back on superb achievements. Since the end of the nineteenth century, numerous other armies had taken the German General Staff and its highly professional attitude as a model. But some peculiarly German characteristics had emerged in its operational thinking, and these must be examined if we are to understand the military planning that led to Barbarossa.[129]

The defining considerations were: the Germans' position in the centre of Europe, the resultant danger of a war on two or more fronts, and the potential for the Reich to be overmatched in terms of both men and materiel. As Schlieffen had seen, however, this central position did have the advantage of geographically separating Germany's two most powerful opponents, France and Russia, from each other. Given Central Europe's excellently developed infrastructure, the Germans might be able to operate on interior lines and defeat their two enemies one at a time. Their numerical inferiority might thus be compensated to some degree by their ability to concentrate their forces on one side at a time. That, however, necessitated a few prerequisites. First among those, they had to have highly trained troops and their tactical-operational leadership had to be superior to the enemy's. Only thus did it seem possible to end this kind of war so quickly that the enemy coalition would have no opportunity to mobilise its superior resources and grind out a victory in a long-drawn-out war of attrition.

The parameters of skilled operational leadership were movement, attack, speed, initiative, freedom to make decisions, concentration of forces, encirclement, surprise and annihilation. The objective was to encircle the enemy's forces in one or more battles close to the German border and destroy them. The destruction of the enemy's 'living forces' (that is, neutralising them, not physically obliterating the soldiers) had to be quick and comprehensive, to prevent the enemy from regenerating and establishing new fronts. In the ideal scenario, the enemy would recognise that he had been defeated and declare himself ready to negotiate a peace.

So it was these considerations that meant any war would have to be won in battles close to the German border, up to a depth of 150 miles into enemy territory. Of course, the German–French war of 1870–1 had already shown that defeating the enemy's armies would not necessarily lead him to surrender. If the Germans wanted to prevent transition to a 'total war', they required a complementary political strategy that would break the enemy's will to resist. Political warfare had been very successful in the east in 1917. The plans of 1934–5 took that as their guide.

To solve the strategic problem of fighting a war on two fronts with a disadvantage in resources, the General Staff had to stick to the principle of arranging decisive battles close to their own borders – or else advise the political leadership not to go to war. But giving that advice could ultimately have ruined the General Staff's belief in their own professionalism and their position in German society. And what conclusions had the leaders of Hitler's Reichswehr drawn from defeat in World War I, in which most of them had been middle-ranking officers in the General Staff? In a collective refusal to recognise their actual strategic circumstances – the fact that their resources were insufficient for the fight to become a great or global power – they interpreted the defeat like this: the kaiser's Reich had had a recipe for success in the Schlieffen–Moltke plan and had merely failed to implement it correctly. After all, the army had remained 'undefeated in the field'.

By criticising the kaiser's generals, the younger staff officers freed themselves from any need to question the ambition of becoming a great power. They believed that they would do better in the next war. For them, the pivotal question was: how could an offensive – which is the way quick, decisive battles would have to be fought – regain its manoeuvrability after an initial engagement? This decision to limit their professional thinking and rethinking was at heart anti-political and assumed that the politicians would take care of securing an international and strategic situation in which war could be declared.

The military had at least learned that an overly strict 'road map' could become damaging. It was actually one of their profession's basic principles that only the advance and the initial phase of a campaign could be planned in detail. After that, Clausewitz's 'friction' began. So Seeckt had restarted the tradition of giving staff officers intensive education. Studies of individual tactical-operational problems, as well as General Staff exercises and war games in which high-ranking officers simulated battles 'on the terrain', all trained the officer's ability to assess a situation and make the necessary decisions himself. Any kind of template was to be avoided; it was a matter of training the commander's flexibility, skill and resolve. These war games were highly valued also as a means of testing, despite all the Clausewitzian friction of manoeuvre, every conceivable and likely option in future warfare. To the historian, these war games provide evidence of how the military was thinking and planning, even when the original blueprints were, as was routine, destroyed after use.[130]

How did Hitler's about-face on eastern policy influence the Reichswehr's plans? As mentioned above, the Reichswehr's leaders found it very difficult to let go of the idea that a German–Russian alliance would guard Germany's rear in the Reich's conflict with the arch-enemy, France. The period of readjustment went on for months. Indeed, the chancellor's efforts to complete the strategic turn against the USSR and win Poland as an ally for a future war of intervention were not to have any great influence within the military until 1935.

It did, however, make it possible to start thinking about an invasion of Czechoslovakia, which a study gave the name 'Operation Training'. The study assumed that Great Britain would stay neutral, in line with the naval agreement, as would Italy, so that a lightning-quick invasion of Czechoslovakia would be able to capture any forward bases of the Red Army and gain a little breathing space in case France could not be intimidated into staying out of the war. Chief of Staff Ludwig Beck, however, criticised the study for lacking both an appreciation of the wider strategic situation and a realistic appraisal of the present level of armament. Until his resignation in 1938, Beck often worried that making isolated operational plans without an overall plan for the war as a whole would lead to recklessness and then to a large-scale war that Germany could not win. Beck was more sceptical than others even about the prospects of a quick and decisive operation against the Czechoslovakian Army. He was not fundamentally rejecting a strategy which intended to begin securing Germany's status as a great power by occupying Austria and Czechoslovakia. But Beck first wanted to finish rearming in order to be able later to strike harder in a more favourable European situation.[131] His solution was 'rapid rearmament plus military alliance'.

In the Wehrmacht's war games from 1935 onwards, it was assumed that the Red Army – given Polish neutrality – would be able to launch attacks via Romania and the Baltic states, and that the Germans would be easily able to contain them. In this way, Poland's anti-Soviet stance, holding the centre, made it possible for Hitler to act against the west and the south-east, preliminaries to eastern expansion.

After 1935, the leaders of the German Navy, in their yearly exercises, also played through scenarios of Russian intervention. To prevent the larger Soviet fleet from breaking out of the narrow Gulf of Finland and making an attack on the western Baltic, the German strategy would be to lay mine barriers in the eastern Baltic and then guard them. That would not be easy, given the breadth of the Baltic and that it would need to be done off the coasts of neutral states.[132] Nonetheless, from the navy's point of view, it was essential that the Russian fleet be locked in, as in World War I. This would secure the strategically vital sea routes across the Baltic and allow supplies, particularly Swedish iron ore, to reach the Reich. The navy considered itself superior to the Soviets in tactics, technology and personnel, and believed that it would take Russia many years to develop a 'naval strike force'.

The threat of Soviet invasion was hardly acute, as the Red Army could not reach the German border without crossing foreign territory. That limited the significance of the Soviet–Czechoslovak assistance pact, even if one imagined that Soviet squadrons would be flown across and stationed in Czechoslovakia.[133] So the idea of an offensive exerted a certain fascination. Polish neutrality created a range of opportunities – and an alliance would have provided even more – for changing the balance of power in the east. The Germans began to consider East Prussia a potential springboard as early as 1934–5. Its small neighbour Lithuania had been at loggerheads with both Germany and Poland since 1920. The Reich demanded the return of the Memel Territory, an important strategic position and a bridgehead on the eastern side of the Neman River. Poland had occupied the area around Vilnius, which, along with other advantages, had straightened the border with Russia. But this had led to a latent state of war with Lithuania, which formally ended only in 1937 when the Lithuanian government gave in. President Antanas Smetona used dictatorial violence on the fascist model to govern a country weakened by attempted coups and agricultural unrest.

Finland and Estonia had long had close military ties with the Wehrmacht. For example, they allowed the Wehrmacht to listen in on the Red Army's radio traffic, almost up to the gates of Leningrad.[134] At a reception for Finnish intelligence officers, Werner Freiherr von Fritsch, commander-in-chief of the army, thanked them for the many years over which they had worked together and assured them that the 'new Germany' would work 'with especial zeal' to 'tackle Soviet Russia as the bearer of the communist idea. […] Our work against Russia now takes the very highest priority.'[135]

Part of the preparations consisted in having the Defence Ministry investigate how propaganda could be deployed against the USSR in the event of war. In either a defensive war fought in Central Europe or, an option that was considered feasible, a military intervention in the USSR by European powers under German leadership, they would play up the nationalist minorities and their own anti-Semitic slogans. Having evaluated the experiences of World War I, they also suggested setting up Ukrainian units under direct German command rather than leaving them in the control of their countrymen. These ideas were indeed partially implemented in 1941.[136]

If the Baltic states and Finland were regarded as potentially under German influence, and if the extent of Poland's eastern border was also factored in, Leningrad and Kiev were absolutely within reach. In 1935, this must still have seemed fairly unrealistic. But what changed things was the decision to shift the focus of strategic deliberations to the east. The former corporal who was now in charge had devoured military literature on World War I – alongside the classics – during his autodidactic training to become the 'Greatest Field Commander of All Time'. While in prison in Landsberg, at the latest, he read a paper by Max Hoffmann. Hoffmann had been commander-in-chief in the east in 1917–18. He had defeated the Russian Army and led the long advance eastward. The general provided a number of examples to show how a quick victory in the east could have allowed the Germans to win the whole war.[137] His most important point was that there had never been any prospect of a rapid victory in the west and that it would therefore have made more sense to focus on the east while remaining on the defensive on the western front.

East Central Europe after the peace treaties of 1919/1922
Oslo
Finland
Helsinki
Leningrad
Stockholm
Tallinn
(Reval)
Estonia
Russian Socialist
Federation SR
Volga
Sweden
Denmark
Latvia
Riga
Moscow
Copenhagen
BALTIC SEA
Lithuania
Vilnius
(Wilna)
Gdańsk
East Prussia
Minsk
Elbe
West Russia
SSR
Berlin
Vistula
Warsaw
Soviet Union
USSR
German Reich
Oder
Poland
Kiev
Prague
Kraków
Lviv
Dnieper
Czechoslovakia
Ukraine SSR
Carpatho-
Ukraine
Vienna
Budapest
Austria
Odessa
Hungary
Romania
Sevastopol
Belgrade
Bucharest
Danube
BLACK
SEA
Italy
Yugoslavia
Sofia
Bulgaria
Rome
Istanbul
Tirana
Albania
Ankara
Greece
Turkey
Athens
Sicily
MEDITERRANEAN SEA
Crete
0
500 km
N

But how was a swift military victory in the east to be achieved? After all, the Central Powers had needed three years to push the Russians out of the Polish 'balcony'. For the men of 1935, alternatives could be found in Piłsudski's successes of 1920.

It was in 1935 that the second volume of Piłsudski's memoirs appeared in German. It juxtaposed his assessment of the 1920 campaign with that of his opponent Tukhachevsky. The foreword was written by the defence minister and commander-in-chief of the Wehrmacht, Major-General Werner von Blomberg. For professional soldiers, he said, this war, which should be considered 'one of the great turning points in world history in the past decades', deserved 'to be attentively traced with the aid of the marshal's gripping account. An abundance of space, a lack of resources and the idiosyncrasies of hastily assembled troops gave this war a unique form.' Even if a war between great powers would presumably be different in nature, there was still a 'profusion of valuable insights' to be gained from this historical case study. The Germans' own study into the war of 1920 was commissioned by Blomberg after this publication and appeared in summer 1940, just in time.

Major-General Werner von Blomberg on the war of 1920:

This war stood strategically and to some extent tactically in the shadow of the World War. The experiences and concepts of the World War had a conscious or unconscious effect on both sides. But the circumstances had fundamentally changed. There were no more mass armies or locked fronts. There was neither an overwhelming deployment of materiel nor the pounding of day- and week-long artillery battles.

Everything depended on adapting the eternal principles of war to new conditions and so uncovering the secret of victory. That seems easy and is yet difficult. It requires a clear head, independent thought and an iron resolve that can transform insights into deeds.

This was where Piłsudski's greatness as a commander showed itself. He freed himself from the obsolete concepts of the recent past. He waged the war as was required by the parameters of space, time and relative strength. He could not seek to decide the war by a mass advance across locked fronts, but instead exploited the huge space available for rapid and far-ranging troop movements. Like all great commanders, he was not shy of giving up his own territory. So he became a master of the war of manoeuvre.[138]

One important feature of the war of 1920, according to Blomberg, was the deployment of large cavalry formations. That may have become outdated, but it gave some valuable pointers on the issue that all European armies were presently arguing about among themselves: how to deploy and repel large manoeuvrable formations, light divisions and armoured groups. Alongside the military lessons, Blomberg reminded his readers that Poland had prevented Bolshevism from spreading to Germany.

'In heavy fighting, Poland threw Bolshevism back into the country of its origin and erected a solid dam between it and the West. In doing so, Poland protected Europe and Germany in particular from collapse, and decisively contributed to the preservation of the entire occidental culture. The National Socialist Germany of Adolf Hitler knows the worth of that accomplishment.'

This assessment was still being popularised in 1937, when a military writer publishing under the pseudonym 'Agricola' (one Alexander Bauermeister) wrote a book about 'the miracle on the Vistula' *in memoriam* Marshal Piłsudski.[139] The slim volume, which was published by a house close to the Wehrmacht and presented like a novel, was based on the war diary of a former officer in the Russian General Staff. It accorded the Polish marshal the highest praise: 'The eerie red phantom was swatted away by Piłsudski like an annoyingly persistent fly.' The author did not spare Tukhachevsky his criticisms, but granted that the Russians' commander-in-chief had been only 26 years old at the time. Tukhachevsky was said not to have had any talent as a field commander, though the defeat had been the fault, above all, of his junior officers. Nevertheless, the merciless forced march from Minsk to Warsaw was to be respected, even if it had been spurred on by an underestimation of the Poles.

The book opens with Tukhachevsky's order to his army group on 2 July 1920: 'The road to world revolution leads over the corpse of Poland! Forward to Vilnius, Minsk and Warsaw!' And it ended with a reminder of 'a wildly agitated time in which Europe's fate hung by a silken thread and Tukhachevsky's red hordes stood at the gates of Warsaw, ready to pounce and drown Europe in an ocean of blood and tears.'

In 1935, the Soviet marshal presented his own 'Führer', Stalin, with a memorandum on the topic of 'Hitler's plans for war',[140] in which he described Germany's rearmament and its enormous military potential. Tukhachevsky analysed Germany's new doctrine of warfare, which aimed to use mass deployment of tanks, aeroplanes and motorised infantry to swiftly destroy the bulk of the enemy's forces, throw his mobilisation into disarray and annihilate his centres of power. To illustrate Hitler's intentions, he pointed to well-known passages in *Mein Kampf* that named Russia as the main goal for the policy of Lebensraum. At the moment, said Tukhachevsky, there was no need to expect direct aggression. Rather, Hitler was trying to weaken the USSR's western borders and prevent a Soviet–French alliance. But, according to their agents, Hitler wanted to gain a free hand in the east in the future. A German–Polish alliance was said to be thoroughly possible, but Stalin crossed out this prognosis, apparently because he thought it unlikely. By all accounts, the Soviet dictator assumed that his Austrian adversary's priority was revenge against the western powers and that Nazi ideology was only a cover for coolly calculating power politics, which would sooner or later lead Hitler, under the influence of the conservative milieux around him, back to the policies of Rapallo. That prediction was both right and wrong, as history would show.

2

A WAR OF INTERVENTION AGAINST THE SOVIET UNION?

1936: 'War-Ready in Four Years!'

The esteem in which German officers held Piłsudski was so great even after his death in 1935 that, when the Wehrmacht captured Krakow in September 1939, the commanding officer paid his respects at the grave and appointed a guard of honour.[1] And the political change of course in Warsaw after the marshal's death did nothing to diminish the Germans' hopes of an alliance. The authoritarian remodelling of the constitution led the colonels' regime further to the right.[2] Their concept of 'Sanacja' included efforts to 'resolve the Jewish question' by means of mass emigration. Anti-communism and anti-Semitism thus provided a stable ideological foundation for a potential partnership with Germany – though, of course, this could not be said of their incompatible territorial ambitions in the Baltic states and the Ukraine. Alongside the new marshal, Francophile Edward Rydz-Śmigły, Foreign Minister Colonel Beck became the actual strongman in Warsaw. In the circle of Piłsudski's former comrades-in-arms, he continued to advocate organising eastern Central Europe into a zone that would provide a basis for Polish foreign policy.

Interest in aggressive expansionism at the expense of the USSR nonetheless remained stronger in Berlin than in Warsaw, where there were very good reasons for remaining reticent and not entering into a dependent relationship in which Poland could probably only lose, at least its western territories and possibly its position as a significant power. But the arms race that had begun between the great powers was already considerably outstripping Poland's ability to expand and modernise its army. Accepting German offers of alliance might have reduced the economic and technological shortfall, but Poland would then have been committed to concentrating its rearmament in the east and taking strength away from its positions on the German border. French capital help remained hesitant and extremely limited, and this severely constrained Poland's efforts to rearm and build up an armaments industry of its own in the country's centre.

In Germany, too, accelerated rearmament led to financial difficulties in 1935–6. Additional, but not unrestricted, wiggle room was gained by a camouflaged system of financing rearmament with promissory notes. A lack of foreign currency inhibited the import of crucial raw materials. The right-wing conservative politician Hjalmar Schacht, Hitler's adviser on finances and the economy, advocated slowing the tempo of rearmament and taking up Moscow's offer to rebuild extensive economic relations.[3] In front of the newly founded Wehrmacht Academy, Schacht expressed the situation with military concision: 'We're permanently broke. [...] If there were war tomorrow, we would have to shut up shop within four weeks.'[4] Schacht pressed for a change of course not only in personal talks with Hitler, but also in letters to the defence minister, whom he threatened by saying the Wehrmacht's ever-larger requirements would not be met. To the governor of Bavaria, Schacht complained that the 'idea of conquering eastern territory' was doing a lot of 'damage'. He, too, supported border corrections in the east, but considered wider-ranging plans for settlement and annexation totally utopian. In these straitened circumstances, the Defence Ministry declared itself willing to lift Hitler's ban on exporting weapons to the USSR. Since Schacht did not hold back in public and the British press was already reporting that German industry demanded closer ties to the USSR,[5] the Führer stepped in. He let the defence minister know that, contrary to the rumours that the higher echelons of the German military were thinking of resuming cooperation with Moscow, 'there can be no question of looking for military affiliation with Soviet Russia in the near future'.[6]

Meanwhile, Göring was in Poland again and making renewed suggestions for a joint march on Russia. Now, however, his proposal had been altered geographically. Poland would 'impose order in the north of Russia'. For Germany he demanded the south. German interest in the 'breadbasket' of the Ukraine and the oil in the Caucasus must have been significantly intensified by the Reich's problems with foreign currency and raw materials. But even for a pro-German faction in Warsaw, the offer of Russia's barren north would not have been especially attractive, even if it included the industrial areas of Leningrad and Moscow as well as the towns along the highway from Minsk to Smolensk. Lipski said later that Göring had had 'more imagination than familiarity with either the problem or the map'.[7] For the Polish side, the only important points were that Berlin was sticking to the idea of a German–Polish alliance and that it wanted to control the Ukraine without involving the Ukrainian nationalists.

Reich Foreign Minister Konstantin Freiherr von Neurath assured the American ambassador to France, William C. Bullitt, on 18 May 1936 that Hitler considered the enmity with the USSR to be insurmountable and that he intended to sit on his hands only until the western fortifications were complete.[8]

Solving all German economic problems by seizing parts of Russia remained a tempting prospect in 1936, but it was not one that could be immediately realised and could not help Germany out of the tight spot it was presently in. Hitler was forced to make a fundamental alteration to his economic policies in order to secure greater freedom with which to rearm and prepare for war against the USSR. In August 1936, he prepared a memo on the 'four-year plan'. It commissioned Göring to do everything he could to increase domestic production of raw materials and synthetic replacements. That was intended to gain substantial autarky for Germany within a short time and so make it able to withstand the coming struggle.[9] The 'permanent solution lies in extending our Lebensraum, that is, our people's resources of food and raw materials. It is the task of the political leadership to some day resolve this question.'

Hitler provided a comprehensive justification of this new policy, which Schacht opposed, as a step towards enabling the Reich to wage 'a promising war against Soviet Russia'. He said the Red Army was undergoing a process of accelerated armament and that Germany would soon have to meet it with the best armed forces in the world. He set two tasks: in four years, the German Army had to be ready for deployment and the German economy had to be ready for war. In parallel to his new economic policy, he worked to find more anti-Soviet allies with whom to complete the encirclement of the USSR and create a favourable starting position for the planned invasion. This made plain that his four-year deadline in no way precluded attacking sooner if an opportunity arose.

At a party meeting in autumn 1936, Hitler explained how he imagined Lebensraum in the east: 'If the Urals, with their immeasurable wealth of raw materials, Siberia, with its rich forests, and the Ukraine, with its immeasurable expanses of grain, were all in Germany, we would, under National Socialist leadership, be swimming in surplus. We would make it productive, every single German would have more than enough to live. In Russia, however, the population is starving, because the Jewish-Bolshevik government is unable to organise production and give the worker practical assistance.'[10]

Joachim von Ribbentrop, German ambassador to London between 1936 and 1938, subsequently foreign minister, explained in his conversations in Britain that possession of the Ukraine and Byelorussia was 'indispensable for the future existence of greater Germany and its seventy million inhabitants'.[11] In a discussion of Hitler's four-year plan in the Council of Ministers at the start of September 1936, Göring justified the economic measures by declaring that war with the Soviet Union was unavoidable.[12] To high-ranking officers of the Luftwaffe, he later explained that Germany was *already* at war with Russia. They just hadn't started shooting yet.[13] The American military attaché in Berlin, Truman Smith, thought it wasn't clear what the next steps would be in Hitler's expansionism, but was certain that this expansion would progress along the lines Berlin–Leningrad and Berlin–Prague–Odessa.[14]

Hitler managed to pull Japan more tightly into the encirclement in a move as dramatic as the pact with Poland. And as with the Poles, he had to overcome considerable resistance within both the Wehrmacht and the Foreign Ministry, which had tended, in view of Japan's aggression towards China, to side more with the Chinese. German military advisers, including for a while even General Seeckt, supported Chiang Kai-shek in hopes of benefiting from China's huge market and its position as a great power in the Far East. In contrast with those advantages, Japan hardly seemed an attractive partner in the global game, and the conservative German officers and diplomats who still regretted the passing of Rapallo did not ascribe any importance to its anti-Soviet troops. Even Göring hesitated for a long time before dissolving ties with China, since it provided imports of crucial raw materials, particularly of tungsten, which Germany, for all its striving for autarky, could not do without.

The Anti-Comintern Pact of 25 November 1936 could have become fatal to the USSR. The initiative had come from the Japanese in 1935 when military attaché Hiroshi Oshima conveyed the suggestion to Berlin.[15] As a precaution, the pact would not be aimed directly at the Soviet Union, but against the Communist International (Comintern) controlled by Moscow. The signing was delayed by a military revolt in Japan in February 1936. The fundamental disagreement between the Imperial Navy, which looked to the south, and the army, which preferred expansion to the north and hence against the USSR, remained unresolved. In a secret supplementary protocol,

Germany and Japan, the first signatories – Italy only joined a year later, on 6 November 1937 – agreed not to help the USSR should one of the participating powers attack it.

Though it was formally a defensive agreement, the partners agreed to coordinate their anti-Soviet policies, albeit without making any more precise commitments. This kept the pact open for the entry of Britain and Poland, with whom (and an agreement with Italy) Hitler would have achieved the international coalition he desired and hoped for.

At the start of June 1936, after a meeting with the Japanese ambassador, Hitler became surer that the situation in the Far East would soon escalate again. To Goebbels he said: 'Japan will give Russia a thrashing.' The colossus would start to totter. The propaganda minister wrote in his diary somewhat sceptically: 'Let's hope that that'll be us finished and the Führer will still be alive. And that something is done.'[16] A few months later, after the announcement of the four-year plan, Hitler's optimism seems to have become more convincing: 'After dinner I have a comprehensive talk alone with the Führer. He is very satisfied with the situation. Rearmament is continuing. We're putting fabulous sums into it. In 1938 we'll be entirely ready. The struggle with Bolshevism is coming. When it does, we want to be prepared. […] We have now completely won over the army. The Führer is untouchable. […] Ascendancy in Europe is now as good as certain. We just mustn't let any opportunity pass us by. Rearm and be ready.'[17]

Until spring 1939, Hitler repeatedly offered Poland entry to the Anti-Comintern Pact. It would be impossible to set up an anti-USSR front without the Poles, even if only on strategic grounds. The formal invitation to join the pact was delivered by Göring on another hunting trip in February 1937. In talks with Marshal Rydz-Śmigły, he even dropped Germany's revisionist claims to the Corridor and Upper Silesia. He said that a strong Poland with access to the sea was important to Germany as a bulwark against the USSR. The Reich would never return to the politics of Rapallo. It would be wise to discover the extent to which German–Polish cooperation could be extended. Here he also mentioned intensifying relations between the two armies.[18]

This was partly a reaction to a visit by Maurice Gustave Gamelin, a French general, to Warsaw in the middle of August 1936. Paris was keen to prevent Poland from crossing to the German side, but did not want to be any more precise about its own commitments. The Polish commander-in-chief, for his part, had to worry about whether France would indeed cover him against

Germany. Rydz-Śmigły had on that occasion presented a Polish deployment plan, which assumed that in the event of a German invasion, the offensive thrusts would be made – as seemed very likely – from Pomerania or East Prussia and Silesia. The Polish Army intended to remain on the defensive.[19]

As regards German plans or even intentions, this was pure fiction, because the German deployment plan in force at that time ('Red') assumed that there would be an attack from France and that German forces would be concentrated in the west, while the border with Poland, which the Germans thought would remain neutral, would be assigned only two weak covering armies.[20]

Warsaw's response to Göring's offer was to keep its cards close to its chest, but it did not refuse so unambiguously that Berlin would give up all hope of deepening the partnership. After all, Poland and Germany, supported by Italy, had already successfully worked together on toppling the Romanian foreign minister, Nicolae Titulescu, who had been a proponent of the 'Little Entente' between Romania, Czechoslovakia and Yugoslavia, and had declared himself willing, if Czechoslovakia needed help, to allow Soviet troops to advance through Romania.[21] By toppling him, the Polish foreign minister, Beck, secured another protective anti-Soviet buffer for his own country, but contributed to the isolation of Czechoslovakia.

9. By mid 1934, construction had begun on the line of fortifications between the Oder and Warta rivers. Anti-tank turrets pictured today at Panzerwerk 717, near Międzyrzecz.

Even if Poland eschewed further anti-Soviet bonds with Germany, cooperation on the levels of politics and ideology continued to function smoothly. A policing treaty, for the signing of which Hitler received the Polish justice minister Witold Grabowski, was concluded to better coordinate the fight against the communists. At the same time, their cooperation was extended to include a youth exchange programme in which the Hitler Youth and the Polish scout movement made trips and set up camps in the neighbouring country.[22]

Poland's interest in having French protection was understandable from a German perspective,[23] but ultimately irrelevant, because Germany was steering towards a war not with France, but with the USSR, expecting that Poland would at least remain neutral and that the Soviet–French–Czechoslovak mutual-assistance pact would therefore not be activated. That was why they directed their first operational plans for a war of aggression not at Poland, but at Czechoslovakia.

First Operational Plans

The events that Polish historiography[24] today interprets as a policy of maintaining an equilibrium between Hitler and Stalin are by no means that clear-cut. The German sources – as has been shown – convey the impression that Warsaw welcomed the idea of an anti-Soviet alliance, but not at the price of making territorial concessions to Germany and potentially losing the opportunity for exerting its power independently in eastern Central Europe. This impression is confirmed by the little-known Japanese sources.[25]

Poland and Japan were natural allies after the end of World War I. Both had managed to defeat the Russian Army. Japan had been victorious in 1905 and had aided Poland in 1919–20. In the 1920s and 1930s, the two powers were strong and mutually complementary bulwarks against the USSR. As Japan expanded its position with the conquest of Manchuria and so drew the attention of the Soviet Union onto itself, it eased Poland's national-security situation. Taken the other way around, a threat on the Soviet Union's western border was something from which Tokyo could profit. So the Hitler–Piłsudski pact was seen by the Japanese as the opportunity for a three-way alliance. A Captain Yamawaki, who had already been in Poland as a military observer in 1919, was appointed military attaché in Warsaw.[26] And the visit of an imperial prince to Berlin and Warsaw in 1934 marked the beginning of consistent Japanese pressure to that end.[27]

The prospect of a German–Polish assault on the Soviet Union again became more distinct in 1937. Two coinciding developments encouraged the idea that the USSR might collapse more quickly than had seemed likely in the 1920s. At the start of the year, the head of the SS, Heinrich Himmler, referring in a lecture to the 'Wehrmacht's education in national politics', said that the main enemy in a future war would be Bolshevism and that Germany had to get ready for a 'war of annihilation' against a 'subhuman opponent'.[28] This was entirely in line with the beliefs of his Führer – and in opposition to Hjalmar Schacht, who undertook another attempt to rebuild beneficial trading relations with the USSR. He had a talk with the head of the Soviet trade delegation, David Kandelaki, who then, on 29 January, brought a declaration to Berlin from Stalin and Molotov. It explained that their politics were not directed against German interests and that they were ready to conduct political negotiations on how to improve their present relations, in total secrecy if so desired.

Schacht's initiative has to be seen against the background of a Wehrmacht study produced in the Defence Ministry in autumn 1936 and explored with the help of the Propaganda Ministry, the interior minister and the 'General Plenipotentiary for the War Economy' (that was Schacht in a different hat) over seven weeks of comprehensive war games. The study took as its starting point an 'eastern scenario in which the Bolshevik states (Russia, Lithuania, Czechoslovakia) were enemies and the anti-Bolshevik states (Germany, Italy, Austria, Hungary, nationalist Spain) were allies, while all other states remained neutral'.[29] In regard to the war economy, the significance of the Russian resources could not be overlooked, which was why the experiences of World War I were highlighted to show that occupying and exploiting Russia's areas of agricultural surplus, especially the Baltic and the Ukraine, as well as the raw material deposits in the Donets Basin and the Caucasus, was indispensable.[30] For the Reich's minister for the economy, the central question was whether, if it became possible to gain access to these resources as part of a trade exchange during the rearmament phase, Germany would be able to say no.

Everything seems to suggest that the intention behind Stalin's offer was to undermine the Anti-Comintern Pact and dissuade Hitler from his policy of encirclement with Poland and Japan. But, unlike two years later, when Stalin repeated his advances, Hitler rejected any kind of contact. His positive assessment of Poland's attitude in 1937 played an important role in that decision. Foreign Minister Neurath informed Schacht after a conversation with the Führer that Hitler feared Stalin would simply use these negotiations to gain a closer military alliance with France and a friendlier relationship with Britain. 'It would be different if things in Russia were to develop towards absolute despotism, based on the military. In that case we would have to be sure not to miss the moment for again involving ourselves in Russia.'[31]

Stalin can hardly have been pleased by this rebuff. And his opponent in Berlin was already 'involving himself in Russia'. The Reich Security Head Office under Reinhard Heydrich was supporting various nationalist organisations among separatists and emigrants with whom the Japanese were also in contact – especially groups in the Far Eastern and Central Asian Soviet republics.[32] The Ukrainians in exile, however, were kept at a distance and largely left to the Poles, who ran their own anti-Soviet leadership centre under the code name 'Prometheus'.[33]

In Germany, the Wannsee Institute, which the SS had founded in 1936, took care of procuring and evaluating, for example, economic data from the USSR, which demonstrated its steep industrial upswing. Heydrich's 'security service' also faked politically charged documents and passed them into the hands of the Soviet government via Edvard Beneš, the unwitting Czechoslovak president. These gave Stalin a pretext for moving against his strongest domestic opponent, Tukhachevsky. The idea was said to have come from Hitler personally.[34]

Tukhachevsky appeared in public for the last time at the May Day parade. On the 26th of that month, he was arrested on Stalin's orders, tortured and, after a show trial, executed. The accusation that he was a German agent was, of course, just as absurd as the imputation that he had intentionally lost the war of 1920. It can hardly have spoken in Tukhachevsky's favour that his recollections as the Soviet commander in that war had been published – certainly without his being asked – in, of all places, the German luxury edition of Piłsudski's memoirs. Whether Stalin cynically wanted to use these allegations to eliminate a rival much beloved among the populace and the army, or whether his paranoid fear of traitors had been unfeignedly directed onto the marshal by the secret service – which surely cannot have overlooked the hopes being placed in Tukhachevsky by others than just the Wehrmacht – is something we will never know.[35]

This trial marked the beginning of the 'purges' in the Soviet Army, which was figuratively decapitated by the murder of its officers, especially those in the higher ranks. From then until the outbreak of World War II, the Red Army experienced such a precipitous decline in both its international prestige and its actual efficacy that foreign military experts assessed it as a shapeless mass that no longer needed to be taken seriously. The Polish ambassador to Moscow considered the progressive weakening of the USSR to mean that a significant military conflict would be too much for the country's forces.[36] This limited the Soviet Union's efforts to find new forms of collective security and encouraged bold speculation among its enemies.

Three weeks after Tukhachevsky's execution, Japan turned up the heat in its simmering conflict with China. An open war broke out in which Germany, after a failed attempt at mediation, took Japan's side (as did Poland), aggravating tensions with the USSR.[37] In Berlin, the Japanese military attaché presided over a conference in which the Germans and Japanese discussed bringing Poland into the Anti-Comintern Pact. They were agreed that Poland's internal conflicts would make that more difficult to achieve. The Japanese suggestion that Germany exert pressure on Warsaw by massing troops on the border and perhaps occupying Lithuania and the disputed Memel Territory was declined by the Germans.[38]

The conference's conclusions are not known, but it had become clear that Japan hoped its belligerent expansion would be supported by an attack on the

10. War in China: Japanese troops before the occupation of Hankou, October 1938.

USSR from its western border, something neither Poland nor Germany could risk – not yet, that is, since they expected the USSR to be destabilised by Japan and that its internal structure would disintegrate. In Berlin, the preparations for war were directed at closer-lying and more easily achievable aims: that is, at Czechoslovakia, the potential Soviet 'aircraft carrier'.

Four years after Hitler came to power, the international situation and the balance of power were considered so favourable that the Germans dared make plans for a war of aggression. The Wehrmacht's leaders had prevented a slow-down of rearmament and Chief of Staff Ludwig Beck now pushed through his demand that Germany's leaders work out an overall concept for operational planning that would include all strategic and international political considerations. Defence Minister Werner von Blomberg signed a first directive for 'unified Wehrmacht war preparations' and had it played through in a study over winter 1936–7.[39]

The heart of the operational plans was an invasion of Czechoslovakia. Beck had already made the necessary agreements with Hungary in 1935 and now the Germans aimed at gaining the help of Italy and Austria – this was all on the basis of Polish neutrality, a crucial prerequisite for rapid operational victory. In 1934, Beck had still hoped for active Polish participation, but three years later he considered that superfluous, especially as he now regarded Polish politics as unpredictable and also commanded sufficient defensive troops on the eastern border to prevent, if necessary, Poland from intervening in alliance with France and Russia.[40] This was unlikely anyway, because relations between Poland and Czechoslovakia were fraught and joint Polish–Soviet military action was unthinkable for Warsaw.

The detailed operational study was overseen by Beck's deputy, Erich von Manstein, who planned for the three allies (Italy, Hungary and Austria) to be deployed under strict German command.[41] A crucial element of Beck's strategy was that the alliances and the nature of the operation would enable them to fight a decisive battle close to their own border. Only if a short, isolated war seemed likely, and an escalation to include France and Britain could be prevented, would he be able to answer for deploying a Wehrmacht that was still under construction. Beck belonged to the minority of General Staff officers whose experiences of World War I had been of trench warfare on the western front. So he was motivated by concern that a new war against the western powers would break out before the Wehrmacht was ready for it and before Germany had consolidated and expanded its position in Central Europe.

On 27 January 1937, Defence Minister Blomberg presented the results of the Wehrmacht study in a three-hour lecture attended by Hitler. Despite the fact that the meeting is inadequately documented, it can be discerned that all of Beck's prerequisites were addressed: completed rearmament, superiority of Germany's political bloc, element of surprise and a quick outcome that would make it pointless for contractually obliged countries such as France and Russia to intervene. He even considered transporting the active forces in East Prussia over the sea from Pillau (present-day Baltiysk) to Swinemünde (Świnoujście) – as was scheduled to be practised in the Wehrmacht's 1937 summer manoeuvres – to build up a sufficient concentration of troops for an attack on Czechoslovakia. All that would be left in East Prussia were the border guards. But regardless of the fact that Beck took every risk into account, a war with the USSR could not be ruled out even under the most favourable circumstances. If Stalin did decide to intervene, the Poles would have to play a larger role. On the other hand, destroying Czechoslovakia would deliver the Transcarpathian Ukraine into German hands, giving it a platform for instigating revolution in the Soviet Ukraine. So they also sketched out propagandist subversion campaigns of the kind that were then actually employed in the German–Soviet war.[42]

Not at all coincidentally, the Wehrmacht again began intensifying its contacts with the Ukrainians in exile. In 1937, German military intelligence recruited more Ukrainian staff. One of these was Colonel Yevhen Konovalets, who, in exile in 1929, had founded the Organisation of Ukrainian Nationalists (OUN), which carried out attacks in the Soviet Union. He was looking for international allies. His discussions with Rosenberg were fruitless until he eventually found sponsors in military intelligence. Konovalets made efforts to unify the Ukrainian exiles and give them more clout, for which the Japanese ambassador to Berlin honoured him with a banquet in January 1938.[43] Konovalets announced a large congress of the OUN to take place in September, but was assassinated shortly afterwards in Rotterdam.

But back to January 1937. After the meeting in the Defence Ministry, Hitler and Goebbels discussed their impressions of the Wehrmacht study, which has not been preserved in detail. The assumption that Germany would fight 'with fascist allies against, if necessary, Russia, the Czechs and Lithuania' had been 'planned out right down to the last detail', according to Goebbels. Even the deployment of civilian commissars in the occupied zone was discussed, as was the important role to be played by propaganda – an indication perhaps that, as in World War I, they would rely on it as a weapon against Russia. The conclusion: 'Führer very satisfied', as Goebbels noted.[44] Intervention by the western powers had to be prevented, in accordance with Beck's strategy. That was something with which Hitler could unhesitatingly agree, as he could with the assessment that Germany should hope for another six years to prepare. But – and this was where he differed from his risk-averse chief of staff – he didn't want 'to miss a particularly good opportunity if one should arise'.

An opportunity to do what? After all, taking Czechoslovakia out of the picture and extending German influence via Austria and Hungary into Romania were supposed to be only intermediate steps towards the actual objective: war against the USSR. In the conversation with Goebbels, Hitler's considerations started from assessments of 'Russia's strength'. As ever, he expected to be able to somehow reach an understanding with Britain, and he praised Italy's 'enthusiastic heroism' before saying that France probably wanted 'reconciliation', which would, however, 'only be permanent once we are strong enough'.

So there was no indication at all that Germany would first have to neutralise the west before being able to turn to the east. On the contrary, Hitler's view of foreign policy evidently agreed with the eastern orientation of the Wehrmacht's study. The growing strength of the USSR and communist propaganda would drive ever more allies into Germany's arms; the Reich would inherit France's 'Little Entente' in eastern and South-East Europe, that is, Romania and Yugoslavia as well as 'Poland to an ever-greater degree'. Hitler evidently expected to be able to draw Poland even more completely onto his side.

In March–April 1937, the Wehrmacht Academy played through plans for a war of 'France, Czechoslovakia and Russia against Germany, Italy, Austria and Hungary', including drafting the necessary orders and sketching out how the troops would be deployed.[45] Imputing the intention to start a war of aggression to the 'Bolshevised group of powers' corresponded to the usual conventions of official language, but was modified by the description of a political situation in which Russia attempted by means of 'unfriendly actions' to 'induce either Germany alone or the group of authoritarian powers as a whole to take steps which in the eyes of the world would be interpreted as an attack'.

In terms of the overall international situation, it was assumed that the tensions with Japan would prevent the Soviet Union from deploying its army in the Far East to Europe. Lithuania would ally itself in every way with

Moscow – which gave the planners their pretext for planning more widely than merely for an invasion of Czechoslovakia, which in the game was engaging in close military cooperation with Russia. The Czech part of the population was assumed to be demanding war with Germany and bloodily oppressing the German and Hungarian minorities.

What's interesting is the assessment of Poland. It was bound by treaties to both France and Germany. Paris would try to broker a Polish–Russian deal that would allow the Red Army to march through Poland, whereby the Red Army would refrain from any kind of Bolshevik agitation whatsoever. East Prussia would be promised to Poland upon the end of the war. The negotiations for this deal would, however, turn out to be almost intractable. Moreover, Warsaw's relationship with Prague would already be tense because of disagreement over the Cieszyn area.

It is evident that, given Polish neutrality – guaranteed by German border troops – and the neutrality of Great Britain and most other European states, the study thought it might be worth taking the risk that war would break out on multiple fronts, even if it was hoped that would not occur. A lightning-quick invasion of Czechoslovakia and Lithuania would improve Germany's strategic position and probably keep France and Russia from intervening. If not, Germany would be in a strong defensive position on the Rhine front, where the bulk of its troops would be gathered, and in the east its occupation of Lithuania and Czechoslovakia, including the Transcarpathian Ukraine, and its close cooperation with Estonia would provide favourable strategic positions against the Soviet Union. An advance of the Red Army through Romania was to be delayed by the cooperation of Hungary and Austria until the mass of the Wehrmacht had been mobilised for a defensive war.

The international situation seemed to improve so much in summer 1937 that while updating his 'directive for unified Wehrmacht war preparations' Blomberg had his planners map out a special scenario in which Austria was seized by force ('Case Otto').[46] For strategic reasons, securing the Austrian terrain seemed the necessary first step of German expansionism. Blomberg's directives display the willingness to use force more clearly than has previously been recognised. The directives say Germany need not expect a war at once, because all Europe's peoples, even the Russians, lacked the desire for war. Germany, however, needed to be constantly ready to defend against sudden attacks and 'to militarily exploit any politically favourable opportunities that may arise'.[47]

If things went badly and the conflict spread to multiple fronts, the war in the west would be fought on the defensive; the fortifications there were considerably improved by the start of construction of the 'western wall'. By deploying vast manpower, the Wehrmacht in 1937 managed to erect a new line of bunkers that could be held with very scant forces, allowing Germany to go on the offensive elsewhere. However, the investment poured into the soil here was therefore not available when it came to building up offensive capabilities – a dilemma that accompanied Germany's war-planning right through to Hitler's death in the Führerbunker in April 1945. On the other hand, the army's leaders in 1937 neglected the further expansion of the eastern wall and instead accelerated the construction of armoured units. This was to create a 'strike force' that could be used offensively in the east and south-east. Chief of Staff Beck assumed that this would not occur before 1941, that is, before the minimum conditions of rearmament had been fulfilled. But he accepted that the political leaders might well spot 'favourable opportunities' far sooner than that. The extent to which the eastern scenario dominated the High Command's thinking can be seen in a statement by General Werner von Fritsch, the army's commander-in-chief, in an argument about who should play the biggest role in the running of the Wehrmacht as a whole. He declared that his branch of the armed forces was most important because victory in a forthcoming war could be achieved only by 'conquests in the east', that is, by the army.[48]

With the murder of Tukhachevsky and the internal paralysis of the Red Army, there was a steep reduction in the danger that the USSR would intervene in a German invasion of Czechoslovakia and that this invasion would thus precipitate a German–Soviet war. And the western powers would not want to get involved without substantial support from the Soviet Union. Hitler did not want to wait for 'favourable opportunities', but worked feverishly at bringing them about himself. As early as 5 November 1937, he inducted the foreign minister and the leaders of the Wehrmacht into his considerations. These contained the germ not of any new strategic approach, but rather of the Führer's intention, now clearly apparent for the first time, to go to war as soon as possible, at the next moment that presented itself. Austria and Czechoslovakia were to be the first objectives of German expansion.[49]

Hitler made no bones about this being only the beginning. He was 'irrevocably resolved' to alleviate Germany's space crisis by the violent means of seizing Lebensraum. That would happen, at the latest, in 1943–4, when

German rearmament would reach its apex, but he said the window of maximum opportunity was narrower than that. Moreover, there is no doubt that by 'Lebensraum in the East' Hitler meant in the USSR, not Poland, because on the same day, 5 November 1937, he received the Polish ambassador Lipski in order to sign a German–Polish declaration on the protection of minorities. The day before, Göring had again discussed extending German–Polish relations, this time with Deputy Foreign Minister Szembek. Although Poland hesitated to put cooperation against the USSR into contract, it was open to the idea of joint action against Czechoslovakia.[50]

Hitler's internal declarations about his further plans, which have become known as the Hoßbach Memorandum,[51] were not contradicted in so far as they applied to the Soviet Union. The defence minister, the army's commander-in-chief and the foreign minister were not, however, convinced by Hitler's argument that the western powers would stay out of it. Blomberg and Fritsch expressed, at times in very strong terms, that it would be disastrous if Britain and France were brought into war by a premature invasion of Czechoslovakia. The foreign minister – like the chief of the General Staff, who was informed of the discussion a few days later – was also extremely concerned by Hitler's open eagerness to act and by the danger that an attack on Czechoslovakia would lead to a new world war.

The Wehrmacht's leaders were also little persuaded by Italy's new willingness to join the Anti-Comintern Pact. From Hitler's perspective, this Japanese–German–Italian alliance now seemed perfect, in that Italy would keep France out of a Central European conflict by tying it up in the Mediterranean. It must have been very disappointing for the Führer that he was unable to win over the leaders of the military. Adopting the Stalin–Tukhachevsky model of dealing with his commanders was not easily practicable for Hitler and, as it happened, his 'purges' were far more efficient than Stalin's parallel attack on the leaders of the Red Army. In the space of a few weeks, Hitler replaced Fritsch, Blomberg and Neurath, while Beck resigned his post in autumn 1938, chiefly because his misgivings had isolated him within the High Command. When, at the Munich Conference, the western powers gave Hitler a free hand in Czechoslovakia, all the existing plans for a military putsch fell apart. The opposition among the army's leadership had made preparations for a *coup d'état* in the event that Hitler's order to attack led to war with Britain and France.

Although Beck had tried to put the brakes on Hitler's drive towards war, he, as chief of the army's General Staff, also made sure that the operational plans did not lag behind the political instructions. Although he considered a war as soon as 1938 to be far too risky, he did at least have his planners thoroughly map out an invasion of Czechoslovakia. He slated an operational war game for the start of the year under the designation 'General Staff Exercise 1938'. Instead of the routine training exercises for staff officers, a small number of generals and higher General Staff officers would play through 'waging a war of aggression against Czechoslovakia, including mobilisation' on paper. And this was to be done explicitly on the basis of the current level of armament, not on a projection into the future![52] The exercise continued until the middle of year, when the game became reality.

Since the problems of a possible military coalition had already been played through in the large Wehrmacht exercises the year before, it seemed sensible to Beck to test the operational side of things. So the Hungarian General Staff was brought into the process. Updating 'Case Green' (the attack on Czechoslovakia) was given the highest priority. In contrast, 'Case Red', a war with France, was put to one side. The army leadership was preparing for the most pressing task. So it is not surprising that Russia is practically not mentioned in either the discussions and instructions of the General Staff or the fragmentarily preserved planning documents. That applies equally to the Luftwaffe's comprehensive plenary studies of Cases Red and Green. The area where the air force might well be deployed on the defensive, or from where it might undertake an aerial war against the enemy hinterland, was southern Germany.[53] In that context, Poland and the USSR were not pertinent.

The German Navy's War Games

In the navy's well-preserved planning and training documents, however, it becomes clearly apparent that the leaders of the Wehrmacht considered war with the USSR plausible and 'doable' in 1938–9, and prepared for it. The very nature of the navy had already predisposed it to wider strategic thinking; furthermore, its operational area, the Baltic Sea, brought it into direct contact with the bases and areas most important to the Soviet Union's capacity for naval warfare. For the leaders of the German Navy, the discussions about securing supremacy in the Baltic were of existential importance, even if the highest priority was still given to the North Sea in the belief that the Royal Navy would be their chief opponent. They were quite certain that a war against Britain could be fought only with Russian help, and a war against Russia only with the aid of the British.[54] Anyone looking for early indications of Barbarossa should not neglect the navy's documents, particularly because close contact was maintained with the other branches of the Wehrmacht during the war games and exercises, meaning the other branches' conceptions of a future war are also recorded.

The aim of the Navy High Command's war games in 1938, beginning at the start of the year – that is, shortly after Hitler's declaration – was to investigate whether there would be an opportunity within the next two years for the Germans to begin a war on two fronts against France and Russia with a 'strategic invasion' that meant victory could be won even in generally unfavourable circumstances.[55] Several groups were to play through the task from the same starting point and compete to find an optimum solution. Extracts from these games were then investigated in tactical detail by subordinate groups. It was the first navy war game in which were embedded overarching considerations of the war as a whole. That included lectures on economic warfare, land warfare and international law.

In his concluding speech, Fleet Commander Admiral Rolf Carls sketched out the political situation that had been posited: after a period of heightening tensions in summer 1940, war with the Franco–Soviet alliance had become unavoidable, but Germany's enemies were trying to delay it until spring of the following year. The Reich's political leaders had then decided to 'exploit a brief, favourable-seeming moment in the national defence situation to stage the inevitable military conflict'.[56] All other states would remain neutral for the time being, and on 5 September Germany would employ the advantages of a lightning-quick surprise attack. At this point, Admiral Carls emphasised that this kind of undertaking would be possible only if the military could make a guarantee of strategic success to the politicians.

As regards war against Russia, Germany found itself in an advantageous position. Its long coast and access to the Baltic Sea gave it numerous operational options, whereas the enemy was practically cut off from any kind of sea routes and had only a single base in, as it were, a far-flung corner. By sealing the narrow entrance to the Gulf of Finland, the Germans could take the Soviet Navy out of the picture. That did mean, however, that Finnish and Estonian coastal waters would have to be mined, as it would otherwise be possible for the Soviets to circumvent or break through the blockade. Moreover, a base would be required in the blockade's vicinity. From this it followed that Finland and Estonia had to be brought onto the German side.

Summing up, Carls said he did not consider this kind of war on two fronts to be likely. In the event of war, Britain would always side with France. At present, Germany would be unable to survive a war like that. On the other hand, neither of those countries currently had any interest in war with Germany. As for the Russians, the admiral made an unambiguous statement that must have elicited particular attention from the attendant representatives of the army, the Luftwaffe and the foreign ministry.

> **Admiral Carls at the end of the 1938 war games:**
> I am also of the opinion that *neither* Germany *nor* Russia is in a position to undertake operations of a *decisive* scale against the other. German operations into Russia will peter out in the vastness of its territory, while Russian operations against Germany, which I do not consider the Russians presently capable of mounting, would shatter on Germany's defences.[57]

At heart, Carls was expressing the scepticism that Moltke and Schlieffen had harboured about operations in the depths of Russian territory. Beck, as chief of staff, presumably shared the views of his predecessors. But Carls's reservations also show that these ideas of exerting influence on Russia from the operational zone of the frontier were already considered as good as self-evident among military thinkers in 1938.

A backdrop to this was provided by the results of the operational war game played by the Baltic Sea naval station under Admiral Conrad Albrecht. It examined a variant in which the war was begun by the USSR. It showed that, given the very limited German forces in the Baltic, a longer war would mean losing control of the western and central parts of the sea. If the Germans wanted to maintain a strategic defence in the Baltic, they would have to lay a dense minefield by Öland upon – or preferably before – the outbreak of war, to protect existentially important trade with neutral countries, particularly the ore imports from Sweden.

As to land warfare, it was calculated that the Red Army would need around three weeks to advance through the Baltic states and cover the approximately 130 miles to the German border.[58] In the course of this advance it would have to fight around 20 divisions of the Baltic armies, which the Germans believed to possess at least some military value on the defensive. After that, the Red Army would appear with some 20 divisions of its own on the border with East Prussia, which was strongly fortified and would fight to the end.

Overall, control of the eastern and central Baltic coasts would probably go to the Russians, which would put the German Navy under so much pressure that it would be unable to fulfil its task of providing support to the war from the North Sea and the Atlantic.[59]

That was why Admiral Albrecht also had his men examine the possibilities of a strategic German invasion. The result was unambiguous. The key to dominating the Baltic lay in the West Estonian archipelago and the Åland Islands. These had to be occupied and defended. That was not possible with the navy's resources alone. Therefore, political and 'greater strategic' plans would have to be put in place in peacetime with the cooperation of all branches of the Wehrmacht. Even if the overall eastern strategy was defensive, a partial offensive would be necessary in the Baltic area. In World War I, the Åland Islands had been occupied only in 1917. In a future war, this step would have to be taken at the outset, to secure the Baltic and give Germany 'a free hand for the strategic offensive in the west and the north, which is what will decide the outcome of the war'.[60]

The prerequisites of victory, he said, were to bring about a favourable political grouping and then to carry out a 'strategic invasion'. The government would have to make sure that England and Sweden had no interests in the states around the Baltic, that Sweden and Poland (!) would maintain benevolent neutrality, and that Finland and Estonia were won over for use in the German war effort. As long as the Bolshevik regime was still in power in Moscow, that would not be impossible. Militarily, it would be crucial to have the army occupy Latvia and gain control of the strategically important ports of Liepāja and Riga, as well as support Estonia in defending Tallinn and lend a hand to Finland. At the same time, the navy and the army would occupy the West Estonian archipelago and important parts of the Åland Islands. The navy would suddenly mine the strait between Tallinn and Helsinki without consideration for Estonian and Finnish sovereignty. In parallel to that, the Luftwaffe would aim to destroy the Soviet aerodromes and the naval base at Kronstadt, as well as to chase the enemy air force from the skies. Kronstadt would have become the Pearl Harbor of a German–Soviet war.

Admiral Albrecht made clear that for Germany the only option was a strategic invasion, that is, a surprise attack to seize important positions upon the outbreak of war. That was how they could get ahead of the Russians. The value of a surprise attack was as indisputable from a military standpoint as from a political one. That had been shown in Manchuria, in Abyssinia and – as regarded Germany – in the occupation of the Rhineland and the recent 'incorporation of Austria'.[61] In conclusion, Albrecht discussed the options Germany would have after this kind of attack had begun. Although Britain would side with France, the German government would be able to evade the danger of an 'overwhelming British–French–Russian' coalition as long as there was no offensive in the west or against the English Channel. 'Decisive victories' were perhaps no longer achievable on the German–French border. The army's task in the west would then consist in preventing the war from being decided by a victory of the enemy's. The overall strategy would entail defence in the west but 'an offensive in the east to conquer the area around the Baltic and so resolve the truly *existential* and decisive issues for the survival of our Reich: the lack of space, the settling of our relations with Poland and the destruction of the global danger that is Bolshevism'.[62]

It is evident that Albrecht was one of those high-ranking officers who considered the slogan of 'Lebensraum in the East' to mean a limited territorial expansion, in his case into the Baltic states, which need not occur at the expense of Poland. The anti-Bolshevik element was the same, but applied instead to a territorially restricted expansion of the German area of control. That did not necessarily mean the subjugation of Russia, but probably the removal of the Soviet regime, by whatever means available. Albrecht led the naval war against Poland in September 1939 and was subsequently dismissed.

The navy's commander-in-chief, Admiral Erich Raeder, who had participated in the Hoßbach discussions five months earlier and had not contradicted Hitler's intention of going to war as soon as possible, pointed out in an address on 12 April 1939 that war games were not just for general training. The war games in 1938, in particular, had been designed so that the tasks of a future war were given a thorough theoretical inspection prior to receiving a practical test in manoeuvres and exercises.[63] In contrast to Albrecht, he emphasised that the British would almost certainly intervene if there were a war with France. That would completely alter the parameters of the naval war. In a war on two fronts, one of those being Russia, the occupation of the Åland Islands, as well as of Finland and Estonia, would still be greatly advantageous, but would require a considerable commitment of resources from the Wehrmacht as a whole. So it still had to be examined whether it might not be more favourable to initially respect these countries' neutrality in order to launch a counter-offensive when the enemy violated it.[64] Raeder did not think there would be a strategic invasion by the Russians of the kind that had been played through in the war games of the Baltic Sea naval station. This was characteristic of the situation in mid 1938.

1938: Hitler's Eastward Expansion Begins

On 12 March 1938, the Wehrmacht, after considerable political pressure, occupied Austria without firing a shot – and the world watched passively. Under the code name 'Special Case Otto', the German General Staff had been preparing to occupy their neighbour since June 1937. Göring had pressed for a rapid Anschluss for economic reasons, to mitigate the Reich's mounting financial and raw materials shortages. The Austrian National Socialists had put the government in Vienna under strain and Hitler had demanded submission. Then he marched in the Wehrmacht. The troops were greeted rapturously by the majority of the population. No other large power wanted to involve itself for the sake of Austrian independence. That also applied to the Polish government, which initially hoped to exchange its acquiescence for German concessions on the question of Danzig. But then it looked to the future and recognised that the next objectives of German revisionism would be Czechoslovakia and/or Lithuania. On that same day, 12 March, Warsaw decided to move against Lithuania.[65] Faced with massive domestic opposition, the Polish government hoped to increase its own popularity by inciting nationalist fervour. In terms of the international situation, annexing Lithuania would both extend the anti-Soviet barrier and strengthen Poland's position on the Baltic as well as prevent Lithuania from coming under German influence. And restoring the historic Polish–Lithuanian union had already been one of Poland's ambitions under Piłsudski.

For years, relations between Poland and Lithuania had been very tense. On the day the Germans marched into Austria, a Polish border guard was shot by Lithuanian troops. The government in Warsaw wanted to use the opportunity to implement an effective hegemony over Lithuania. It demanded by ultimatum that the corresponding treaties be signed and was plainly willing to begin a military invasion.[66] Soviet, French and British pressure eventually made Poland give up further-reaching demands, but it insisted that Lithuania resume the diplomatic relations it had broken off over the struggle for Vilnius. The Polish government simultaneously reassured Berlin that it would be consulted if the conflict escalated again. Hitler took that as an opportunity to have his forces prepare the military occupation of the Memel Territory, claimed by Germany.

And he was concerned that if Lithuania were subjugated by Poland, an old idea of his own would become obsolete: to persuade Poland to give ground over Danzig by offering it Lithuania as compensation.[67]

The German–Polish line of demarcation in Lithuania that was projected on 18 March 1938 by the Supreme Command of the Armed Forces went beyond Germany's original revisionist claims. German politics had no interest in aiding Poland's desire to have a second point of access to the Baltic.[68] If Germany's policy towards Russia had been essentially defensive, protecting East Prussia could have been left to Poland. As things stood, however, it was important to make sure that an offensive through the Baltic states towards the USSR would not find its way blocked by an expanded, probably neutral, Poland. The Memel bridgehead, however, did not fall into German hands in 1938, because the Lithuanian government complied with the Polish ultimatum. Warsaw declared itself satisfied by the restoration of diplomatic relations.

After this brief Lithuanian episode, attention turned back to Czechoslovakia, especially because Berlin had already gained the impression in November of the previous year that Great Britain might be willing to allow Prague to fall into the German sphere of influence. That would push the USSR out of Central Europe and give the Germans a free hand in the east, as long as they pledged to refrain from a politics of *faits accomplis*. This kind of appeasement policy failed to recognise either Hitler's desire for war or the exorbitance of his aims.

A rapid agreement was again reached with the Polish neighbour. Göring had already brought up the 'Czechoslovakian problem' on his customary hunting trip in February. Foreign Minister Beck had expressed interest in the parts of Czechoslovakia settled by Poles. If Czechoslovakia was going to be dismembered, Warsaw did not want to be left out. Eliminating Soviet influence on Prague was less of a priority for Poland than the territorial claims about which Warsaw was already conducting precautionary negotiations with the Hungarian government, which was, in turn, interested in controlling Slovakia.[69]

Göring's renewed attempts to further joint German–Polish interests at the expense of the USSR were met with polite refusal from Rydz-Śmigły. However, he also delivered a suggestion of Hitler's, that the non-aggression pact be extended to a term of 25 years, which aroused Beck's interest. But in exchange Beck expected 'commensurate action on the Danzig problem', that is, that Germany relinquish its desire to alter the status quo. That requirement would have been hard for Hitler to fulfil, not least for reasons of strategy and domestic politics. Although historians have generally explained Poland's behaviour at that time as motivated by the desire to avoid becoming a satellite state of the Reich's,[70] those concerns evidently played no role in summer 1938. The question of Danzig took a back seat behind the joint dismemberment of Czechoslovakia.

During the escalation of international tensions caused by Germany's anti-Czech agitation in July and August 1938, Chief of Staff Ludwig Beck had reason – as did the navy – to bring the USSR into the considerations for war. The army was facing the prospect of immediate deployment against a neighbouring state which was dug into a well-fortified defensive belt and had an alliance with Moscow. When Beck, in his memorandum of 5 May 1938, firmly criticised Hitler's risky route to war, he was not doubting Germany's ability to subjugate Czechoslovakia in an isolated campaign. His concern was that if the campaign went on for longer, it might attract the intervention of the great European powers, which the Wehrmacht, at its present level of armament, would not be able to resist.[71]

The supreme commander of the Wehrmacht, Adolf Hitler, was enraged when he was informed of these reservations on the part of the chief of the army's General Staff, because he believed that 'he wants to keep me from my intention of war'.[72] It was the first step towards Beck's dismissal. Nor did Hitler like that the extension of the western wall he had ordered had been projected to take 20 years. The dictator believed that the General Staff was sabotaging his commands. On 28 May Hitler again presented his intentions and arguments to the heads of the Wehrmacht and the diplomatic service: 'It is my unshakeable intention to make Czechoslovakia disappear from the map.' He justified that policy not only with the need for Lebensraum but also by pointing out that, in the event of war with the west, the strategic situation would make it Germany's most immediately dangerous opponent. Beck could agree with that, though not with Hitler's announcement that, if war broke out, Germany would extend its access to the coast into Dutch and Belgian territory, and also attempt to recover its colonies.

It is apparent that Hitler had no definite mid-term strategic concept. He was seeking another success as quickly as possible. To gain one, he needed the west to hold still. So he rejected any arguments questioning that it would. It was also significant that he knew he had Poland on his side in the present crisis. After the speech, Hitler is said to have approached Generals Brauchitsch, Keitel and Beck, and explained: 'So we'll do the job in the east, then I'll give you three to four years and we'll get down to the big job in the west.'[73]

What did Hitler mean by 'the east'? Applied only to Czechoslovakia, this statement makes little sense. It is more probable that he was referring to an idea he had been thinking about and repeatedly sketching out for years, and which the Wehrmacht was already preparing for: using 'favourable opportunities' to overrun Czechoslovakia and so gain a southern avenue for attacking the Ukraine, as well as to secure Danzig and the Memel Territory as a northern avenue for an advance against the Baltic states and north-west Russia. If Poland participated in an interventive attack on Bolshevism, so much the better; if it stayed neutral and covered the centre, then the Wehrmacht – in the best-case scenario, supported by parallel Japanese intervention in the Far East – would decisively defeat the Red Army near the border and speed up the disintegration of the USSR by deploying various political measures.

On his visit to Rome at the start of May 1938, Hitler remained reticent towards the Italian leadership. However, his foreign minister spoke 'incessantly and to everyone about waging a war, albeit without a definite enemy

11. Polish ambassador Józef Lipski (standing) at the diplomatic reception for the NSDAP's party conference in Nuremberg, on 10 September 1938. At the table: Reichsführer SS Heinrich Himmler; Annelies von Ribbentrop, the wife of the Reich foreign minister; British ambassador Nevile Henderson; and Joseph Goebbels, Reich propaganda minister.

or a clear aim. Now he wanted to destroy Russia with Japan's help. Then he wanted to fall on France and Britain. Then again he threatened the United States,' noted Mussolini's foreign minister, Galeazzo Ciano.[74] Ribbentrop heralded the destruction of Czechoslovakia and emphasised Germany's good understanding with Poland. Germany would accept the Corridor's existence 'for an indefinite time' and would even like 'to see Poland's power increase [...] so as to strengthen the protective anti-Bolshevik wall'.

Poland's readiness to militarily participate along with the Hungarians in the defeat of Czechoslovakia created a very favourable starting position. It reinforced Hitler's belief that the western powers would not intervene. The Polish Army could field an independent operational group with a strength of more than 35,000 men, plus around 100 tanks and the same number of aeroplanes.[75] In the event that tensions increased to the point of war, these troops were to occupy the territories claimed by Poland. In preparation, the secret service deployed subversive groups to undermine Czechoslovak authority in those areas with a Polish minority.

The Wehrmacht prepared in similar fashion. The parts of the Sudeten German population that had already been radicalised were given support by the Reich.[76] At the outset of September 1938, Hitler gave the order to methodically escalate the clashes already taking place. The climax was an unplanned uprising on 12 September by the Sudeten German National Socialists, who were supported close to the border by local units of the SS and the SA. But the uprising had come too early, as the Wehrmacht had been ordered to be ready for intervention only by 1 October. After it was put down, Hitler, as he did in Austria, settled on the creation of a Sudeten Freikorps, which would assist the Wehrmacht's invasion with targeted military operations. In a very short time, this corps attained a strength of more than 40,000 men.

Even the renewed misgivings of his chief of staff had not put Hitler off preparing the military assault. Beck stuck to his assessment that it would not be possible to keep the war from spreading.[77] He also pointed out that the new form of warfare coordinating the army and the Luftwaffe – a prerequisite for ending the war quickly – had not been sufficiently practised. Göring's Luftwaffe was gathering only limited experience of aerial bombardment in the Spanish Civil War. Indeed, the exercises and war games in summer 1938 had shown that these two arms of the military had highly divergent ideas of how this coordination would work.[78] The army expected the Luftwaffe to provide its units with massive support from the first day of war. The Luftwaffe's preparations, however, were aimed at first destroying the enemy's own air force. If it came to war with France, the army would have to do without any support from the Luftwaffe's combat units for a considerable length of time. And there was still a wide diversity in opinion even about how the armoured units were to be deployed. Overall, these were not good conditions for a 'lightning-quick' defeat of the Czechoslovak Army. But in the subsequent 'General Staff Exercise 1938', the games played by the army's leaders gave a surprising result: only seven days into war against the Czechoslovak Army, the German victory would be assured and the first German units could be redeployed as reinforcements to an imaginary western front.[79]

So the army's leadership plainly had little faith in Hitler's assumption that the western powers would not intervene in Case Green. But Beck's hope that the army's commander-in-chief would therefore dissuade Hitler from the plan of attack was not fulfilled. There were others who shared his concerns. The state secretary in the Foreign Ministry, Ernst Freiherr von Weizsäcker, proposed instead that Czechoslovakia be subjected to a 'chemical, rather than mechanical, process of disintegration',[80] but Hitler wanted action. Admiral Raeder nonetheless managed to make the Führer accept that from the navy's perspective the main potential enemy was Great Britain, whether it remained neutral in the case of Czechoslovakia or not. To be able to withstand a future global combat, the German Navy required a costly and long-term building programme. Although the emphasis would be on the army and the air force in the first phase of Hitler's envisaged expansion, the navy was given the highest priority for its building programme. Hitler also had the armament programme as a whole accelerated further.

What the dictator demanded of his General Staff was not a master plan on the model of the famous Schlieffen plan of 1905, nor for decisive battles against the west or the east, but rather the readiness to prepare quickly for isolated campaigns and operations. This actually suited the German General Staff's particular qualities and experiences, which stood the test until well into World War II. Even Alfred von Schlieffen himself, the chief of the kaiser's General Staff, had been prompted by the danger of a war on two fronts to lay out his plans in a number of variations.[81] But even then the Germans had lacked a coherent strategy, a diplomatically and economically coordinated war plan. In view of the failure of the German war effort between 1914 and 1918, Beck justly concluded that the country needed a political directive that would correspond to what was militarily possible – something that could be accurately judged only by the General Staff. The argument was thus partly about Hitler's claim of political primacy and the Army General Staff's contradictory claim to leadership, which the dictator began to undermine by transforming the Supreme Command of the Armed Forces, under Keitel, into his personal team of advisers.

At the high point of the crisis, on 18 August 1938, Beck handed in his letter of resignation. Franz Halder surprisingly became his successor. This highly diligent 'desk general' with weak nerves had, like many others, fewer scruples than Beck about risking a war.[82] He, too, however, feared that the Sudeten crisis could escalate into a world war. But Halder did distance himself from the hope expressed to him by a group of conservative nationalist officers, that if Hitler gave the order to attack, he would be at the head of a *coup d'état*. This military opposition would, anyway, soon have the ground pulled out from under its feet by the agreement Mussolini brokered with the western powers on 30 September 1938 at the Munich Conference.

Czechoslovakia was forced to give the Reich its areas with a German-speaking majority. Poland hurried to occupy the Cieszyn area after an ultimatum, and Hungary occupied areas with a Hungarian population in the country's south. The Czechoslovak government was forced to bow to the diktat of the three great powers, Great Britain, France and Germany. Stalin's offer of help went unanswered and would in any case not have been of much military use. In retrospect, Hitler repeatedly lamented that he had accepted a diplomatic solution rather than unleashing the war he had prepared.[83] What war did he forgo in 1938? Why did he regret only triggering war a year later? One possible answer: a decisive battle in Bohemia would, with the expected non-intervention of the western powers, have made Hitler a successful field commander, one who, strengthened by considerable booty and prestige, would have been able to show generosity to his Polish and Hungarian partners, something that would have allowed him to confront his main enemy from a more strategically advantageous position. If the western powers allowed him a free hand in the east, the Baltic states and the Ukraine would stand open to him.

So Hitler considered Munich only a partial success, since Czechoslovakia continued to exist despite the relinquishment of the border areas it had heavily fortified to defend against, in particular, the Reich. The Wehrmacht was not in Prague and the German border had not moved further east. When the dictator promised the western powers that Germany had no further revisionist demands, he had, of course, not meant it. The euphoric belief of British Prime Minister Neville Chamberlain that peace had been secured once and for all must have made Hitler smile. The consequence of having compromised at Munich, however, was that any further territorial expansion, especially by use of force, risked prompt intervention by Great Britain. The danger of unleashing a general war increased significantly.

3

THE TURNING POINT IN GERMAN–POLISH RELATIONS

As contact between Japan, Germany and Italy again intensified in summer 1938 and a military alliance seemed imminent, Hitler must have been well pleased. An alliance would provide the ideal conditions for the planned expansion. An anti-Soviet bloc strong enough to force Poland to collaborate and Britain and France to stay neutral would be able to attack the USSR. At the end of July, there were initial clashes between Japan and the Red Army at the Battle of Lake Khasan in Mongolia, no more than an 'incident' in military terms, but surely a test by the Japanese. In September, Poland arranged large-scale manoeuvres in Volhynia as a warning to Moscow not to meddle in the 'resolution' of the Czechoslovakian 'problem'.

That, however, was the product of a rather more defensive attitude in Polish politics to both the Soviet Union and the Reich. It was true that Poland indicated its interest in continuing the dismemberment of Czechoslovakia beyond what had been agreed at Munich, and that Foreign Minister Beck considered the neighbouring state a 'bridge to Russia', as he put it in instructions to his ambassador to Berlin when the diplomat was invited for a discussion with the Reich's chancellor.[1] But Beck wanted to indirectly make it difficult for the Germans to use this bridge. He was thinking that Hungary could annex both an autonomous Slovakia and, in particular, the Transcarpathian Ukraine. That would create a Polish–Hungarian border and incorporate Hungary into the defensive anti-Soviet front which the Poles wanted and in which they were presently trying to persuade the Romanians to join them.

At the same time, Beck wanted to stabilise German–Polish relations at the status quo without having to offer any further-reaching concessions. That applied, among other things, to Danzig. What he expected from Berlin was a commitment to the current shared border; in exchange he proposed an early extension of the 1934 pact. In his discussion with Lipski at Obersalzberg on 20 September, Hitler did not seem forthcoming. For him it was now a matter of emboldening Poland to join an invasion of Czechoslovakia. In the event of Soviet intervention, Poland could count on German support.[2] The occasion was used to again suggest to Warsaw that it join the Anti-Comintern Pact.

Hitler's Last Overtures to Poland

After the signing of the Munich Agreement, Berlin became more explicit. On the question of the Transcarpathian Ukraine, Hitler had for a while been indecisive. It might, after all, be possible to fulfil Poland's ambitions in exchange for political concessions. But here the Supreme Command of the Armed Forces (the OKW) intervened, because it wanted to keep the 'bridge' to the Ukraine and South-East Europe open for itself. That was why rump Czechoslovakia, including the Transcarpathian Ukraine, should come under German influence. Within the OKW, this was advocated above all by military intelligence, which had begun preparing the way for German expansion by intensifying its contacts among exiled Ukrainians. In 1938, ever more Ukrainians were being trained for armed combat.[3] The Foreign Ministry supported this policy and conceived of the Transcarpathian Ukraine as part of an independent Slovakia or indeed as the starting point for a potential 'greater Ukraine'.[4]

Hitler was in favour of concealing German ambitions and declared to a representative of the Hungarian regent, Miklós Horthy, that: 'If Germany were to form a large bloc with Hungary and Poland, nothing would be irrevocable and it would still be possible to make border adjustments.'[5] It is plain that the dictator was continuing his attempt to open the gateway to the east and to bring Poland on side. That was not primarily in order to dominate Poland or reduce it to the status of a satellite, but to construct a joint anti-Soviet front. As long as Poland, even if neutral and defensive, blocked the centre against the USSR, the German strategy could unfold along the northern and southern flanks. If, however, the Poles succeeded in binding Hungary and Romania into their own passive bloc, German expansion would have to proceed solely along the narrow northern avenue, making it dependent on the bottleneck of Danzig and the Corridor. But Poland's efforts in Romania went awry, because Bucharest rejected anything that would extend the power of its rival, Hungary.

The German government made considerable efforts to be correct and accommodating in its dealings with Poland. Walther Funk, who was named

Schacht's successor as economics minister in February 1938, explained to the Polish ambassador on a visit to Turkey in October that, although Poland needed access to the Baltic Sea, Germany also required a closer connection to East Prussia. Moreover, he pointed out that the USSR was, after all, a natural area for Poland to expand into.[6] To the Polish ambassador, Lipski, Foreign Minister Ribbentrop proposed a 'general solution' of contentious bilateral questions, something that did not seem impossible.[7] The discussion was to prepare the ground for a visit by Foreign Minister Beck. After all the previous proposals that Poland had avoided, there now began what Andreas Hillgruber called 'the decision-making phase'.[8]

Hitler now definitively wanted Danzig to 'come home' to the Reich and, for reasons of domestic politics, refused to accept Polish dissent.[9] And Berlin's other demands, an extraterritorial connection by motorway and multi-line railway, did not seem unreasonable given that Poland was to be compensated with extraterritorial concessions in the Danzig area. Ribbentrop also offered numerous other compensations derived from previous Polish suggestions, such as extending the 1934 pact and recognising the shared border. This last concession, in particular, meant giving up on revisions demanded by even Stresemann and the Weimar Republic, because it entailed renouncing other disputed regions, such as East Upper Silesia, that the Treaty of Versailles had given to Poland. What is especially macabre with hindsight is the willingness of both sides to work together in forcing Poland's Jewish population to emigrate. Lipski promised Hitler 'a nice monument in Warsaw' if he could find a solution to the 'Jewish question'.[10] Hitler seems to have been convinced that the Polish government would ultimately accept his offer.

Warsaw, however, continued to be coy over Danzig and ignored German pressure to finally join the Anti-Comintern Pact, because taking that step would have significantly constrained Poland's room to manoeuvre. That would ultimately have made the country an 'anti-Russian trench' (in the words of the Italian foreign minister, Count Ciano)[11] and had incalculable repercussions for its future. Whether accepting this German 'general settlement' would have indeed meant the end of Poland as an independent power will have to remain an open question. In any case, the Polish foreign minister's grand vision of founding a 'third Europe' between east and west under Polish leadership had no chance any more, given the shifts that had occurred in political power. Poland's place in a German-dominated Central Europe would certainly not have been insignificant, even if Hitler's assurances were not to be trusted.

Berlin was apparently ceasing to place much hope in the idea that Poland would play an active role against the USSR and join the military alliance that Japan, Germany and Italy kept discussing. In autumn 1938, the General Staff distributed a *Handbook of the Polish Army* 'for the use of troops in the field'. The comprehensive and comparatively objective description of the Polish forces made clear that they were expected to mobilise on the German as well as the eastern border.

The General Staff on the Polish Army in autumn 1938:
The Pol. soldier is willing, brave, tough, undemanding and patriotic. He will commit himself fully.

In difficult situations, however, the troops will require strict leadership, because the individual soldier, given the low standard of national education, will generally be unable to take independent action. Schematic tactical leadership makes the troops vulnerable to rapid and surprise attacks, particularly if they are aimed at the flanks and rear.[12]

When Poland eschewed closer ties with Germany after the first joint action against Czechoslovakia, Japan stepped in to mediate. The ambassador, General Oshima, asked for Hitler's assurance that he was still willing to maintain friendly relations with Warsaw. Tokyo obviously assumed that Hitler would undertake further aggression, which, given the current state of affairs, could only be directed at stricken Czechoslovakia. This naturally brought Poland's strategic interests into play, because if Slovakia and the Transcarpathian Ukraine went to Hungary, that would prevent the Reich from gaining ground around Poland.

In December 1938, the Japanese diplomats pressured the Polish government to reach an agreement with Berlin, on the grounds that Hitler and Ribbentrop intended to advance into the Ukraine. If Warsaw continued to refuse the German offers, there was a chance that, after the dismemberment of Czechoslovakia, Hitler might use the Transcarpathian Ukraine as a base for guerrilla incursions into Poland.[13] The American chargé d'affaires, Raymond H. Geist, later recalled that the new chief of the General Staff, Franz Halder, had told him at length in December 1938 that Hitler's eastern programme was now set in stone and directed primarily at the Ukraine, which was to become a German province.[14] Oshima travelled to Rome with the compliments of Ribbentrop, where he explained Japan's intention to 'carve Russia into so many

12. Polish Foreign Minister Józef Beck visits Hitler at the Obersalzberg on 5 January 1939.

states that any thought of revenge would be vain and nonsensical'. In response to Oshima's insistence that the Anti-Comintern Pact finally be turned into a military alliance, Mussolini requested a few weeks' thinking time.[15]

After this mediation by the Japanese, the Polish foreign minister, Beck, found Hitler in a conciliatory mood when he arrived on 5 January 1939 for a discussion at the Berghof. According to Beck's account, Hitler explained that there was a comprehensive overlap between Germany and Poland's interests.

'Hitler says that, for Germany, Russia is equally dangerous whether tsarist or Bolshevik. Bolshevik Russia is perhaps more dangerous because of Bolshevik propaganda. However, tsarist Russia was militarily more dangerous and more imperialist. For these reasons, a strong Poland is a simple necessity for Germany. Every Polish division deployed against Russia frees up a German division.'[16]

The German minutes of the discussion with the Polish delegation read similarly: 'Germany will be interested under any circumstances in maintaining a strong nationalist Poland, quite apart from how things develop in Russia. Regardless of whether Russia is Bolshevik or tsarist or anything else, Germany will always regard that country with the greatest caution and is therefore interested in seeing Poland's position maintained. In purely military terms, the existence of a strong Polish Army on the Russian border considerably eases the burden on Germany; the divisions that Poland stations on the Russian border save Germany the corresponding military commitments.'[17]

Hitler placed great emphasis on allaying Polish concerns about a rival German ambition in the Ukraine. He said that Germany had no interests beyond the Carpathians and that it did not matter to him what was done there by countries interested in those regions. If it were possible to find a sensible solution to the problems of Danzig and the Corridor, the Germans could provide Poland with a contractually regulated border guarantee. Hitler also brought up their common interest in solving the 'Jewish problem'. 'He, the Führer, is determined to remove the Jews from Germany.' If the western powers accommodated him on the colonial question, he would be able to provide a territory in Africa 'which could be used for the settlement of not only the German, but also the Polish Jews'.

In his responses, Beck underlined that Poland had to find a 'sustainable modus vivendi' with its Russian neighbour. But Poland would never place itself in Russian dependency. As for the Ukraine, he cited Piłsudski's warning about the 'Balkanisation of Central Europe'.

'Poland recognises that the agitators now active in the Transcarpathian Ukraine are its old enemies and fears that that territory could develop into the source of so much unrest for Poland that the Polish government would see itself induced to intervene, something from which further complications might arise.'

He said that was why Poland wanted a border with Hungary. The question of Danzig was one on which Beck declined to comment. 'He would like to consider the problem calmly in his own time.'

On the following day, the Polish foreign minister was able to continue the discussion in Munich with his German opposite number. Here, Beck opened the talks by immediately broaching the topic of Danzig. He said he had not yet found a solution and warned against a 'tactic of *faits accomplis*'. According to Ribbentrop's notes: 'Beck then moved on to the question of a greater Ukraine and said he had been satisfied by the Führer's reassurance that we have no interests there, as indeed it had given him heartfelt pleasure to note the Führer's clear and consistent line on a friendly understanding with Poland.'[18] Ribbentrop repeated the German offers for a resolution of the Danzig/Corridor problem, without eliciting anything encouraging from Beck. Then he said 'the policies to be adopted towards Russia by Poland

and Germany, and, in this context, the question of a greater Ukraine', would be a necessary part of the proposed general settlement of German–Polish relations.

> **Ribbentrop to Beck on shared anti-Russian interests, 6 January 1939:**
> I assured Beck that our interests in the Soviet Russian Ukraine extended only in so far as that we tried to inflict damage on the Russians wherever we could, just as they did to us, and we therefore of course maintained relations with the Russian Ukraine. Never had we ever engaged with the Polish Ukrainians, but rather, had always very rigorously avoided doing so. After all, the Führer had laid out our negative stance on a greater Ukraine. The difficulty seemed to me to be that anti-Russian agitation in the Ukraine naturally also entailed considerable repercussions for the Polish minority as well for the Ukrainians in the Transcarpathian Ukraine. In my opinion, this could be altered if we and the Poles worked together in everything to do with the Ukrainian question. I could imagine that, in an altogether generous settlement of all problems between ourselves and Poland, we could certainly be willing to regard the Ukrainian question as being under Polish privilege and to support Poland in every way in its handling of that question. This, on the other hand, did of course presuppose an ever clearer anti-Russian position on the part of Poland, since otherwise a common interest would hardly be present.[19]

At this stage, Ribbentrop again posed the crucial question: whether Poland would join the Anti-Comintern Pact. From a German perspective, it was important, while making preparations for transforming the pact into an anti-Russian military alliance, to clarify what role Poland would play in an intervention. The fact that the Ukraine kept being brought up made plain to the Germans what price the Poles would ask for their cooperation. Beck did not completely rebuff this approach, but emphasised again the necessity of tranquil relations with Russia, which his country required for its own 'peace of mind'. Ribbentrop noted: 'I asked Beck whether they had given up Marshal Piłsudski's aspirations in that direction, that is, in the Ukraine, to which he laughingly answered that they had, after all, been in Kiev before and that there was no doubt these aspirations still existed today.'

It seems clear that Hitler took war with Russia into account in spring 1939 and that a military alliance with Poland, whether aggressive or defensive, was of the greatest importance in allowing him to carry forward his policy of expansion. From his perspective, the demand that Poland relinquish

Danzig was not unreasonable, as he himself was willing to relinquish the South Tyrol to forge an alliance with Italy. As for the South Tyroleans who opted for Germany, he wanted, as we know from his later efforts, to settle them in the Crimea. It initially seemed that Great Britain could be willing to let Danzig go to Germany and to steer Hitler's expansionist urges eastward. The German ambassador to London, Herbert von Dirksen, had the impression in January 1939 that Britain would, 'in line with the basic trend of Chamberlain's politics, accept a German policy of expansion in Eastern Europe', particularly if a Ukrainian state were to be created with German aid – including military aid – and if the Ukraine's right to self-determination were emphasised in the process.[20]

That Hitler now intended actually to implement the plans for war against the Soviet Union had also been made quite clear by a report of Oshima's.[21] And although Poland's leaders were evidently not absolutely disinclined to participate, they did not want to be drawn into this kind of adventure, especially as they had recently been encouraged by American diplomats to instead become part of the anti-German front.[22] Since the Munich Conference and the brutal repression of the Jews in Germany, Roosevelt had instituted a policy of containing any further expansion by the Third Reich. The American press reported at the outset of 1939 that the Germans intended to march into the Ukraine as they had done in 1918. Observers were said to be unanimous that this would be Hitler's next step.[23] In 1928, Warsaw had already begun to ease tensions with the USSR.[24] Although the Americans' idea of erecting a Polish–Soviet dam against German ambition did not convince the Polish leadership – their anti-Russian sentiments ran too high for that – this American support did encourage them to adopt a tougher stance towards Hitler. The critical voices in the British leadership, too, were becoming louder. The British ambassador to Berlin drew attention to the ideas in *Mein Kampf*. He interpreted them as meaning that an eastward extension of the Reich would lead to a collision between Germany and Russia in which the Germans would assert their paramountcy over the Ukraine. Whether the USSR would be sufficiently powerful to defend the Ukraine was not certain, according to the *The Times*.[25]

The ever-greater support offered by the Anglo-Saxon powers ended the discussion that had been taking place within some parts of the Polish government about whether to accept the Germans' proposals for Danzig. In the middle of January, Beck and Marshal Rydz-Śmigły decided to decline the German government's suggestions for Danzig and the Corridor, although this had recently become a question of secondary importance. It was a conscious change of course, one that factored in the risk of war even though Poland's position would be hopeless.[26]

In his return visit to Warsaw on 25 January 1939, Ribbentrop tried in vain to make compensation in the Ukraine for German annexation of Danzig an appetising prospect for the Polish government.[27] Even Poland's wishes in Slovakia and the Transcarpathian Ukraine could be granted. Beck said he wanted to 'carefully consider' the proposals, but again declined to join the Anti-Comintern Pact.[28] The Polish leadership had decided to regard Danzig and the Corridor as its most sensitive western pressure points in order to compel Germany to respect it as an equal power. Ribbentrop returned to Berlin empty-handed.

Beck was probably not as hard with Ribbentrop as he made himself out to have been. To the Japanese ambassador to Warsaw he admitted that he had told the German it might not be impossible to reach an agreement on making the Soviet Ukraine independent. He had also been satisfied by the absence of German interest in the Transcarpathian Ukraine.[29] So Berlin could well believe that the Polish government might yet join an anti-Soviet front and alter its position on the question of Danzig. But the Reich also had opponents who were trying to stoke up mistrust of Germany's Ukrainian policy, going so far as to create false documents that, despite being false, were completely accurate in their assessment of German intentions.

The Prague archives contain the record of a speech supposedly given by Ribbentrop at 'a meeting with the Imperial German generals' before his departure for Warsaw. The striking turn of phrase, 'meeting with the Imperial German [*Reichsdeutsche*] generals', which does not correspond to the terms then used by the military, gives a clue to the identity of the forger, who a few months later also circulated (this time in London and Moscow) a speech supposedly made by Halder, with the claim that the report originated from a former officer of the Austrian Wehrmacht. But more on that below.

Ribbentrop was said to have spoken on 22 January 1939 about how a 'greater Ukraine' was the 'ideal aim of Germany's eastern policy'. This would comprise the Ukrainian-inhabited regions of Poland, Russia and the Transcarpathian Ukraine. This state would be barely able to maintain itself against Russia and 'the rest of Poland', and would therefore become a German vassal. The Transcarpathian Ukraine was only the first stage on the road of 'divide and rule'. Germany would nonetheless be forced to 'sustain the friendliest of relations with Poland' because it would need Polish neutrality in the event of war with France. That consideration was hindering Germany's moves to resolve the Ukrainian question.[30]

In a speech in the Reichstag on 30 January 1939, Hitler again made conciliatory noises and declared that in the crises of the previous year, 'the friendship between Germany and Poland [was] one of the most promising elements in the political life of Europe'. But he announced at the same time that he would continue the struggle against the Versailles system. That struggle's objectives included Poland, which cannot have been surprised by this speech, given that Warsaw had in fact rescinded the 'friendship' that Hitler had been trying to construct for the last five years.[31]

Even Heinrich Himmler made the effort on 18 February to go to Warsaw. He conceded that Germany did indeed support Ukrainian nationalists, both financially and with propaganda broadcasts, but also suggested that in a general settlement of all German–Polish issues, it would be easy to reach agreement on the Ukraine.[32]

So the Germans did not yet consider the bridges to have been burned, even though Berlin attentively noted that Poland was now intensifying its relations with Great Britain. Japan reacted with great concern and supported a visit to Warsaw by the Italian foreign minister, Ciano, because if Poland openly shifted onto the side of the western powers, that would strengthen the USSR's position and disencumber it in dealing with tensions in the Far East. But all attempted mediation by Germany's partners in the Anti-Comintern Pact proved to be in vain. In his discussions in Warsaw at the end of February, Ciano had the impression that 'despite all Beck's political efforts, [Poland is] fundamentally and thoroughly hostile to Germany. [...] Tradition, feeling and interest bring it into opposition with Germany. A Catholic country with large Jewish groups, unsettled by strong German minorities, is one the fates have given everything that stands in contradiction to Teutonic imperialism.'

The talks with Beck led the Italian foreign minister to conclude that Poland wanted to maintain good neighbourly relations with Germany, but that a solution for Danzig 'could only proceed out of free diplomatic negotiations'. He reported that, in private, Polish thinking was dominated by 'concern about the Ukrainian problem' and that Beck had not been convinced by Hitler's reassurances. In conclusion, Ciano said that although Poland had not yet been won for the Axis, it was not to be considered an enemy: 'When the general war breaks out, Poland will for a long time merely keep its guns to hand, and only when the outcome has been decided will it fight for the winning coalition. It does well to plan in that way, as it is a country with friends and enemies on both sides.'[33]

Plans for 'Case East' – Even without Poland

The received interpretation of Hitler's intentions at the start of 1939 is that he wanted to control Poland as a forward base in the east so as to first undertake an offensive in the west and then subsequently wage war against the USSR.[34] But there were no especial military measures or plans in place for an imminent war against the western powers. The Wehrmacht's activities continued to be directed eastward and aimed at preparing the ground for an expansion into the USSR. Hitler's decision to order a gigantic naval building programme and his recent emphasis on Germany's demand that her colonies be returned did not contradict this orientation on the east. These moves were not those for a proximate war against the western powers, but rather those of appearing to present a threat and of making Germany able, at a far later date, to wage the war for world domination. German fleets and aircraft carriers were not scheduled to be ready before 1944 and would have required quantities of raw materials that the Reich did not come close to possessing, especially as the Luftwaffe was also implementing a vast upgrade plan.

Even the augmented production of artificial substitutes as overseen by the four-year plan could not make up the shortfall for years at a time. The decision to first extend Germany's Lebensraum eastward and seize the raw materials required to subsequently wage a larger, global war was therefore far more obvious. And the colonial demands will not have been more than the gamesmanship needed to reach the coveted agreement with Great Britain. The best guarantee of good odds in the next phase of German expansion would still have been British passivity, for which Hitler could have offered to exchange the relinquishment of these colonial claims. The offer to Poland (Danzig for parts of the Ukraine) fitted in with the German desire to make a deal with Britain: Germany would renounce its former colonies if Britain agreed to allow Hitler a free hand in the east. That was what the dictator had made the basis of his foreign policy programme in *Mein Kampf*.

And at the start of 1939, France was no longer a threat. The French did not seem opposed to coming to an understanding with the Reich, or to respecting eastern Central Europe and South-East Europe as an area of

German interest. The French General Staff saw no means of containing Germany's eastern expansion, as the USSR and Poland could not be relied upon. The Maginot Line and Great Britain seemed reliable guarantors of France's own safety.[35]

Should Hitler's calculations prove to be wrong, his strongest security against the western powers – alongside the massively extended western wall on the Rhine – would be his three-way alliance with Italy and Japan, which he also made efforts to enhance. After all, the Anti-Comintern Pact was not directed solely against the Soviet Union, but also – as Hitler understood it – against Great Britain. An alliance with Italy would pin down the Franco-British military potential in the Mediterranean; an alliance with Japan could divert Great Britain into Asia and contain the USA in the Pacific.[36] The mere threat of that scenario might persuade the western powers to stay out of it while he waged his war for Lebensraum against the USSR; the west would hardly take the risk in order to prop up ramshackle Soviet communism. This thinking certainly did not aim to defeat the west in order to be able to then march into the east.

The efforts to complete negotiations for a three-way alliance did not make much ground at the start of 1939, because the three partners did not manage to coordinate their interests and create the mutual trust on which to base a powerful partnership. Tokyo endorsed striking at the Soviet Union, but wanted to avoid provoking Great Britain and the USA. Rome, too, showed little inclination, despite all its demonstratively emphasised 'friendship', to hitch itself to Hitler's wagon and take on the role of a buffer in the Mediterranean and East Africa. Italy and Japan both feared the risks of a war with the western powers, but they warmly encouraged the German drive eastward. If Hitler made advances there, his two partners would be able to profit from it and perhaps extend their own room to manoeuvre. The 'friends' negotiating here all wanted to minimise risk to themselves at the expense of the others. There is no doubt it was Hitler who pushed for war, who wanted finally to attack and who was thinking on the grand scale. His partners were not in such a rush, and Poland, courted by the Axis, continued to give nothing away. In a secret speech to troop commanders on 10 February 1939, the Führer made plain that the small steps taken so far were only part of a very much larger plan. It was a matter of 'the fate of our race in the centuries to come', and the 'next battle' would be 'completely a war of ideologies'.[37] Did that indicate he had decided to turn on Great Britain and prioritise the war in the west? It's hard to imagine that could be the case. As long as Hitler could assume that Poland would ultimately bind itself more closely to the anti-Soviet front, his steps make sense as leading towards a conflict with the USSR. In winter 1938–9, the time was not yet ripe for that attack. If he waited until May–June 1939, he could hope not only for better weather conditions and further enhancement of the Wehrmacht's strength, but also for more favourable opportunities to invade or to undermine and isolate the enemy. 'Disposing of rump Czechoslovakia' had been scheduled as the Wehrmacht's next task soon after the occupation of the Sudetenland.[38] The army and Luftwaffe had been told to be ready to do so at any moment. The attack was to occur as suddenly as possible and as an ostensible 'pacification'. Although the Supreme Command of the Armed Forces tried to hold fast to the principle of making unified preparations, Hitler did not want to specify its subsequent tasks and the resultant preparatory measures until later. In this way, he avoided bothersome discussion of overall strategy, something that might break out again even after Beck had resigned as chief of staff. Hitler is said to have ordered the army's leaders to put aside planning for deployment and devote themselves entirely to the armaments programme.[39] But this probably refers to general plans for a full-scale war. The Supreme Command of the Armed Forces did indeed limit itself to regulating the ongoing task of securing the borders and providing aerial defences. But the army's commander-in-chief, Walther von Brauchitsch, signed the deployment order for Case East as early as 30 January 1939. This set out detailed plans for using the 2nd Army to secure the German–Polish border and for mobilising defensive forces in the event of war.[40]

As for future aggressive operations, Hitler did name some definite objectives.[41] These were 'disposing of rump Czechoslovakia' and 'taking possession of the Memel Territory', as well as 'occupying Danzig in a *coup de main*'. This robbed the Wehrmacht's plenary work and the armaments programme of their overall coherence – albeit that this was only rudimentary anyway. Supreme Commander Hitler was an erratic leader for the Wehrmacht, making changes to suit the short-lived opportunities of the moment and avoiding war with the western powers for as long as possible. Case Red – a war with France, which had still played a large role in the plans of 1937 – was not mentioned in the directives of spring 1939. In the west, the army's only consideration now was 'border security', although the navy and the Luftwaffe still had to engage intensively with the problem of waging war against Great Britain. For if the policy of persuading the western powers to tolerate further German expansion were to fail, these two branches of the Wehrmacht would be the first to come into contact with the enemy.

The army, however, updated and intensified its preparations for a military conflict in the east. Hitler had ordered that the army be ready for a lightning attack on Czechoslovakia as well as the sudden occupation of the Memel Territory and Danzig, and the army had implemented the concomitant directives to achieve that readiness as early as January 1939. The units stationed in central and eastern Germany were always kept at a high degree of readiness in any case. Large-scale mobilisation would not be necessary, because the surprise attack would be over before any opposition could be mustered. In planning the destruction of Czechoslovakia, the Germans no longer needed to worry about any serious resistance from the weakened and demoralised Czechoslovak Army. Intervention by the west or the USSR could also be ruled out.

The situation in Danzig and the Memel Territory looked very different. Lithuania might try to put itself under Moscow's protection. Then the Wehrmacht would not only have to defeat the Lithuanian forces, but would also have to brace itself for a collision with the Red Army. In that case, Poland's attitude would be crucial, because there was no Lithuanian–Soviet border. The Polish-occupied Vilnius region lay like a bolt between the two countries. At least, in view of the Polish–Lithuanian tensions, there was no need to factor in Polish intervention on the Lithuanian side. The government in Kaunas found itself in a visibly hopeless position. If the Germans went on the offensive, not even Soviet paratroopers would be able to rescue it. If, as was possible, Lithuania and the USSR attempted to use Polish neutrality to reconquer the Memel Territory after the Germans had occupied it, the Wehrmacht would immediately begin an offensive 'to destroy at least parts of the Lithuanian Army before it assembles'.[42]

Far more problematic for the Army High Command was the case of Danzig. Although Hitler made sure that the National Socialists in the city were noisily demanding a 'homecoming into the Reich' and secretly arming themselves in preparation for a putsch, the Führer still wanted to avoid direct conflict with Poland as far as possible. So he made political efforts in January–February 1939 to try to persuade the government in Warsaw to accept a German operation, even a violent one, in Danzig. On a military level, preparations were being made to occupy the city with a '*coup de main*'. This was to support a putsch that would take place as soon as the League of Nations, as seemed imminent, gave up its responsibility for the city. The subsequent Wehrmacht occupation was to respect the Polish positions as long as no weapons were used against them, for example from the Westerplatte peninsula. If there was nevertheless a military entanglement with the Poles, it would be necessary to try to 'take away' the Corridor. The Army High Command, however, particularly stressed the care needed to avoid starting any entanglement of that sort through misunderstanding or provocation – by irregulars, for example. Crossing the Polish border was forbidden under any circumstances.

The body responsible for working out and preparing the measures to be taken in war was the High Command of the I Army Corps, stationed in Königsberg. It had initially planned the defence of East Prussia – against a Polish attack until 1934, and against the Red Army after that. Its main tasks had consisted in driving forward a fortification programme and preparing for a defensive war. Now, at the start of 1939, it was ordered to switch over to planning aggressive operations. These were definitely not aimed at Poland, on whose neutrality or passivity the Germans still counted, but at recovering a secure avenue of advance in the north-east, which would be indispensable for an attack on the Baltic states. Organisationally, this entailed setting up a High Command of the 3rd Army, which would direct the war from East Prussia. In peacetime, this High Command existed only on paper. The core of the 3rd Army would be formed by the existing I Army Corps, which would be suitably strengthened by the mobilisation of reserves. The High Command in Königsberg was thus the brains for a war against the USSR, which – even in spring 1939 – was seen as more likely than a conflict with Poland.

That is confirmed by the parallel planning for the as yet still theoretical 2nd Army, which in Case East was to secure the German border in Silesia against the Poles.[43] If the Poles attacked, the 2nd Army was to slow them down and make a fighting withdrawal to its lines of fortification. Here, where the main thrust was launched against Poland in September 1939, the Wehrmacht was still, at the start of that year, making plans for defence. Both Armies, the 2nd and 3rd, were to be under the control of Army Group Command 1 in Berlin, which had already been set up. For Army Group Command 3, in Saxony, the task looked somewhat different. On 4 February 1939, it issued 'Directives for First Deployment', which were aimed at subjugating Czechoslovakia. On 'Day Y', Army Group 3 was to 'suddenly take control of the Czechoslovakian border garrisons [and make a] surprise concentric attack on Bohemia, with the main emphasis on the northern front', then rapidly take Prague, disrupting connections with Moravia to prevent the Czechoslovak forces from making an orderly withdrawal.[44]

Hitler did not involve himself in this kind of planning. And in 1939, after the personnel changes of the previous year, the division of responsibilities functioned smoothly. The High Commands of the Wehrmacht's branches drew up their blueprints in line with the political directives issued by their supreme commander and developed a high degree of initiative in the process. Russia had been discussed as the target of an attack since 1935 and, in 1939, it seemed the time had come to bring their 'forward pickets' to within range of the enemy. Poland still stood between the Wehrmacht and the Red Army and had, since Warsaw's change of strategy in the middle of January, been less inclined than ever to make an aggressive move against the USSR or even to at least adopt a neutral benevolence to German intentions and so not stand in the way of Hitler's drive eastward.

Roman Knoll, who had been close to Piłsudski as a politician but had fallen out with his successors, wrote in March 1939 that a joint German–Polish campaign against the USSR would be a suicidal undertaking. It was still in Poland's interest for the USSR to disintegrate into separate nation states and, if the balance of power were different, Poland would be able to benefit from German assistance. But in the present circumstances, a large-scale German operation directed against Russia would be a threat, above all, to Poland. As long as the USSR existed and didn't cooperate with Germany, it would be better not to undertake anything against it, since it was impossible to know whether whatever replaced it would be better or worse.[45]

The Polish General Staff also had to respond to the altered political situation. Their current 'western operation plan' had to be urgently updated, especially since the pressure from Germany meant a military conflict could not be ruled out. On the other hand, they could not remove all their troops from the eastern border with the USSR. Mobilising in both directions at the same time would have overextended the forces available to Poland, whose options were extremely limited as it was because of ongoing economic and political crises.[46] A detailed elaboration of the plans for war in the west, ordered by the inspector general in 1939, never lasted long, because the Polish preparations kept having to be altered and accelerated because of German activity and changes to the strategic situation. Ultimately, the leaders of the Polish Army did not manage to fully lay out their operational plan in writing, nor did they manage to familiarise their subordinate commanders with it.

The turning point came in March 1939, when Germany – without, as previously, informing Poland and inviting it to participate – first conquered Czechoslovakia and then occupied the Memel Territory a few days later. These operations employed the methods used successfully in the past. At first, subversive activities were escalated to provoke anti-German action that, in turn, delivered the desired pretext for the Wehrmacht to march in. Under massive pressure, the governments decided against military resistance. This proved to be enormously beneficial, particularly in the case of Czechoslovakia, because the complete inventory of Czechoslovak equipment and weaponry fell into German hands. That made it possible for the Wehrmacht to set up a further 20 divisions and provided it with an additional modern armaments industry. The brutality of German actions and the breaking of Hitler's promise shocked the British government and strengthened its resolve to prevent the dictator from making any further expansion.

After Slovakia declared its independence under the aegis of the Reich, the Poles had to severely stretch their line of anti-German defence and place another army in the Carpathians. The Transcarpathian Ukraine briefly became a source of unrest. Ukrainian nationalists sought to turn the area into a mustering point for their independence movement, which the Germans considered premature. Hungary violently asserted control. But although Hungarian intervention had previously been Poland's preferred option, there was now little cause for satisfaction in Warsaw, as Hungary officially completed its move into the German camp and declared that it had joined the Anti-Comintern Pact.

Hungary had been aided in making this decision by an extremely advantageous economic deal with the Reich, just as had Romania, which agreed to deliver strategically important oil in exchange for German weapons. Italy now urged the 'global political triangle' of itself, Germany and Japan to begin the necessary General Staff discussions.[47] Rome was preparing to annex Albania and so obtain its own springboard into South-East Europe.

The Wehrmacht's southern avenue now seemed to stand open; Danzig remained a bottleneck in the north. Poland was under massive pressure to accept an obviously imminent Wehrmacht invasion of the city. Ribbentrop explained to Ambassador Lipski on 21 March 1939 that the Führer was bewildered by 'Poland's strange attitude'. What it came down to was that 'he did not get the impression that Poland was simply unwilling'.[48] This conversation is usually interpreted as meaning that the Poles were to be forced into the same position as the Czechoslovakians, which understandably prompted Warsaw to seek backing from the UK. But was it really a matter of subjugating and dismembering Poland so that Hitler could turn his unhindered attention to the conflict in the west? Lipski interpreted the German demands as meaning 'that the Germans have decided to soon implement their eastern programme' and therefore wanted to know 'what attitude Poland will definitively adopt'.[49]

What did he mean by the German 'eastern programme'? Peter Kleist, secretary of the German–Polish Association in Berlin and a colleague of Foreign Minister Ribbentrop, explained the situation to contemporary journalists like this: 'In the further development of German plans, war against the Soviet Union will remain the ultimate and crucial task of German politics. Although it was previously hoped that Poland could be drawn onto our side, Berlin is now convinced that Poland cannot be used as an aid against the Soviet Union in its current political condition and at its current territorial extent. It is clear that Poland must be territorially divided (i.e. detachment of regions formerly belonging to Germany, establishment of a West Ukrainian state as a German protectorate) and politically organised (appointment of Polish leaders who are reliable from a German standpoint) before it will be possible to begin the war against Russia with and through Poland.'[50]

In Berlin, Poland's definitive rejection of an anti-Russian partnership led to a complete volte-face. Hitler evidently considered Warsaw to have deceived and disappointed him. Now he had to mentally adjust to postponing the clash with the USSR until after the 'Polish question' had been resolved. As Poland, after 23 March, strengthened its military presence in the Corridor and near Danzig, giving a clear signal that it would not tolerate a sudden Wehrmacht occupation of the city, Hitler's task became considerably harder. But even now he did not want to risk using force, as he explained to the army's commander-in-chief on 25 March, because he 'did not want to drive Poland into the arms of the British. He still hoped that Poland would give in to pressure and accept a takeover of Danzig. 'But we will have to grasp the nettle and guarantee Poland's borders,' said Hitler.[51] Three days later, the Polish foreign minister made it unmistakeably plain that German use of force in Danzig would mean war.[52]

A war of this sort was not one that Hitler fundamentally eschewed, because he was also thinking that in 'especially favourable political circumstances' the Wehrmacht might smash Poland so thoroughly 'that it won't have to be taken into account as a pol[itical] factor for decades to come'.[53] This smacked of chagrin for his failed partnership project. What 'especially favourable circumstances' could those be, which would allow him to clear his recalcitrant neighbour out of the way? In Hitler's political thinking, it was a matter of whether Britain afforded him a free hand in the east.

It must be noted that here, at least, he discussed neither the maxims of racial ideology nor an irrevocable devastation of Poland. It was an option reminiscent of Kleist's interpretation, as quoted above. Unlike during the era of the pact with Piłsudski, Hitler wanted to reduce the refractory Poles to auxiliary status.

On 26 March, Poland's rejection of the German proposals arrived in Berlin and on the 31st, the British prime minister, Neville Chamberlain, announced in the House of Commons that Britain would guarantee Polish independence. It was the long-awaited sign of British resolve – not uncontentious in Britain itself, but welcomed in Poland as the backing it had been hoping for. Although British forces would not be able to help Poland directly if the Germans were to invade, Hitler would now have to factor in the possibility of a war on two fronts. Hitler may have dismissed Britain's move as insignificant, but it nourished his growing aversion to Poland. On 3 April, he ordered the Wehrmacht's Supreme Command to extend 'Case White', the previously drawn-up plan for 'securing the eastern borders', in such a way that 'any threat from that side can be ruled out for the foreseeable future'. The plan had to be ready for implementation 'at any time' from 1 September.[54]

Was this the irreversible decision to invade Poland and so create a border with the USSR that would enable the Germans to make a wider advance into the east? If Hitler wanted to use the next six months to bring about 'politically favourable circumstances', was that in order to underpin an advance into the east or to cover his back for a full-scale attack on the west? There was one person in Europe who had recognised the looming danger to himself and the new possibilities that had emerged from Poland's change of course. On 10 March 1939, Stalin publicly declared that, in view of the international tensions, he was not prepared to 'pull the chestnuts out of the fire' for anyone else and that he did not see any threat to the Soviet Ukraine. If the western powers thought they could transform Poland into an anti-German trench supported by a Soviet rearguard that would itself become the target for the German attackers and draw them ever further into the east, then the Soviet dictator would turn the tables. The fact that it took his adversary in Berlin some time to realise what this nod meant was presumably because Hitler was still fixated on his 'eastern programme'.

4

PREPARATIONS FOR THE WAR IN THE EAST

If Poland's leaders in March 1939 had adopted the political stance that Hitler had counted on, he would have been able in May to risk the war against the USSR that had been secretly negotiated and speculated about for the past five years.[1] A German–Polish military partnership – given Western neutrality – would have had good prospects of success. Covered in the rear by the recently completed western wall, the Wehrmacht would have had at least 50 combat-strength divisions at its disposal, as well as the bulk of its armoured forces and the Luftwaffe, along with an approximately equivalent number of allied Polish divisions. That would have given the Germans a military force superior both in numbers and quality to the Red Army in the western part of the Soviet Union. The German General Staff estimated the combat strength that the Red Army could muster at short notice to be no more than 80 to 100 'good' divisions. Since the Soviet Union was also tied up in the Far East, it would hardly have been able to transfer additional units to its western border.

An advance by this German–Polish force, starting – according to the weather conditions – on, say, 1 May 1939, would necessarily have made it possible to involve the Baltic states and reach agreements with Romania and Finland. So the attack could have begun at the gates of Leningrad and Minsk, with the mass of the German armoured units deployed in the north and south, while the Polish Army and its 50 infantry divisions formed an Army Group Centre, tying up the Soviet enemy in the swampy and heavily forested areas of Byelorussia. Overall, this would certainly have been a far more advantageous starting position than that of 22 July 1941. But these hopes were permanently dashed when Poland broke ranks. War against the Soviet Union continued to be played through nonetheless.

Alexander Cadogan, British under-secretary for foreign affairs, in May 1939: Germany is not presently capable of starting a war on two fronts. If, however, it had a free hand to expand into the East and take control of the resources of Central and Eastern Europe, it could become powerful enough to attack the Western countries with overwhelming force.[2]

The Albrecht Plan

As mentioned above, the Army High Command's documents survive only in fragmentary fashion, but the German Navy's completely preserved strategic war games and studies give solid indications, at least in some places, of what options and considerations, what ideas and plans the Wehrmacht's leaders had in 1938–9 for a collision with the Red Army.

A strategic navy exercise led by Admiral Erich Raeder in September 1938 had still assumed that there would be conflict with the Royal Navy over control of the North Sea and lines of supply.[3]

That was the worst conceivable grouping of powers, which could not be ruled out but was hardly desirable from a German standpoint. The operational leadership of the naval war was to be split into two group commands, east and west. Raeder later wrote: 'Since a conflict in the east seemed to be most immediately imminent, Group Command East was created first and provided with the necessary personnel. As the Führer did not in 1939 expect war with the west until much later, only one analyst was initially assigned to do preliminary work for Group Command West.'[4]

So a comprehensive and highly detailed study by the High Command of the Baltic Sea naval station in March–April 1939, which built on the experiences of the war games in spring 1938, went beyond the realms of a mere exercise. In April 1939, this option – designated as a 'plenary study' – was taken to a higher level of practical preparations for war and used as the basis for further discussions on how to win the struggle for the Baltic. As in 1938, the planners concluded that a strategic assault was the most advantageous solution. The potential problems arising from international law were dismissed as minor. Moreover, the political conditions for an attack on the USSR might change abruptly at any time.[5] Admiral Conrad Albrecht justified the line taken in the study by saying that the studies in previous years had always been of a war on two fronts against France and Russia with Britain as neutral. Now, however, Britain had entered the arena as a probable enemy. Because that posed a severe threat to supply lines across the North Sea, the routes across the Baltic, especially those bringing stocks of Swedish ore, became so important they could 'decide the war'.

The defensive attitude planned hitherto for the war in the Baltic thus had to be abandoned, because, he said, it no longer accorded with the Reich's war aims.

Admiral Conrad Albrecht in the study 'War in the Baltic', April 1939:
Knowing the objective of the war is the premise for any strategy; it determines what tasks the military is given, the evaluation of potential theatres, the allocation of forces, mobilisation and the actual warfare of both the Wehrmacht as a whole and its individual branches.

The chief aim of German politics is seen as being the consolidation of Europe from Germany's western border to European Russia, inclusively, under the military and economic leadership of the Axis powers. A Central and Eastern Europe of this kind would be strong enough to nourish itself even in wartime and to use its own means and its own power to defend itself without requiring raw materials from other continents.

The achievement of this objective means departing from an overseas policy directed at the west and turning towards the east, a development that is now in progress. Overseas trade and colonies are thus questions that could have served to strengthen our economy and military *in peacetime*. In war, they would not be of decisive strategic importance, since they can provide no economic advantages worth naming and only very limited military ones.

If this objective is achieved, then alongside a unified and independent Central and Eastern Europe under leadership of the Axis powers, there would also be:

a) The British Empire
b) France with its colonial empire
c) North and South America
d) Asian Russia
e) The Asian empire of the yellow race

These are all the significant opponents.

The political objectives in the east can be realised only *against Russia*; whether it is Bolshevik or authoritarian is not a decisive factor, since Germany requires Russian territory and raw materials. Russia is therefore to be considered the most likely enemy.[6]

Britain, according to Albrecht, would make every effort to prevent Germany from attaining a global position on the basis of Eastern Europe, but would be unable to defeat this 'Europe' on the Continent itself, just as France would be unable to. The position of the USA remained ambiguous, but in view of their animosity towards the authoritarian states, the Americans would have to be taken into account in a future war. The Asian powers, however, would be directly or indirectly bolstered by the formation of a large-scale German empire.

> It is highly likely that our main enemies in the coming war will be Russia, Britain, France and the United States. Our war aim as regards Britain, France and the United States will be – to reduce it to a phrase – a free hand in Central and Eastern Europe. As regards the European states: attaining their incorporation into an Axis-led Central and Eastern Europe reaching from the Rhine to the border of Asian Russia.
>
> In my understanding, achieving this goal on land fundamentally requires defence in the west, attack in the east.
>
> There are two main possible lines for an attack by land against the principal Continental enemy, Russia.
>
> a) An advance against South-East Europe via Romania.
>
> b) Via the Baltic states towards northern Russia.
>
> An advance on Romania would primarily accomplish the short-term objective of securing oil and food supplies, and would then reach the potential settlement areas and the important raw materials of the Ukraine, providing a starting point for further operations designed to force Russia to relinquish its influence on Europe.
>
> An advance via the Baltic states accomplishes the short-term objectives of controlling areas of settlement for German farmers, securing the unprotected wing in the Baltic theatre and providing a starting position for either an attack on Russia or for defence.
>
> One thing seems certain: an attack along only one of these lines will almost necessarily result in a counter-attack along the other. This is of far-reaching importance for the Baltic theatre.

Albrecht sketched out a naval and aerial attack on the USSR across the Baltic. The most important target was the single Soviet naval station, at Kronstadt, which was to be neutralised with aerial bombardment and ongoing contamination by chemical weapons. (Finishing off the besieged city of Leningrad by using poison gas was again investigated by the Army High Command in December 1941.)[7] It would have to be assumed that in the event of a German–Soviet war both the Baltic states and Poland would attempt to preserve their neutrality. Despite the military partnership it had now concluded with Britain, Poland would take sides only when it became apparent who was going to win. Because of Poland's considerable military potential, both Germany and Russia would respect their neighbour's neutrality so as not to push Poland into the arms of their enemy. However, if the East Prussian port of Pillau, a naval base from which to fight the Soviet fleet, were to be neutralised, then Germany would have to demand the use of Danzig.[8]

Since Russia would be forced, in defence of its naval strategy, to occupy Estonia and Finland, it would be necessary to draw up plans with the Luftwaffe and the army for beating the Russians to it. Engaging in the concomitant negotiations with the armies of the Baltic states should also be considered. Albrecht requested that his staff be made responsible for undertaking the offensive in the Baltic Sea by sealing the Gulf of Finland.[9] He had to wait a year for that to happen, until autumn 1940, when his successor had to plan the attack on Leningrad under much worse conditions. That was decided on the political level, where the revolutionary developments about to be initiated by the Hitler–Stalin pact were still unthinkable in April–May 1939.

A proximate invasion of the Soviet Union, a 'Barbarossa 1939', did not yet have any clear contours. But there is no doubt the idea was in circulation among the military's planners, who were working to meet recognisable political intentions with corresponding proposals. The Albrecht Plan was fundamentally accepted as an option by the Navy High Command, as long as the political prerequisites were met. That could of course change at any time. In the present situation – that is, from the standpoint of April 1939 – it was assumed that a war on two fronts was 'the more likely' development.[10] If that did indeed occur, the task of confining the Russian fleet by sealing the Gulf of Finland would be impossible to carry out. But operational preparations were to be made for all conceivable scenarios.

The requested transfer of additional warships to the Baltic at the expense of the North Sea theatre of war was out of the question. Albrecht's insistence that the navy's leaders always make sure to remind the government how important it was to bring Swedish ore safely across the Baltic was to have significant repercussions for Barbarossa in 1941, because Hitler used precisely that point to exert influence over the army's operational planning. It was also one of his arguments in 1939–40. So we can see that Hitler did remain sensitive to the strategic problems. The operational staff of the Baltic Sea naval station continued to make preparations for an aggressive solution until they again became relevant in autumn 1940, albeit under extremely worsened conditions. The Führer had paid a very high price for his pact with Stalin and ceded the entire Baltic coast to the USSR. Stalin demanded Finland, too, and after the Winter War of early 1940, he obtained valuable strongholds along its coast. But it was not only the navy that had to rearrange itself after the National Socialist government's switch to an anti-Polish policy in April–May 1939.

The task Hitler gave the army's leaders at the end of March 1939 – to prepare for the possibility of war with Poland – was doubtless a reaction to the steps taken by the Polish government, which had for years hinted at a possible military alliance with Germany, only to now rush into the arms of Great Britain. On 28 April, Hitler cancelled the non-aggression pact. But Warsaw, placing its trust in the west, did not budge. This was perhaps the moment in which the dictator decided to treat Poland as he had Czechoslovakia, isolating it and then eliminating it as a strategic factor and hostile outpost.[11] His desire to wage a war for Lebensraum on Soviet soil, understood more or less correctly by the Albrecht Plan, was set in stone. At the parade for his 50th birthday on 20 April 1939, the Wehrmacht appeared both highly equipped and ready for war. This evidently induced in Hitler a kind of personal fear of missing the boat and a new resolve to begin his great game within that same year.[12] Anything that stood in the way of his march to war was to be ruthlessly destroyed. The spectacular terminations of the Anglo-German Naval Agreement and the non-aggression pact with Poland on 28 April were supposed to demonstrate that he was not bluffing.

It is remarkable that, unlike the kaiser a quarter-century before, he did not even now consider whether it might be possible to win the war by attacking France while leaving only a few covering divisions to counter the potential threat on Germany's eastern border. In this, Hitler found himself in complete agreement with the army's leaders, who in April–May 1939 feared nothing more than a conflict in the west, which, in the worst-case scenario, would be another war of trenches and attrition.

Indeed, Hitler had to repeatedly reassure the generals of his confidence that the western powers, as in the year before, would decide against military intervention; he emphasised again that Britain and France were far too weak to present a serious threat to Germany anyway. To pre-empt any possible

13. Military parade in Berlin to mark Adolf Hitler's birthday, 20 April 1939.

sceptics in the General Staff, he let them know that, should his prognoses prove to be incorrect, Germany would strike decisive blows against France and Great Britain. This, however, was the expression only of his absolute desire for war, not of any considered or mapped-out strategy. Raeder must have asked himself in private how and with what the navy would be supposed to carry out such a task. And even Göring himself presumably did not believe, despite all his outspoken optimism, that the Luftwaffe would be able to land the 'devastating blows' that would force the British to their knees. In the last months of peace, in any case, he exerted himself behind the scenes to try and catch up to Great Britain.

The army's leaders, too, tried to promote a realistic assessment of the options and had to trust that the politicians would again be as successful as they had with all their previous diplomatic manoeuvres, military threats and applications of pressure. After the occupation of Prague and the Memel Territory, it was a matter of getting a firm grasp on Danzig, a further step to enhance Germany's strategic position in the area where, according to the army's received operational thinking and the experiences of World War I, it would be most easily possible to decide the war with battles near their own border. Polish neutrality would, as the Albrecht Plan shows, be a sufficient condition for war against the USSR as well as for the occupation of the Baltic states and the Ukraine, which was vital for the war economy. Since Great Britain had guaranteed Poland's existence but not its borders, there was recognisable wiggle room in which a solution for the Danzig bottleneck might yet be found.

The dictator's harsh reaction and his order that the military prepare for an attack on Poland did not necessarily alter the general strategic targeting of the USSR. It would, however, be a risky move to conquer Poland and then have to do without 50 Polish divisions on a future Russian front. The Wehrmacht would be able to make up this loss only if no parallel mobilisation was required in the west. So the hope that the western powers wouldn't intervene was understandable, but that didn't change anything about the fact that the Germans would have to leave a covering army behind the western wall. The army leadership's reaction at the start of May 1939 shows that they did not yet interpret Hitler's instructions as a definitive decision to wage war against Poland and so did not take into account the consequences for the overall strategic situation.

The Points Are Set, May 1939

The first General Staff exercise overseen by Franz Halder as chief of staff in May 1939 was of decisive importance for subsequent war-planning. This specific variant of the war game has been preserved only in the obscure account of a Luftwaffe liaison officer and not yet been assessed in the academic literature.[13] Halder took the least favourable possibility (intervention of the western powers, Lithuania and the USSR on behalf of Poland) as his starting point.[14]

It focused on the task – similarly to the operational plans for Czechoslovakia in the previous year – of destroying the Polish Army to the west of the Vistula with a sudden pincer movement. It should be noted that the objective was a decisive battle in the area near the border: they aimed to capture favourable

14. Chief of the General Staff Franz Halder, around 1938.

'starting positions' (!) for further operations to the east of the Vistula. The Red Army's mobilisation would be completed twelve days after the operation began. But the planners expected motorised Soviet troops to advance to Lviv and Siedlce before that.

So the army group attacking from East Prussia was to proceed east of Warsaw and occupy the Brest–Białystok area, while the southern army group was to advance on Lviv. One of the Luftwaffe's tasks would be to attack railway movements and mobilisation centres in eastern Poland. The war against the Polish and Russian air forces and the destruction of the Red Army's advancing motorised units was 'absolutely pivotal to the entire war', and pivotal at least to the battle west of the Vistula against the Polish Army. In a war on two fronts with western intervention, the Poles would still only be able to receive direct support from the Russians. By using delaying tactics, they might be able to exploit the considerable size of their country to hold out until they were relieved by pressure from the west. So it was a matter of forcing the bulk of the enemy's units to give battle and neutralising them as quickly as possible with a single devastating blow.

That was in line with classic operational thinking and left open the question of how to continue the war on the eastern front, that is, against the USSR. The various potential scenarios had been drawn up long ago. They now only needed to be activated and implemented, albeit without Polish assistance. But it seemed that neutralising the Poles would be possible without any great difficulty. Even a resultant confrontation with the Red Army was apparently not considered alarming. As described above, the model of a decisive battle in the eastern Polish–Byelorussian area was deeply anchored in the staff officers' thinking. Ludwig Beck commented on his successor's war game in May 1939 only with the laconic statement that 'when the first German soldier has crossed the Narew, the Vistula and the San, the Russians will form up'.[15] That was precisely what Halder prepared for. From his perspective, the dangers of war with the western powers were very much greater. But the Führer reassured him that he would succeed in inducing Britain to give him his free hand in the east.

The Army High Command's plenary documents demonstrate a persistent respect for the forces that in previous years had been considered a potential ally. Three hundred and fifty copies of a *Comprehensive Handbook to Poland*, updated to 1 May 1939, were secretly printed and distributed to the most senior operations staffs.[16] It contained a detailed description of Poland's armed forces. The evaluation of the Polish Army's efficacy was still conducted in objective terms and without any political or ideological denigration, even if particular attention was accorded to the lack of unity in the Polish officer corps. That was said to create 'uncertainty in operational and tactical thinking. The *younger officer corps* is recruited by and large from the country's best circles. It forms a more complete whole than the older officer corps and is fresh, industrious, athletic and disciplined, though less thoroughly trained than young German officers.'

From the *Comprehensive Handbook to Poland*:

The excellent *status of the Army among the populace* deserves to be particularly noted. The army is the most important bearer of the state.

The army has been a school of life not only for the leading figures of the state, but for the whole nation, one from which the farmer or labourer, having started at what by western standards is a very low standard, returns home having learned

> order, cleanliness and patriotism, proud of his weapon and willing to use it for his fatherland.
>
> Their material resources do not yet correspond to modern requirements.
>
> *Conclusion*:
>
> The Polish Army has been trained to attack. Due to its mediocre leadership and its as yet insufficient level of armament, however, it is not capable of large operations against a modern opponent. It is highly unlikely that the Polish Army will stand up to any severe strain on its morale.[17]

Halder's war game of 17 May 1939 did not lead to the desired result: the Polish Army could not be decisively beaten to the west of the Vistula. The officers of the German General Staff had not yet mastered their discipline to the required degree. In other words, the Polish Army's fighting retreat was easier for the German planners to conduct than their colleagues found simulating the Wehrmacht's attack. Halder's list of failings was long:

- A lack of faith in the operational possibilities of rapid troops;
- Hesitancy in moving against a defensively prepared enemy, too much concern for the flanks and about counter-attacks;
- Attacks not made in operationally effective directions;
- Choice of terrain unfavourable for tanks;
- Diversion from the predetermined direction of attack to destroy parts of the enemy's forces;
- Loss of time and wearing-out of materiel in excessive reorganisation.

It is not known whether the chief of staff informed the supreme commander of this result. But while Halder exerted himself over the next weeks to improve the army's training and preparations, Hitler took care of obtaining more favourable political conditions for unleashing the war. He needed a solution that would leave the western powers or Russia – or indeed both of these – out of it. That would allow him to isolate and subjugate Poland as he had Czechoslovakia. Paris, London and Rome contemplated another 'Munich', which might induce Poland to acquiesce on the question of Danzig as long as Hitler refrained from violence. He, however, wanted to finally give his Wehrmacht a military victory and to prove himself as a commander.

On 22 May, he concluded the 'pact of steel' with Italy, believing Italy to be fully on his side as a counterweight to the western powers. In mid May,

Japan had seized the initiative in East Asia and engaged the Red Army in a struggle for Mongolia. Would the spark leap into the West? Again Germany and Japan evidently neglected to coordinate strategically or to engage in General Staff discussions, for neither the first nor the last time. Tokyo ultimately hindered the further-reaching outcome – that is, the transformation of the Anti-Comintern Pact into a military alliance – because it did not want to present Hitler with carte blanche to bring Japan into a war against Great Britain. When Ribbentrop later threatened the Japanese by saying that, in that case, Germany would have to reach an agreement with the USSR, he only alienated them further.

But Hitler still believed in the success of his global triumvirate. Just one day after Italy signed the pact, he gathered the leaders of the Wehrmacht in his office at the new chancellery. The minutes taken by the duty adjutant, Staff Lieutenant Colonel Rudolf Schmundt, were presented to the tribunal at Nuremberg as a crucial document proving Hitler's absolute desire for a war of aggression.[18] Of course, the caveat must be made that the minutes are not a verbatim transcript, but only a paraphrase of Hitler's arguments. His declarations also have to be understood within the context of how the situation was assessed at that time, that is, on 23 May 1939. Many of his prognoses and announcements were not fulfilled, because things developed differently from what had been predicted. Moreover, the idea of this as a firm, irrevocable programme is further undermined by the Führer's later behaviour, in that, although he presented himself to his military leaders as absolutely decided on his course of action, he did now and again allow himself to be persuaded of necessary modifications.

Hitler's statements on 23 May 1939 also have to be understood as a personal appearance with which he overcame the trying experiences during the first discussion announcing war, on 5 November 1937. This time, his declarations brooked no contradiction, no misgivings. At the end he even declared that he was going to create a 'small plenary staff' under his personal control within the Wehrmacht Supreme Command. This would take on the 'theoretical preparations for operations of the highest level' as well as ensuing technical and organisational repercussions. 'The aims of specific directives have nothing to do with anyone outside that staff.' In certain cases, the three commanders-in-chief or chiefs of the General Staffs might be brought into the discussions. This staff would provide a study of the 'overall problem', of which steps to take, the means necessary and the training required. 'This staff must consist of men with the greatest imagination and specialised knowledge, as well as of officers with a soberly sceptical cast of mind.' The precepts for this work:

1. No one is to be involved who does not need to know about it.
2. No one is to be allowed to discover more than he needs to know.
3. What is the last moment at which someone affected can be told? No one is to be allowed to know anything sooner than he needs to know it.

The responsibility for working out an overall strategic plan, which Ludwig Beck, the former chief of the General Staff, had demanded in vain a year previously and tried to reclaim for the Army High Command, Hitler, as supreme commander of the Wehrmacht, now wanted to make his own. This announcement was a clear affront above all to the army's leaders, who in these new circumstances would not be able to bother the Führer with their reservations and question his authority as a war leader. In the end, it was not as bad as some, particularly Halder, had feared. Although the Wehrmacht Operations Office was in February 1940 renamed the Wehrmacht Operations Staff, its responsibilities remained very limited. Even at the top of the Wehrmacht, departmental insularity was so persistent that it did not prove possible to create a stringent structure before 1945.

Hitler's speech on 23 May 1939 served not only to strengthen his military authority, but also to present his intentions, and was guided by the need to anticipate any possible misgivings, with which, after all, he was not unfamiliar. So he built up his argument like this:

1. War is unavoidable.
2. Germany is well prepared.
3. Poland is no longer an adequate barrier to Russia. It is domestically divided, unreliable and, despite the friendship pact, has always at heart had an antipathy to the Reich. The option of sparing Poland therefore no longer exists.
4. Poland has to be neutralised at the next opportunity. Unlike in Czechoslovakia, this will be possible only with force. But success is possible only 'if the west stays out of the game'.
5. The situation cannot be allowed to develop into a conflict with France and Britain at the same time.

6. If at some point, as now seemed likely, it came to a war between the alliance France–Britain–Russia and Germany–Italy–Japan, Hitler would strike 'Britain and France a number of devastating blows'. Hitler devoted particular attention to this issue. He envisaged suddenly occupying Holland and Belgium, defeating the French in northern France and then constructing a new front against Britain. If need be, they would have to be ready for the war to last ten to fifteen years.
7. The best option would be to strike the chief enemy, Britain, a heavy blow right at the outset. But a surprise attack would be possible 'only if we don't "skid" through Poland into war with Britain'. Otherwise the navy and the Luftwaffe would have to cut Britain's supply routes in order to force the island to its knees. Nor did he rule out the use of poison gas. In situations where new weapons technology could not be considered decisive, he said, they would have to put their faith in surprise and 'ingenious' tactics.

If Poland was to be neutralised at the next opportunity, without Germany's 'skidding' into a war with the western powers, what would be the first step? Occupying Poland up to its eastern border would, after all, place the Wehrmacht within reach of Russia's core, the Baltic states and the Ukraine. Hitler's statements on 23 May 1939 are usually interpreted as meaning that he wanted to isolate and invade Poland so as to then (!) turn his attention to the west.[19] This is not a compelling conclusion.

Hitler to the Wehrmacht's leaders, 23 May 1939:
Danzig is not the objective that this is about. For us, this is about extending our Lebensraum in the east and securing a food supply, as well as solving the problem of the Baltic states. Food can be supplied only from places that are sparsely populated. Using the fecundity there, thorough German cultivation will vastly increase the surpluses. There is no other possibility in sight in Europe.[20]

Hitler had not previously applied the slogans 'Lebensraum in the East' and 'securing food supplies for wartime' to Poland,[21] and the first assessments of the economic conditions in which a war could be begun left no doubt that occupying Poland would – as in World War I – not be enough to secure German food supplies. Despite all its investment, the Third Reich in 1939 was not invulnerable to blockade. In a war, it would need the 'breadbasket of the Ukraine', the ores of the Donets Basin and the oil of the Caucasus. The OKW's war economy staff pointed out in a study completed in April 1939 that, in the event of a war on multiple fronts, Germany would not be able to command sufficient oil supplies and would therefore have to not only occupy the Romanian oilfields immediately after war was declared, but also seize the wells in southern Russia and the Caucasus.[22]

Carl Krauch, the chairman of the powerful company IG Farben, and Göring's 'Plenipotentiary of Special Issues in Chemical Manufacture' (effectively the Third Reich's chemistry minister), had told the four-year plan's general council that it would be necessary to 'exploit the Ukraine for the war economy in the event of a conflict'.[23] And the calculations made by other civil economic institutions confirmed that, even if Sweden was willing to deliver important ores, Germany would still be vulnerable to blockade if it was 'without economic access to Russia'.[24] Even without Hitler's long-term political programme, the outbreak of a war with these objectives would have meant that seizing the Baltic states and the USSR, in particular the Ukraine and the Caucasus, was indispensable. The experts in the Wehrmacht's Supreme Command, in any case, had no doubts that doing so would be necessary. A report produced there in May 1939 stated that, if Germany found itself facing a hostile coalition including the USSR, it would have to occupy the Ukraine immediately after the outbreak of war to weaken the Soviet regime and bolster the German war economy through the exploitation of the occupied Russian territories.[25]

It is not recorded whether the Führer took any notice of these experts' assessments, nor whether at least their conclusions were passed on by his closest confidant, Göring. Despite being chancellor, he had not held any cabinet meetings for years. The occasional meetings of the four-year plan's general council did provide a certain amount of discussion on the economy. But Hitler did not need to be told that Europe's resources would be indispensable to him in the event of war. So his argument of 23 May, that there were no other options for gaining agricultural surplus and areas of German settlement, should not be seen as limited to Poland and the Baltic states. The appeal of the Ukrainian breadbasket was deeply rooted in his mind – making war with the Soviet Union unavoidable. When Hitler mentioned the 'problem of the Baltic states', it was a matter not just of agriculture and settlement, but of controlling the eastern Baltic Sea and the consequent implications for securing important Swedish ores, one of the main concerns of the navy and the war economists.[26] Seizing the Baltic states also meant being able to use the northern avenue of attack against the Soviet Union.

From the industrialists' point of view, the economic shortfall could of course also be made up by resurrecting trade relations with the USSR. Some of the Foreign Ministry's diplomats were already working feverishly on a return to the Rapallo option, which would perhaps prevent conciliation between Stalin and the western powers. Although the Polish government evidently relied on the assumption that ideological differences would make a German–Russian agreement impossible, this most improbable of options did remain at least a potential means by which Hitler could exert pressure. In his speech of 23 May, Hitler addressed this point by saying that economic relations with Russia would be possible only when political relations had improved.

Göring's adjutant, General Karl-Heinrich Bodenschatz, who was present at the speech on 23 May, subsequently warned the Polish military attaché in Berlin, Colonel Antoni Szymański, that Hitler was convinced Poland would reject his demands and that he was therefore willing to come to an agreement with any partner, 'even the devil himself', to have Poland destroyed.[27] The possibility of partitioning Poland for a fourth time, with the help of the USSR, did not, however, make any strategic sense, unless it was to threaten the west into staying out of the war for Poland itself.

So why subjugate Poland first and take the risk of colliding with the USSR, as Halder's war game assumed would happen, only to then take the risk of attacking the west and only after that again turn back east against the USSR, the chief objective of all his plans? His ally Mussolini was less than enthusiastic about war against the western powers as it was. The ink was hardly dry on the 'pact of steel' when, in a memo on 20 May 1939, Il Duce rejected Hitler's military deliberations. The western powers, he wrote, had bunkered themselves in and were invulnerable to army operations. Defensive positions should be taken up on the Rhine. A dynamic war could be fought only to the east.[28]

There is considerable evidence that Hitler's plans for war were in no way definite in May–June 1939. The precise formulation of his statements on 23 May is just as ambiguous as the slogan 'Lebensraum in the East'. What is certain, however, is that he did not want to begin a global war against the western powers if it could be avoided, but hoped that they would remain passive or neutral. The road to war was anything but a one-way street and

Hitler's strategies still encompassed the possibility that, if the circumstances were right, he would not only clear Poland out of the way, but also carry on into waging his most important war right away.

The War of Nerves

While Hitler explained the situation and his intentions to his leading officers on 23 May, the Japanese had just begun new skirmishes against the Red Army near the Mongolian village of Nomonhan. The conflict escalated slowly and the spark of war did not make the leap to Europe, because although Hitler considered the Japanese problem grave, Tokyo's hesitancy about entering a military alliance now led him to hesitate in turn. It was 'in Japan's own interest to make an early attack on Russia'.[29] Why did he say 'early'? Stalin, at any rate, reacted at once and had a plan drawn up for driving the Japanese out of the disputed area. At the same time, he signalled to Berlin that he was willing to settle their conflicting interests.

On 1 July, the Japanese Kwantung Army mounted a large-scale assault, but was driven back by the overwhelming numbers of the Soviet–Mongolian troops.[30] There was a ceasefire until 22 August 1939, when Stalin had Zhukov launch a huge counter-offensive, the first successful blitzkrieg, which led to the destruction of the Japanese 6th Army within a matter of days. At the same time, Ribbentrop landed in Moscow to conclude the sensational pact with Stalin. The Soviet dictator was the clear victor in summer 1939's war of nerves.

The western powers' efforts to bring Moscow into an anti-German military alliance had been dragging on. Discussions had begun as early as April.

15. Soviet offensive against Japanese forces in summer 1939.

On 24 June, these led to the conclusion of a French–British–Soviet mutual-assistance pact. This was a piece of chicanery from all sides, as neither Paris nor London was in a position, or seriously willing, to enter into wide-ranging military obligations. Their interest, rather, was in diverting the first blow from the well-armed German military machine away from themselves, and in creating additional fronts in Europe's east or south-east, as there had been in World War I. The idea of passively accepting German expansionism, and even Hitler had now partly understood this, no longer came into consideration. Nor, it must be said, did the west's military experts expect the Red Army to be capable of undertaking a territorial advance towards Central Europe. Stalin, for his part, proved anxious to negotiate a high price for any possible intervention and to make sure the western powers would be the first to commit themselves to any massive war effort. At the same time, he entered into secret negotiations with Berlin, which soon led to rumours that spread throughout Europe and were suspiciously well suited to driving up the price paid for his favour.

In a memorandum to Stalin on 10 July 1939, Boris Shaposhnikov, the new chief of the Red Army's General Staff, laid out four possible forms the war could take: (1) a German attack on France and Great Britain; (2) an isolated German attack on Poland; (3) a German invasion of Romania with Hungarian and Bulgarian support; (4) a direct German attack on the USSR via Estonia, Latvia and Finland.[31] The Soviet leadership was thus entirely aware that a 'Barbarossa' was possible in 1939 and, indeed, of the potential German avenues of attack, via the Baltic states and Romania. They did perhaps overestimate the Polish Army's defensive capabilities; otherwise, they would have had to take into account the consequences of a rapid German victory on the Vistula and a Wehrmacht advance to Poland's eastern border.

Warsaw's strict refusal even to contemplate allowing the Red Army into the country for a joint resistance to the German aggressor can hardly have been a surprise to Stalin. Nor can the unfriendly attitude of the Romanian government. If Poland were indeed to lose its nerve at the last minute and give in to the pressure of its western allies, that would present both dictators with a problem: Hitler, because if the Poles relinquished Danzig and the Corridor, he would have lost his pretext for invasion; Stalin, because if the Poles allowed him to advance to the Vistula or East Prussia, he would come into direct contact with the Wehrmacht while Zhukov was still waging his offensive against the Japanese in the Far East.

The Soviets would have preferred to induce the western powers to fight a battle for the Ruhr and make a thrust at central Germany, which would leave them, as it were, on the lee side of the western war and – covered by the main Polish front on the Vistula – free to advance on East Prussia via Vilnius. They wanted the western powers to pressure the Baltic states, as well as Poland, into allowing the Red Army to transport troops through their territory. Shaposhnikov wanted to deploy only 30 per cent of Soviet forces to fight the German Navy in the Baltic Sea and take control of the coast. It was the precise counterpart of the Albrecht Plan. In other words, the commanding admiral of the Baltic Sea naval station had correctly assessed the operational possibilities open to the Soviets. If the Soviet leadership, in its negotiations with the western powers, had stuck to this plan, and if Poland had been willing to allow the Red Army to advance through the Vilnius region, the German military could have activated the Albrecht Plan and responded with a preventive strike on Leningrad and north-western Russia. If the Albrecht Plan was not already known about in Moscow, then this was at least a case of very astute 'forward defence' by the Soviets.

What role would actually be played by the southern flank was not made clear by the Soviet side. They demanded merely the right to march through Romanian territory – something that the Germans had been taking into account for years as a possible means of Soviet advance. But although the Red Army would have marched into Romania and Polish Galicia in the event of an allied war, securing its political influence and access to the oilfields, German–Hungarian counter-measures would then have forced the Soviets to put off making the risky advance into the area around the Danube. A defeat of the Red Army on its banks would have severely weakened Stalin's position – even in alliance with the western powers – and could have led to a new 'Munich' at his expense, including the risk of German intervention in the Ukraine. It would not be clever to expose himself too much, either by having the Red Army attack heavily fortified East Prussia or by committing himself to a broad advance into South-East Europe.

If, however, the first German blow was instead directed at the western powers and they succeeded in beating back a German offensive over the Rhine, perhaps even advancing on the centre of Germany, Stalin would then have easy victories in the Baltic states, Vilnius and Bessarabia, an unbeaten army and good prospects of holding onto his booty. If the western powers' struggle with the German aggressor turned into a protracted positional conflict on the model of World War I, which the majority of military experts at the time considered the most likely development, then the Red Army, with easily defended outposts in East Prussia and Galicia, would again be in an excellent position for bringing itself more fully into play. There is no doubt that Stalin was a clever strategist, who thought out every move as if at chess, not at all a gambler like Hitler – and the lord of the Kremlin had time on his side.

For a long time, it was not clear which way the war of nerves in summer 1939 would go. When in Moscow, on 12 August, the Soviets and the British and French military delegations began negotiating a joint plan for a defensive war against further German aggression, anything was still possible, even if it was a matter of the greatest difficulty to yoke the three allies' interests together. The Germans could not completely rule out that these negotiations would indeed be successful. It would have been reckless in the extreme to trust solely in Hitler's prognosis that it would be possible to isolate and rapidly subjugate Poland, and then, as it were, simply return to barracks afterwards. His declaration that he would otherwise begin a large-scale offensive in the west could hardly be taken seriously in view of the forces available. In the worst-case scenario, the Reich might, as in 1914, have found itself entangled in a world war within a matter of days. According to Brauchitsch's memoirs, Hitler said: 'I would have to be an idiot to skid into a war over Poland, like those incompetents in 1914.'[32]

What conclusions did the Army High Command draw from Hitler's speech on 23 May? The May war game had assumed that the USSR would intervene, and Halder must have been dissatisfied with the results, because it had been shown that the army had not yet mastered the art of mounting a surprise invasion with massed, rapid troops and far-ranging operational aims. So the Army High Command augmented the measures it was taking to mobilise, train and prepare the troops. A large-scale 'Movement and Combat Exercise for Motorised Units' was to be conducted in September 1939.[33] Preparations for war were already secretly running at full speed. After all, Hitler had demanded on 23 May that the Wehrmacht be ready to invade neighbouring countries, as it were, straight out of the barracks. Meanwhile, he announced a 'party conference for peace', which as well as pulling the wool over the public's eyes also gave him the option of climbing down in either an unexpectedly favourable situation (very quick success against Poland, no war beyond that) or an unfavourable one (Germany being left with no allies) and so gaining momentary relief from this war of nerves, the outcome of which might be real war on a global scale.

For the planners of the Polish campaign, the prospect of being drawn into battle with the Red Army continued to loom large. That was evident in their 'war reconnaissance plan', which contained detailed instructions for front-line troops on how to make reports on the enemy. The Polish Army naturally took centre stage, but it was presented as a matter of course that information would also be gathered about Russian troops in Poland, especially about paratroopers – their weapons, their organisation – and about border railway stations, where the difference in gauge meant everything would have to be transferred over[34] – all important knowledge for a tactical air war. Last but by no means least, the planners wanted any and all information about how communist propaganda might influence the Polish theatre of war after an intervention by the Soviets.

The army's deployment plan for Case White, from 15 June 1939,[35] presumed that the Polish Army would be destroyed by a surprise blow landing to the west of the Vistula. Tactically and operationally, this involved movements and objectives that had already been tested in Halder's war game. The army's commander-in-chief declared that the intention was to pre-empt the enemy's mobilisation and deployment. The planned destruction of the Polish Army with concentric attacks from Silesia and Pomerania–East Prussia corresponded to the familiar pattern. In a pincer movement of this type, the Germans would have to reckon with a counter-attack from out of Galicia. So it was a great boon that Slovakia's cooperation meant an additional army could be directed at that area.

The remarkable thing about these considerations is that on the one hand there was no plan to bring in the Hungarians and so involve the Transcarpathian Ukraine; on the other, the 3rd Army, advancing south from East Prussia, was to ignore the weak Polish forces on its left flank in the Vilnius region, or at most distract them with a feint. Given that the deployment plan envisaged holding East Prussia's Lithuanian border with a minimum of troops, it is plain that the planners were preparing for intervention by the USSR and a Soviet advance on East Prussia via Vilnius and Lithuania. Unfortunately, the 3rd Army's own files shed no light on this early phase of planning for the Polish campaign, because they were destroyed by fire in 1942.[36] They would have been able to give us an idea of the plans for a military collision with the Red Army in north-eastern Poland, something that was still a realistic prospect in June 1939.

The OKH's deployment plan says merely that the 3rd Army is to advance from East Prussia on Warsaw and then 'eastwards'. In this we can recognise

the arrangements made in Halder's war game, which had envisaged creating east-facing positions in that area. What would happen after that was left open? It was possible that the remnants of the enemy's forces would reassemble in the enormous Polish territory east of the Vistula and continue the fight from there, perhaps with the support of the Red Army. That would have made a second operation necessary, either starting on the defensive along the Vistula (perhaps on the model of 1920) or continuing out of the army's ongoing advance in pursuit of what was left of the Polish Army.

Historians have so far neglected General Guderian's 1939 'Movement and Combat Exercise for Motorised Units'. This exercise was intended to solve the problems that Halder's war game had identified in May. The chosen training ground was in northern Bavaria, laid out from north to south along the Main River. The starting position was that the 'blues' (i.e. the Germans) had been forced by a numerically superior enemy to retreat onto well-fortified positions on the northern bank of the Main, and had to brace themselves for the enemy's continued assault. However, the blue army group intended to switch to counter-attack, directing the 3rd and 10th Armies against the flank and rear of the enemy's right wing. This counter was to defeat the enemy's right wing and so 'allow the destruction of the enemy's main forces, which will have advanced north to either side of Bamberg'.[37]

If you swap the Main with the Vistula and Bamberg with Warsaw, this is the blueprint for another 'miracle on the Vistula'. The identifying numbers of the armies were those of the two most important armies in the Polish campaign. Given that the selection of the terrain itself will not have been an accident either, it is also possible that they were training for a defensive battle on the Rhine, substituting it with the similarly hilly and thickly forested Palatinate. But the army numbers used, if nothing else, speak against this second possibility, as does Hitler's statement in May that there would not be an offensive in the west.

In mid June, Hitler received a memo from the NSDAP's Office of Foreign Affairs entitled 'The Eastern European Issues'. In it they bemoaned that, among all the purely military preparations, the political questions had until now been neglected. It was of the highest importance, they said, to treat the population of the future eastern territories in a manner that would further German interests. In the expected German–Polish war, eastern Poland would be 'a gathering point and preparatory glacis [the flat ground in front of a fortification] for a subsequent destruction of Russia [...] and of the utmost significance. Because at some point the Soviet paradise will suffer an inner paroxysm (perhaps even initiated by the demise of Stalin), in which all the nationalist political elements repressed by the Soviet regime will spring back into life.'

It was therefore crucial to use Byelorussians and western Ukrainians to force 'Muscovy' into retreat.[38] Rosenberg's department also complained about the lack of coordination when it came to activities in the Ukraine and did not pass up the opportunity to note that the Polish Jews 'exist in their densest concentration' in Galicia and Volhynia. This was probably 'the greatest Jewish reservoir. A collateral, not to be underestimated, of the Jewish nerve centre.'[39] The memo said only the Führer could decide on the matters raised and order the concomitant preparation.

Hitler did not take up this offer in summer 1939, but activated Rosenberg and his expert staff only in spring 1941, when military plans for an invasion of the USSR were already well advanced. As this memo from Rosenberg's people shows, however, the occupation of Poland and the resultant opportunities for interventionist politics in the USSR were already being discussed among the party's elite in June 1939. It seems that Hitler paid attention to the memo, as Rosenberg's argument that the collapse of the USSR could begin with 'the demise of Stalin' was repeated in Hitler's speech to the Wehrmacht's leaders on 22 August, of which more below. Why the Nazi regime should be making calculations based on Stalin's death, when he was in the best of health, remains unclear. Presumably, they thought the Red dictator might fall victim to another internal power struggle.

It is hard to say whether this mention of using the 'Jewish nerve centre' in eastern Poland as 'collateral' influenced Hitler's actions. In the negotiations in Moscow in August, he unhesitatingly relinquished any claim to this 'collateral' and, as regards the Jews in his own territories, seemed to have settled on forced emigration and deportation (the 'Madagascar Plan'). Two years later, however, in August 1941, the high point of Operation Barbarossa coincided with the decision to extend and systematise the mass murder of the Jewish population in what had been eastern Poland. In Hitler's crude logic, he was using the 'collateral' he had taken from Stalin to destroy the 'Jewish nerve centre'. He now returned to the prognosis that his anti-Semitic hate sheet *Der Stürmer* had publicly announced in May 1939:

> **From an article in *Der Stürmer*, May 1939:**
> A punitive expedition has to fall upon the Jews in Russia. A punitive expedition giving them the same just deserts as any murderer or criminal has to expect: a death sentence, an execution! The Jews in Russia have to be killed. They have to be ripped out root and branch. Then the world will see that the end of the Jews is also the end of Bolshevism.[40]

In summer 1939, an invasion of Poland was becoming ever more likely, something shown not least in the changes to the German image of the Polish Army. A potential ally was transformed into an enemy. In April 1939, the department 'Foreign Armies East' (FHO) had delivered an extra print run of its 'Concise Overview of the Polish Armed Forces' as of 1 March 1939. To the evaluation of the Polish Army quoted above (trained to attack, not capable of large-scale operations, unable to withstand much pressure on its morale) was added this statement: 'It seems essential to deal the Polish Army a heavy blow right at the outset of the war. If the enemy manages to play for time, that will considerably strengthen the Polish Army's self-confidence and its psychological ability to carry on fighting.'[41]

On 1 July 1939, the department released a 'Fact Sheet on Characteristics of Poland's Armed Forces', which was to be distributed along with other materials as far down the military chain as company level. Alongside the hitherto objective information, rabble-rousing clichés were presented about the Poles and their army, something obviously intended to extinguish the Germans' previously positive image of their future enemy.

> **From the 'Fact Sheet on Characteristics of Poland's Armed Forces', 1 July 1939:**
> The Polish populace is fanatical and hate-filled, capable of both sabotage and direct attacks. Any successes, even of the smallest kind, make the Pole presumptuous and belligerent; defeats quickly make him a pessimist. Any accommodating treatment is soon perceived as weakness. The main rabble-rousers are generally the Catholic clergy. There are many groups opposed to the Polish state, quite apart from the ethnic Germans: many Poles and Kashubians from former German areas and, above all, the Ukrainians. The numerous Jews see the Germans as their personal enemy, but are capable of anything in exchange for money. The minorities will become a danger to the Polish Army if it suffers defeats or if the war carries on for a longer period.
>
> We can assume that they will undertake an extensive evacuation of the western parts of Poland and destroy all valuable centres of industry and transport links. The destruction and poisoning of food supplies has to be expected.
>
> *Conclusion*
>
> The Polish Army is not yet a fully combat-ready organisation. Its weapons and equipment, specifically its heavy artillery, tanks, aircraft and bombs, are not yet up to modern standards. It is uncertainly and schematically led. The Poles underestimate the effects of enemy fire while in all respects overestimating their own capabilities. These weaknesses are partially offset by the fanaticism of the officer corps as well as by the soldiers' toughness, their undemanding nature and their willingness to self-sacrifice.

While the Wehrmacht's leaders made intensive preparations for the invasion of Poland – including the tried and tested deployment of a 'fifth column', which was already staging various incidents along the border and inflaming the psychological situation – hectic activity on the diplomatic stage meant that there were still various strategic possibilities.

Poland might yet cave in to the pressure and come to an arrangement with Hitler. That would have enabled Germany to launch a 'Barbarossa 1939', whether as a joint German–Polish project, as had been discussed with Warsaw since 1935, or using benevolent Polish neutrality to underpin a strategic assault via the Baltic states and into the Ukraine.

Poland could also, in the event of war, rescind its objection to having the Red Army's units enter Polish territory and so open the door to a four-way military alliance. Even in that case, Hitler would certainly not have given up his expansionist ambitions. The only promising means of breaking out of the encirclement and putting a swift end to the war would have been to advance into the east. That would have meant subjugating the Polish Army and then carrying the fight to the USSR – while the western powers presumably remained passive on the Rhine. Halder's war game had been along these lines.

In publishing a secret speech of Halder's, the historians Christian Hartmann and Sergej Slutsch asserted that, until then, no documents had been found indicating that the Germans considered using the forces assigned to the Polish campaign for a subsequent assault on the USSR in 1939. The document they themselves present is from the Special Archive in Moscow and, although it discusses precisely that eventuality, it is in all likelihood a British forgery.[42] Its author was probably the British journalist Henry Wickham Steed, who was in charge of British propaganda against the Habsburgs during World War I. After that, he was editor of *The Times* for a few years and was seen as an expert on Eastern Europe, one who had been early to sound the alarm about Hitler. This speech of Halder's had supposedly been recorded by an Austrian former officer of the Wehrmacht Academy. The notes were passed on to official channels in London and Moscow, but seem not to have elicited any attention.

If this speech of Halder's, as it is recorded in the Moscow Special Archive and London's Public Record Office, is real, it confirms the thesis put forward here: that a campaign against the USSR in 1939 was a very real possibility. As 'Halder' puts it, after the subjugation of Poland, 'a triumphant army, charged with the spirit of victory in tremendous battles, will stand ready to either confront Bolshevism or, using the advantages of interior lines, be flung into the west to, quickly but indisputably, win the battle there.'[43] If, however, the speech is a forgery by British specialists, it at least displays a contemporary assessment of the German Army's abilities and intentions.

The western powers' real efforts to gain time without entering into any obligations to Stalin ultimately played into Hitler's hands. It kept his options open and encouraged his hope that he would be able to isolate and crush Poland without unleashing a world war on numerous fronts. This ideal outcome would have led the Wehrmacht, after a short struggle, to the gates of Minsk and deep into the Ukraine, which, alongside the Baltic states, would have provided a springboard for war against the USSR.

5

FROM THE HITLER–STALIN PACT TO OPERATION BARBAROSSA

The disappointment about Poland aligning itself with Great Britain in March 1939 made Hitler think anew about the role of the USSR. He needed a tactical move that would prevent Stalin from reaching an agreement with the western powers about creating a joint front against Germany. The Soviet armed forces were not an especially significant factor in that they did not present any real threat to the Reich. The question of economic relations loomed larger in Hitler's calculations. Negotiations about a new trade agreement at the start of the year had more or less petered out.[1] Stalin's surprising announcement on 13 March that he was not willing to 'pull the chestnuts out of the fire' for the western powers immediately prompted the German embassy in Moscow to point out how valuable Soviet raw-materials reserves could be to the German preparations for war. The Soviet side continued to show itself in a cooperative light and the news agency TASS hinted that, in the event of a German–Polish conflict, the USSR might be prepared to deliver raw materials to the Reich.

The Foreign Ministry in Berlin tried at once to test the reliability of the surprising signals being received from Stalin. During the two sets of negotiations that Moscow was conducting in summer 1939, on military cooperation with the west and on matters of trade with the Reich, the German diplomats, needing to rejuvenate the economic discussions, offered a partition of Poland. At the end of June, Moscow additionally demanded the Baltic states and Finland, and Hitler hesitated. If there was a war against Poland, the occupation of its eastern part by the Red Army would not have any adverse strategic repercussions for the Wehrmacht. This new extension to Stalin's territorial demands, however, was designed to hinder a later German attack.

When the USSR concluded its mutual-assistance pact with the western powers at the end of July, Hitler found himself forced to act. On his instructions, the Foreign Ministry initially concluded the German–Soviet Credit

Agreement. In this treaty of 19 August, the Soviet Union committed itself to delivering raw materials to the Reich's war effort for two years in exchange for industrial goods. Whether the economic exchange would actually work was, from Hitler's standpoint, immaterial. The mere prospect was enough to dispel the concerns in leadership circles about Germany's economic prospects in the event of war. It also forced the western powers to consider that, in the event of a military incursion into Poland, the planned blockade on the Reich would prove ineffective, which, Hitler calculated, might convince them not to declare war.

In exchange for granting the credit agreement, Stalin wanted more territorial assurances from the Germans. So Ribbentrop flew to Moscow on 23 August and signed the German–Soviet non-aggression pact, which made the French–British–Soviet military pact obsolete. With it, the USSR appeared to adopt a neutral position on the German invasion of Poland. That was enough to enable Hitler to start the war. But Stalin insisted on a secret additional protocol, the existence of which Soviet historians denied for more than five decades to come. It delineated 'spheres of interest' in eastern Central Europe. These encompassed more than the mere partition of Poland, envisaging a Soviet grab for Finland, Estonia, Latvia and Bessarabia, roughly corresponding to the territorial extent of Russia in 1914. Lithuania was assigned to the USSR's sphere of interest only later, in a second agreement on 28 September.

Until the Soviets demanded it in August 1939, there had been no indication that Hitler would be willing to renounce eastern Poland, Finland and the Baltic states. In order to quickly secure the propaganda coup of a German–Soviet agreement, he had given his foreign minister the power to pay any price requested as long as the non-aggression pact would come into effect immediately. Everything else was beside the point. From his perspective, dividing Poland along historical lines was only temporary anyway.

Does Hitler's willingness to reach an agreement with Stalin on the partition of Eastern Europe really indicate that he had put his aggressive intentions towards the Soviet Union on hold and instead definitely wanted to attack the western powers after the victory over Poland? In his speech to the military's leaders on 22 August 1939, he was concerned above all with persuading the generals and admirals collected in the great hall of the Berghof that the pact with Stalin meant there was no longer any danger of a war on two fronts. He trusted that the shock felt by the western powers and Poland would indeed allow him, after everything, to complete an isolated conquest of Poland.

16. After the signing of the Hitler–Stalin pact on 23 August 1939. From left to right, Reich Foreign Minister Joachim von Ribbentrop, Counsellor Andor Hencke, Joseph Stalin, Counsellor Gustav Hilger and Soviet Foreign Minister Vyacheslav Molotov. Hitler had written only twelve days before, 'Everything that I undertake is directed against Russia.'

The non-aggression pact assured him at least on paper that the Red Army would not assist the Poles if they were subject to a German attack. The great advantage for the moment was that Moscow's military discussions with the British and French were now dead and buried. Poland's military situation seemed hopeless, unless Britain and France were willing to mount a hasty counter-offensive in the west. To combat that threat, the Wehrmacht had deployed some of its few battle-ready divisions behind the western wall. But that was only to cover Germany's back. Nobody now expected a serious threat from the west.

To the senior commanders of the Wehrmacht who had gathered on 22 August 1939, as ordered, in civilian clothes, along with the most important commanders of armies and army groups, what Hitler wanted to demonstrate, above all, was his resolve to attack. Admitting that he had been wrong in his plans vis-à-vis the USSR and also in his assessment of Poland's attitude would not have been a good psychological start to the most crucial internal meeting he had had as chancellor. It would perhaps have encouraged dissent, which he could not afford at any price. Hitler spoke standing up, his manner relaxed, his right arm resting on a grand piano, for around 90 minutes. After they all had lunch together, there was another speech, now mainly about the military operation against Poland.

The documentary record of this speech is not unproblematic.[2] It also contains a contradictory explanation of his decision to turn on Poland.

> **Hitler in his speech to his senior commanders, 22 August 1939:**
> I made the decision in spring, but thought I would first, in a few years [!], turn to the west and then only after that to the east. But the sequence cannot be conclusively laid out. And one cannot close one's eyes to threatening situations. I wanted to maintain tolerable relations with Poland for the time being, so as to fight the west first. But that plan, which appealed to me, proved impossible to implement when some essential aspects changed. It became clear to me that in a conflict with the west we would be attacked by Poland. Poland desires access to the sea. After the occupation of the Memel Territory another development emerged, and it became clear to me that a conflict with Poland might come upon us at an unfavourable time.[3]

Were Hitler's efforts in Poland really only intended to facilitate war with the west? That is highly unlikely because, although the Wehrmacht had undertaken a covering deployment, it had worked out no plan for an offensive against the western powers. The men the Wehrmacht had in action there were engineers, diligently pouring concrete into the western wall. Moreover, arrangements had been made for mass evacuation of the westernmost parts of the Reich, to allow the Wehrmacht to fight on their own territory. It was equally unlikely that Poland would fall on Germany's rear. Ten days earlier, Hitler had given a quite different explanation to Carl J. Burckhardt, the League of Nations high commissioner for Danzig, on his way to London via the Berghof.

> **Hitler to Carl J. Burckhardt, 11 August 1939:**
> I have no wish to dominate. Above all, I want nothing from the west, not today and not tomorrow. I want nothing from the densely settled regions of the world. I seek nothing there; once and for all: nothing in the slightest. All the ideas that people ascribe to me are inventions. But I must have a free hand in the east. [...] Everything that I undertake is directed against Russia; if the west is too stupid and too blind to understand that, I will be compelled to make an agreement with

> the Russians, overpower the west and then, after it has been defeated, gather my forces and turn on the Soviet Union.[4]

That meant that if the west would hold still and Poland were to give in, the Wehrmacht would be able to take on its real opponent, the Red Army, at once.[5] He would strike at the west only if compelled to do so by Great Britain's refusal to give him his 'free hand in the east' and its attempts to shackle him instead.

When and to whom was the dictator speaking honestly? Hitler's speech to his military leaders on 22 August was just as self-contradictory in what it said about Russia. He pointed out Stalin's interest in long-term cooperation and Germany's urgent need of Soviet raw materials, also claiming that Stalin could not risk a war against Germany because it would lead to the collapse of the USSR. Then – almost in the next breath – he added that he would do the same to Russia as he would to Poland. 'After Stalin's death, he's a very ill man, we'll break the Soviet Union. That will be the dawn of Germany's global domination.'[6] Stalin, as is well known, outlived Hitler by eight years, and the German dictator wouldn't dream of delaying the planned invasion for very much longer. Hitler's strange speculation about Stalin's death is at least an indication that he had paid attention to the Rosenberg memo cited above.

According to another account of the speech, he said: 'I was convinced that Stalin would never accept the Brits' offer. Russia has no interest in maintaining Poland and Stalin knows that his regime would be finished when his soldiers came back from a war, regardless of whether they came back victorious or defeated.'[7] His long-standing anti-Soviet programme reveals itself in this sentence, because in what war could Stalin's soldiers suffer defeat other than one against the Wehrmacht? Moreover, it demonstrates his assumption that a single blow would be enough to precipitate the Soviet regime's collapse – a fatal error, which would influence the planning of Barbarossa a year later and contribute to the eventual failure of Hitler's war in the east.

Everything seems to indicate that the Führer considered it wise not to unsettle his military leaders by telling them that what he had in mind was a broadening of his eastern war. For the moment, he had to use Stalin's neutrality and economic support to allay the officers' fears about a war on two fronts. As for the rest of the speech, he boasted triumphantly about the weakness of his enemies, who would not dare go to the aid of Poland. Even the concerns about the effects of a long-term blockade were dismissed as unfounded. Giving his words particular emphasis, he demanded a rapid victory against Poland

and that the Wehrmacht advance uncompromisingly until the enemy had been completely destroyed.

Some of his statements in this context have been interpreted as indications of his racially ideological strategy of annihilation. But phrases such as 'maximum harshness' and 'a brutal approach', when examined more closely, can be seen to apply not to the civilian population, but to the Polish military. Hitler evidently thought it necessary to warn against 'compassion'. Later, in spring 1941, he found the right formula for dealings with the soldiers of the Red Army: 'no cameraderie'. The Russians were said to be 'no comrades' – the slogan could just as easily have applied to the Poles in 1939. As regards the possibility of war against the Soviet Union in 1939, it is especially striking that Hitler repeatedly said it was not a question of 'reaching a particular line' and that military operations should take no account of future borders. And in reference to the subsequent border with the USSR, his noteworthy formulation was that the Wehrmacht could consider setting up a 'protectorate as a forward zone'. So the Polish option was still open.

When Ribbentrop flew to Moscow a day later, the agreement with the Soviets was easy to achieve, partly because Stalin's demands were still very vaguely expressed. The secret additional protocol sketched out merely a 'demarcation of the two spheres of interest in Eastern Europe'. Finland, Estonia and Latvia fell into the Soviet area, whatever 'sphere of interest' was supposed to mean. Lithuania was to fall into the German area, including the Vilnius region. One of the more concrete passages was the intended partition of Poland along the San, Vistula and Narew Rivers, which approximately corresponded to the Curzon line that had been drawn at Versailles but was not recognised by Poland. These discussions on 23 August 1939 initially remained loose declarations of intention and were still subject to later change.

This agreement was thus initially no more than a 'moratorium' (Klaus Hildebrand) between the two parties, the outcome of the forced situation into which Hitler had manoeuvred himself with his anti-Polish volta – and which Stalin had adeptly exploited for his own ends. To his officers, the Führer naturally presented himself as the superior strategist, one who had already won this war of nerves. Now it was the soldiers' turn. His most important adviser on the east, Rosenberg, was not convinced, but disappointed. Of course, he did not fail to understand that 'transitions' might be necessary in reaching the ultimate aim of carving up Soviet Russia. Three months earlier, he had come to an understanding about that with Göring in a long conversation about the imminent conflict with Poland.[8] Both had lobbied hard since 1935 for a policy of anti-Soviet intervention and thus for collaboration with Poland, Britain and Japan. If Poland was now out of the picture and Japan's position remained opaque, it was more important than ever to get Britain on side.

So Rosenberg asked himself whether, instead of this – to his mind – embarrassing and dangerous entente with Moscow, it wouldn't have been better to pursue the other potential solution: namely, making an explicit renunciation of the German colonies – in line with the plan of 1934 – to persuade Britain to accept German expansion into the east.[9] Göring and Rosenberg agreed that Ribbentrop was an arrogant fool who lacked National Socialist credentials and whose anti-British disposition was exerting a baleful influence on the Führer.

Rosenberg on the signing of the German–Soviet non-aggression pact, 25 August 1939:

I have the feeling that sooner or later this Moscow pact will avenge itself on National Socialism. It was not a step taken as a free decision, rather one made in a predicament, a plea for help from one revolution to the head of another revolution whose defeat has been the ideal held out in front of us for twenty years of struggle. How can we still talk about saving and shaping Europe when we ourselves have to ask Europe's destroyer for help? And nor can we openly say that we will use this agreement to gradually bring about a change in Russia, to really gain influence over the Russian people. If we also have to cede the Pol[ish] Ukraine to the Soviet Union, that will be, after the Transcarpathian Ukr[aine], the second blow we have struck against the strongest anti-Muscovite power. Though this may not have any effect at the moment, it will in years to come. But since a conclusive decision has been made, that, and much else, is now unavoidable.

And again the question presents itself: did it have to come to this? Did the Polish question have to be solved now and in this form? No one today can provide an answer to that. For my part, I consider Ribbentrop to be like the criminal Izvolsky, who created the 'reasons' for his political position out of wounded vanity.[10]

On 22 August 1939, while Hitler was making the decisive speech to his senior commanders on the Obersalzberg, Staff Colonel Eduard Wagner, who had been commanding Artillery Regiment 10 in Regensburg for the last few months, arrived in Berlin. It was a routine posting for an officer who had been working as a departmental chief in the army's General Staff since 1936. Under the quartermaster general in previous years, he had been responsible for planning the evacuations of East Prussia and Silesia in the event of a threat to the eastern border. The order to invade Poland and the 'Russian pact' in August 1939 made these preparations superfluous. Upon mobilisation, Wagner, who was to become one the the key figures in Operation Barbarossa, had been made Quartermaster General Eugen Müller's chief of staff. So he became familiar with the army's entire logistical structure as well as with organising military administration of enemy territory. One of his first tasks was to negotiate with Reinhard Heydrich about the deployment of the SS and the police in Poland.

Wagner's diary distinctly brings out the dejected mood in the General Staff. In the chaos of the orders in the last days before the outbreak of war, only two assumptions seemed certain: Russia would not intervene and the Führer was confident that the western powers, too, would hold back when the attack on Poland began. The last discussions with the British gave Wagner the impression that an agreement with London might be possible, but the 'Führer hopes to still be able to clobber Poland'.[11] Göring nonetheless made intense efforts until the end of August 1939 to bring about a last-minute British–German consensus. This consensus would have extracted some concessions from Poland and subjected it to German influence, that is, turned it into an anti-Soviet 'trench'. But Hitler wanted to have a war at last: that was beyond doubt. And since April 1939, he had been resolved to neutralise Poland as a military factor. The final decision had been prompted by disappointment about his fruitless efforts to create a joint anti-Soviet front, not by any considered overall plan for war.

A war against Poland was popular among Wagner and most officers of his generation, despite the official 'friendship' of the years before. It could also be seen as a valuable, unproblematic field test for the new army, which had been built up with fervid haste. And even if the Germans were not afraid of the USSR's military strength, it would still be useful to have the Soviets remain neutral, especially if, contrary to expectation, the conflict did escalate to include war against the western powers. From his department's perspective, Wagner saw another advantage: the Russian pact would spare the Wehrmacht the need to deploy a large number of security divisions to the expanses of eastern Poland. Let the Russians quarrel with the rebellious Poles.

Naval Group Command East under Admiral Albrecht was also very relieved to hear Hitler announce on 22 August 1939 that a pact had been concluded with Stalin.[12] Four weeks later, when the insiders found out what secret price Hitler had been willing to pay for his enormous bluff, the dismay must have been particularly intense in the Baltic Sea naval station.

September 1939: Will Hitler Get a Free Hand in the East?

When the invasion of Poland eventually began on the morning of 1 September, there were still several possibilities as to how things would turn out. The road to war was no one-way street. Until 3 September, Hitler was evidently convinced that the western powers would not follow through on their threat to declare war. When they did indeed demand that Germany retreat from Poland, he went completely silent and motionless, as if frozen, and asked his foreign minister: 'What now?'[13]

After the declaration of war on 3 September 1939, Hitler could still hope that there would be no serious military action in the west. If the Polish Army capitulated after a brief resistance, then Hitler – assuming the western powers stayed passive – would be able to occupy the whole country and gain a favourable position from which to launch an advance on the USSR. He might perhaps even have been able to agree some sort of cooperation with the Polish government, as he did nine months later with Marshal Pétain's government after the defeat of France. After all, what did he care about a paper agreement with the 'devil' Stalin? This kind of Polish–German cooperation would not necessarily lead to an immediate exchange of blows with the Red Army. It would, in any case, be the wrong time of year for that. But why should Hitler allow Stalin to occupy strategically advantageous positions in Finland, the Baltic states and the western Ukraine if he could come to an understanding with the western powers and free himself of the need to cover his back? Official German 'peace propaganda' was aimed primarily at France, which had a large army standing battle-ready on the Rhine. Goebbels gave instructions that the term 'war' was to be avoided as much as possible in the German press, to deceive the German populace and international opinion about the Nazi government's intentions and so weaken the enemy's desire for a fight. In the Army High Command, too, there were many who still hoped that the politicians would be successful.[14] Then the Wehrmacht would be free to move in any direction it chose. A free hand in the east: this objective that German politics had striven for since 1933 still seemed tantalisingly close.

The campaign against Poland went triumphantly at first. The forerunners of the 10th Army reached Warsaw's city limits on 8 September and a rapid occupation of the Polish capital seemed possible. That could have ended the campaign after only a week. But the Poles' tenacious resistance pushed Hitler into closer cooperation with the USSR than he can have originally planned. East Prussia had mobilised the 3rd Army, which had constituted the important northerly wing of the attack in Halder's war game. In May, the plan had been for the 3rd Army not to advance directly on the Polish capital, but aim to the east of it, between the Vistula and the Bug, in order to 'gain an advantageous starting position against the Russian armies that are expected to arrive subsequently from the east'.

As late as August, the leaders of the Red Army, in their talks with the western powers, had floated the idea of making an advance via Vilnius to East Prussia, something that would have meant a direct strike at the flank or rear of the German 3rd Army. New confidence that the Soviets would remain neutral caused the Germans' military arrangements to be changed within a matter of days.[15] Securing the flank against the few Polish troops in the Vilnius Region was a task that could be left to a number of small reserve formations, consisting – as in 1914 – mainly of forestry officials.

So the 3rd Army under Artillery General Georg von Küchler was able to direct all its active units south and assault the fortifications of Modlin and Warsaw, which protected the core of Poland. On the old battlefield of 1920, the Germans got into considerable difficulties, despite their technological and operational superiority. For nearly three weeks, the Poles fought hard and self-sacrificingly for their heartland. Only on 28 and 29 September did the two strongholds capitulate. Their fate had been sealed on 6 September, when the French Army undertook only a half-hearted advance on the western front, and was doubly sealed when the Red Army, on the 17th, fell on the Polish Army's rear. No definite military agreements had been made between the Soviets and the Germans on 23 August. Assuming that they would win a swift victory, the Germans had had little interest in involving Soviet troops. When, after ten days, however, Polish resistance stiffened and a relief attack, albeit a weak one, was made by the western powers, Berlin began to get nervous. While Stalin could afford to wait and see how things developed, the Army High Command advocated a speedy switch of focus to the west. That seemed to necessitate asking the Red Army to intervene in Poland and free up German troops. Stalin responded to the

17. German and Soviet soldiers at the joint victory parade in Brest-Litovsk, 22 September 1939.

German request by having his armies advance across a broad stretch of the Polish border.

In the first week of the campaign, the troops of Army Group North also made a rapid advance.[16] Alongside the 3rd Army in East Prussia, this included the Pomeranian 4th Army, which was to occupy the Corridor and secure the link to East Prussia. It was then to support the advance of the 3rd Army from the east bank of the Vistula. Fedor von Bock, the commander-in-chief of Army Group North, managed on 5 September to gain acceptance for his idea of forming a second eastern wing. This would advance towards Brest-Litovsk and Lublin to enable the Germans to encircle any enemy troops gathering in central Poland. At this point, it was still wholly unclear whether the Red Army would intervene on the side of the Wehrmacht. To make the advance work, the army group was given permission to take the motorised forces of the 4th Army, which had just broken through the Corridor, out of the line and move them behind the 3rd Army to the area around Giżycko. These motorised forces were in fact the XIX Army Corps under Heinz Guderian, the 'creator of the German tank force'. With his two motorised infantry divisions and an armoured division, he proceeded to give an exemplary demonstration of the potential for rapid and far-ranging operational movement – something for which the Germans had lacked the confidence during Halder's war game in

May. Guderian and his corps had reached the Vistula from Pomerania within a few days, then liberated Danzig and been transported more than 120 miles to Giżycko, from where they advanced nearly 180 miles behind the Polish front, travelling on the eastern bank of the Bug via Brest-Litovsk to Włodawa. While the battle for Warsaw was being fought, he and his forces covered the 3rd Army from the east until the Red Army arrived. By conquering the area between the Narew and the Bug, Guderian had secured the projected northern avenue of advance right up to the Pripet Marshes, which – in both World War I and the military plans of the 1930s – had been considered the point of departure for an attack on the Baltic states and the Russian heartland. History does not record what Guderian was thinking during the subsequent joint German–Russian parade to mark the handover of that area to the Soviet armoured divisions. In any case, he and his troops withdrew from a part of Poland to which he would turn his attention again almost exactly a year later, when he took on an important role in the planning and preparation for Barbarossa.

On the projected southern avenue, the 14th Army had advanced via Krakow towards the Ukraine, crossing the San and reaching the Bug within a fortnight. The right flank (i.e. the southernmost German group) was made up of the XVIII Army Corps. Because of the terrain, the partly motorised corps included a mountain division. Together with the Slovakian Army (three divisions and a rapid detachment), they had advanced from Slovakia to move as quickly as possible down the old military road to Lviv, the capital of the western Ukraine. The attempt to capture it failed on 16 September. The Germans could not hold their positions and had to fall back. On the following day, the Red Army began its own advance into the Ukraine. It turned into a race to take Lviv. On the 19th, the Germans and Russians ran into each other. Eduard Wagner noted in his diary: 'The encounter with the Russians by Lviv today was extraordinary. Two Russian armoured vehicles shot up by us and an officer of our First Mountain Division dead. Accidentally, because the positions on the Russian maps were wrong and the Russian combat vehicles were assumed to be Polish. After all that had been cleared up, a friendly greeting took place as prescribed.'[17]

The orders for the first armed meeting of the Wehrmacht and the Red Army on Polish soil stated that a German officer was to proceed to the foreign troops and make the following announcement in Russian: 'The German Army greets the Soviet Russian troops. As soldiers, we wish to enter into good, soldierly relations with the soldiers of the Soviet Union.

We have always held the Russian soldier in high regard. That is to hold for the future as well.'[18]

The Wehrmacht did not keep this promise. In September 1939, however, the agreed lines of demarcation, at least, were respected. Wherever the Germans had raced past their goal, they had to withdraw, for example out of Lviv and Galicia. The gateway to the Ukraine stayed locked. The race for Lviv was to be repeated in summer 1941.

At the start of the bitter struggle for Warsaw, the German 3rd Army expected reinforcement from the Red Army in order to complete and secure the eastern encirclement of the Polish capital. The 3rd Army's commanders even prepared to incorporate Soviet units into their front. On 23 September, Hitler ordered the Wehrmacht to take Warsaw from the west and the Luftwaffe made heavy preparatory bombardments. The 3rd Army was to hand over its positions in the industrial suburb of Praga and outside Nowy Dwór to Russian troops as soon as they could arrive in sufficient numbers. Their own forces were to concentrate on assaulting Modlin.[19]

But nothing came of this joint Wehrmacht–Red Army attack on Warsaw. Stalin evidently wouldn't dream of risking an advance that far west and kept his troops on the Bug near Brest. Instead he suggested that the Germans swap Warsaw and Lublin for Lithuania. This led to a new round of negotiations starting on 20 September, which created, as it were, the fifth partition of Poland. In view of the strategic situation, Hitler found himself in an extremely awkward position. He urgently needed a rapid end to the fighting in Poland in order to throw the bulk of his forces against the west. However, he had already made hasty preparations to extend German influence on Lithuania. There had been secret negotiations about bringing it under the 'protection' of the Reich. By occupying Vilnius, the old Lithuanian capital, and giving it back to the Lithuanians, he could have consolidated relations with this strategically important neighbour.

Now Stalin was insisting on being the one to give Vilnius back to the Lithuanians and to exert control over the country. Given that the battle with the Polish Army was dragging on and that the Soviet troops were advancing slowly, Hitler hardly had any other choice if he was to swiftly close down one side of this war on two fronts. In his 'Directive Number 4', on 25 September, Hitler announced: 'The decision about how to continue the war will be made very shortly. Until then, measures taken by the branches of the Wehrmacht, whether in regard to organisation or armaments, cannot run counter to any of the various possible outcomes. The ability to wage the war offensively in the west at any time must be preserved. Enough troops must be kept ready in East Prussia so that Lithuania can be quickly occupied even in the event of armed resistance.'[20]

One of these 'possible outcomes', as is clear in the passage cited here, was to continue the offensive in the east by occupying the gateway to the Baltic states, Lithuania, which the original German–Soviet partition of Poland on 23 August had left open.

When Hitler was eventually forced by Stalin to give up on Lithuania, he could at least hope to obtain some extra profit from the ongoing trade negotiations. After three weeks, the effects of the British blockade were beginning to be felt and the economic experts considered it all the more important to secure Moscow's willingness to make generous deliveries of strategically crucial goods in a new trade agreement.

When Britain and France declared war, contrary to Hitler's expectations, on 3 September, it compelled him for the second time (the first being the great *coup de main* of 23 August) to become closer to Stalin than he was happy with. Now the understanding with Moscow had to be maintained and extended, at least for the time being, while it was still uncertain how things would develop on the western front. The Saar region was being evacuated of hundreds of thousands of people, all of whom were being transported deeper into the Reich, and for several weeks the Wehrmacht was indeed fighting a war on two fronts. The quick victory against Poland had been achieved, but solely because they had had to conquer only a part of the country. And what was to happen next? Would it be possible in the west, too, to fight a decisive battle near the border, as Hitler imagined, or would it be more sensible to settle into the western fortifications? For Eduard Wagner, the lack of a clear organisational structure for the occupation of Poland meant that the Red Army's advance was simply a welcome reduction of the area to be administered. He was 'happy every day that this territory has been taken away from us. So now it's about face and quick march into the trenches.'[21]

Since Paris and London had declined to declare war on Stalin, too, after the Red Army's entry into eastern Poland on 17 September, Hitler again saw his strategic options narrow. If Warsaw had fallen into German hands in the first assault and had a Polish Pétain been found, then Hitler – who was certainly unscrupulous enough – would have had the chance make a political U-turn and, covering his back in the west, attack the Red Army as it advanced into eastern Poland, then have himself celebrated as the rescuer of Europe from Bolshevism. Alternatively, if the western powers had declared war on Moscow, that would have made Stalin more heavily dependent on the Germans.

So Hitler used his visit to Danzig on 19 September to broadcast a speech in which he appealed to Britain to make peace. He gave justifications for the campaign, which he claimed had now finished, and reminded them of his pact with Marshal Piłsudski. He said the marshal's successors had poisoned relations between the two peoples. Poland had chosen war and fought bravely, at least the soldiers and the junior officers had, even though the Polish High Command had ordered an insidious sniper campaign. A situation had now been created in which it might be possible to 'one day speak reasonably and calmly with representatives of this nation'.[22]

He then praised the agreement with Russia, which had not been willing 'to jump into the breach for the ideals of Western democracy' and make an alliance with the western powers. It was a British lie that Germany intended to 'rule Europe up to the Urals'. The agreement with the Soviet Union also debunked the assertion 'that Germany wants or wanted to conquer the Ukraine'. What it sought was 'a relationship of sincere friendship' with the British people. That he sought this 'friendship' only in order to wage his war for Lebensraum in the east was something he naturally omitted to mention. But you could, of course, read all about it in his writings.

Since there wasn't much sign that the British were receptive to his overtures, it would have been unwise to alienate his new 'friend' in the east. He sent Ribbentrop to Moscow with the mission of suggesting a military alliance; in doing so, he was toying with a diplomatic strategy of overawing the western powers and so bending them to his will after all. But given that Paris and London had reacted with silence to the Soviet intervention in Poland, it was impossible that this game would succeed. The western powers stayed quiet vis-à-vis the USSR and appeared determined to continue the war against Germany at any cost. This put Stalin in a better position than Hitler.

The only option left to the Führer was to remove his operational forces from the east and, for now, fight the war in the west, especially as he was lacking the support he had hoped he would receive from Italy and Japan. So he paid a high price. The withdrawal to the Vistula from Lviv and the southern Bug, combined with the decision to give up on Lithuania, amounted to a strategic defeat. This conclusion may seem strange, because there still does not seem to be consensus on who gained the most in the dictators' poker game of September 1939. Lev Bezymenski, the recently deceased doyen of Russian Barbarossa researchers, who was close to the most powerful figures during World War II and had access to Stalin's private archive, put forward the thesis during the Soviet era that Stalin had used the pact with Hitler to give the USSR time and space to prepare for war. In his last book, in 2002, he said the Soviet Union had later had to pay a dreadful price for this breathing room. He explained this by saying that the Wehrmacht had then eventually fought the Red Army on the expanses of Byelorussia, the western Ukraine and the Baltic States, where the Soviets had not yet been able to construct any fortifications.

But the Polish campaign had already shown that fortifications were not to play any major military role in World War II. Even the German–Soviet war was decided by the movement of massive motorised armies. That, moreover, lends credence to the idea that the Hitler–Stalin pact gave the Red Army useful territory from which it could draw greater strategic advantages than the Wehrmacht.

The German strategy of fighting decisive battles within around 150 miles of the border now applied to the eastern part of Poland; that is, its target terrain was shifted westward by the alterations to the USSR's border. The long-term objectives of Leningrad, Moscow and the Caucasus thus shifted further east. The reconquest in June–July 1941 of the ground occupied by Stalin in 1939–40 required considerable time and effort, which may even have decided the outcome of Operation Barbarossa. Subjugating the Baltic states in 1941 involved the Wehrmacht in weeks of heavy fighting, and Army Group North ultimately did not have the strength to then take Leningrad. The 180 miles from Brest-Litovsk to Minsk did allow Guderian's armoured corps to win a superb victory over two Soviet armies. But the distance was equivalent to that from the Reich's western border to the English Channel and so marked the limit of Germany's capability to carry out extensive blitzkrieg operations. From here on in, the road to Moscow became ever more arduous. Here, too, the Germans' forces proved insufficient. Finally, Army Group South, in conquering Galicia in 1941, expended the strength that it then lacked in November when it tried to advance from Taganrog to the oilfields of the Caucasus, its actual target. So the Red Army won its first victory in World War II in September 1939, at the cost of only 700 dead, and occupied a territory that the Wehrmacht in 1941 paid 200,000 lives to conquer!

Occupied Poland as an Additional Deployment Zone against the USSR

Even in the speech to his military leaders on 22 August 1939, Hitler had alluded to gaining 'forward-lying neutralised states, possibly a Polish protectorate' as a war aim – he could also have mentioned the Ukraine and the Baltic states. This was reminiscent of similar German ideas in World War I and allayed the conservative-nationalist army leadership's fear that the war would escalate. A Polish satellite state – perhaps along the lines of Slovakia – might have made it possible to come to an arrangement with the western powers. A moderate peace settlement might even have made this Poland into an ally against the USSR, and the same applied to an independent Ukraine. Moreover, the western powers were in no way indifferent – as they had been to the Red Army's invasion of eastern Poland – to the massive Soviet pressure exerted after October 1939 on the Baltic states and Finland.

There was now a German–Russian border for the first time since 1919, albeit only on Polish soil for the time being. The potential of the Polish Army to act as an anti-Soviet buffer or vanguard had been destroyed. Its 50 divisions could not be replaced from the Wehrmacht's own forces as long as these were needed on the western wall. Nonetheless, the Polish booty could be used to equip some extra units. Was Poland's anti-Soviet potential ultimately extraneous to Hitler's continuing expansion or could it still be somehow exploited despite Poland's defeat? This question arose every time over the next two years that the Wehrmacht conquered another country or gained another foreign ally. From today's perspective, it may seem unrealistic, but it was not necessarily so in September–October 1939. And what is often overlooked is that the answer was by no means certain.

For one, the Wehrmacht had not conducted the Polish campaign as an ideologically aggravated war of annihilation. Unlike two years later against the Red Army, the rules of the Hague Convention were largely respected, although there were some excesses and abuses. The Wehrmacht, SS and police acted with brutal ruthlessness against Polish partisans as well as against political activists in the former Prussian provinces. The enemy's military leadership was viewed with a certain contempt on account of its professional failure and supposed arrogance. But the Germans recognised a high degree of courage in the ordinary Polish soldiery, just as their own earlier evaluations had predicted.

After all, more than a few of them had worn Prussian uniforms in World War I. The captured Polish officers were treated with respect. In September 1939, this was no bad start for a continuation of the anti-Russian brotherhood-in-arms that had existed between Germany and Piłsudski-led Poland from 1914 to 1916. The memory of that partnership was symbolised by the Wehrmacht's laying a wreath and mounting a guard of honour at Piłsudski's grave.

These thoughts must have been in the minds of at least the older officers, especially as they had suffused German–Polish relations since 1934, as was demonstrated by the spectacular 'Marshal Edition' of Piłsudski's memoirs, distributed to the German leadership elite in 1936–7 with respectful forewords by the most senior officers of the Wehrmacht. The Nazis' anti-Polish propaganda about hatred and atrocities had of course inflamed the public mood, but it can hardly have deeply altered the image of Poland for these rationally calculating generals. The thesis that other options were not unthinkable in September 1939 could have been proved by either of two developments: firstly, a massive attack by the western powers, perhaps with the active assistance of the USA, something that would undoubtedly have mobilised the German military opposition to Hitler and his incautious willingness to start a war. The plans for a coup in 1938, drawn up before the Munich Conference to prevent the outbreak of a global conflict, were still in circulation and – as was demonstrated in the leadership crisis of November 1939 – thoroughly up to date. A military dictatorship after Hitler's arrest or execution, possibly with Göring, the Poles' hunting companion, at the helm, could have fallen back on the 1916 model: 'Congress Poland' as an independent, anti-Russian state 'under the Reich's protection'. A similar outcome might have been reached if the bomb set off on 8 November 1939 in the Munich Bürgerbräukeller by lone assassin Georg Elser had indeed killed Hitler and those closest to him.

There is another question here that is hard to answer: whether, in the shock of military defeat, it would have been possible to gather enough Polish troops willing to put themselves under the command of a collaborationist regime. It must be said that the Germans neither made a concerted effort in this direction, nor, until the start of October 1939, entirely ruled this option out. Unlike Hitler, Stalin had from the outset shown no interest in 'forward-lying neutral states' or a 'Polish protectorate'. In the German–Soviet Treaty of Friendship on 28 September, and again in the secret additional protocols, which contained some minor changes, Moscow drew a clear demarcation of its interests. Since the western powers supported the Polish government-in-exile, which had been formed in France on 17 September after the leaders had fled Poland, and so aided continuing Polish struggle against the aggressor, Hitler publicly mentioned the idea of making Poland a satellite state only once more, in his so-called 'Call for Peace' on 6 October. This was an attempt to link the conclusion of the Polish campaign with the offer to reach agreement with the western powers. He made quite explicit that he would provide 'order' in 'his' part of Poland, just as Stalin had already begun profound repression in the eastern part. The issue of Poland would be dealt with solely by Russia and Germany, he declared in the Reichstag. Hitler now ended the chaos that had reigned in the German occupation. He made sure that the campaign, which had been planned and waged as a normal war by the Army High Command, albeit accompanied by certain excesses right from the outset, was now transformed into a scheme of radical Germanisation and exploitation. Even here, the Führer did not have any well-developed ideas, but instead reacted to prompts and pieces of information as and when they arrived from his subordinates.

What is particularly telling is a long discussion that Hitler had in the Chancellery with Rosenberg on 29 September, one day after signing the treaty with the Soviet Union.[23] He began by describing his impressions during his visit to the front and admitted that he had 'learned a lot in these past weeks'. This referred partly to his idea of Poland. The country was lousy and squalid. 'The Poles: a thin Germanic layer [!], then dreadful material underneath. The Jews, the most horrible thing you could even imagine. The cities clogged with dirt.' This was no longer the desirable alliance partner that Hitler had been wooing only half a year before. What had he been told or shown? Or was this the hauteur of his victory?

As for the future? He wanted to divide the occupied zone into three strips: in the easternmost part, between the Bug and the Vistula, he would collect 'the entire Jewry' including the Jews from the Reich and 'all other in some way unreliable elements'. They would provide the forward zone in front of 'an impregnable eastern wall' on the Vistula, 'even stronger than in the west'. This was an absurd notion, which can be explained only as the result of uncertainty and the need to come up with a coherent strategy for continuing the war. For the western part of the occupied zone, he intended a broad swathe of Germanisation and colonisation close to the previous border to the Reich – the work of decades. Between the ominous eastern wall on the Vistula and this area of settlement, the task would be to construct a Polish 'statehood'.

Since he was familiar with Rosenberg's reservations about the pact with Moscow, Hitler emphasised in this discussion that he had given it 'very deep consideration'. If Stalin had entered into an alliance with Britain, Germany would have been unable to prevent the Russians from seizing a number of Estonian ports – an argument reminiscent of the navy's misgivings and war games. He also had a German advance into the Baltic states in mind. He had, he said, chosen the lesser evil and 'gained an enormous strategic advantage' – presumably the USSR's neutrality. On the following day, Goebbels wrote in his diary: 'We could expand into the Baltic countries, but the Führer doesn't want to attack yet another country; anyway, we have enough to digest for the time being. That does not mean we're relinquishing the Baltic states.'[24]

Hitler's derisive remarks about the Red Army show that he did not consider his new neighbour in the east to be either an ally or a potential danger. They had sent him a general, he told Rosenberg, who in Germany wouldn't have been allowed to command so much as a single battery. Stalin had 'purged' the uppermost officers and was therefore afraid of war. A defeated Red Army would be just as dangerous to the Red dictator as a victorious one. There was no need to fear the Russian Navy; only the Soviets' masses of infantry had to be taken into account. Was it to counter this nugatory threat that he needed an 'impregnable eastern wall'?

The quartermaster general's efforts to establish a conventional military administration in occupied Poland, one taking responsibility for order and reconstruction as well as a fruitful relationship with the populace, swiftly became a 'struggle against dark forces'.[25] His adversaries in the SS and the police had the support of Hitler, and the Army High Command ultimately gave way to the dictator. It was all the easier for the Army High Command to distance itself from these 'political' questions because Hitler was pushing it to begin an assault on the west as soon as possible.

As early as 27 September, while Warsaw and Modlin were capitulating, he explained his assessment of the situation to the army's leaders in the Chancellery.[26] Continuing the war in the west was something he regarded as in itself undesirable, and he seemed to trust in the efficacy of his calls for peace. But, he said, they also had to take into account that circumstances might change. The only thing that 'always counted' was success, power. Time was against Germany, so the High Command should be prepared to 'act aggressively in the west'.[27] The troops returning from the east were not to be sent into an attritional war on the western front. They were the most powerful part of the Wehrmacht, filled with the confidence of the victory they had won. This proven force should be deployed as soon as possible to win a decisive battle on the old battlefields of northern France. His willingness to stake everything on one card and deal France a 'great blow' as soon as the end of October, in order to wrap up the world war he had been 'forced into' by the end of the year, provoked utter horror in the High Command.

Unlike in 1914, the army had no operational plan for the west at its disposal, and it was only with great reluctance that its leaders came round to this new line of thought. They doubted that it would be possible to break through the Maginot Line and warned about the political consequences of advancing through Holland and Belgium. If a rapid success proved unattainable, Germany would be economically finished within 18 months. But Hitler would not tolerate debate and gave the impression of having already thought through all the problems and options. It would be a limited operation, defeating the French field army and then occupying northern France, Belgium and Holland. From this position, they would be able to wage an aerial and naval war on Great Britain, while also protecting the vital Ruhr valley.

For the first time, Hitler took on the role of field commander, not only marking out the framework of a campaign, but also involving himself in all important deliberations. The army's leadership was required only to implement the plans and clarify matters of particular detail. It was the beginning of a silent struggle over the General Staff's demand for autonomy in operational planning. They submitted a comprehensive list of problems with Hitler's instructions. Not least among these were the condition of the troops and their lack of combat readiness. A few days later, and even before Prime Minister Chamberlain rejected the offer of peace, the Führer again laid out his arguments in a memorandum to the High Command. He was intensely irritated by the OKH's hesitancy and presented himself as determined to overcome all internal resistance, even though his decision had evidently not yet been definitively made.

He said that he did not fail to see the advantages of concluding a peace treaty on the basis of the territorial expansion already achieved in the east, but claimed this would be short-termist. Even written agreements were not a secure foundation on which to base prognoses of the future. The enemy had to be beaten down to a point where he would no longer be able to oppose any kind of future developments in the east. Ultimately, the USA's antagonism and the USSR's doubtful attitude also had to be borne in mind.

From Hitler's memorandum and guidelines on war in the west, 9 October 1939:
Russia: No treaty and no agreement will ever definitely secure the lasting neutrality of Soviet Russia.

At the moment, everything indicates that they will not abandon their neutrality. In eight months, in a year or even in several years, that might change. The negligible value of contractual agreements has been demonstrated to everyone in the past few years more than ever before. The greatest security against a Russian attack will be a clear manifestation of German superiority, or indeed a rapid demonstration of German power.[28]

It must be remembered that Hitler's decision to turn west was intended to inflict a rapid operational defeat close to the border and thus free up his troops for conflict with the USSR. Russia's neutrality was important to him for the moment, but not as an end in itself. Contractual commitments meant nothing to him and he was entirely convinced of the Wehrmacht's military superiority. He dismissed the Army High Command's complaints about the units' lack of combat readiness. He consistently reiterated that the real enemy was in the east. In order to attack him, Hitler needed the powerful military force that had neutralised Poland and was now tied up in the west.

His orders and the decision he made in mid October 1939 clearly reflect this thinking. In his 'Directive Number 6', of 9 October, he gave the OKH its task in writing. And on 17 October, Hitler decided that it was time to end the military administration of Poland. The party-dominated civilian administration was to act as a 'General Government' (a term borrowed from World War I) and keep occupied Poland as completely under the heel as it could. It was to neutralise the Polish intelligentsia and prevent 'the formation of nationalist cells'. He explicitly rejected the contacts that German officers in Krakow had made with the episcopacy and the old ruling feudal class. 'These problems do not have a social solution. [...] All efforts to consolidate relations must be eradicated,' ordered Hitler.

From Hitler's instructions on 17 October 1939 for future relations between Poland and Germany:
Our interests consist in the following: making provisions to ensure the area, as a forward-lying glacis, has military significance for us and can be used for deployment. The railways, roads and communication links must be maintained and exploited for our purposes.[29]

Since an invasion had been ordered in the west, what mattered in the east was securing against a possible Polish uprising and militarily upgrading the defences on the new border with the Soviet Union. This would be done in part by setting up garrisons in stable strongholds, following the example of the Teutonic Knights. The other priority was to upgrade routes of advance. But why? If the bulk of the Wehrmacht had been sent to try to end the war in the west – though it was ultimately unknowable which way the scales would tilt, as even Hitler, despite his ostentatious optimism, did not wholly deny – then was there not also a risk of attack from the east? Was it absolutely certain that Stalin would not use a favourable situation to exchange one alliance for another?

The question of the Hitler–Stalin pact's stability could not but be in German minds. And the advance of Soviet troops after October 1939 into the sphere of influence accorded them by Berlin could not leave anyone indifferent, as the takeover of the Baltic states and Finland denied the Wehrmacht one of its most important avenues of assault for a war against the USSR. The navy had only just given up its arguments for a preventive strike to secure the eastern Baltic Sea and so provide a basis for the war against Great Britain. Only a year earlier, the Luftwaffe had still been reckoning with the danger that Czechoslovakia would be used as a Soviet 'aircraft carrier'. Now the Soviet Air Force had moved its airstrips so far westward that it was within range of every corner of the Reich. And the army, too, was now face-to-face with the Red Army.

Colonel Wagner took part in the meeting at the Reichstag on 6 October and, after Hitler's 'Call for Peace', did not share the optimism of the many who thought the end of the war was in sight. That evening, he noted in his diary: 'Russia is undertaking a significant westward expansion and is gradually taking the Baltic states "under its protection". That means it has regained its lost provinces without bloodshed and made a considerable advance into Europe. If the friendship pact holds, then all well and good. But unfortunately the delivery of raw materials is taking a very long time because, firstly, the Russians need them themselves and, secondly, the railway network over there is a catastrophe.'[30] Nevertheless, he believed – like the proponents of a Rapallo policy – that an alliance with the USSR could be of strategic benefit to Germany if it were possible to direct Moscow's energies towards India, which would put Great Britain under pressure and force it to come to terms.

Max Ludwig, artillery general, chief of the Troop Office in the 1920s and one of the most important figures in the secret German–Soviet collaboration on armaments production, when writing as executive editor of the September 1939 issue of the *Military Technology Monthly*, celebrated the 'Führer's ingenious decision to alleviate the tensions and return to our long-established friendship'.[31] Nowhere in the world were there two economies that complemented each other so well. As for supplies of raw materials, he said, Soviet Russia was 'Germany's natural hinterland' – which of course was no argument against war with the USSR. Oskar Ritter von Niedermayer, Seeckt's representative in Moscow in the 1920s, now employed as an adviser by the OKW, wrote in the semi-official *Review of Military Studies* to extol the economic potential of the Soviet Union and the long tradition of German–Russian friendship.[32] Behind the scenes, he drew up new plans for a German–Russian advance towards the Persian Gulf and India, which was seriously discussed in the Foreign Ministry and the OKW, and expressly encouraged by Hitler and Rosenberg.[33]

That kind of strategy, to which Hitler, under the influence of Foreign Minister Ribbentrop,[34] was very receptive, and which had supporters among the leaders of the NSDAP and the Wehrmacht, was by no means based on the assumption of long-term partnership with the Soviet regime. The conflict with Great Britain was not supposed to destroy the British Empire, but only to force London to recognise German dominance of Continental Europe and provide Hitler with his free hand in the east. Even though there were some powerful political groups who dreamed of a German overseas empire, Hitler saw Germany's future colonies as lying in the east. But he let the Africa and overseas enthusiasts carry on lobbying nonetheless. As his rage mounted about Britain's stubborn refusal to come to terms with him, and as he became increasingly determined to force the British government to its knees, he began to think more globally. But his options for striking a decisive blow against Britain remained limited, which meant that the war of conquest against the USSR had to be postponed into the indefinite future. He had of course never considered a lasting collaboration with Stalin. But now that the bluff of August 1939 had to be maintained and gained a certain momentum of its own, the situation compelled him to make compromises and take measures that were hard to reconcile with the eventual switch to war in the east.

The intractable trade negotiations are a good example of this. The new agreement was concluded, on 11 February 1940, only after the German side had declared itself willing to exchange its most advanced military technology for the Soviet raw materials urgently needed by Hitler's war economy.[35] The agreement entailed very large quantities of goods and secured Germany's grain and oil requirements for a year, even though that only partially compensated for the overseas deliveries lost as a result of the British blockade. Since the German deliveries were scheduled to begin later, this agreement practically meant that Stalin was credit-financing Hitler's attack on the west. And the increasing obligations to provide these deliveries made the Reich economically dependent on the Soviet Union, which narrowed the time frame in which the war in the east could be started. Plus, if the German advance in the west found itself bogged down, that dependency would become ever more painful.

The agreed resettlement of the ethnic Germans from the territories allocated to the USSR began in eastern Poland and the Baltic states and was later extended to Bessarabia and the Bukovina. Hundreds of thousands of people of German descent were transported 'home to the Reich' and settled in what had formerly been western Poland. On 7 October, Hitler had appointed Heinrich Himmler his 'Reich Commissioner for the Strengthening of German Nationhood' and given him practically free rein to undertake a ruthless Germanisation of occupied Poland, a task whose objectives were actually very long term, but meant in the short term that the resettled Germans were lost as a potential fifth column in the areas they had been living in. Stalin thus gained a security advantage while Himmler merely used the German settlers to replace the Polish farmers driven from the General Government to the 'Incorporated Eastern Territories'. A great number of these ethnic Germans spent years in transition camps. These mass deportations not only created unrest but also had such grave economic repercussions that the Wehrmacht and Göring intervened to put the brakes on Himmler's enthusiasm.[36]

Stalin's conquest of the Baltic states and his attack on Finland on 30 November 1939 also prompted considerable disquiet in the highest German circles. In the 'anti-war group' among the conservative opposition and the generals, more than a few had hoped to reach a peace accord with the western powers in which Germany would revert to its eastern border of 1914, perhaps beside a central Polish state. In some, this hope was combined with an aversion to both the SS's atrocities in Poland and Hitler's, from their standpoint, foolhardy 'pro-Bolshevik' policy. Former ambassador Ulrich von Hassell and the former mayor of Leipzig Carl Goerdeler, two representative members of the upper-middle-class civilian opposition, considered Hitler's desire to attack the west with Stalin's backing to be 'criminally reckless and this form of politics with Russia to be a tremendous danger'.

They argued that, in order to escape a momentary predicament, Germany had 'sacrificed all the most important positions: the Baltic Sea and the eastern border. Even leaving aside the politically indecent handover of the Baltic countries, our dominium maris baltici is now severely threatened, as the supply of ore from Sweden will be in the event of war with Russia. All this, however, pales in comparison with the blithe offering up of a large and important section of Europe, partly of German-Lutheran culture and partly a remnant of Old Austria, to the Bolshevism that we were supposedly fighting to the death in far-off Spain. Widespread Bolshevisation has already begun in formerly Polish areas.' It was probable 'that Hitler in his heart of hearts still reserves the right to attack the Soviet Union. That only confirms the criminal character of his politics. The advance of Bolshevism along the whole front and indeed up to our borders, together with the necessary socialist consequences of a war economy, will have the most dangerous of domestic political repercussions for Germany.'[37]

Ludwig Beck, who had resigned from his post as chief of the army's General Staff a year earlier over the hazardous course Hitler was taking towards war, was of a similar opinion. He thought it would be impossible to end the war in the west and predicted either a massive allied offensive or a long-drawn-out war of attrition, which the Reich would be unable to withstand. In that case, Russia's hand would grow ever stronger and decisively restrict Germany's strategic options. 'If no adequate Polish buffer state is maintained, Germany will in future have the heaviest of debts on its account, the return of Russia into Europe', he wrote in a memorandum after the end of the Polish campaign.[38]

Beck's successors had other worries. Franz Halder was under permanent pressure from Hitler to start an offensive in the west, preferably before the end of the year. On 3 November, he began a General Staff exercise involving the most important leaders of the army, which concluded that not one senior commander thought an attack would be successful. At a discussion of the situation with the army's commander-in-chief two days later, Hitler reacted to this assessment with fury and threatened the army's leaders with personal consequences for disobeying his will, only to rescind the order he had already given for an attack on 7 November and then, a few days later, reinstate it again.[39] Overall, the start of the western offensive was postponed 29 times in the following months – one symptom of the dogged wrangling between the leaders of the Wehrmacht and their supreme commander about the necessary means and preconditions of such an operation.

The army's leaders were not above exaggerating their reports on the poor state of the German troops to dissuade Hitler from his order.[40] Although there had indeed been significant wastage, particularly among the motorised troops, and although the battles in Poland had shown up considerable gaps in the army's training, these problems were emphasised by its leaders because they doubted whether they would, in their present state, be able to attack and 'annihilate' the French armed forces. Moreover, a long period of nothing but defence in the west might yet provide the right circumstances for a political settlement with the enemy.

Even though Nazi propaganda promulgated a very different picture, the rapid expansion of the Wehrmacht had created an intensely heterogeneous war machine. The erstwhile elite of a well-trained 100,000-man army had become the scaffolding for a force that increased its size eight-fold in three years and then been increased another six-fold before the outbreak of war. Only a few divisions had a high level of equipment and training and were fully prepared for mobile warfare. Ninety per cent of army units still advanced on foot or on horseback, and only half of them were considered fully battle-ready. The majority of soldiers had had only a brief period of instruction and did not at all correspond to the young, dynamic front-line soldiers of Nazi propaganda.

The Polish campaign had revealed shortfalls in equipment and, above all, training that went far beyond the expected Clausewitzian 'friction'. Unlike in 1914, especial problems emerged in the carrying out of operations and attacks. The bottom end of the command chain was often too hesitant and uncommitted in deciding to attack, meaning that momentum was easily lost.[41] Coordination of the Luftwaffe with the ground troops was 'severely lacking'. The air force often bombarded their own side. Even some of the armoured units had not grasped the technique of fighting with massed force, as was demonstrated outside Warsaw and on the Bzura. The tanks were often – in contradiction of the new doctrine – split up into small groups to support the infantry, which led to failures and unnecessary losses. So the artillery, in particular, had played an increasingly important role and proved to have an extraordinarily intense effect on the enemy's morale. However, it required better support from the motorised forces.

The shortcomings were equally grave when on the defensive.[42] Intelligence and security duties were regularly neglected; surprise attacks and setbacks were the consequence. The support services and the supply units were largely unarmed and reacted to enemy attack with brutal mistreatment of the civilian population. When on the march, there had been constant and enormous traffic jams. And it had been shown, to the detriment of the Polish Army, just how vulnerable massed units in close formation were to attack from the air. The Wehrmacht's organisation in that regard had been no better than the Poles. This was not the state in which to step into the western arena.

The Army High Command responded in October 1939 by organising a training offensive that is almost without parallel in military history. It involved all ranks, but was aimed primarily at battalion commanders.[43] As well as training leadership skills, the exercises were focused on practising combat with massed forces and on enhancing attacking capabilities. The infantry was reorganised and given better weapons. Tank tactics were modified to make it easier to join up different units and concentrate forces on a single point. The introduction of larger and more powerful armoured trucks was accelerated and coordination with the Luftwaffe put onto a far more effective footing. It was these improvements that made it possible for the Wehrmacht to win the victories it did in France in May 1940.

In October 1939, the Army High Command still considered the situation very unpromising. Only a small proportion of the troops could be given sufficient munitions for a large-scale conflict along the lines of World War I. There would not be enough to storm the Maginot Line or for a long-lasting battle in northern France. The result was intense pressure on the armaments industry to increase its munitions production, even at the expense of tank manufacture.[44] And yet, the deficient state of the Wehrmacht would not have made it unable to withstand battle in October–November 1939. It was certainly well enough armed for a conflict with the Red Army, something which, given how late it was in the year, could now be ruled out until the following spring. The Soviet assault on Finland in November would soon show how misplaced Moscow's euphoria had been about the 'easy' successes in its conquest of Poland. These had given no real indication of the Red Army's capabilities. In its deployment against Poland after 17 September, the Red Army had been fighting a force that had actually already been beaten. The Polish reserves displaced into the east of the country were ordered by their leaders to avoid battle and to fight only in self-defence. So the Russians had encountered little resistance and were able to advance 180 miles west in a matter of 12 days. The Poles lost up to 7,000 dead, the Red Army supposedly only 737.[45] When the Poles had stood and fought, the Red Army had left much to be desired. When subjected to enemy fire, the troops panicked; the Soviet artillery was inadequately motorised; the railway troops were a failure. In fact, there was no cause for euphoria, as was then demonstrated a few weeks later in the attack on the overwhelmingly outnumbered Finnish Army. It was only after a long struggle and heavy losses in the teeth of tactically astute Finnish operations that the Russians were finally able to assert themselves and force Helsinki to relinquish parts of its territory.

The Wehrmacht's leaders used the time gained by their own ongoing intransigence over the attack Hitler had ordered on France to thoroughly evaluate the experiences in the Polish campaign, and to improve their training, equipment and tactics accordingly. The Red Army's leaders, in contrast, made sweeping rulings based on isolated observations. For example, finding that the cavalry had advanced more swiftly into eastern Poland than the ponderous armoured corps led them to conclude that armoured brigades should be reduced in size. The decision to restructure these vital units in line with 'the principle of deep operations' is today regarded as having been an egregious error. In the campaign against France, the German armoured divisions again proved their worth as the motorised spearhead of rapid, far-ranging operations, whereas the smaller tank brigades created by the Soviet side were shown in 1941 to be too weak to be useful.[46] There was no need for the Wehrmacht in 1939 to fear an exchange of blows with the Red Army.

Hitler Postpones His Anti-Soviet Plans

When Hitler, in a speech to his senior commanders in the Chancellery on 23 November 1939, again emphasised that he was 'irrevocably resolved' to attack France and Britain, the army adjutant in the Führer Headquarters, Major Gerhard Engel, noted this meant that all 'possibilities of ending the war and of a separate peace with the Polish government', which Hitler had 'often discussed', were now finished.[47] Although attempts to negotiate did continue via various channels,[48] Hitler had now firmly settled on the idea of forcing Britain and France to their knees. This would finally give him a free hand in the east, and on his own terms at that. Never again did he want to have to tolerate peace conferences and compromises as he had in Munich in 1938.

In these circumstances, his 'friendship' with the Soviet arch-enemy must have seemed even more insufferable. But as long as Britain was not willing to accept his Eastern policies and remained able to fall on his rear, his troops would be tied up in the west and unable to march on the USSR. It was impossible to prevent Stalin from exploiting the situation to cash in the strategic gains he had been promised, unless Hitler dared to undertake another about-face like the one in August 1939. But what could he have offered the west other than the restoration of Polish and Czech sovereignty 'under the Reich's protection', which would not have been enough for the western powers? His impression that they meant to destroy his Third Reich sparked furious concentration on implementing the order to attack on the western front: 'I want to defeat Britain, whatever the cost. And that is what my every thought and action strives towards. I no longer know the meaning of cinema, theatre, music. Defeat Britain!'[49]

Would it have been completely unrealistic to make an about-turn in autumn 1939 and go for Stalin? In his foreign politics and ideologically, Hitler's present anti-western orientation threw up far greater hindrances and objections than an anti-Soviet course would have. A test of strength against the USSR would by no means have necessarily led immediately to an exchange of blows. As mentioned, it was already too late in the year for that. But despite the unusually bitter winter, which put the German war economy in all sorts of difficulties, it would have been possible to again adopt an anti-Soviet stance and extend German influence into the Baltic states and the Ukraine. After all, how binding was the secret additional protocol on spheres of interest in eastern Central Europe? The powerless League of Nations in Geneva had ejected the USSR after Stalin's attack on Finland. There was no authority to whom Stalin could complain if Hitler broke the agreement, especially as the USSR's propagandist pretext for annexing eastern Poland – a supposed plea for help from the Byelorussian and Ukrainian populace – would be discredited if the agreement became public.

No, Stalin would have had to keep the additional protocol a secret even if there had been a Cold War with Germany in winter 1939–40. Anyone to whom that seems improbable should ask themselves what kind of policy would have been pursued by Göring if Georg Elser's attempt to assassinate Hitler on 8 November 1939 had been successful. He had always lobbied in favour of Poland and an agreement with Britain. He was also involved in an escalating dispute with Heinrich Himmler, whose ruthless deportations were radicalising and complicating the occupation of Poland, particularly in regard to its economics, for which Göring was responsible.

Of course, if Germany had changed course against him, Stalin could have exerted economic pressure by stopping the Soviet deliveries of oil, though these were only arriving in small quantities as it was. Germany could have made up that shortfall by taking a stronger grip on Romania. If Hitler thought it possible in October 1939 to prepare and begin a western offensive within four weeks, how much more lightly could he have decided to carry out a campaign in the east? There can be no argument that the Wehrmacht would not have been capable of it in 1939. It was rather that Hitler preferred to tackle the far more difficult task of dealing with the west. He could have decided quite differently. And he must have been privately aware of that.

Continuing the war in the east would also have been an ideologically simpler idea to sell than this alliance with the Bolshevik nemesis. Moscow, meanwhile, was making considerable propaganda efforts to attack the western powers and support the German position. After the Comintern Congress at the start of November 1939, which branded the western powers warmongers, Paris countered with an elaborate fraud. According to the French reports, Stalin had made clear to his most important functionaries on 19 August – that is, before the signing of the pact – that the USSR must encourage Germany to wage war on the western powers and try to ensure that this war would drag on until both sides were exhausted. Until then, propaganda work would be stepped up in those countries so that the Soviets would be well prepared when the moment was right. This announcement elicited no particular reaction in Berlin,[50] but the Italian press attacked the Comintern's appeal to the proletarian masses in no uncertain terms. Seeing Fascist Italy, which did not want to follow Hitler into the world war, now emerge as Europe's leading opponent of Bolshevism – while Nazi Germany stood silent – was a bitter pill for the Reich's propaganda minister to swallow. Goebbels noted: 'It does sometimes become a little uncanny, this association with Moscow.' And he decided to play it like this: 'Laid out our position on Russia before the press conference. We have to be very circumspect. No more pamphlets and no books about Russia, neither positive nor negative.'[51]

The topic of Russia must have pained Hitler, particularly because he had nothing to set against Stalin's gradual advance and had to feign indifference and dispassion even to his most intimate confidants. After a talk with the Führer, Goebbels noted his attitude: 'We have no cause to intervene on behalf of Finland. We are not interested in the Baltic states. And Finland has always behaved so badly to us in the past years that helping it is out of the question.'[52] But the maligned Finns knew how to help themselves and put up a remarkable resistance to the overwhelming numbers of the Red Army. One day after Elser's unsuccessful assassination attempt, which Hitler had survived only by chance, he declared to his propaganda minister: 'Russia's army is not worth much. Badly led and worse equipped. We don't need any military aid from them.'[53] Three days later, on 14 November 1939, he repeated this diagnosis.

Goebbels after a discussion with Hitler, 14 November 1939:
He again pointed out the catastrophic condition of the Russian Army. It is as good as useless in battle. That presumably explains how the Finns are holding out. Also, the level of intelligence in the average Russian presumably does not allow for modern weaponry. In Russia, just as everywhere else, centralisation, the father of bureaucracy, is the enemy of all individual development. There is no personal initiative there any more. The farmers were given land and all they did was laze around. The fallow fields then had to be conglomerated again into a kind of state holding. It was similar with their industry. This malady affects the whole country and makes it incapable of assessing its own abilities correctly. What nice allies we've chosen.[54]

Judgements of this kind beg the question: why, then, didn't the Germans attack their supposedly weak arch-enemy and why did they instead initiate the much-feared global war with the western powers, especially in view of Hitler's unswerving conviction that 'our enemy is in the east'? The most plausible explanation is that Hitler thought it was less likely that the Red Army would fall on his rear while he attacked the west than vice versa.

After his speech to the senior commanders on 23 November, and after a long, grave discussion in which he again tried to convince the army's commander-in-chief that attacking the west was the right option – and had to reject Brauchitsch's offer of resignation – Hitler moved into the large situation room. In the presence of Luftwaffe Adjutant Nicolaus von Below, he paced up and down as he recapitulated his thoughts. His main worry was that the western powers would significantly raise their level of armament in the coming months. That was why he was pressing his generals to attack as soon as possible. Below later remembered the moment: 'Hitler also wanted to have the army free again in the spring for a large operation against Russia. This was the first mention I had heard of Russia from Hitler. It seemed very utopian to me. But these were obviously plans he had been considering for a long time and that he now intended the Wehrmacht to carry out.'[55]

As indifferent as Hitler presented himself as being to the Finns' defence of their country, it must have been deeply embarrassing to him that Mussolini, his most important ally, wanted to support Finland while remaining neutral in the war against the western powers. On 5 January 1940, the Führer received a letter from Il Duce. Mussolini reminded him that the soil was still fresh on the graves of the Germans and Italians killed fighting Bolshevism in the Spanish Civil War and that thousands of Italians had now volunteered to go to the rescue of Finland. He then pointed out that Britain was scoring propaganda points by emphasising two things: that the German–Russian pact was practically the end of the Anti-Comintern Pact and that the Poles under German rule were suffering terribly.

From Mussolini's letter of 5 January 1940 to Hitler:

A people that has been shamefully betrayed by its governing military-political class but which continues to fight bravely, as you yourself gallantly recognised in your speech in Danzig, deserves to be treated in a way that does not give our enemies room for speculation. It is my conviction that creating a modest, disarmed and exclusively Polish Poland (which has been relieved of the Jews, for which I thoroughly approve of your plan to collect them all in a large ghetto in Lublin) will never present a danger to the Greater German Reich. But doing so would be very significant in removing the large democracies' justification for continuing the war and would eliminate the laughable Polish Republic that the French and British have set up in Angers. Unless you are irreversibly resolved to wage this war to its utmost, I believe that creating a Polish state under the German aegis would contribute to ending the war and provide a sufficient basis for peace…

The treaties with Russia.

No one knows better than I, after forty years of political experience, that politics demands tactical concessions. This applies even to the politics of a revolution. I recognised the Soviets in 1924; in 1934, I entered into a trade and friendship agreement with them. So I understand that you, after Ribbentrop's predictions that Britain and France would not intervene were not fulfilled, have avoided having to face a second front. Russia, without striking a blow, has been the war's great beneficiary, in Poland and the Baltic countries.

But I, who have been a revolutionary from birth and have not altered my standpoint, say to you that you cannot constantly sacrifice the principles of your

> revolution to fit the tactical requirements of a particular political moment. I feel that you cannot give up the anti-Semitic and anti-Bolshevik banner that you have held up high for twenty years and for which so many of your comrades have laid down their lives; you cannot deny the gospel in which the German people have placed their blind faith. It is my duty to add that a further step forward in your relations with Moscow would have catastrophic consequences in Italy, where the general anti-Bolshevik sentiment, particularly among the Fascist masses, is absolute, iron and indestructible.
>
> Let me assume that that will not be the case. The solution to the problem of your Lebensraum lies in Russia and nowhere else, in Russia with its enormous expanse of 8 million square miles and only 9 inhabitants for each. It does not belong in Europe. Despite its size and its population, it has no strength; it has a weakness. The mass of its population is Slavic and Asiatic. In a previous era, the Balts were the element that bound them together; today it is the Jews. But this explains everything. It is Germany's task to defend Europe against Asia. That is more than just a theory of Spengler's.[56] Only four months ago, Russia was global enemy number one; it cannot have become friend number one, nor is it that. This has intensely agitated the Fascists in Italy and perhaps also many National Socialists in Germany.
>
> On the day on which we annihilate Bolshevism we will both have remained true to our two revolutions. Then it will be the turn of the large democracies, who cannot survive the cancer that gnaws at them and that is making itself felt in migration, in their politics and in their attitudes.[57]

This admonition from his former role model, who had taken power in his country in 1922 while the erstwhile Corporal Hitler was still giving speeches to a little gaggle of followers in Bavarian beer halls, must have been extremely irritating for the Führer. The Polish option was now out of the question for Hitler and he refused to hear any doubts about his anti-Bolshevik position. Mussolini's proposal that he first expand into the East fell on deaf ears. Hitler had become fixated on destroying Britain with a single devastating blow – the revenge of a spurned suitor. It took him two months to reply to Mussolini's letter. His own missive was even longer than Mussolini's and full of justifications for what he was doing, all diplomatically couched and without a hint of personal accusation. After all, he did still hope to persuade Italy to join the war against the western powers.

In his letter, Hitler had to do a lot of dissimulating and presumably did not even himself believe in many of the predictions and prognoses he expressed. But mobilisation in the west forced him to rule out any doubts about his resolve to attack France and Britain, which also meant that he had to present his friendship with Russia in the most favourable light. He again justified the invasion of Poland as necessary to defend himself against British machinations and as a means of 'utterly eliminating the Polish state as a source of danger and so freeing up the German rear'. It had been a matter only of 'absolutely securing the Reich's eastern border'. He had had to take on the 'ballast' of administering Poland because chaos would have broken out otherwise, and he reassured Mussolini that Germany wanted to give up this responsibility when the war ended. In reference to Russia, he underlined the shift that had supposedly occurred there since the removal of the 'Jewish-international leadership'. 'If Bolshevism in Russia develops into a Russian-nationalist state ideology and economic principle, it will constitute a reality we will have neither any interest in, nor any reason for, fighting against.' Russia was a valuable aid for the time being in the struggle against the western powers. The economic supplements it provided were comprehensive and Germany had undertaken a clear demarcation of zones of interest: 'None of which will ever be changed again.'[58]

On 24 January 1940, Hitler, as in the previous year, gave a speech to around 7,000 officer cadets. This time he chose Frederick the Great's birthday as a point of reference from which to emphasise – after the usual observations about Lebensraum and the necessity of struggle – how advantageous it was for Germany to be fighting on only one front. 'We have two states as our enemies: Britain and France. [...] The Europe that is directed by the mercy of Britain and France begrudges our nation the things it needs to exist, because they do not want to tolerate Germany as a great power and do not believe that they can tolerate it. However we constrain ourselves, we will never be able to placate France and Britain. [...] Today, for the first time in Germany history, the German giant, better armed than ever before, has to face only a single front. They thought they would be able to again bind us into a war in every direction of the celestial [i.e. compass] rose, but this time our alliances and treaties have prevented them from doing so.'[59]

Of course, Hitler could not openly expound his war plans. But his explanations show that he thought the war against the western powers had been forced upon him and could have been avoided if they had given him a free hand in the east. Another note in Goebbels's diary shows that the war in the west was supposed to be only a brief diversion to establish Germany's predominance on the Continent before it attacked the real enemy and conquered its Lebensraum in the east. One day after Hitler's speech to the officer cadets in the Sportpalast, the two talked over lunch and immediately brought up 'the Russian question'. 'The Russians' behaviour towards us is increasingly loyal. They have good reasons for that. They cannot now pull out of the war against the Finns, even if they have been making severe tactical errors. The Führer believes they will defeat Finland within a few months. Britain neither can nor wants to help Finland. London has too much trouble of its own.'[60]

If these kinds of report accurately reproduce what Hitler said, then they demonstrate at the very least that he was avoiding making warlike pronouncements even to his most intimate circle. This was not the result of a change in opinion, but rather because it kept him safe from follow-up discussions that might have questioned his present aggressive intentions in the west. Only rarely do a few treacherous phrases betray his real purposes. At a secret conference of the NSDAP's Gauleiters and Reichsleiters on 29 February 1940, Hitler said he was convinced that victory against the west would be won before the end of the year. There was no need for concern about whether the eastern border was covered, because the Russians 'wouldn't mount an attack in a hundred years'. Tellingly, he added: 'Even if moving the border were ever to come into question, it would only be further to the east. But that would be a matter for the future'.[61]

So, in spring 1940, Hitler was completely focused on the imminent western offensive, which he was taking an ever-larger hand in planning. While the Army High Command was still wrangling over which was the correct operational blueprint for France, Hitler took personal control of the plans for invasion of Denmark and Norway. After his announcement in May 1939, a special plenary staff was founded within the Supreme Command in accordance with his 'wishes'. This was to work 'under his direct personal influence and in the closest cooperation with the leaders of the war as a whole' on plans for the enterprise subsequently known as Operation Weserübung, the assault on Denmark and Norway. This plenary staff was also to be the 'core of a future operations staff'.[62] This organisational interference at the expense of the army was to have repercussions when it came to preparing for war against Russia.

Meanwhile, what had become of the much-trumpeted 'impregnable eastern wall' on the Vistula? Did this absurd notion emanate from a desire to stay on the defensive against the USSR? It can be safely assumed that, for Hitler, this was merely a slogan with which to allay fears that the Red Army would advance westward. In fact, what the military was actually planning could hardly have been more different. Hitler's order on 17 October 1939, that Poland was to be used as a 'forward-lying glacis' and that the Wehrmacht was to prepare for mobilisation, is often incorrectly interpreted as a routine act of national defence, rather than as a measure against the USSR.[63] In his diary, Halder described Wagner's report on discussions with the Führer: 'A German deployment zone for the future'.[64] Hitler's concept of the 'glacis' is reminiscent of Rosenberg's memo in June 1939, cited above, in which he described Poland as a 'preparatory glacis for a subsequent destruction of Russia'.

Three days later, on 20 October 1939, the army's commander-in-chief ordered his engineers to upgrade the lines of defence on the Vistula, the San and the Narew, as well as on the East Prussian border. The security divisions left behind after the bulk of the troops had been redeployed to the west had to be able to use these positions to hold off an attack until reinforcements could arrive. So it was important also to repair or enhance rail and road connections running west–east.[65] This was still a means of providing cover for the western offensive. But the line of fortification could not be described as an 'impregnable eastern wall'. It consisted – and even at that, only along some sections – of trenches and barbed-wire obstacles. No one could seriously expect to hold up the Red Army with that. Would the western reinforcements be used only for defence? That is very unlikely, because, as we have seen, defence was only ever temporary in the army's operational thinking. The orders for the improvement works in the occupied Polish territories correspond to the kind of warfare planned for in the 'Movement and Combat Exercise for Motorised Units' in September 1939. Starting from a sparsely occupied line of defence, Guderian had wanted to use rapid motorised units for a counter-offensive that would strike at the enemy's flank and allow the destruction of his army. The planning documents drawn up and then worked through in detail in June 1939[66] did not contain any completely new operational thinking. They bear traces of the lessons learned from the Battle of Tannenberg in 1914 and from Piłsudski's victory outside Warsaw in 1920, but could be easily reused for a battle on the western front. Erich von Manstein was thinking in a similar way in October 1939. He developed a strategy of tempting the western powers into an attack, leading them to suffer heavy losses in front of the western wall – after which they would be defeated with a highly mobile counter-attack.[67]

Hitler's first ideas for the western offensive show that he was by now intimately versed in the army's operational thinking. In a memo on 9 October 1939, he sketched out an operational plan, the essentials of which could have been used against Russia and indeed reappeared a year later in the preparations for invasion of the USSR. His plans convey an impression of how a campaign in the east might have looked in 1939: a surprise attack by massed forces; the enemy front ripped open with two armoured spearheads; the attack then continued on a broad front to prevent the enemy from mounting a coherent defence; the overall objective of destroying the enemy's 'active forces' in one movement.

'It is not possible to develop an operational plan any further, i.e. to recognise and pre-emptively account for future events and the decisions and actions crystallising out of them. It is, however, possible and necessary to be familiar from the very outset with the overall task, which can be directed only at destroying the enemy's active forces. If this destruction should fail for reasons that cannot now be anticipated, then the secondary aim will be to secure territory that can serve as the basis for successful warfare in the longer term.'[68]

An Offensive Solution to Eastern Border Security: The Halder Plan in June 1940

After almost all battle-worthy units had been redeployed to the western front, only a weak defensive force of ten reserve divisions remained in Poland. That was apparently considered enough to temporarily ease the High Command's ongoing misgivings. After all, Stalin could still have waited until the Wehrmacht was tied up in the west and then risked an invasion of his own. So Franz Halder gave the eastern commander's chief of staff, Major-General Karl Adolf Hollidt, the task of predicting how a Soviet attack might look.[69] In his study, Hollidt assumed that the Red Army would risk an advance on Germany only if the Wehrmacht had suffered heavy casualties on other fronts. The Russians would have around 80 divisions at their disposal. Because their operational training was rudimentary, they would undertake a simple operation in which two army groups headed towards Warsaw and East Prussia. Since the Red Army was adjudged to have only very modest abilities – an evaluation that seemed to be confirmed by the Finnish campaign, which took place while Hollidt was working on the study – the eastern commander-in-chief had no doubt that he would be able to engage this theoretical danger with only his own meagre forces.

The basis for Hollidt's study was a document produced by the General Staff's Foreign Armies East bureau, which Halder had ordered to assess the future of the USSR's relations with Germany as quickly as possible. According to these experts, the Red Army in Poland was deployed in such a way that it would be able to both resist an offensive and carry out a westward operation of its own. The Soviets would actually attack, however, only once their Polish base of operations had been improved, once their Far Eastern relations with Japan had been settled, and once the internal consolidation of the USSR had been completed. This was naturally a very flexible list of preconditions, but certainly one that did not indicate any imminent danger.

What's important here is the assessment that the Wehrmacht would face around 80 enemy divisions in the event of war. At the start of 1940, the Wehrmacht had at its disposal a total of 116 deployable divisions, each of which could be sent either east or west depending on what was required. By May, these were reinforced by a further 41 newly assembled divisions. If that is compared with Halder's prospect in October 1939 of engaging France with 75 divisions, it is plain that the German Reich had nothing to fear from the Red Army. Conversely, this also meant that defeating the Soviet forces in the European part of the USSR seemed a relatively straightforward task, nothing like the decisive battle against the western powers, which, fully mobilised and ready for defence, were waiting for a German attack in the fortifications of the Maginot Line. On 10 May 1940, at the beginning of the western offensive, the Allies fielded 151 divisions while the Germany Army deployed 135, 45 of them held in reserve.

In spring 1940, Hitler was completely focused on the west, forced by various factors (weather, a transport crisis, etc.) to repeatedly delay the invasion. He also had to bear in mind that Britain and France might seize the initiative at any time and bring the German war machine into disarray by means of diversionary attacks. Indeed, there were Allied plans to occupy Norway and disrupt the German transports of Swedish iron ore, as well as to strike the German fuel supply line at one of its most sensitive points by attacking the Caucasus. Moreover, in the secret agreements with Stalin, Hitler had promised him Bessarabia, which the Soviet dictator might demand from Romania at any moment and which he might use – as in the case of Finland with the strategically important nickel mines in Petsamo – to bring that country and its vital oilfields under his influence.

So there were good reasons for keeping a close eye on the situation in the east. But Hitler remained anxious not to place any strain on the relationship with the USSR so long as the war in the west had not been concluded. That was why he refrained from making aggressively anti-Soviet statements, even to his intimate circle. His instructions of October 1939, that occupied Poland was to be prepared as a deployment zone for the future, had prompted a number of measures that did not make military sense and were caused by differences of opinion between rival groups within the German administration. Hitler's contradictory ambitions and aims contributed to this state of affairs. The measure that set the tone for the future was the dissolution in autumn 1939 of the military administration and the division of the occupied territory into zones under different authorities. This encouraged a proliferation of agencies and organisations that Himmler's cadre came increasingly to dominate. Organising the military's requirements under these circumstances was no easy task for the eastern commander-in-chief (in July 1940 retitled the military commander in the General Government).

The routine creation of new training grounds on which to drill replacement units for the western front provided the first opportunity for the military to make certain areas autonomous of the civil administration and simultaneously to channel the wild resettlement schemes of the SS. By setting up the security strip Hitler had ordered, the army also created an extraterritorial, as it were, corridor along the Vistula and the Narew, which ran straight through the General Government. Keitel, as Hitler's closest military adviser and head of the OKW, took responsibility for approving these measures.[70] The various branches of the Wehrmacht and Himmler's SS were instructed to provide a clearer idea of what their intentions were. Himmler's office of the 'Reich Commissar for the Strengthening of German Nationhood' was pursuing plans to transport just under 7 million Poles from the Reich's 'incorporated eastern territories' into the General Government; the 'Polish reservation'. The NSDAP's Office of Racial Policy, however, summed up the party's ideas in a settlement plan that would create a large number of 'defence farms' in a 120-mile-wide strip on this side of the Reich's new border.

At a joint meeting of civilian and military authorities in Łódź on 16–17 January 1940, the High Command presented its own plans connected with the creation of the eastern security zone. Hitler had already agreed that this zone would be considerably widened along the rivers, but did not want to have any ethnic Germans settled there. Himmler found himself forced to scale back his plans to deport Polish sections of the population because of difficult conditions in the General Government. Furthermore, Hitler had approved the suggestion that veterans of the war would be given priority in settling the east, which could of course not be put into practice until after the war was over and so obstructed the SS's current resettlement policies. At the meeting in Łódź, the High Command's representative also claimed 400,000 German families from the Reich for the army's own resettlement plans, which intended to provide a political anchor for the large training grounds and the security zone among the populace in the heart of Poland. This was not a matter of an eastern wall, in the sense of the previous lines of fortification, but of creating a mobilisation zone. Active troops would also continue to be stationed east of the Vistula and 'in the unlikely event of a conflict with Russian units, would be given the task of defending the border'.[71] That would give the army a forward line of defence directly on the border and a main defensive position along the line Narew–Vistula–San. West of that, the planned training grounds would provide important garrisons and muster areas for reinforcements.

Himmler recognised the danger that the Wehrmacht would take control of resettlement, as had been the case in the eastern territories during World War I. For him, there was no doubt that the east had to belong to the SS. So he had his men urgently draw up the first sketch of a 'General Plan East', which would regulate settlement in the east after the end of the war. To improve his relationship with the army, he made a move designed to uncouple the settlement mission from the tasks assigned to the military. Himmler's idea was to build anti-tank fortifications as a military bulwark directly behind the German–Soviet border, and he offered to deploy 2.5 million Jewish forced labourers to make it happen. Since the army wanted to get the Jews out of the planned security zone and the general governor was bristling at the idea of bringing all the Polish Jews into his area, this 'Jewish Wall' would provide an apparently meaningful justification for deporting them and would also disguise the enslavement and annihilation of the Jewish population as military necessity. It was the start of the process that, a year later, with the invasion of the USSR, made the Wehrmacht into accomplices in the Holocaust.

The Army High Command had this proposal of a 'Jewish Wall' evaluated. The engineer general responsible for doing so expressed serious concerns. The commander in charge of the central section of the front considered the project superfluous and did not want to have any 'Jewish columns' deployed, because it would put the military's central task of national defence in the hands of the SS.[72] The Army High Command made a concealed withdrawal. There was

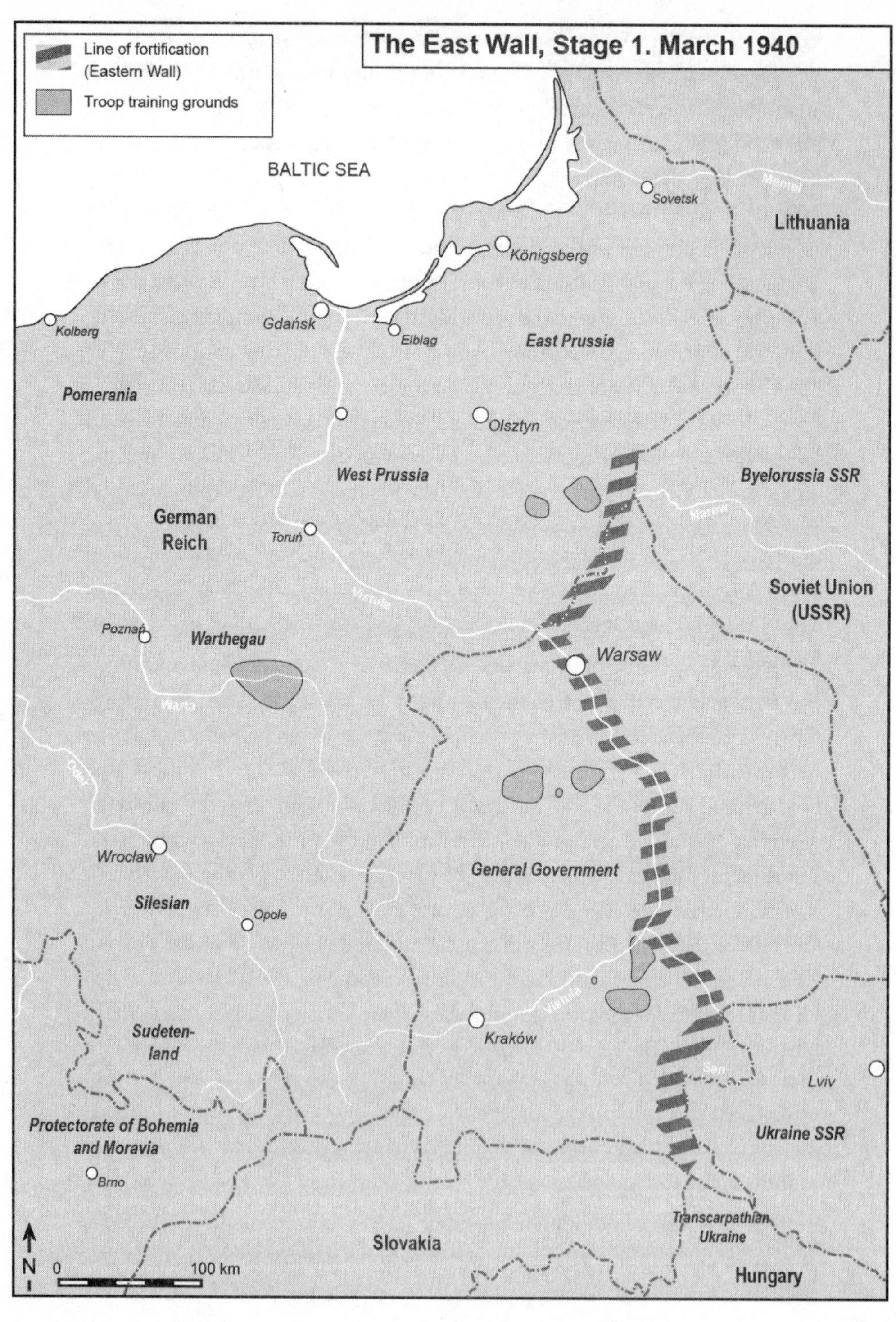

The East Wall, Stage 1. March 1940
Line of fortification
(Eastern Wall)
Troop training grounds
BALTIC SEA
Sovetsk
Memel
Lithuania
Königsberg
Kolberg
Gdańsk
Elbląg
East Prussia
Pomerania
Olsztyn
West Prussia
Byelorussia SSR
Narew
German
Reich
Toruń
Soviet Union
(USSR)
Vistula
Poznań
Warthegau
Warsaw
Warta
Oder
Wrocław
General Government
Silesian
Opole
Vistula
Kraków
Sudeten-
land
San
Lviv
Protectorate of Bohemia
and Moravia
Ukraine SSR
Brno
Transcarpathian
Ukraine
Slovakia
N
0
100 km
Hungary

no more talk of them having their own settlements and Himmler was given the opportunity to make a speech to the most senior generals about the SS's racial mission in the east to improve mutual understanding between the two organisations.[73]

The OKH agreed in principle to the projected 'Jewish Wall'. It is not clear what role was played in that decision by Staff Major Reinhard Gehlen, who, as leader of the territorial fortification group, was Halder's protégé in the operations department. Shortly afterwards, Gehlen was given a crucial post in the planning and implementation of Operation Barbarossa. General Johannes Blaskowitz, the eastern commander-in-chief, resigned and suggested sarcastically that the eastern part of the General Government could just be left to the SS. Halder did not want to go that far and was in charge of finding Blaskowitz's replacement. The two organisations came to an agreement. The SS's Jewish construction battalions were assigned to shorter sections of the front. They began by building anti-tank obstacles on the south-eastern border, between the Bug and the San. By the start of 1941, construction of the 'Jewish Wall' had reached a mere eight miles and was militarily pointless, since it was amateurishly designed and wholly unoccupied.[74] Himmler had taken Hitler's idea of chasing the Jews into the Pripet Marshes, the area in front of the 'eastern wall', and made of it his 'Jewish Wall' project, out of which the death camps later developed.

On 9 April 1940, the triumphant offensive in the west finally began. It led initially to the occupation and conquest of Denmark and Norway. On 10 May, the Benelux countries and France were attacked. After a surprising breakthrough near Sedan, German armoured units raced forward all the way to the Channel, encircling the entire Allied expeditionary force, which had advanced into Belgium. The attack that became a legendary example of the German blitzkrieg was a tactical and operational success, unexpected by either Hitler or the Army High Command.[75] It came about because the enemy's leaders were out of their depth; although they had greater numbers at their disposal, they could not keep up with the tempo of the decisions forced upon them and employed an obsolete defensive strategy.

The German victory also owed much to the preparations of the preceding months and to an audacious operational attitude instituted by General von Manstein. In the wrangling with Hitler about the offensive in the west, he had finally convinced the dictator of his own ideas. These were to tempt the Allies into entering Belgium and then to make a surprise attack through the

Ardennes and towards the Channel. Encircling the enemy's mobile troops seemed to offer a chance of winning a swift victory in the west. The Army High Command, however, derived from the experiences of World War I the belief that the offensive in northern France might well seize up after some initial successes into a static positional war. The campaign's entire armaments programme was designed to reach its peak only in spring 1941. More resources were made available for building fortifications and emplacements than for tank production. The German economy's orientation on war was to be increased further when the expected 'mass battles' began.[76] This also explains Hitler's reticence in spring 1941 when it came to prognoses about the planned war against the USSR.

The rapid collapse of the French Army and the British withdrawal to their island came as a complete surprise to the German leadership. Their euphoria about entering Paris and France's offer of an armistice was indescribable. In World War I, the German Army had been bled out by four years of heavy fighting in northern France. That had not been outweighed even then by the effortful victory over the Russians in 1917–18. Now, in June 1940, nothing seemed impossible any more. Wasn't it obvious that now was the time to again confront the last remaining potential enemy on the Continent? On the other hand, it was still possible that German–Soviet relations would soften and develop to mutual benefit. Stalin was covering the German rear while it calibrated its sights on Britain, which now stood alone against Hitler's war machine. Churchill's strongest weapon against Hitler, the blockade, had been blunted, because after the difficulties of winter relented, the Soviet supply trains had begun to roll into the west.

How did the Wehrmacht now shift itself from the former western to the future eastern front? Was it really just a routine measure as part of providing territorial defence, a 'completely normal process'[77] out of which the plan for Operation Barbarossa and the great war for Lebensraum in the East developed step by step? And did the initiative for that development come from Hitler, as a broad consensus of historians has assumed for decades?[78]

Wouldn't one indeed expect Hitler, after the ceasefire in France on 22 June 1940, or even a week before that, when German troops marched unopposed into Paris on the 14th, to tell his Army High Command about his intention to now begin the 'build-up in the east'. In fact, there is no evidence for that whatsoever. In both his discussions of the situation with the military and in his talks with Goebbels, he was entirely focused on the thought of how to end the war with Great Britain as soon as possible. This cannot come as a surprise, since it meant returning to the strategy of summer 1939, when he had hoped to be able to reach an understanding with the British and gain their acceptance for his projects in the east.

The 'peace' that he called for was in no way intended to fulfil the German population's longing for peace, but rather to allow him to finally implement the central idea of his political programme. After he had now, as he must have seen it, chastised the British and chased them off the Continent, he could hope again that his strategic calculations would come good. When and how the 'eastern problem' would be resolved, however, remained an open question.

But the new prime minister, Winston Churchill, proved to be of a different calibre from the men Hitler had encountered at Munich only two years before. The British government continued to refuse outright to consider recognising German dominance on the Continent, and would certainly not do so on Hitler's terms. The only two options remaining were to use constant military pressure to demoralise the British until they finally relented, or to conquer the British Isles – both very risky and demanding propositions. No wonder that the only thing the Führer had in mind after the armistice with France on 25 June 1940 was preparing a 'speech for peace' that might yet persuade the British to come around. There did, after all, appear to be a 'peace faction' in Britain. Directly after the enormous victory parade in Berlin on 7 July, he set to work on the speech while simultaneously casting his eye over preparations for a possible invasion of Great Britain. On 16 July he issued a directive to that effect (Number 16, Operation Sea Lion); three days later, he appeared in the Reichstag.

In these four weeks, there had also been more than enough opportunity to consider Germany's future attitude towards the USSR. As the Wehrmacht marched into Paris, the Soviet Foreign Ministry suddenly became extremely active and hurried to take up the concessions Hitler had made in the previous year. Having already occupied the eastern part of Poland in September 1939, they now demanded by ultimatum that the Baltic states join the USSR and also that Romania hand over Bessarabia and northern Bukovina. The German dictator did not seem unsettled, though those around him certainly were. On 5 July 1940, while the victory parade in Berlin was being set up, Goebbels noted in his diary: 'Slavism is extending right across the Balkans. Russia is seizing the moment. Perhaps we will have to step up to the Soviets at some point after all.' And a few days later: 'We can now impose order on Europe.

Russia is trying to gulp down as much as possible before closing time. We'll have to keep an eye on that.'[79]

Having to step up to the Soviets at some point after all – does that indicate that the Führer had already made a definite decision? Hardly. The months June–July 1940 can now be considered a turning point in World War II, because Britain decided to continue the war against Germany, alone if necessary, and at the same time the German war machine began to be transferred into the east. From today's point of view, this moment can be seen to be even more dramatic than the situation in September–October 1939, when the Wehrmacht began to prepare for an assault in the west. At that time, there had been heated disagreements between Hitler and the High Command. The dictator had made powerful pronouncements to underline his resolve for a western offensive, and he had been dragged into comprehensive discussion of the possible problems, the strategic approach, the methods and objective of his western offensive.

Nine months later, in summer 1940, the picture was very different. The military plans and preparations did not start with a definite, comprehensively expressed decision that they were to begin getting ready at once for the eastern offensive. There was rather a sort of spiral of decision-making, which began almost imperceptibly and gained momentum only after weeks and months. How did the High Command assess the situation and what conclusions did it draw? At the start of June, Hitler had already spoken about having a 'peace-time army' of around 70 divisions. He wanted to reduce Germany's level of armament, so that its people could taste some of the fruits of victory.[80] The Reich's Ministry of Economics made preparations for switching to a postwar economy. In all the economic committees and companies, plans began to be drawn up for a 'Reorganisation of the Greater German Economic Zone'.

As early as 15 June, one day after the Wehrmacht entered Paris, Hitler ordered that the army begin reducing its size from the current 155 divisions to an initial figure of 120, because 'the enemy's imminent collapse means the Army's task is complete and that we can carry out the restructuring of enemy countries into the basis of the new peacetime order at our leisure.'[81] The Luftwaffe and the navy would be given the task of 'continuing the war against Britain by themselves'. Although Halder may not have shared the Führer's optimism that the other branches of the Wehrmacht would be able to bring the British to their knees, he could not as chief of staff contradict the release of personnel and materiel, and had to make the best of the situation. The main

18. Lieutenant Colonel Reinhard Gehlen, who was head of the OKH's territorial fortification group at the start of 1940 and became head of the West German Federal Intelligence Service after the war. Photo from around 1941.

force of the army remained tied up from Norway to the Spanish border in securing the Continent against the British. The rest were to be sent home, partly to be discharged, partly to be reorganised to improve their training and equipment, especially their provision with motor vehicles.

If we examine this situation – which was the starting point for the planning of the war against the Soviet Union – we can see that it corresponded to the one already described and was in this sense truly 'routine'. On 18 June, three days after Hitler's order to reduce the size of the army, Halder had a discussion with Lieutenant Colonel Reinhard Gehlen from the OKH's territorial fortification group. Gehlen was also Hitler's adjutant. At the start of October 1940, he became a group leader in the operations department and, after 1942, chief of the Foreign Armies East bureau, the mysterious body responsible for assessing the Red Army and its intentions. Later, as head of the Federal Intelligence Service, he played an important role in the history of West Germany. In his memoirs, he may well have had reason to pass lightly over his actions as Hitler's assistant in June–July 1940 and subsequently as one of the central planners of Operation Barbarossa.

In June 1940, Gehlen and Halder discussed the progress of the fortification works on the eastern border. The meagre forces available to the military commander had not yet achieved very much and even the SS's ominous 'Jewish Wall' was still at a rudimentary stage. Halder noted the principle that only a minimum of one's own forces should be used for fortifications. 'Whatever one has must be used for attack.'[82] There followed a long list of defensive measures such as the construction of tank obstacles along rivers, the laying of minefields and, above all, the organisation of a mobile force that would be ready, should the enemy break through, to be rapidly deployed to plug the gap or indeed be used for a counter-offensive – standard military practice on a tactical level. These mobile forces had not yet been available in the Polish territory behind the German–Soviet border. The third-class reserve formations left there would have served at most to occupy the few defensive positions on the Vistula.

Gehlen's briefing was doubtless also a reaction to the fact that Stalin had increased the pressure on the Baltic states and Romania four days before, in order to implement what he had agreed with Hitler. There was no need for immediate concern, as the Soviets' military actions were plainly not directed at the Reich. It did mean, however, that the Wehrmacht and the Red Army, which had already been facing each other in Poland since the previous September, now also became neighbours on the East Prussian border. By drawing up Soviet forces in front of Romania, the USSR hoped to pressure Bucharest into relinquishing Bessarabia and the Bukovina. Berlin was forced to ignore the Romanian government's pleas for help, something that embarrassed and angered people such as Goebbels.

It must have been far harder to pay the price for Soviet support now that France had been defeated and it seemed the war with Britain would soon be resolved. From the sober standpoint of the German chief of staff, Russia's advance entailed the painful recognition that both avenues of attack against the USSR were now blocked. So it was all the more important to create a set of political circumstances that would restore the options of 1938–9. Since the army also now found itself in the process of becoming a peacetime force in line with Hitler's instructions, a 'build-up in the east' could only mean a return to the status quo of 1939, that is, to being ready to engage the USSR at any time, whether as part of an aggressively conducted defence or as part of a larger struggle for political power.

In any case, there is no sign that in June 1940 Hitler was thinking of reorganising the Wehrmacht for an imminent war against the Soviet Union. The changes to the strategic situation in the east did not come as a surprise, or in a threatening form. There is nothing to indicate that he was disturbed by them. On the same day as Halder spoke to Gehlen, Hitler met Foreign Minister Ciano. The Italian wrote in his diary afterwards: 'Hitler is now like a gambler who has broken the bank. He wants to stand up from the table and not risk anything more.'[83]

His discussion of the situation on 23 June concerned a long list of practical questions that had arisen from the end of the fighting in France. The word

'Russia' does not appear in Halder's notes, though it does in the account of Lieutenant Colonel Bernhard von Loßberg, who was the man in the Wehrmacht Operations Staff responsible for army matters. According to him, Hitler was convinced that Britain would soon give in, because the British could have no hope of success if the USA and the USSR stayed out of the war.[84]

Is the logical consequence of that line of thinking that this was the time to attack the USSR? It would have made sense if they had managed to obtain an agreement with London beforehand, because otherwise, if the war against the British continued, then a German attack on the enemy in the east would naturally embolden the remaining enemy in the west. If, however, they could be quite sure of subjugating the eastern power in a very short time and of being able to keep the British contained during that phase, so as to turn back to the west after a victory over Moscow, then the strategy also made sense. This had nothing to do with Nazi ideology or a step-by-step plan of Hitler's. It simply followed from the logic of Germany's central position in Europe,

19. Hitler with his personal staff, May or June 1940. From left to right in the first two rows: SA Obergruppenführer Wilhelm Brückner; OKH Adjutant Major-Gerhard Engel; Press Chief Dr Otto Dietrich; personal physician to Hitler, Karl Brandt; head of the OKW, Major General Wilhelm Keitel; Luftwaffe Adjutant Major General Karl Bodenschatz; Adolf Hitler; Wehrmacht Adjutant Colonel Rudolf Schmundt; General Alfred Jodl, head of the OKW's operations staff; SS Gruppenführer Karl Wolff; Martin Bormann, the head of the party Chancellery; personal physician to Hitler, Theo Morell; OKW Adjutant Captain Nicolaus von Below; SS Adjutant SS Gruppenführer Julius Schaub; NSDAP Reich photographer Heinrich Hoffmann.

which had already prompted Schlieffen before World War I to base his plans on using minimal forces to hold back one enemy in either the east or west while forcing a victory with a mass of troops on the other front – a concept that had permeated German strategic thinking ever since.

The argument that Russia had to be eliminated as a potential British 'Continental sword' – that is, to obviate the danger that the USSR, under British influence, would turn on the Reich – is indeed one that Hitler later often repeated to justify his decision to prepare for an eastern war, but whether he was already thinking like that on 23 June is far from certain. This consideration could of course also imply that the Germans would be well advised to maintain their understanding with Stalin, because doing so would demoralise the British more than anything else. That was not a new line of thinking either. Fifteen years previously, while writing *Mein Kampf*, Hitler had argued that Imperial Germany's greatest mistake was to become involved in a war on two fronts, instead of having reached an understanding with one of the sides, either Britain or Russia.

Two days after the talks with Hitler, Halder and his departmental chiefs in the OKH outlined the consequences of the reduction and reorganisation of the army that the dictator had ordered: 'Meanwhile new standpoint: strike force in the east.' This is where we should prick up our ears. In the published edition of Halder's diary, the editor, historian Hans-Adolf Jacobsen, added the comment in 1962 that this 'reinforcement of the eastern front arranged by Hitler (including 9 rapid div.) is presumably to be seen as a reaction to the Soviet advance into the Baltic states'.[85] In the meantime, research has made clear that the measure was initiated by Halder himself.[86] In the restructuring order signed by the army's commander-in-chief, the eastern border is treated as an in-no-way-dramatic secondary consideration. While eight armies remained stationed in the west to deal with Britain, only one was to guard the eastern border. It would be made up of troops primarily from the reserve divisions already stationed there, as well as of divisions from the seventh wave of mobilisation. These were the new units formed at the end of 1939, which had been intended as reserve divisions for the French campaign and consisted chiefly of older men in the so-called white year groups.[87]

Three days later, Halder made his thoughts slightly more distinct while speaking at a small meeting. During this discussion in Versailles, he explained that the war in the west was over. 'There are no victories to be won in the west for a long time.' The focus of the war was now the struggle against

Britain. But the right conditions first had to be created for the army's deployment.

'Only the 18th Army's High Command (AOK 18) will be given a particular military assignment in the east. This will initially be a case of "documenting the presence of the German Army in the east". However, it will be important not to openly display any hostile attitudes.'

The way the minutes[88] are formulated seems to indicate that Halder expressed his intentions with all manner of circumlocution. The main topic of this discussion was the disbanding of 35 divisions as well as a restructuring that would take the army to a low level of armament. As regards the motorised divisions, the decision to create new units by halving existing divisions was to have grievous repercussions for future German warfare in the east.

On 29 June, Brauchitsch signed this special directive for the 18th Army's High Command. It was made 'responsible for securing the eastern German border against Russia and Lithuania'. Moreover, it was to make preparations for delaying an enemy advance and bringing it to a halt on the San–Vistula line and at the East Prussian border, in order to then allow a counter-attack by rapid reinforcements from the 'Guderian group' to retake the surrendered territory. But they were on no account to 'give the impression that Russia is threatened with attack' – apparently a routine military statement, yet still an indication that, as in 1939, the scenario was considered possible. The first step was to provide the 18th Army with seven general commands and 15 infantry divisions.[89] This was certainly enough to mount a 'normal' (i.e. peacetime) guard on the eastern border, but, given that they were facing an enemy who had ten times as many troops deployed, the worries about giving 'the impression that Russia is threatened with attack' do seem extremely overconfident.

On his birthday, Sunday, 30 June, Halder received the Foreign Ministry's secretary of state, Ernst Freiherr von Weizsäcker. He noted the results of the meeting in his diary, including several points that the editor, Jacobsen, in 1962, presumably in agreement with Halder, ascribed to supposed statements by Hitler and the personal opinions of Weizsäcker, something not compellingly presented as such in the original text. In this way, the following two points are ascribed to Hitler: 'c) Eyes turned sharply to the East; d) Britain will probably require another demonstration of our military power before it relents and frees up our rear for the East.'[90]

The content of these remarks could equally have come from Halder himself; after all, they paraphrase the strategic situation that the Wehrmacht had already found itself in in 1938–9, when a first demonstration of this kind was made with the invasion of Poland. And why? The main aim in 1939 was the same as in 1940: to strike at the Soviet Union. If this argument comes from Hitler, that would make it the dictator's first mention in 1940 of possible intentions in the east. But even then, Halder would still have beaten him to it by a few days.[91] Nonetheless, it is understandable that Halder, who only narrowly escaped the Nuremberg trials, would think it important to explicitly ascribe the phrase 'frees up our rear for the East' to Hitler. In the literature, the following sentence is often overlooked: 'Overall satisfaction with containment of Russia.'[92] The Weizsäcker papers, which emerged subsequently, do not mention the meeting with Halder.

The later efforts to obscure who provided the initiative for an eastern campaign was thoroughly systematic. At Nuremberg, the charge of preparing a war of aggression threatened not only the necks of those on trial, but also the reputation of the General Staff and of the entire military leadership. Ascribing all the responsibility to Hitler as supreme commander took the blame away from the military, all the more so if they attributed defensive strategic motives to his decision and so, as it were, made Stalin the main culprit. It is no wonder that Halder and many others worked at promoting this interpretation.

In 1949, Halder published a small text, *Hitler as a Field Commander.*[93] The former chief of staff was now working as an adviser to the US Army and was considered the highest of authorities due to his former contact with the military opposition to Hitler and because of his reputation as the supposedly last representative of the fine traditions of the German General Staff.[94] In his analysis, Halder glossed over July 1940, argued that there had been a growing threat from Stalin, pointed out Hitler's Barbarossa order of December 1940 and claimed that Hitler had made his definitive decision to attack only in April 1941. Halder said Hitler had refused to listen to the warnings of his military advisers. Then he described his own plan, under a series of misleading dates, as the purportedly realistic option. It is not hard to make out that this was based on the older concept of a war of intervention.

Franz Halder on Hitler as a field commander, 1949:

At the beginning of the year 1941, the German forces that could have been made available in the east – while sufficiently securing all other fronts – would have been enough to decisively defeat the opposing Russian contingent, which was

> the great majority of Russia's European forces, and so rule out any military activity by Russia for a significant length of time. These forces would have sufficed to occupy a strategic forward zone in front of the German and Romanian border, i.e. in western parts of the Ukraine, of Byelorussia, and the Baltic states, and so also gain *collateral for peace negotiations.*[95]

This was Halder's reaction to a statement by Alfred Jodl, the former head of the Wehrmacht's Operations Staff, who had said in 1946 that the army had drawn up an operational plan even before Hitler gave the order to do so.[96] Halder had considerable interest in concealing his own initiative and disguising Hitler's motives.

If even the army's then chief of staff certified that the Führer had mainly been reacting to the looming threat of a Soviet attack, there was no need for Hitler's adjutants to be reticent. So David Irving cites Nicolaus von Below, the Luftwaffe adjutant, as telling him that during a rainy walk through the Black Forest near the Führer HQ Tannenberg, Rudolf Schmundt, the Wehrmacht's chief adjutant, had related in a sombre mood that the Führer had mentioned in passing that he was toying with the idea of beginning a campaign against Russia. This scene does not appear in Below's memoirs. Rather, he records his belief that Halder and Brauchitsch accepted Hitler's decision without a single word of protest – despite knowing that the idea was impossible – in order to let 'Hitler run on into his own disaster'.[97]

Memories of such statements by Hitler are actually not surprising when we remember that Hitler had been toying with the idea of a war against the Soviet Union for many years. But the right-wing extremist writer David Irving has tried – as have many others on his trail and in the German generals' memoirs before him – under the heading 'The Great Decision' to argue that the initiative for a campaign against the USSR came from Hitler personally.[98] Another officer with good reason to conceal the impulse for what became Operation Barbarossa was Lieutenant Colonel Bernhard von Loßberg, the army specialist in Hitler's plenary staff. He was responsible for an independent study of a projected eastern campaign, about which there will be more to say below.

In his memoirs, which appeared in 1949, he passed over this study and claimed that he had expressed 'grave military concerns about a war on two fronts' to the chief of the Wehrmacht Operations Staff. He added that of the representatives of the three branches of the Wehrmacht – 'without exaggerating' – all three had been against the Russian campaign, but they had not presented a united front and so lacked the power to assert themselves against Hitler.[99] In a private letter in 1956, he made comments to the effect that he had already begun his work as early as July 1940. He had kept quiet in his memoirs because Helmut Greiner, who had been in charge of the OKW's war diary, had pressured him to make Hitler solely responsible for the planning of the Russian campaign.[100] Writing to the historian Andreas Hillgruber in 1954, Loßberg said that Hitler had been of the opinion in summer 1940 that, after a settlement with the British, he would no longer be able to put the exhausted German people 'back on their feet' for a war against Russia. In Hillgruber's standard work on Hitler's strategy, this became an 'essential reason' for Hitler's decision in July 1940 to favour an eastern campaign – although Halder's diary does not contain a corresponding statement by Hitler until 17 February 1941.[101]

The constant rivalry between the OKW and the OKH continued after the end of World War II, because although the leaders of the OKW had to appear at the Nuremberg trials, the OKH was largely spared. So it goes without saying that Walter Warlimont, the former acting head of the Wehrmacht Operations Staff, used his own late memoirs (1962), which have been accorded much attention by historians, to put forward his own spin on events. This served mainly to exonerate his former boss, Alfred Jodl, who was executed as a war criminal, of any wrongdoing. The chapter on the eastern campaign is titled 'The OKH's Precedence' and begins with the following words:

From Walter Warlimont's memoirs, published in 1962:

One of the most extraordinary phenomena in the history of the German headquarters was that the highest staff in the Wehrmacht and its supreme commander, in the period from the end of July to the start of December 1940, played only a minimal role in the preparatory work for the largest campaign of World War II. Neither was there a fundamental, thoroughly evaluated plan of the sort created by the old Prussian–German General Staff, nor had Hitler, unlike before the western campaign, revealed his intentions about how the operations should be conducted, other than in a few words casually expressed. From the very beginning, the development of the concept, just like the entire deployment plan and the setting of the first attacking objectives, was left completely to the OKH, which itself drew the Luftwaffe and the navy into its considerations when the time came.

The Wehrmacht Operations Staff stood apart from all this. Not invited even as a guest or observer to the great eastern war games organised by the army's

> General Staff in autumn 1940, General Jodl did not, according to all accounts, undertake any steps whatsoever to assert for himself a leading position in these developments, as would have been in accordance with the general responsibilities and nature of his staff.

He claimed that Loßberg's study was presented to Jodl only in mid November 1940. Moreover, the entry in the OKW's war diary, placing this on 19 September, he said was a mistake made by the man responsible for the diary, who was not informed about the plans for an eastern campaign until very much later and had therefore added an entry retrospectively under an inaccurate date.[102]

The confusion about responsibilities and dates is obviously deliberate. General Georg von Sodenstern, himself the author of a study on preparing for war in Russia, about which there will also be more to say below, told the historian Karl Klee in 1955 about a statement of Hitler's that is now often and eagerly circulated. Hitler was said to have visited the commanders of Army Group A in Charleville on 2 June 1940. In a private conversation with Gerd von Runstedt, the army group's commander-in-chief, and Sodenstern, then chief of the army group's General Staff, Hitler had said that after the expected peace treaty with Britain he would finally have his hands free for his great and one true task: the attack on Bolshevism. The question had been only: 'How do I tell my child?', meaning the German people, not the Army High Command. To give an idea of how important this source is, Sodenstern explained to the historian that 'he had not told anyone about the contents of this conversation until now for political reasons, but its significance meant he could remember precisely what was discussed'.[103]

Lieutenant Colonel Hermann Böhme, who in June 1940 was the representative of the German Armistice Commission's chief of staff, reported a quarter of a century later, in a study prepared by the Munich Institute of Contemporary History, that Hitler spent the last few hours before the beginning of the ceasefire on the evening of 24 June with an intimate circle of colleagues in Führer HQ Brûly-de-Pesche and, moved by this historic moment, said: 'The war in the west is finished. France is defeated, I will soon be able to come to an understanding with Britain. Then all that's left is the conflict with the east. That is a task which throws up global problems, such as our relations with Japan and the balance of power in the Pacific Ocean; it is something we won't be able to get down to for perhaps ten years, perhaps I will have to leave it to my successor. For years to come we will have our hands full digesting and consolidating what we have achieved in Europe.'[104] This personal recollection cannot be verified either.

Back to the situation at the end of June 1940. What's certain is that over the next three weeks, Halder, without any influence from Hitler, gave the military's plans a distinctly offensive character. 'Because ultimately it was not about an aggressive defence as part of an ongoing campaign, but about an act that meant starting a war.'[105]

If we turn to the officers who now took over planning the war against the USSR, we discover the 'blueprints' drawn up for a war against the Soviet Union in 1939. This option was something that, as discussed above, had been in the minds of the leadership even before then. So much so that we have to ask whether anything and, if so, what was changed, rather than simply updated, in the initial planning of Barbarossa. How much had the Red Army changed since 1938 and what intentions did Stalin now have? These were important questions, crucial to the methods and strategy adopted for a future military engagement.

Obtaining information about the military capabilities of the USSR and then drawing conclusions from it about the enemy's intentions and the options open to Germany was the task of the Foreign Armies East bureau in the army's General Staff.[106] It had been created in autumn 1938 and analysed a whole smorgasbord of countries that could not be geographically classified as eastern, including sometimes Italy and, until 1942, even the USA. The FHO worked in parallel to the Foreign Armies West bureau, and both were under the control of Departmental Chief IV, Staff Colonel Kurt von Tippelskirch. He, however, only very rarely wrote strategic analyses and reports for his own superior, Halder. He received information not only from the intelligence officers in the army staffs who were responsible for observing the enemy, but also from the active reconnaissance and spying activities of the Abwehr, a department under the control of the OKW.

Tippelskirch was Halder's adviser on the Red Army in the first phase of planning for Operation Barbarossa. Then, in 1941, he was transferred to become commander of an infantry division, the most important step for any General Staff officer hoping to become a general. This personal ambition brought about a break in the continuity of evaluation, even if his successor, Staff Colonel Gerhard Matzky, previously military attaché in Tokyo, did bring valuable experience to the task.

That also holds for Eberhard Kinzel, who was head of the Foreign Armies East bureau from 1938 to 1942. In the Defence Ministry in the 1920s, he had become familiar with the military-political view of the Red Army and had in 1932 even got to know Tukhachevsky. Between 1933 and 1935, he was then 'assistant' to the German military attaché in Warsaw and sometimes acted as his temporary replacement, though he was seen by his subordinates as a carefree bon vivant. The position of 'Group Leader II' in the FHO, the one responsible for the USSR, Scandinavia and the Far East, was left entirely vacant from October 1939 to the start of July 1940! Staff Major Erich Helmdach, who had been earmarked for this post, reported to Fontainebleau, the FHO's then headquarters, only after Halder began the planning process. In the 1970s, Helmdach emerged as a public proponent of the preventive war thesis.[107] In the important working group he led after July 1940, the only people investigating the Red Army were two older so-called supplementary officers (appointed in the 1930s) and an auxiliary officer, who all spoke Russian or Polish. With this meagre personnel, no rigorous observations could be formulated for the chief of the army's General Staff, especially if changes to the situation required a rapid response. Was this the result of neglect or of a deep-rooted sense of superiority? It certainly implies an underestimation of the potential enemy in the east. The German leadership was plainly unconcerned by what happened in Moscow or by what resources of manpower or materiel the USSR had at its disposal. In autumn 1939, Hitler is supposed to have forbidden the Abwehr to send agents into the Soviet Union or to infiltrate the leadership in Moscow.[108] The embarrassment if they were exposed would apparently have outweighed any potential gain.

The Germans' image of the Red Army did not change after the outbreak of World War II; on the contrary, the encounters with Soviet troops in eastern Poland and the Red Army's failures in Finland confirmed the previous assessment: untrained commanders, 'their Asiatic behaviour only thinly masked', the common soldiers undemanding and bovine.[109] What is interesting is not so much the suspicion that conceitedness on the part of the German General Staff led them to dangerously underestimate the Red Army,[110] but that the German experts could draw similar conclusions from the Polish General Staff's confiscated archives.[111] Independent of their evaluation of the enemy's morale, what proved fatal for the eastern campaign was that German military intelligence failed to note the introduction of modern heavy tanks in the Red Army. The T-34 had already been deployed in summer 1939 against the

Japanese, but was not shown at military parades and was not used in the war against Finland. It was the greatest surprise for the Wehrmacht during the eastern campaign in 1941.

The first task Halder assigned in preparing for a possible war against the USSR went to the 18th Army's High Command in June 1940. This is where the first sketches of the campaign were prepared. What qualified this particular army, or rather its general staff, AOK 18, for this assignment? They were in large part officers who had already had to engage with the possibility of war against the Red Army in June 1939, and it is hard to believe that they did not draw on the documents they had previously worked up. These were staff officers who, until summer 1939, had been responsible for organising the defence of Military District I (Königsberg) for East Prussia, a task that – as described above – had already considered offensive action towards the Baltic states and north-western Russia in 1938. In August 1939, this specialist group made up the General Staff of the newly formed 3rd Army under the command of Artillery General Georg von Küchler.[112]

Küchler (born 1881) was one of the older generals in the Wehrmacht who had gathered his experiences during World War I on the western front. As early as 1919, however, he had taken up posts in the Baltic area and later in East Prussia. An officer from the Hessian military nobility, he remained closely engaged via various assignments with the eastern 'outpost' of the Reich and in 1937 became commander of Military District I. In 1939, he used the East Prussian units as part of the 3rd Army to complete the encirclement of Warsaw to the east of the Vistula. After the end of the Polish campaign, a part of the Königsberg staff was used to form the General Staff of the newly created 16th Army. It fought around Luxembourg and Verdun. After the end of the French campaign, the 16th Army applied itself to planning Operation Sea Lion, the proposed invasion of Britain. When the attack on the USSR began on 22 June 1941, the 16th and 18th Armies formed Army Group North and advanced from East Prussia to the gates of Leningrad.

In November 1939, Küchler had been given command of the new 18th Army. Its General Staff consisted of the High Command of the previous Central Border Section, which had been responsible for securing the Reich's eastern frontier where it ran through Polish territory. The 18th Army was transferred to the western front and conquered Holland and Belgium. Its chief of staff was Major-General Erich Marcks. Born in 1891, he, too, had been a young staff officer during World War I and had, like Halder, made his career in the

Reichswehr of the 1920s. Chief of staff for the VIII Army Corps since 1935, he was involved in the advance into the Ukraine during the Polish campaign.

To put it bluntly: by choosing the 18th Army for special tasks in the east, Halder secured in Küchler a commander-in-chief experienced in the northern avenue of attack from East Prussia through the Baltic states, and in Marcks a chief of staff who was familiar with the southern avenue into the Ukraine. Both were also representatives of the conservative old elite of the army's General Staff, which Halder trusted, and did not belong to the group of swashbucklers and National Socialists who were particularly close to their Führer.

The first volume of Halder's edited diaries ends with the entry for 30 June 1940, perhaps a coincidence, but entirely apt in the context of this investigation. 'Eyes turned sharply to the east' and 'free up our rear for the east' are the phrases already quoted above from his discussion with the Foreign Ministry's Ernst von Weizsäcker. These were commonplaces about the present political situation and should be related to the crisis in Romania; whether they actually convey Hitler's reaction is more than dubious. They may well correspond to Halder's perspective.

In the following days, Halder precisely defined the task assigned to the 18th Army's High Command. There is no sign of Hitler's influence in these instructions, though there certainly are indications that he was drawing on older ideas about a war against the USSR. Amid the many urgent questions related to the war against Great Britain, to the military administration of occupied France and to the reorganisation of the army, Halder noted in his diary on 1 July: 'Russian–Polish War: Ask at OKW whether publication is allowed.'[113] It is surely no accident that he thought it important right at that moment to make this previously internal historical study of the war available to all officers.

Two days later, on 3 July, Halder and the head of his operations staff, Colonel Hans von Greiffenberg, discussed the most pressing questions for a proposed invasion of the British Isles. He wanted to treat the 'eastern question' in relation to it. According to Halder, it was a matter of how 'to strike a blow against Russia that would compel it to recognise Germany's dominant role in Europe. Alongside that, particular viewpoints, such as Baltic or Balkan states, could give rise to variations.'

Contrary to later claims made by Halder – which will be examined below – this war plan cannot be attributed to Hitler. For the dictator, it was never about a mere 'blow against Russia'. In his programmatic writings and in his political declarations, he never once mentioned that he wanted Russia's 'recognition' of German dominance in Europe. What Halder referred to as 'particular viewpoints' evidently meant military action against the USSR in the Baltic states and in the Balkans. These were precisely the variants that had been circulating in military thinking in the preceding years. These were considerations Halder was familiar with when he talked to the head of his own operations staff about the tasks to come. It was strategic and power-political thinking that drew Halder's gaze to the east, not Nazi ideology, and his concerns were with maintaining the initiative in the war against Britain, so as to bring it to a rapid close and consolidate the German gains in Europe. At that time, on 3 July, Halder could still assume that the war with Britain would soon be resolved in one way or another, after which – this was his line of thought – it might yet be necessary to strike a quick 'blow against Russia'. It will be shown here that this traditional anti-Russian model influenced the planning process for Hitler's eastern war more fundamentally and for far longer than the standard interpretations have realised.

On 4 July, as the British attack on the French fleet at Oran was throwing Berlin into a commotion and being interpreted as an act of desperation, Küchler and Marcks reported to Halder for initiation into the duties of AOK 18. These consisted of tactical and organisational details, measures to ensure that the deployment already beginning in the east would soon develop into combat readiness. In addition, there was a lecture by Kinzel about how the Red Army's troops were set up. It is impossible to overstate the importance of this assessment by the FHO bureau, because in the following months Kinzel's information was used by the German leadership as the basis for its decisions. His information was incorporated into a map that the AOK used for its planning process and was probably also referred to in discussions with Hitler at the end of July. Glancing at this map offers us the chance to look over the decision-makers' shoulders, as it were, and trace how they reached their conclusions.

What are particularly striking are the concentrations of Red Army forces by the Baltic and in Bessarabia – the result of the territorial changes agreed in the Hitler–Stalin pact. Other than that, there was a relatively weak garrison in eastern Poland as well as reserves near Moscow and in the centre of the Ukraine. Numerically, the Baltic area contained around 24 infantry and cavalry divisions as well as ten tank brigades. This approximately corresponded to the strength of the Red Army as estimated in 1938. The difference was that, on 8 July 1940, Soviet units were already standing directly at the border with East Prussia. The Polish centre had 12 rifle and nine cavalry divisions and, by the standards of the day, formed a group that was barely combat-ready and certainly not capable of mounting an attack. The Soviet Bessarabian group was a very different proposition. Its 30 rifle divisions, nine cavalry divisions and ten tank brigades were more than capable of putting the Romanian Army under pressure and would have been well suited to large-scale operations. The meagre reserves in the rear could be dismissed as negligible.

From the perspective of AOK 18, the following conclusions could be drawn from this state of affairs: with their own reinforcement by 15 infantry divisions and the Guderian group's motorised forces, it would be more than

possible to maintain a traditional territorial defence. It would be necessary, however, to strengthen the positions in East Prussia and develop the central stretch's capability to make a fighting retreat to the Vistula and then repulse the enemy with a counter-attack. The Soviet forces in the south-east were tied up opposite Hungary and Romania. From a standing start, the Red Army would hardly be able to count on receiving reinforcements from the Russian interior.

In the eyes of the German chief of staff, who had just won an unexpectedly superb victory over France and expected the British to give in at any time, this situation was a downright temptation. In line with the traditions of German operational thinking, there now seemed to be opportunities to destroy the enemy army with decisive battles close to the frontier and so regain the territories that had been handed over to Stalin in 1939 despite their – as in World War I – still belonging to the German sphere of interest. Anyone occupying the line Tartu–Minsk–Kiev and the lower reaches of the Dnieper would be able to command the most valuable economic resources in European Russia and advance easily into the oilfields of the Caucasus. According to this assessment of the situation, Moscow would then be barely protected and, if one assumed that the giant empire in the east was a 'colossus with feet of clay', it seemed a rapid end to the war could be counted on.

Halder's diary shows that at that time he was busy with an abundance of other issues. For that reason, if no other, it is hardly likely that he could have developed entirely new ideas for AOK 18 and the 'eastern problem', or indeed been prompted to do so by Hitler. That would have triggered a whole set of other activities to prepare for the eastern scenario, as in October 1939 with the decision to invade France.

As it was, however, Halder merely informed Küchler and Marcks that there was no 'political reason' for haste, but that the AOK should nonetheless prepare a proposal for how to fight the war.[114] A deadline was not specified; as it turned out, the 18th Army's commander and chief of staff needed only six days. That indicates a high level of professionalism and also implies that they drew on extant documents and analyses. In any case, it again demonstrates how quickly a battle plan could have been drawn up in summer and autumn of 1939 if considered necessary. If we re-examine Halder's war game of May 1939, its concentration of force east of the Vistula and the shape of its front against the Red Army provided a similar set-up to what the AOK was facing in June 1940.

20. General Erich Marcks, who, as head of the 18th Army's General Staff, presented the first draft of Operation Barbarossa on 5 August 1940. Photo from around 1941.

What did this handful of staff officers, only recently installed in the military academy in Bromberg, the new headquarters, make of this assignment? Marcks, the seasoned soldier, got to work. In a first brief sketch given to Halder's operations staff on 9 July, Küchler conveyed the 18th Army's intention to deploy four divisions to defend the East Prussian border and another four along the upper reaches of the San. The body of their own forces – around eight divisions – was to be kept available in the eastern part of the General Government, so that 'Russian attack preparations beyond the border of our zone of interest can be destroyed by *an attack of our own*'. This was a qualitative difference from the initial task and laid open the possibility of a preventive strike against the USSR. Marcks assumed that it would possible to form two assault groups, one attacking to the south-east, that is, along the familiar route into the Ukraine, and another to the north-east, which would instead set out from Warsaw rather than East Prussia. This was a new operational solution, because, unlike in 1939, there was a Soviet group in the formerly neutral Baltic states on which it would be unwise to launch a frontal assault. The Guderian group was to be deployed in such a way that it could be used to support both the northern and southern assault groups.[115]

This was the operational result of Halder's idea for a brief war and it was supposed to be capable of activation within 48 hours. It was clear, however, that implementing these plans would still require significant preparation time. They still had to meet the organisational requirements, such as coordinating with the territorial military commanders and improving infrastructure, and address the question of where to accommodate troops in the mobilisation areas, something that had already led to certain tensions with the SS. But this disguised plan of attack had the advantage of allowing the Germans to fool the USSR, because they needed to deploy only a numerically small section of their forces to the east, while in fact the reserve formations stationed there were being replaced with combat-ready troops. Moreover, the Wehrmacht was prepared to move up a large number of units within a few days of war breaking out and so give extra force to the offensive. The 'eastern glacis' had been undergoing preparation for this eventuality since 1939. That was how AOK 18 was able, drawing on older documents, to prepare a detailed map of all the major and linking roads to the front, as well as one of the unloading zones, as early as July 1940. The distribution of these unloading zones shows an unmissable emphasis on the south-east, towards the Ukraine, and the north-east, towards the Baltic states.

It remained an open question how far and with what objectives an offensive would be carried out, as did whether it would be possible to count on further reinforcement from the Reich. Since the army leadership had to prepare for the possibility of invading Britain, the Halder plan presented two options: firstly, protecting the rear in the event that Stalin, while the bulk of the army was deployed to Britain, attempted to exert pressure on Germany's eastern border; secondly, if Great Britain were to give up in the near future, transporting the mass of the troops into the east. That would – as in October 1939, though in the opposite direction – require several weeks, and would not go unnoticed by the enemy. That spoke in favour of making an initial attack with a smaller part of the available forces and then gradually reinforcing and extending the offensive. In October–November 1939, Halder had had to develop this kind of plan (for France) very quickly because of intense pressure from Hitler. For this current about-face, he evidently wanted in June 1940 to get ahead and have a plan ready so that he wouldn't again be standing there empty-handed when the Führer gave the order.

The army's commander-in-chief gave his approval to the proposed plans on 11 July. In the fully elaborated formal 'deployment directive', checked and endorsed by Halder, a number of tweaks had been made. Now the introductory statement read: 'In the event of conflict with Russia, *significant German forces* will be deployed to the east. Until they arrive, AOK 18 will secure the eastern German border.'[116] That already entailed a considerable increase in the scope of a possible attack and went beyond the previous framework. What remained in place was the projected offensive campaign with two assault groups led by AOK 18. 'The objectives and implementation of these operations are to be determined in detail' only in 'an emergency situation' and depending on the enemy's movements, political conditions [!] and the strength of their opponent. But even now they were envisaging an advance into the Lviv–Tarnopil area and another by the northern group towards Białystok in a generally eastern direction. These were the spearheads of a territorially limited operation by the 18th Army, which would be followed by 'significant German forces'. The Eastern Army,[117] based on its numbers on 22 July 1940, would include 11 infantry divisions in the front line, parts of the Luftwaffe, heavy artillery and four armoured trains, followed by three infantry divisions in reserve, and tactical control of two reserve (*Landesschützen*) divisions providing cover on possible fronts in East Prussia, as well as five infantry divisions provided by the commander in the General Government. To this was added Guderian's group of four armoured divisions and two divisions of motorised infantry – all in all, a pretty respectable fighting force.

The deployment directive contained an appendix with information about the Russian armed forces, including the map printed above and the assumption that the USSR's territorial expansion had led it to gather the majority of its rapid combat groups, as well as two-thirds of the rifle divisions in its European side, close to the Soviet Union's western border. It was not explicitly mentioned that this offered the possibility of destroying them. Küchler emphasised that the Soviet state was not currently planning a westward or south-westward offensive. But that could change at any time.

The 23 copies of the directive circulated among the army's leaders already contained definite orders for the units under their command. They were to test their ability to overcome water obstacles on either side of the border and request the concomitant supplies, and use the directive as the basis for their own studies, war games and terrain evaluations. Küchler scheduled a 'Führer war game' for August to assess the army's leadership structure. August was not far off and this implies that he was working from the idea that he might have to implement the Halder plan in August–September 1940. That would still have been more than early enough in the year for the limited 'blows' they had planned. Come October–November, the weather would make any large-scale operations impossible. That had been learned during World War I. But the campaign against their previously feared arch-enemy, France, had been concluded in just four weeks. So surely they would not need more time than that to defeat the apparently feeble Russians. (A year later, they counted on the campaign – i.e. the decisive battles – taking four to six weeks.) So if an eastern war was begun in August 1940, the forced pause in operations from October onwards might come at just the right moment for the Germans to take up negotiations with the Soviet regime, perhaps in Brest-Litovsk, as at the start of 1918. We cannot rule out that Halder was thinking along these lines.

At the Berghof on 13 July 1940, Hitler had himself briefed on how the preparations for an attack on Britain were coming along. This was one of the preliminary discussions before his 'Call for Peace', in which he had placed much hope. Halder was ready for the meeting. His ideas were approved by Hitler and turned into a formal directive. In the discussion of the political and strategic situation, the Führer gave the army's leaders many ideas of his own about how to put Britain under pressure, but left none of them in any doubt that the prospect of subjugating the British militarily was not an appealing one. The collapse of the British Empire would bring no benefit to Germany.[118] Halder's diary makes quite clear that he and Brauchitsch reinforced Hitler's assumption that the British were being persuaded to hold out by hopes of Russian intervention. Brauchitsch suggested that 20 of the 35 divisions the Wehrmacht was planning to disband not be fully disbanded after all; their soldiers should merely be given leave and used as a workforce to speed the production of armaments. These 20 divisions could then be called on at any time. They could also be reserves for the east, should the bulk of the army remain tied up in the west.

At that time, Hitler was evidently worried by the idea that the British government would cling to the hope that a German–Soviet conflict would relieve the pressure on them by enmeshing the Reich in a war on two fronts, as in 1914. So in his public speech in the Reichstag on 19 July 1940, he emphasised that it was unrealistic to imagine hostilities between Germany and Russia.

From Hitler's speech in the Reichstag, 19 July 1940:

The relationship between Germany and Russia has been conclusively defined. The reason for this act of definition was that Britain and France, supported by certain smaller states, continually accused Germany of intending to conquer territories that actually lie outside the German sphere of interest. Now they said Germany wanted to occupy the Ukraine, then that Germany wanted to march into Finland; on another occasion they claimed that Romania was under threat and in the end they even feared for Turkey. Under these circumstances, I considered it correct to soberly lay out our interests, with Russia in particular, to make plain once and for all what Germany believes it must consider its sphere of interest for the future and what, on the other hand, Russia views as important for its own existence.

This clear delineation of the two sides' spheres of interest was followed by a reorganisation of German–Russian relations. Any hopes that the implementation of these agreements will lead to new tensions between German and Russia are childish. Neither has Germany taken any step that would lead it outside its sphere of interest, nor has Russia done so.[119]

In the following days, the question of Britain was at the centre of Halder's work. After all, the Führer had issued some urgent directives. As his 'offer of peace' failed to meet with a positive response from Whitehall, the commanders-in-chief of the army and the navy were summoned to a situation meeting on 21 July. Hitler did not want to lose the military-political initiative.[120] He was facing the decision of whether to carry out Operation Sea Lion in the autumn or postpone it to the following spring. For the navy, an early attack would entail enormous risks, which Admiral Raeder essentially shied away from, recommending postponement. But what Hitler was burning to know was why Britain was not backing down. It was almost in passing that Britain's 'Russian hope' was mentioned. London might encourage Moscow to attack the Reich's fuel supplies. According to Hitler, however, there was no sign that was happening. So he decided in favour of continuing to focus the war on Britain.

Nevertheless, it behoved Hitler to issue the instruction: 'Tackle the Russian problem. Make theoretical preparations.' In that moment, the preparations Halder had started to make long before all paid off.

From Halder's war diary. Entry for 22 July 1940:

The Führer has been informed that:

a) Deployment will take 4–6 weeks.

b) Russian forces are to be defeated or, at least, as much Russian territory occupied as is necessary to prevent enemy air attacks on Berlin and Silesia's industrial areas.

Desirable to advance far enough for our Luftwaffe to destroy Russia's most important areas.

c) Political objectives:

- Ukrainian Empire;
- a Baltic federation;
- Byelorussia;
- Finland.

Baltic states 'thorn in the side'.

d) Require 80–100 div.: Russia has 50–75 good div.

If we attack Russia this autumn, the aerial pressure on Britain will be relieved. America can supply Britain and Russia.

e) Operations: What operational objectives can we decide upon? What forces?

Duration and extent for which they will be needed?

Operational avenues: Baltic states, Finland – the Ukraine.

Protect Berlin and Silesian territories.

Protect Romanian oil centres.[121]

Here, too, Halder succeeded after 1945 in confusing the interpretation of these diary entries and in having them read as showing Hitler's initiative for a war in the east.[122] But we must bear in mind that this is a 'report' from Brauchitsch in response to Hitler's instructions that 'theoretical preparations' be made for solving the 'Russian problem'. Hitler was apparently concerned that, if Göring's aircraft were tied up in an attack on Great Britain, the Soviet air force might present a threat to the Reich's vital interests. Everything that was reported about the deployment – the forces available, the political objectives and the operational avenues – can be unambiguously attributed to Brauchitsch. It corresponded to the Halder plan for a limited campaign, this folly that had already been circulating much earlier. The political objectives make plain that this is a manifestation of the military's old concept, not of Hitler's Lebensraum programme. A 'Baltic federation' as a 'thorn in the side' of Russia?

It is apparent that Hitler discussed the Halder plan only briefly with Brauchitsch. The argument about the aerial war probably came from him, as he was at that time wholly preoccupied with the necessity of establishing aerial superiority before attempting an invasion of Britain. The outline and tone of the diary entry do not indicate that Hitler issued new instructions or, for that matter, ordered a fundamental change of strategy.

After the report, however, Halder evidently felt this was a chance to implement his idea of making a quick assault on the Red Army as soon as the coming weeks. After all, the preparations for Operation Sea Lion were tying up 40 divisions, which, if the invasion was postponed, would be available for use elsewhere. So he directed his own operations staff and Kinzel to give further consideration to the 'Russian problem'. Moreover, he summoned Marcks to Fontainebleau to discuss the preparations made so far by AOK 18.[123] Most of the units assigned to the 18th Army had already arrived. The ideas that Marcks took to Halder are shown by an entry made in the war diary by Staff Colonel Arthur Schmidt, the senior General Staff officer and a close colleague of Marcks's.[124] Schmidt was another staff officer with experience of the former East Prussian headquarters. Two years later, he was the 6th Army's chief of staff and became the fanatical minder of his commander-in-chief, Friedrich Paulus, during the siege of Stalingrad.

In July 1940, Schmidt considered it impossible that the Wehrmacht would suffer a surprise attack from the Soviet group in the Baltic states, especially as the Red Army's units there had already been partially withdrawn. If there was a 'crisis in the German–British war', the USSR might occupy Romania, which the Reich would not tolerate. After a victory over Britain, the Reich would be able to demand that the Russians give back the Bukovina, as Stalin's occupation of it went beyond what had been agreed. Then the following opportunities might emerge: either the Soviet Union would give in to the pressure of German deployment – that is, be forced to do so in a war with limited means and objectives – or, as a last resort, war could be declared along the entire front, which would mean a 'march on Moscow'.

Here, too, we can see the familiar folly of a limited war, as had been in circulation in 1938–9. On 26 July, despite the torrent of details requiring his attention for the projected invasion of Britain, Halder had himself briefed by Kinzel about the deployment of the Red Army's forces. Kinzel's map did not fail to make its implications to Halder, either. To him, the most promising type of operation seemed to be an advance that would 'take Moscow with support from the Baltic Sea and then come from the north to force the Russian units in the Ukraine and by the Black Sea to fight with their front inverted'.[125] On the following day, the head of his operations staff, Colonel Hans von Greiffenberg, presented a different idea: namely, to attack with a stronger southern group.

But Halder stuck to the obviously fascinating idea of a northern group that would fight a quick battle and fall on the enemy's rear.[126]

This exchange about operational 'ideas' was one freed from considerations of time, space and troop numbers – no more than that – but perhaps this last iteration, the 'march on Moscow', was the point at which Halder hesitated. After he had been informed about the possible lines of attack, he invited Marcks to a late breakfast on 29 July and inducted him into his new task of subjecting these ideas to more rigorous analysis.

On the same day, Hitler asked Jodl, his closest military adviser, whether it would indeed be possible to attack Russia in the coming spring (remember this was Halder's idea, not Hitler's). Jodl spontaneously ruled it out completely, but was prompted to subsequently inform his staff of the discussion and order them to carry out studies of their own.[127]

The next meeting with the Führer was scheduled for 31 July. It could be expected that more strategic decisions would be made. On the evening beforehand, Halder and Brauchitsch discussed the situation. They agreed that the navy would not manage the leap to Britain, at least not in the coming autumn. But it would be an error to relinquish the initiative. So they discussed a range of attacks on British positions in the Mediterranean, namely on Gibraltar, the Suez Canal and Haifa. They could 'set the Russians' on the Persian Gulf.

From Halder's discussion with Brauchitsch, 30 July 1940:

d) The question of whether – if the war against Britain cannot be brought to an end and there is a danger that Britain will ally herself with Russia – the ensuing war on two fronts should be waged against Russia first ought to be answered with the statement that it would be better to retain Russia's friendship. A visit to Stalin would be desirable. Russia's efforts to control the straits and the Persian Gulf do not concern us. In the Balkans, which fall into our economic sphere, we can avoid each other. Italy and Russia will not harm each other in the Mediterranean.

In those circumstances, we could strike decisively at the British in the Mediterranean, push them out of Asia, help the Italians construct their Mediterranean empire and use Russia's help to build up the empire created in Western and Northern Europe. We can then confidently prepare for the war against Britain to be a long one.[128]

There are good reasons for thinking that this conventional strategy was Brauchitsch's work. It suited the interests of Raeder and the navy. They had certainly not forgotten the old enemy in the east; nor had they forgotten the bases on the Baltic Sea left unprotected since their troops had been sent to the western campaign. The Navy High Command naturally held fast to the old idea of turning the Baltic Sea into a *mare nostrum*. The head of the navy's operations staff, Rear Admiral Kurt Fricke, also reached for the desk drawer in his 'Observations on Russia' of 28 July 1940, and brought out the proposals from 1938–9.[129] In order to neutralise the 'danger of Bolshevism', and place Germany's supplies of important Russian raw materials on a sounder basis, the Wehrmacht ought to make use of the forces freed up by the victory over France. He assumed that the politicians intended to 'clean things up in the east' and construct a zone of German economic autarky. After annexing the Baltic states and a part of the Ukraine, as well as consolidating their influence on the Balkans, the Germans would be able to 'dictate the peace while in possession of these areas'. The occupation of the Baltic states and Leningrad would remove the basis for the Russian fleet and lead it to collapse. A surprise attack, he said, would offer an opportunity to narrow the Soviet fleet's room to manoeuvre and destroy the Soviets' heavy naval forces in their harbours. This was the Halder plan applied to the seas. The 1938 war game had set the fictive start of an invasion of the USSR on 3 September 1940. That might now become reality.

The Fricke Memorandum was not given to Hitler. It served to help the navy's leadership form their opinions and prepare Raeder for the discussion, scheduled for 31 July, in which Hitler would ask him for a definite statement on Operation Sea Lion's chances of success. So in his study, Fricke reminded his readers of a familiar alternative strategy, turning their attention to the east. It could be seen as certain that the Führer, in his indecisive search for a means of ending the war against Great Britain, would also take this alternative into consideration.

Back to the discussion between Hitler and Artillery General Alfred Jodl, who, as head of the Wehrmacht's operations staff, was in charge of the small group of officers from the various branches of the military whom Hitler considered his personal cadre, responsible for coordinating the planning of large-scale operations. After this conversation, Jodl is said by his deputy, Colonel Walter Warlimont, to have informed his extremely surprised colleagues that the Führer had decided to rid the world 'once and for all' of the Bolshevik threat, and to do so in May 1941. The circumstances in which the OKW became involved in planning a war against the USSR rest on equally dubious accounts. In 1945, Warlimont had spoken candidly to American interrogators about these activities, but then explicitly apologised in his memoirs, published in 1962, for having contributed to the material used to prosecute his former superiors. He then attributed the sudden about-face to Hitler and referred to a purported memorandum issued by Keitel and Jodl, in which they said the time required, the terrain to be covered and the weather that would be encountered made a war of aggression against the Soviet Union impossible.[130] This memorandum has never been found – but Hillgruber, supported by Warlimont's memoirs, considered that there is 'no doubt about its importance for the timing of a possible eastern campaign'.[131] The reality may well have been that the OKW took up Brauchitsch's report to the Führer on 21 July and formulated its own opinion on the Halder plan. On the evening before the crucial meeting, Hitler apparently accepted the belief that an attack on the USSR in August–September 1940 would not have any broader repercussions.

The army's commander-in-chief, a former imperial page, had counselled caution in the previous discussions with Hitler about the western offensive and presented himself as explicitly in favour of avoiding conflict.[132] Only a few days before, Brauchitsch had had friendly words to say about the USSR in a set of instructions to the officer corps. Whether that was really intended to camouflage the deployments to the east or corresponded to his personal opinions is an unanswerable question. After all, the Führer himself had publicly said in his 'Call for Peace' on 19 July that 'the relationship between Germany and Russia has been conclusively defined'.[133] The Army High Command's conclusion of 30 July, that it would be better to retain Stalin's friendship, certainly takes that line. But neither Brauchitsch nor Halder informed the Führer of this opinion during the pivotal meeting on the following day.

As an interim conclusion, we can certainly say that, in June 1940, Halder drew on the old idea of creating a 'strike force' in the east, whether to provide strategic cover for the eastern border or to keep open the option of an offensive against the Soviet Union. At first, those requirements seemed to be met by deploying 17 divisions arranged around the core Guderian group. It was an effective short-term measure to make the Germans ready for a possible exchange of blows with the Red Army in the Polish–Byelorussian area, a 'small-scale' solution, which was supposed to lead to the occupation of foreign territory and give the Wehrmacht control of 'collateral' that would allow them to quickly 'conclude a peace treaty after winning victories in the east'.[134] Underpinned by the line of defence on the Vistula, the operation could lead either towards the Baltic states or into the Ukraine, in accordance with military and political thinking before 1939. The military strategy would be accompanied by a political one aiming to support the nationalist movements on the periphery of the USSR, to set up local governments under German protection and, after the destruction of the enemy's 'active forces', to rapidly force a dictated peace upon him. Whether Hitler could still be persuaded to accept a war of intervention on the model of 1918 was to be put to the test at the Berghof on 31 July 1940.

The Myth of 31 July 1940: Hitler's Decision to Go to War in the East

Hitler's midday meeting at the Berghof near Berchtesgaden on 31 July 1940 lasted only around 90 minutes. The participants were Wilhelm Keitel and Alfred Jodl for the OKW, Erich Raeder as commander-in-chief of the navy, and Walther von Brauchitsch and Franz Halder for the army. The make-up of this group is striking, because the Luftwaffe was not represented at all and the army's commander-in-chief – unlike in the previous discussion on 21 July – brought his chief of staff with him. It was plainly about Halder and the plans he had made for a war against the USSR. This meeting is seen today as a turning point in World War II, because it was here that Hitler announced his decision to invade the Soviet Union and gave the first concomitant operational and political instructions.

It has become a historian's dogma that this was the starting point for Operation Barbarossa.[135] With that is connected the idea that the war was ultimately an ideological decision of Hitler's, who was enacting the final step of his Lebensraum programme. The German military now moved swiftly along a fixed course to a racially ideological war of annihilation. Among historians, there has, however, been disagreement for decades about whether, in the following months, Hitler was acting out of an inability to achieve his aims or pursuing an interim strategy intended to push Britain into a corner and conceal his real intentions from Stalin – that is, whether his 'final' decision to actually implement the plan for an invasion of the USSR, even though the war against Britain was still going on, was made then or only after he was visited by Molotov, the Soviet foreign minister, in November 1940.

In the context of this investigation, the questions to be examined are what concept Hitler had of a war in the east on 31 July 1940 and how binding the alterations he made to the Halder plan were. The chief of staff's records are, when examined closely, very telling. In the first part of the meeting, Raeder discussed the state of preparations for invading Britain.[136] He delineated the grave technical problems and the differences between the operational approaches employed by the navy and the army. Again he expressed misgivings about whether the operation could be successfully carried out and this time wanted Operation Sea Lion postponed until 15 September, a time of year that would only make matters more difficult. In any case, the Germans first needed to gain aerial superiority above the Channel. So Raeder proposed a postponement until the following May. Hitler still could not decide about the invasion and first wanted to wait and see what would happen in the aerial battle. A postponement seemed to be probably the best solution.

After Raeder had left, Hitler continued the discussion with the army's leaders and the heads of the OKW. The question was what to do if Britain did not give up soon. Winning the war by intensifying the aerial and naval battles could, in his opinion, take as long as two years. It had to be considered that this would give Britain time to recover its strength and that both the USA and the USSR might be disposed to intervene – in any case, the hope of

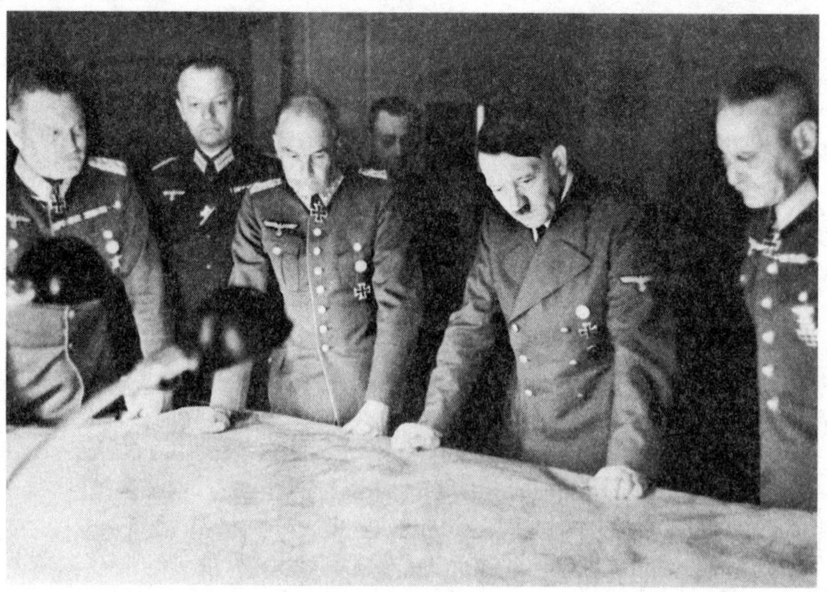

21. Hitler in the army commander-in-chief's headquarters after the end of the French campaign. From left to right at the map table: Field Marshal Wilhelm Keitel, Field Marshal Walther von Brauchitsch, Adolf Hitler, General Franz Halder.

intervention seemed to be spurring the British government on, even though, Hitler said, Britain was actually finished. The dictator had obviously thought about the wider strategic implications in the preceding days and returned to earlier ideas. These led him to assume that, if the USSR were neutralised, the USA would have to stop lending support to Britain, because Japan – freed from its confrontation with the USSR – would pursue its imperial ambitions in the Far East unhindered and so mount a challenge to the Americans. This would take away both sources of British hope and lead them to give up at last. From his perspective, that did not mean the destruction of Great Britain, but rather the agreement he had always wanted about how the world would be divided.

So it was only in a very general sense that Hitler was making changes to his political programme, while concealing that he was considering breaking a monstrous taboo, namely a war on two fronts. He used strategic arguments exclusively and avoided bringing up any ideological dimensions. If he had used the language of anti-Bolshevism, anti-Semitism, of racial ideology and Lebensraum, Halder would have noted them in his diary, particularly as the dictator subsequently came to accept the plans Halder had already made.

From Hitler's statements to the army's leaders in the discussion on 31 July 1940:

Decision: In the course of this conflict, Russia has to be eliminated. Spring 1941.

The faster we destroy Russia, the better. Operation only makes sense if we can severely damage the state with one blow. Territorial gains alone are not sufficient. Being stationary in winter dangerous.

Therefore better to wait, but definite decision to eliminate Russia. Necessary also because of the situation in the Baltic Sea. A second great power on the Baltic is not acceptable. May 1941. 5 months for implementation. This year preferable. But impossible, if operation is to be implemented in coordinated way.

Objective: Annihilation of Russia's active forces. Divide into:

1st attack Kiev support on Dnieper. Luftwaffe destroys crossings Odessa.

2nd attack satellite states in direction of Moscow

Finally meeting from north and south.

Later smaller operations in Baku oilfields.

Extent to which Finland and Turkey involved remains to be seen.

Later: the Ukraine, Byelorussia, Baltic states to us. Finland up to the White Sea.[137]

These minutes show that Hitler accepted Halder's principle of a rapid switch to the east with a short-term war against the USSR. He did, however, have other ideas about the time and troops required. But if the navy would not be ready for an invasion of Britain until 15 September, that meant there were only four weeks available for the limited offensive prepared by the Army High Command before the highly risky seaborne invasion would require all forces to be concentrated on the Channel. In the worst-case scenario, German troops would be stuck simultaneously at the chalk cliffs of Dover and in the swamps of Byelorussia, which could place the German bridgeheads in both the east and the west in great difficulty come the winter. If the British invasion took place successfully at the end of September, it would already be too late in the year for a subsequent attack on the east.

Pushing the start of an eastern operation back to the spring, however, offered numerous advantages. By then, the conflict with Britain might have resolved itself. If so, the Wehrmacht would be able to undertake a comprehensive deployment in the east. 'The more divisions we come with, the better. We have 120 plus the holiday divisions,' declared Hitler. And in the eastern parts of the Reich, it would be possible to muster another 40 divisions composed of 'battle-tried units'. The dictator had been thinking about this. The bottom line was that the offensive in the east would have 120 divisions at its disposal. Hitler believed Britain would be able to field around 35 divisions by spring 1941, which would be facing around 60 German divisions in the west. That would give him a sufficient capacity to fight on both sides.

As for the eastern campaign's operational and political objectives, Hitler's ideas essentially did not go beyond the Halder plan. Unlike that planned by AOK 18, it was to be a unitary operation carried out in one swoop, just like the one recently carried out in France with unexpectedly complete success. In this sense, Hitler's eastern war in 1941 became the first 'blitzkrieg'[138] campaign planned as such by the Wehrmacht – the subjugation of small European states did not have those dimensions. All of Hitler's other ideas drew on the older deliberations about a war against the USSR: forming two operational spearheads in the north and south, which would join up later; bringing in Finland and Romania; making a later small-scale strike at Baku and its important oilfields. The operational approach even still contained the old model of an 'anti-Russian trench' on Polish territory, in so far as the central section of the front was apparently supposed to remain defensive until the two spearheads met east of the Pripet Marshes.

Of course, they did not have the 50 divisions of Piłsudski's army at their disposal, but the Wehrmacht was now more than capable of providing the necessary troops itself. Unlike Halder's idea that the eastern campaign would have limited objectives, as had been the case in France, where the terms of the armistice recognised the French government and left them a part of the country, Hitler wanted Russia to be completely destroyed as a potential power. He was familiar with the navy's old ideas of how to fight a war against Russia. So he used the argument that the USSR had to be 'disposed of' in order to force the Russians away from the Baltic Sea. The other objectives, too, were oriented on previous conceptions: occupying the Baltic states, Byelorussia and the Ukraine, which were to be incorporated into a greater German political sphere.

It is striking that Hitler mentioned conquering neither Moscow nor any part of Russia further to the east, but rather had in mind an operational line running Leningrad–Smolensk–Kiev–Dnieper, which roughly corresponded to the model of 1918. When discussing the advance through the Baltic states, he talked merely about the 'direction of Moscow', which could mean that, after the two spearheads met, they would take up positions facing the Russian capital. In the following months, the question of Moscow led him and Halder into an unresolved dispute that contributed to the failure of the campaign in summer 1941.

It is equally remarkable that in Hitler's deliberations at that time there is no talk of the racially ideological war of annihilation that the German–Soviet war became. The context of the easily misunderstood formulation about 'destroying Russia's life force' makes unambiguous that this referred to power and strategy, and so it must be seen as military terminology of the day. Nor can the territorial objectives be classified as typically National Socialist. Political questions about, say, administering the occupation, were evidently not even brought up; if they had been, then Halder – after the previous trouble in Poland – would surely have diligently noted it. The remaining question is what to make of the formulation 'definite decision'. It isn't known whether this phrase was actually used by Hitler or whether it expresses how Halder interpreted the meeting. When assessing the decision taken on 31 July 1940, we must use for comparison the discussion on 23 November 1939 in which Hitler informed the Army High Command that he was 'irrevocably resolved' to attack France. Then, he had been reacting to the hesitation and worry of his officers; now, he was taking on their suggestions and fundamentally approving them. The corresponding formal directive in 1940 was not produced until five months later (Directive No. 21: Case Barbarossa, of 18 December 1940); in 1939, the directive (No. 6 for the military) had been issued six weeks before the pivotal meeting, on 9 October 1939.

So it can be seen that in the discussion on 31 July 1940, Hitler was essentially reacting to deliberations already made by the army's leaders. The strategic situation after the British government decided to continue the fight against Hitler prompted them to again focus on the 'eastern problem' and examine anew the ideas for a war against the USSR that had already been in general circulation in the previous year. Hitler's statements could equally have been made, or similarly made, on 31 July 1939, when the prospect of cooperation between the British and the Soviet Union gave rise to concomitant military preparations. Of course, it goes without saying that these meetings and decisions have to be interpreted in the context of Hitler's general political objectives. The belief widespread today that the criminal war for Lebensraum in the USSR should be attributed to Hitler's 'definite decision' on 31 July 1940 actually conceals the continuity in the conception of the war that had existed since 1934. The war in the east – and this is the crucial point – was not an undesirable, misunderstood project that the Führer presented to the army's leaders on that day. This myth, successfully propagated by Franz Halder after the war, disguised the military leaders' initiative and culpability, as they worked towards the Führer in carrying out the largest and bloodiest war in world history. The impulse came not from Nazi Lebensraum ideology, but – despite all affinity with National Socialism – from simple military routine. The claim that Hitler, on 31 July 1940, decided to go to war for ideological reasons is a construction that essentially goes back to the historian Andreas Hillgruber, who by putting it forward in 1954 qualified and complemented Halder's myth about Hitler's strategic reasoning.[139]

Wrangling over the Operational Plan

Halder's notes on 31 July 1940 do not indicate that there was any exchange of ideas with Hitler. Brauchitsch kept his insight of the evening before – that it would be better to retain Russia's friendship – to himself. His chief of staff, for his part, hurried back to Fontainebleau to adjust the already ongoing planning for the eastern war. To complement the operations planning, Halder now had his staff theoretically prepare both the logistics of a large-scale offensive in the east and the outline of a military administration. It is again evident here that

Hitler made no indication that this war would have an abnormal character; nor did he say anything about how to treat the conquered populace. So Wagner and the Quartermaster General's office could work along habitual lines.

Hitler's use of the word 'Moscow' was of the greatest significance to Halder. If the Führer was not willing to negotiate with a Russian government – even a post-communist one – as at Brest-Litovsk in 1918, about German annexation of the Baltic states and the Ukraine, that had far-reaching consequences for the operational plan. Hitler himself had presumably not yet given this any thought. Even if it was assumed – as it had been for years – that the Soviet system would collapse soon after the outbreak of war, the question still arose: who would rule the larger, unoccupied part of Russia's vast territory? The answer Hitler gave a year later was that the entire European part would be comprehensively occupied and transformed into German Lebensraum, which would be secured by a military border extending much further eastward, on the model of the Austro-Hungarian Empire's possessions in the Balkans – that is to say, constant skirmishes and conflicts with newly formed regional powers on the far side of the Urals. Halder had not yet got that far on 1 August 1940. Rather, he saw the necessity of ending the war quickly in order to free up the troops deployed in the east for a conflict in the west. According to traditional thinking, a rapid end to the war required that the capital be directly assaulted and occupied. That would mean the military's task had been by and large completed, and things would go back to being the politicians' responsibility.

A brief overview of the ongoing plans for the war in the east show that the old ideas were altered only gradually. Right after his return from Berchtesgaden, Halder invited General Marcks to give a presentation on the state of planning for the Russian operation. Halder placed particular emphasis on the formation of an Army Group Moscow, which would participate only in passing in the battle for the Baltic states. An operational group also had to be directed at Kiev. Within three days, Marcks presented a comprehensive and detailed 'Draft Operation East' with numerous appendices.[140] It is hardly feasible that this – as far as we know – first campaign plan was created only in the short time since the meeting with Hitler. It can be assumed that Marcks drew extensively on previous designs and blueprints. This is proved by the tone and the details.

Marcks saw the 'point of the campaign' as 'defeating [the Red Army] and making Russia unable to be an enemy of Germany's for the foreseeable

Draft Operational Plan East (The Marcks Plan) for 5.8.1940
Key:
Stage 1 (400 km, lasting approx 3 weeks)
Stage 2 (100-200 km, lasting 2-4 weeks)
Stage 3 (300-400 km, lasting 1-2 or 3-4 weeks)
The ultimate goal after stage 4. Total duration of the campaign between 9 and 17 weeks.
Murmansk
Kola Peninsula
White Sea
Kem
Archangelsk
Northern Dvina
Kotlas
FINLAND
NORWAY
SWEDEN
Petrozavodsk
Lake Onega
Lake Lagoda
HELSINKI
OSLO
STOCKHOLM
Leningrad
Sukhona
Vologda
Tallinn
Narva
ESTONIA
Veliky Novgorod
Gothenburg
BALTIC SEA
Pskov
Volga
Kalinin
Gorky
Riga
LATVIA
Liepaja
Copenhagen
Velikiye Luki
SOVIET UNION
MOSCOW
Daugavpils
LITHUANIA
Western Dvina
Polotsk
Vitebsk
Kaunas
18.A
Gdańsk
Königsberg
Vilnius
Smolensk
Orsha
Dniepr
Tula
GERMAN REICH
6.A
Res. AOK 9
H.Gr. North
Minsk
Hrodna
Mogilev
BERLIN
Res. AOK 1 u.2
Res. 11.A
Białystok
Bryansk
Vistula
Poznań
4.A
Rogachev
Brest-Litovsk
Gomel
WARSAW
Kursk
Voronezh
Wrocław
General-Government
Pripet
Chełm
Oder
Prague
Protectorate of Bohemia
Rivne
Don
Krakow
H.Gr. South
16.A
Kiev
Kharkiv
Zhytomyr
Lviv
Ukraine
SLOVAKIA
Cherkasy
Donets
Vienna
Dnieper
Stalino
Danube
Dniester
Dnipropetrovsk
Chernovitsy
Budapest
Prut
Rostov on Don
HUNGARY
Iași
Mariupol
Szeged
Klausenberg Cluj
Mykolaiv
12.A
Only deployed 14 days after the outbreak of war
Zagreb
Odessa
ROMANIA
Krasnodar
Crimea
Belgrade
YUGOSLAVIA
Bucharest
Danube
BLACK SEA
0 100 200 300 400 km

future. In order to protect Germany against Russian bombers, Russia is to be occupied up to the line lower Don–middle Volga–Northern Dvina.' He assumed that a Russian state would continue to exist somewhere to the east of the projected line of operations. The economic, political and emotional centre was the area containing Moscow. 'Conquering it would tear apart the cohesion of the Russian empire.' The industrial areas further east were not yet up to scratch and could be discounted as an alternative base of power – one of Marcks's many mistaken assessments.

As for how it would play out militarily, Marcks did not think that the Russians would 'do us the favour of mounting an attack'. This, too, is a remnant of older thinking, which wanted to solve the 'eastern problem' with a counter-attack launched from defence. Marcks assumed that the Red Army in the occupied parts of the western USSR would make a fighting withdrawal to the old border's fortified Stalin Line. To protect its 'sources of strength', the enemy would then have to give battle there.

'Since the Russians do not this time, as in the Great War, possess numerical superiority, it can be assumed that once their lines are broken, they will no longer be able to gather their forces, which are spread out along a long line, for coherent counter-measures, and in the ensuing isolated battles will soon succumb to superior German troops and leadership.'

This assumption that the Wehrmacht would be superior even in numbers is astonishing. But Marcks was banking on the Red Army having to station a third of its forces in the Far East to guard against Japan, meaning that there would be 96 infantry divisions, 23 cavalry divisions and ten motorised–mechanised brigades facing the Germans. In opposition to that, just the German forces available on the eastern front in spring would amount to 147 divisions. Marcks gave as little thought to the Japanese as his predecessors had.

The draft operation did not foresee a German advance along a wide front, but wanted to deploy 35 divisions to Army Group South and 68 divisions to Army Group North. A good third of the Eastern Army, 44 divisions, was to be held in reserve. Both spearheads would be forced by the geographical situation to concentrate themselves on only a few roads, which with a deployment in depth meant it would be possible to have correspondingly large reserves. That would also solve the mobilisation problem. The deficient infrastructure in eastern Central Europe and the need to keep their intentions secret meant that only step-by-step mobilisation would have been possible anyway.[141]

The fact that Marcks had previous documents at his disposal is shown by his referring to 'Study South-East' from 1938, which provided details of what capacity the Romanian and Hungarian railways could offer the German mobilisation. His statements about the participation of the navy and the occupation of the Baltic ports were also along very familiar lines. And not least did he mention the need to step up the Abwehr's activities to mobilise indigenous forces that could prevent the Red Army from destroying things as it retreated. Finally, his study says: 'A military administration has to be prepared for the occupied territories. For the Ukraine, Byelorussia and the Baltic states, it is envisaged that there will be a transition to indigenous, non-Bolshevik government.' This point in particular again confirms the assumption that Hitler did not express any definite political intentions on 31 July.

Equally noteworthy is Marcks's approach to the parameters of territory and duration. The concept of fighting decisive battles close to the border had merely been extended with extra phases for the pursuit of a defeated enemy. Hitler's 'large-scale' solution to the eastern problem thus did not give rise to any new strategic ideas. Marcks assumed that the decisive military encounter with the Red Army would take place in the first phase. Against a retreating enemy, who would be withdrawing to his old defensive positions, the mass of the German infantry would need around three weeks to cover a distance of some 250 miles. The armoured divisions would have to advance far and quickly to prevent the enemy from setting up a closed defensive front. This thinking has clearly been shaped by the experiences of the Polish and French campaigns.

Marcks imagined the second phase as consisting of a battle for the rivers and forest regions, taking place up to a depth of 120 miles and lasting up to four weeks. The Germans would either 'force the decisive breakthrough or defeat one at a time the sections of the Russian Army scattered by the first phase'. In the third phase, it might be a question of merely 'keeping the defeated Russians on the retreat, taking Moscow and Leningrad and advancing deep into the eastern Ukraine'. If large sections of the Red Army were still fit for action, the German forces would have to pause for three to six weeks to be resupplied. After those battles had been concluded, the pursuit would lead them to the Don, the Volga and the Northern Dvina, which meant covering another 250 miles in the south and as much as 500 miles in the centre and the north.

From Major-General Erich Marcks's 'Draft Operation East', 5 August 1940:
After we take Kharkiv, Moscow and Leningrad, cohesive Russian armed forces will no longer exist. Complete occupation of this territory is not possible and not necessary. Rapid troops and inf. div. advancing by train will be chiefly responsible for maintaining the pursuit. Time required: 2–4 weeks. Total time required for the campaign until the eventual objective will be between 9 and 17 weeks.

If the Soviet regime does not collapse or sue for peace, it could become necessary to continue advancing up to the Urals. Even if Russia is not capable of actively waging war after the destruction of its armed forces and the loss of its most valuable European regions, it could still, supported by Asia, remain in a state of war for an unforeseeable length of time.

This assessment, which from today's perspective may seem to be a case of puzzlingly deluded military megalomania, can be understood as the thoroughly rational calculation of an experienced staff officer only in the context of the contemporary image of war in the east. At the end of the 1930s, the instability of the Soviet system and the weakness of the Red Army were apparently secure principles, and not just in Germany. Marcks's belief that the Wehrmacht would be not only qualitatively but also numerically superior to the Red Army during the eastern campaign was due to an all-too-optimistic assessment of the enemy's position. Because of this image of war in the east and the experiences of 1917–18, there was an unshakeable assumption that, after a few heavy defeats, the Red Army would disintegrate into a number of isolated clusters and be chased through the country like a squadron of horse-whipped Cossacks. This extreme underestimation of Stalin and the rest of the Soviet leadership's capabilities may be due to anti-Bolshevik stereotypes or other ideological influences, but even considered objectively from the standpoint of 1940,[142] the USSR had done nothing to demonstrate any sort of military efficacy. The impressions gleaned from the Polish and Finnish campaigns had rather underlined this disdainful assessment.

Alongside a comprehensive appendix dealing with training and organising the troops on the basis of the experiences gathered so far, Marcks's study also contained another text that may be surprising, the relevance of which becomes immediately distinct in the context of this investigation into how the war in the east was planned. It was an extract from Mikhail Tukhachevsky's text *Advance across the Vistula*, which describes the war of 1920 and was recommended to the Wehrmacht in the mid 1930s as useful reading in conjunction with Marshal Piłsudski's account. The extract from Tukhachevsky contains a military assessment of the Pripet Marshes, which led Marcks, right from the outset, to want to divide the German attack in two.[143]

This natural barrier could be used by defenders to concentrate their forces for dangerous flank attacks on the northern and southern offensive groups. How big a risk that was to the campaign depended on how easy it was to move large units around this swampy, forested region. Tukhachevsky's experiences came from a time when war had been waged primarily with cavalry and infantry; twenty years later, this information was not necessarily sufficient. Marcks was still dealing with the question.

Eberhard Kinzel, head of the Foreign Armies East bureau, pointed out in his evaluation of 10 September 1940 that the leaders of the Red Army were convinced they would be able to make use of the region even given the switch to motorised warfare, but he himself did not think the Russians would be capable of creating troop concentrations either north or south of the marshes.[144] Later, even Hitler noticed that this might present a problem, and so he had a study commissioned. In response, Foreign Armies East delivered a collection of quotes from easily accessible sources. Halder had the draft worked over and the version ultimately given to Hitler omitted a crucial passage. Although the original version underscored the region's importance as an obstacle for attackers and said that defenders might be able to start a local war there, it also stated that railway connections meant the defenders would be able to move their troops in every direction. A threat to the flanks and rear of the attacks on Moscow and Kiev was 'certainly in the realm of the possible'.[145] By repeatedly downplaying this possibility to Hitler, Halder kept in place his own operational plan focused on Moscow.

In autumn 1940, AOK 18 took on the practical and plenary preparations for a large deployment in the east. At the same time, the fortifications near the border had to be upgraded as a counter to an unlikely but certainly feasible preventive strike by the Soviets. We know today that in spring 1941 the Soviet General Staff was thinking about making just this kind of strike to combat the ever more clearly visible German mobilisation, but Stalin shied away from it. Otherwise, the Red Army would have done the Wehrmacht that 'favour' (Marcks), allowing it to destroy the Soviets' attacking forces from a defensive position and then press its own offensive into the east. Direct command on the eastern border was taken up in September 1940 by a group from AOK 18. Halder's suggestion that Marcks be made this group's chief of staff, in order to provide continuity in the planning process, was rejected by Hitler, who mistrusted Marcks because he had been the chief press officer of the Reich's Defence Ministry at the end of the 1920s and a close confidant of General Schleicher, a political rival whom Hitler had had murdered in 1934.[146] Marcks took over an infantry division in 1941 and was badly wounded in the first days of the eastern campaign.

It cannot be ruled out that Hitler's intervention stemmed from Heinz Guderian. The headstrong tank general and his corps were subordinate to AOK 18, but he nonetheless pursued his plan of building up an independent armoured force to act as a spearhead against Moscow. Guderian had presented his impressions and reports on the 1939 advance to Brest-Litovsk to Hitler in person and had also discussed with him his encounter with the Red Army. These reports added to the adverse image of the Red Army's equipment and attitude. Its armoured vehicles were, according to Guderian, old and obsolete. And Guderian, like so many others, was not keen to remember the part he played in preparing Operation Barbarossa when it came to writing his memoirs after the war. Between the end of the French campaign and the visit from Molotov there is a striking blank. Guderian presents the barefaced claim: 'I had no contact with the OKH or the General Staff, and was not consulted on the question of reorganising the armoured groups or in reference to how the war would be continued.'[147]

Hitler thought a lot about Guderian's experiences in Poland; they confirmed his belief that 'If [...] you really get to grips with this colossus, it will break apart far more quickly than the whole world realises.'[148] But he did not now concern himself more closely with the planning of a war in the east. His interest was focused on the aerial war against Britain and on the German advances in the Mediterranean.

On 15 September, the 'Day of the Eagle', Göring's Luftwaffe failed in their attempt to achieve aerial superiority over the Channel. Operation Sea Lion now had to be postponed to the spring. At the Berghof, Hitler had a long talk with Göring about the situation. The 'Reichsmarschall' still thought it possible to subjugate the British from the air and demanded a further acceleration of aerial armaments production. Harsh words were aimed at Raeder and the navy, who were 'scared' of the invasion. Then the talk moved on to Russia. The army adjutant noted: 'Both see Russian forces as meagre. Guderian's report on impressions in Brest-Litovsk. Intention perhaps to attack Russia in order to deprive Britain of any potential alliance.'[149] A few days later, Hitler conferred with the navy's commander-in-chief. Raeder proposed using the winter to bring the whole Mediterranean under the control of the Axis powers. The Russian problem would then look very different. Since Moscow was basically 'afraid of Germany', an attack on the USSR 'from the north' might no longer be necessary. 'Führer fundamentally agrees', state the navy's records.[150]

So how are we to assess Hitler's 'definite decision' on 31 July? Halder was not in a rush to prioritise the plans for the east above his many more urgent tasks. Since he could no longer assign the ongoing preparatory work to Marcks, he involved a man from his own circle, Lieutenant General Friedrich Paulus, the newly appointed deputy chief of the General Staff. This diligent and highly talented staff officer, who would lead the 6th Army into Stalingrad two years later, concerned himself above all with questions of tactics and personnel. As Halder's right-hand man, he became one of the 'godfathers' of Operation Barbarossa.[151]

Wilhelm Keitel, head of the OKW, had been present at the meeting on 31 July 1940. On the following day, he ordered additional measures to be undertaken in his own field, which had repercussions for all the armed forces. One of these was 'Plan Otto', which concerned the upgrading of infrastructure in the eastern mobilisation zone. Issued as an order about 'build-up in the east' on 9 August 1940, it became binding and was used by the Nuremberg trials as evidence of Keitel's co-culpability in planning a war of aggression.[152] Keitel was executed, while Halder, the actual initiator of the plans, was not touched. At the start of August 1940, Keitel brought one of his subordinates, General Georg Thomas, head of the War Economy and Armaments Office, up to speed. They needed to redirect armaments production in such a way that, come the following year, a landing in Britain, a war against the USSR and a conflict with the USA would all be manageable.

But because the Führer was not willing to tighten up the economy to benefit armaments manufacture right after he had loosened it following victory over France, the Wehrmacht had to organise its armaments programme within the existing framework. Since the Luftwaffe and the navy retained priority in the distribution of resources because of their fight against Great Britain, all the army could do was shift things around within its own share. The production of munitions was slowed down in order to slightly accelerate the manufacture of tanks. In order to equip additional divisions, the army resorted to relying extensively on materiel captured during the previous campaigns.[153] Since the priority of the Luftwaffe and the navy was reconfirmed at the turn of 1940–1 and again shortly before the start of Barbarossa, even the OKH's modest armaments programme could not be fully carried out. As a result, the Eastern Army's equipment was reminiscent of a patchwork quilt. Only a small proportion of the troops had modern arms and gear. And despite the priority given to aerial production, the Luftwaffe was only just managing to make up the heavy losses it had sustained in the Battle of Britain. So, on 22 June 1941, the invasion army standing ready in the east was no stronger than the army that had marched against France a year before. That did not worry the army's leaders, as they were expecting a victory as rapid as it was overwhelming against the apparently inferior Red Army.

The OKW was, in any case, paying more attention to the other theatres of war. Nevertheless, after the meeting on 31 July 1940, Keitel commissioned the Wehrmacht Operations Staff to prepare their own study for a war against the USSR. The small staff, which reported directly to Hitler, was generally able to work only from the documents and drafts produced by the OKH. So the study produced by Lieutenant Colonel Bernhard von Loßberg in parallel to Marcks's drew much the same conclusions.[154] The Soviet enemy was said to be neither ready nor willing to attack. The advantage he had was the vastness of his territory, but the Red Army would nonetheless give battle near the border. Once beaten, its leaders would no longer be able to mount organised resistance. To accelerate the enemy's collapse, Loßberg brought up the old idea of harnessing the non-Russian minorities, especially the Ukrainians, for the Germans' purposes. He also made the case for launching an additional attack from southern Finland and for strengthening Army Group South. In line with Halder, however, he wanted the main thrust to be made centrally, against Moscow, with numerically superior German forces that could also be given secondary assignments on the way. Loßberg considered it possible for some of these troops to swing northwards; Marcks thought they might swing south. This thinking had far-reaching repercussions for the further planning and the actual results of the operation.

In autumn 1940, the plans, armaments production and mobilisation orders proceeded at a cautious tempo, and the few in the military who knew about it did not have the impression that Case East represented an unalterable decision of the Führer's. Rather, Soviet Foreign Minister Molotov's public visit at the start of November 1940 indicated that the USSR might join the Tripartite Pact with which Germany, Italy and Japan had recently been trying to coordinate their wars against Great Britain. A treaty by which Moscow agreed to pressure the British around the Indian Ocean could have been the move that convinced London to give in. Then, according to Hitler's previous ideas, they could 'settle things' with Russia. But Molotov would not have the wool pulled over his eyes and insisted that any closer partnership would have to satisfy further Soviet interests in Europe. That was something Hitler, in view of German interests in Romania and Finland, would not agree to, if only for economic and political reasons. Unlike in the previous year, a diplomatic coup at Britain's expense was not important enough for him to pay the high price demanded by Moscow.

In the end, both dictators were disappointed. The new trade agreement was only a superficial addition to their strategic partnership. By all accounts, Stalin trusted that Hitler would not dare to attempt a war on two fronts, and therefore discounted his intelligence services' many warnings that the Germans were mobilising in the east. Nevertheless, he did hastily reorganise and rearm his troops. The resulting increase in the concentration of forces in the occupied westernmost territories, however, tactically played into Halder's hands, because this increased his chances of destroying the largest part of the Red Army in battles near the border during the first phase of the campaign. Albeit that Stalin assembled his main force in the south, to protect the Ukraine. This would threaten the flank of Halder's central thrust at Moscow.

At the start of December 1940, Paulus had the operational arrangements tested in a three-day map exercise with the heads of the General Staff.[155] It became apparent that the enormous encirclement planned near Minsk would succeed only if a strong infantry contingent was available to close off the pocket and free up the armoured units for a further rapid advance. Putting a swift end to the campaign by taking Moscow would be achieved only if the northern and southern army groups made it their priority to cover the flanks of the strong central thrust, and if the stricken Red Army pulled back to defend the capital – conditions that were not met in summer 1941.

The officers were not unaware of the risks involved in the Halder plan. But the chief of staff would not be deterred. Nor did another study for an eastern campaign, presented on 7 December by Infantry General Georg von Sodenstern, the future Army Group South's chief of staff, lead to any alterations in it. Sodenstern went back to the old idea of remaining static in the centre – that is, in the Polish 'trench', in front of the Pripet Marshes – and instead attacking over favourable terrain with two armoured groups in the north and one in the south, in order to take control of the most important economic and armaments areas and then encircle the outstripped Russian centre.[156]

This older concept disappeared into a drawer. Two days before the Sodenstern study, Halder had already presented his operational intentions to the Führer.[157] In a long monologue, Hitler showed himself to be far more concerned with the numerous other conflicts and theatres of war, though he emphasised at the same time that domination of Europe would ultimately be won in the 'fight against Russia'. But he was clearly not thinking of concentrating all his forces on that objective. Hitler declared himself generally in agreement with Halder's operational ideas, only to then engage with the details in a way that revealed great differences in their conceptions of the war. These related chiefly to the second phase of the campaign. In contrast to Halder, whose gaze was fixed on Moscow, Hitler saw it as necessary to first clear up the situation in the Baltic states. The chief of staff avoided a more comprehensive discussion, apparently confident that he would be able to implement his concept when it actually came to the fighting.

In accordance with procedure, OKW Lieutenant Colonel Loßberg presented a draft of 'Directive No. 21', in which Hitler set out guidelines for the Wehrmacht. In the final version, of 18 December 1940, his fingerprints can again be seen in places where he overruled Halder's intentions.[158] For Hitler, too, the destruction of the Russian Army close to the border was the first priority, but the next most pressing task was to secure the Baltic Sea by occupying the states on its shore. Only after that was the Wehrmacht to take simultaneous possession of Moscow and the economically important Donets Basin. The Urals were taken into consideration, but there was no talk of the Caucasus. Overall, the brief directive corresponds most closely to the standpoint of the OKW, which can be seen not only in its economic elements but also in the emphasis on the deployment of the Luftwaffe and the navy. The directive went from Hitler to his commanders-in-chief with the requirement that they inform him of the actions they intended to take as a result. The statement that preparations had to be complete by 15 May 1941 did not represent a definite decision in the Wehrmacht's usual methods, especially as the preparations for Operation Sea Lion were running undiminished and under intense pressure to meet the same schedule.

So the army's commander-in-chief had the army adjutant ask the Führer whether he intended to actually carry out the campaign or whether it was just a 'bluff'. Major Engel got the impression that Hitler himself was not sure how things would proceed. He distrusted the leaders of the military. He was constantly preoccupied by his disappointment about the 'toughness of the British' and by the lack of clarity about Russia's actual strength. 'But repeatedly stresses that he reserves all rights to make decisions. Molotov's visit showed that Russia wants to get its hands on Europe. He cannot afford to give up the Balkans, Finland's dependency is already enough of a danger. The pact has never been honest, because the ideological chasm is too deep.'[159] By sending a military delegation to Romania and renewing his contact with the Finns, Hitler had long been making efforts to secure his strategic interests. He was aware of Stalin's rival interest, but he obviously did not consider himself to be in a predicament that would force him to launch an attack on the USSR.

The information from the army adjutant could have prompted its leaders to encourage Hitler to first make sure that Britain was persuaded or forced to provide cover for an advance – the guarantee the Germans had been seeking since the mid 1930s. But Brauchitsch did nothing, even though the worries about a war on two fronts, now being expressed by the navy, were hardly new to him. In their presentation to Hitler on situation 'Barbarossa', he and Paulus, who was standing in for Halder, were pleased to find agreement on how the forces were to be deployed and where concentrated. Albeit that Hitler dug in his heels 'very deeply on north and south'. 'Economic arguments keep coming to the fore, as well as ideological ones: oil and grain in the south, and in the north the destruction of the ideological fortress Leningrad.' Hitler was thus more attached to the concepts of the previous years than the army's leaders were. But the dictator's decision not to wage a limited campaign and not to dictate peace to a Russian government meant that Halder became fixated on Moscow, because he considered taking it to be the only possible means of putting a rapid end to the war.

The Führer, however, apparently still did not have any definite ideas of how to complement the military strategy with a political programme, and instead clung to the familiar economic arguments. That was something for which the army's leaders had a lot of sympathy. But again Brauchitsch omitted to discuss with Hitler the contradictions that had emerged in the plans and concepts. Instead, he shared Hitler's highly optimistic assessment of the two armies' relative clout: that the Red Army possessed only meagre combat strength, outdated equipment and very few aeroplanes.[160] It seems that the two men not only talked at cross-purposes but also, in their reciprocal distrust, preferred to put a positive spin on everything so as to achieve artificial consensus.

Hitler mentioned even important strategic decisions as if in passing. In the 1930s, Japan had always played an important role as a hostile power on the Soviet flank and a means of eventually dragging the USSR into a war on two fronts. In 1939, Tokyo had been extremely angered by the surprise pact between Hitler and Stalin because the Japanese were already engaged in hostilities with the Red Army at the time. After the victory over France, Hitler had seen Japan as merely a spearhead against Britain and made no effort to construct a front against Stalin in the Far East. In the meeting on 9 January 1941, he declared Japan 'ready for serious collaboration'. What he meant was that Japan would have a free hand against Britain in the Far East if Germany tackled the Russian question.

Two months later, he issued the secret 'Directive No. 24 on Cooperation with Japan'. The objective as regards the Tripartite Pact was to 'convince Japan to take active steps in the Far East as soon as possible' resulting in the 'occupation of Singapore'. In conclusion it said: 'No indication can be given to the Japanese of the Barbarossa operation.'[161] This was another mistake ultimately dating back to the Halder plan, which did not envisage Japanese support for a campaign against the USSR. A front in the Far East would perhaps have been superfluous in Halder's original plan of a brief campaign in autumn 1940, but Hitler's broadening of the operation led to no change in the strategic approach.

On 28 January, Halder gathered together a large group of generals from the economic and armaments departments to discuss the progress in preparations for Barbarossa.[162] Their focus was on the enormous logistical problems. Halder considered victory 'guaranteed' if they could manage to conduct the extensive operation in one fell swoop. The Russian Army had to be broken from the border to the line of the Dnieper. It could not be allowed to come to rest. The distance to the Dnieper was approximately that from Luxembourg to the mouth of the Rhône. At a meeting with his officers a week beforehand, Quartermaster General Wagner had been unable to find a solution to the many problems they were facing. There was a shortage of fuel, of tyres, of spare parts; in short, of the material requirements for a largely motorised war fought over vast distances. There would be enough for mobilisation and two months of operations. But what then? If Halder's discussions did not come up with a solution, the Führer was to be asked to make a decision – at least, that was what Wagner hoped.[163]

The chief of staff must have recognised that the army's reluctance to allocate resources put the Barbarossa plan in extreme jeopardy. In the subsequent conversation with Brauchitsch, Halder showed that he was fully aware of the dangers: 'Barbarossa: point of it not clear. Will not affect the British. Our economic basis will not significantly improve. The danger in the West cannot be underestimated.'[164] When the two men, barely a week later, on 3 February, met Hitler to present their progress, this would have been the opportunity to discuss their misgivings and the predictable Clausewitzian 'frictions'. Instead, both omitted to mention the risks. Halder presented his operational planning at length: in great detail where Hitler was not expected to intervene, otherwise cursorily. Hitler took the numerous maps and other documents to examine them more intensively later. He also requested a special map on which were marked the areas most important for the USSR's armaments production and its economy. This played a guiding role in his subsequent operational decisions.

In February–March 1941, Hitler definitively set out the campaign's general political and economic parameters. Here, too, the documents produced by the military's operations staffs had prompted the Führer to intervene, because he had got the impression that the military were working with unsuitable criteria. Of course, this primarily entailed bringing out the ideological nature of the war. Of course, the ideological aspects could, as in the Polish campaign, have been given attention after the military action had been concluded. But the internal conflict about the military administration of Poland made it seem more sensible to Hitler to install a better system of interaction and more narrowly define the military's responsibilities from the outset.

An important consideration for him was the estimate of how long the campaign would take. Since he was counting on a rapid advance and the total destruction of the Soviet state, in order to free up the Wehrmacht for the tasks it would be required to perform after Barbarossa, he thought it necessary to treat the Russian population with brutal decisiveness. Moreover, that was the only way the Wehrmacht could quickly extract enough Russian food supplies and raw materials to support the 'war against continents'. The older conceptions of a war of intervention on the model of 1918 and Halder's 'small-scale' solution had, for their part, required the occupation to pursue a policy of compromise and consideration as well as of placing greater trust in local elites and securing the cooperation of the populace. A rapid and total victory made a policy of moderation seem superfluous; indeed, it offered a chance to use the pressures of war to lay the foundations of a 'new order' right away. For Hitler, the model to be followed was not what had been done in France, but in Poland.

The army's leaders did not contradict this assumption that victory would be swift. Right up to the start of the campaign, Halder was careful to keep the contradictions and problems in the operational plan hidden from the dictator, so as to obviate the risk that he would intervene. That was why he did not take the logistical and armaments problems as a prompt to ask Hitler to make fundamental decisions. If there was a shortage of petrol, the army would just have to reduce the scope of its driving school. If its modest armaments programme could not be carried out, they would just have to reduce the amount given to the troops and use captured materiel instead. Measures such as these were assuredly not conducive to rapid, motorised warfare.

At least as dramatic were the changes relating to the character of the war and the occupation. The quartermaster general, who was responsible for a future military administration, had had orders drawn up and then played through in a war game at the start of February 1941.[165] These orders were oriented primarily on the conventional principles and were thus in line with the contemporary customs of war. That meant the army would take complete responsibility for the occupied areas and would concentrate on military tasks. Police units were to be used for security, albeit deployed to normal police duties rather than en masse. Any resistance from the civilian population was to be 'nipped in the bud. Confident and ruthless action against any anti-German elements will be an effective preventive measure.' But it would also be necessary to quickly discover 'which parts of the population the German troops can rely on. Those hostile to the Russian regime are to be used to further German interests, including by granting certain freedoms and material advantages.'

The only difference from France was that the vast extent of Russia's territory would make it impossible to create a close-meshed administration. They also considered treating the various regions differently. The Baltic states and the Ukraine could be placed as soon as possible into the hands of 'an ordered administration. Public life and the economy are to be started up again. Industry and agriculture are to be encouraged so that they become able as soon as possible to strengthen the German war economy with their goods.' The 'creation of an independent state with its own government under German suzerainty' was envisaged. Moreover, 'Prisoners of war are a useful workforce'. If they provided 'willing work', they were to be 'rewarded with adequate provisions and a good level of care'.

The OKW had summed up these plans for military administration in its draft 'Guidelines on Special Areas'. These were rejected by Hitler on 3 March and reformulated in line with his instructions. In the concepts he expressed on this matter we can see ideas that he and Rosenberg had at least hinted at in the previous 15 years, but which were fundamentally different from what the military had been planning hitherto. In view of all the wrangling over occupation policy since the beginning of the war, he had also already given thought to how to restrict the responsibilities of the military's – to his mind – conservative and reactionary leadership and so prevent it from getting in his way.

Hitler's instructions for occupation policy, 3 March 1941:

This coming campaign is more than just a struggle between armies; it also entails a conflict between two ideologies. The size of the territory means that defeating the enemy military will not suffice to end the war. The whole region must be dissolved into separate states with their own governments, with which we will be able to make peace.

The formation of these governments will require a great deal of political skill and, in general, a well-thought-through approach.

Every revolution on a grand scale creates facts that cannot simply be wiped away. Today's Russia cannot be imagined without the socialist idea. It alone can provide the domestic political basis for the formation of new states and governments. The Jewish-Bolshevik intelligentsia, the previous 'oppressor' of the people, must be eliminated. The former bourgeois-aristocratic intelligentsia, which continues to exist, particularly among emigrants, must also be discarded. It has been rejected by the Russian people and is ultimately anti-German. This applies especially to the former Baltic states.

Moreover, it must be avoided at all costs that the place of the Bolsheviks is taken by a nationalist Russia, which, as history has shown, would ultimately be hostile to Germany.

It is our task to use a minimum of military strength to rapidly build up a set of socialist states dependent on us.

These tasks are so difficult that the army cannot be expected to take them on.[166]

Politically, Hitler had by no means yet wholly given up on traditional ideas. When he mentioned the formation of new states and governments with which peace could be concluded, this still corresponded to the older thinking. What did the Führer mean by the 'socialist idea' without which Russia could no longer be imagined? It was probably no more than an additional argument against the concept of returning to the relations of 1917. The old leadership elite was not to be returned to power with German help. But, unlike in Poland, he was not thinking of murdering them. His fantasies of annihilation here were limited to the 'Jewish-Bolshevik intelligentsia', evidently not yet encompassing the entire Jewish population. Although they are not expressed, we can recognise the subliminal stereotype of dull masses that the German ruling class would be able to use as a workforce. All this does not yet give the impression that he had an overall concept for the war. Moreover, these thoughts were in reaction to the military's plans, which no longer met with his approval in 1941, now that war in the east had been decided upon and secret mobilisation was already in progress.

Hitler did not want any debate over this from Halder or any of the other leading officers. So he immediately gave Göring complete responsibility for economic exploitation, which he accorded the highest priority because he worried that the looming ration reduction within Germany would make it impossible to 'rouse' the population to new efforts. Moreover, the ambitious armaments programmes of all branches of the Wehrmacht were lacking necessary raw materials. In March–April, Göring combined the civilian and military economic portfolios and had a radical policy of exploitation drawn up, which took into account that millions of civilians and prisoners of war in the east would starve to death. This resulted from the operational idea of a rapid, far-ranging campaign that would by and large force the Wehrmacht to 'live off the land' and give over their supply lines to fuel and materiel.

As early as 3 March 1941, Hitler also announced that he was going to give Himmler's police independent tasks to carry out in the hinterland. They still needed to test whether they would also be needed in the operations zone alongside the army's secret military police.

'The necessity of rendering all Bolshevik chiefs and commissars harmless as soon as possible speaks in favour of doing so. Military courts should be kept out of all these questions; they are to concern themselves only with the judicial issues within the soldiery.'

In general, the army's activities were to be limited to the operations zone. Behind that, he wanted to set up a civilian administration with German 'Reich commissars'. This gave Hitler the pretext for including Rosenberg, his foremost thinker on eastern questions, in the planning process. In 1934, Hitler had already commissioned him to make sure Germany would be ready when the march into Russia began. But in recent years, Hitler had hardly paid attention to Rosenberg, whom he valued as a theorist and supposed authority on the country. Although he did not credit him with any practical or organisational abilities, he designated him the future 'Reich Minister for the Occupied Eastern Territories' in April 1941.

Rosenberg proved able to produce large studies for the future Reich Commissariats and the new National Socialist order in a very short time. But for Hitler, the initial priority was to fill the Reich commissar posts with uncompromising party officials or Gauleiters whose 'pistols sat lightly' and who could promise to plunder the territories under their control with total ruthlessness. All the new order's other political, racial and resettlement objectives, which were so important to Rosenberg, were secondary considerations for Hitler. But because Rosenberg, like the military, counted on the collaboration of the non-Russian minorities, particularly the Ukrainians, he was involved in some fragmentary coalitions of interest that attempted – albeit only after the blitzkrieg had failed – to persuade Hitler to accept some modifications to this plan. These concerned the agricultural majority and dissolution of the collective farms, efforts towards an at least partial reconstruction of the economy, food supplies for the civilian population, the deployment of prisoners of war and volunteers (Hiwis) as a labour force and the mustering of local military units.

In March 1941, Hitler was not interested. As head of the OKW, Keitel hastily signed the new version of the 'Guidelines on Special Areas' on the 13th. Three days later, he attended a meeting with Hitler, where Wagner and Brauchitsch put forward the army's concept of a military administration. It developed into one of the ferocious confrontations that the army's commander-in-chief had so feared. The army adjutant Major Engel noted that there had been an 'unpleasant discussion' of the draft, which the Führer had rejected with 'very harsh words'.

'Military administration is good for nothing. He will put administration in political hands on a case by case basis, because the Army does not understand much about politics. C-in-C tries to contradict but his views are profusely and severely dismissed, and he resigns.'[167]

Hitler stuck to his decision that the Wehrmacht's area of command would extend only as far back as the rearward troops.

Two weeks later, he gathered a large number of generals in the Chancellery to initiate them into his ideas for the imminent war against the USSR.[168] His intention was evidently to obviate any possible misunderstandings or dissatisfaction about the new form of the war before they arose. So he again explained his resolve to 'clear up the Russian situation' in order to crush Britain's hopes and, within two years, provide Germany with 'the equipment and personnel needed to master our tasks in the air and on the world's oceans'. After giving this strategic justification for the campaign, he analysed the relative strength of the two countries and began to talk about the 'problem of Russia's size'. The massed deployment of tanks and aircraft at crucial points would make it possible to defeat the enemy. Evasion would not be possible. The threat posed by the Pripet Marshes was to be warded off by the laying of minefields – Hitler had not lost sight of the Achilles heel of the Halder plan. After the end of the campaign, it would be possible to withdraw and disband 100 divisions to facilitate a massive increase in aerial and naval armaments production. Then it would be the turn of Gibraltar and Africa – there was no more talk from Hitler of Operation Sea Lion.

In his notes, Halder paid particular attention to Hitler's explanation of the new character the eastern war would have. This represented a clear break with the military's approach in 1918 and the following 15 years of secret cooperation with the Red Army.

Halder's notes on Hitler's remarks about the war in the east delivered to assembled generals in the Chancellery, 30 March 1941:

Fight between two ideologies. Devastating judgment on Bolshevism, it is no different from anti-social criminality. Communism enormous danger for the future. We must move away from the idea of soldierly camaraderie. The communist is not a comrade beforehand and he is not a comrade afterwards. This is a war of annihilation. If we do not approach it accordingly, we will still defeat the enemy, but in 30 years the communist enemy will be facing us again. We are not waging war to preserve our enemies.

Future organisation of states: Northern Russia belongs to Finland. Protectorate of the Baltic countries, the Ukraine, Byelorussia.

Fight against Russia: Annihilation of the Bolshevik commissars and the communist intelligentsia.

The new states will have to be socialist states, but without their own intelligentsia.

A new intelligentsia must be prevented from forming. A primitive socialist intelligentsia will suffice.

We must fight against the poison of subversion. That is not a question for military courts. The troops' leaders will have to know what matters. They will have to lead in this struggle. The troops will have to defend themselves by the means with which they are attacked. Commissars and GPU [Soviet secret police] people are criminals and to be treated as such.

So the troops will not need to go beyond their leaders. The leaders will have to issue their instructions in accordance with the feeling among the troops.

The struggle will be very different from the struggle in the West. Harshness is mild is the East's future.

The leaders must make the sacrifice of overcoming their misgivings.[169]

Misgivings about the military switch to the east and about this kind of warfare did continue to exist, albeit in an isolated way. They persisted in the Foreign Ministry and among the navy's leaders, in the Supreme Command of the Wehrmacht and in the Army High Command. But critical comments, such as those by Helmuth James Graf von Moltke, the OKW's expert on international law and one of the main figures in the civilian resistance, and Lieutenant Colonel Henning von Tresckow, chief operations officer of Army Group Centre and one of the most active members of the military resistance,[170] could not be openly discussed. There was, not least, a lack of support from their superiors. After discussions with Himmler's people, Halder and Brauchitsch appeared to be satisfied that this division of responsibilities with the SS could have its advantages for the army, because it would leave the troops free to concentrate solely on the fighting itself. This again dovetailed with the need to employ all their forces to attain a rapid operational victory. The idea that they were being freed from what they doubtless considered ballast-like questions of politics and policing turned out to be a fatal illusion. The army's leaders took responsibility for criminal orders whose consequences not only contributed to the failure of the campaign but also to the ignominious downfall of the Wehrmacht.

The Wehrmacht's senior officers were, of course, familiar with the historical precedent: Napoleon's Russian campaign, which ended in failure in Moscow, had also set off on 22 June. In private, a certain anxiety troubled men such as General Friedrich Fromm, commander-in-chief of the Reserve Army and head of armaments: 'Our German Army will be no more than a breeze across the

Steppe.'[171] Others may have considered it ominous that the German invasion had been given the code name 'Barbarossa', a reminder of the high-medieval German emperor who set off on a crusade and died before he even got there.

The Barbarossa Plan Fails in August 1941

The Barbarossa plan was the product of older ideas about fighting the USSR, which could have been realised in 1939, and of Hitler's decision to extend the war. In plumping for the Napoleonic solution – that is, a direct and massive advance on the enemy capital – Halder had begun a dangerous game that can hardly be counted a masterstroke on the part of the German General Staff. Although they had almost a year to prepare, the operational concept contained any number of contradictions and questionable assumptions. In order to make sure of success, Halder bet everything on one card.

On the face of it, he seemed to agree with Hitler that an invasion of the USSR would be 'child's play'. The German armoured divisions would tear through the units the Red Army had stationed near the border, encircle the majority of the Soviet western front, destroy it, and advance further east as fast as possible to prevent the Russians from setting up another coherent defence. The rest would be taken care of with advances into the Caucasus and the Urals, which would then set up a military border to the east of Moscow that could be held with a small number of troops. The body of the Eastern Army would return home to forge the weapons with which to fight the Anglo-Saxon powers for global domination.

The plan was as bold as it was foolhardy and entailed neither support nor reserves. Two-thirds of the Eastern Army were concentrated in the middle. The force and speed of Army Group Centre were threatened not only by natural barriers, but also by the weakness of the flanking Army Groups North and South. They commanded only one armoured division each; the centre had a second armoured group at its disposal alongside Guderian's. The three army groups were meant to and indeed had to attack simultaneously, trying to all progress at the same speed so that the centre would not be threatened by enemy attacks on its flanks. Halder had pushed the few reserves he had very far forward to give as much force as possible to the first and decisive blow.

The price paid for concentrating troops in the centre was the inclusion of a large number of allied troops, of whom most were deployed, other than on the Finnish front, in Army Group South. Hitler had a low opinion of

the Hungarians and Romanians, but they were nevertheless supposed to tie up the majority of the Red Army's forces in the Ukraine and then, together with the German 6th Army and Armoured Group 1, destroy them on the western side of the Dnieper before making a long advance to the oilfields of the Caucasus. This southern German wing was weakened even before the beginning of the assault, because a military coup in Belgrade prompted Hitler to set aside Yugoslavia's unsteady neutrality and launch an attack on Greece that would drive the British out of South-East Europe entirely. He had to redeploy a whole army that had been meant to support Romanian Army Group Antonescu.[172] The units sent to the Balkan campaign on 6 April 1941 either never reached the Romanian front after this detour or arrived late with their equipment in tatters.

To maximise the shock of the attack and accelerate the collapse of the Soviet regime, any sign of resistance from the population was to be repressed using the most brutal of methods, the communist elite was to be liquidated and the Jewish intelligentsia was to be murdered. Hitler wanted this war to be waged as an uncompromising campaign of destruction and exploitation, which meant intensifying and radicalising the warfare, something that the military leadership, despite some qualms, went along with. The political concept was just as half-baked and contradictory as Halder's operations plan. While Rosenberg whittled at his plans to dismember Russia and Goebbels pontificated about the 'true socialism' that Russia was to have the joy of experiencing, Hitler at least recognised the danger of moving away from the old model of a war of intervention. By deciding to destroy not only the Soviet Union and the Bolshevik system, but also the Russian soul, he was provoking a total war and, in doing so, gambling everything, including the future of his own regime, on one throw of the dice.

Goebbels on a conversation with Hitler on 16 June 1941:

Russia will not have tsarism reinstituted, but rather true socialism will replace Jewish Bolshevism. It gives every old Nazi a deep sense of satisfaction to know that we will live to see it. Cooperating with Russia was actually a stain on our honour. That will now be washed off. This thing we have fought against for our whole lives we will now destroy. I said that to the Führer and he agreed with me completely. [...] The Führer said: whether we do it rightly or wrongly, we have to win. That is the only way. And it is right, moral and necessary. And once we have won, who will ask us about our methods. We have so much on our slate as it is that we have to win, because otherwise our entire nation, including us at the top and everything we hold dear, will be wiped out.[173]

Hitler's eastern armies mobilised in the greatest secrecy and Stalin, despite numerous warnings from his intelligence services, continued to let important supplies roll across the German border until the very last minute. As late as May, he ignored his generals' proposal that the ever-more-obvious German deployment be countered with a preventive strike.[174] That would actually have done Hitler a great 'favour', because the Wehrmacht was extremely well prepared to ward off just such an attack and destroy the enemy by the Vistula and in Masuria – where there were still mass Russian graves left over from the battles of 1914 and 1920. Politically, too, this kind of suicidal attack by the Red Army would have been very welcome as an opportunity to put a better spin on the war both domestically and internationally, and to allow the Germans to begin their own campaign with victory in a huge defensive battle. But Stalin, unlike Hitler, was not a gambler and understood the art of biding his time. Moreover, he obviously did not yet believe that Hitler would violate his own fundamental principle by starting a war on two fronts. Stalin's shock was all the greater when he realised that the reports of German attacks on the morning of 22 June 1941 signalled the opening of a massive war of aggression.

Militarily, the start of the campaign was a complete success. The approximately 3 million soldiers of the German Eastern Army, supported by around 690,000 allied troops, had at their disposal 625,000 horses, 600,000 trucks, 3,648 tanks and 7,146 artillery pieces. With their qualitative and quantitative diversity of equipment and combat efficacy, they were arranged in three army groups with ten army high commands and four armoured groups, a total of 150 divisions. In the Soviet Union's western military districts alone, they were facing four army groups with ten army high commands; a total of 145 divisions and 40 brigades consisting of 2.9 million men and around 10,000 tanks. The numerical superiority of the German attack, an important assumption of Halder's, existed only in the most fleeting way. Behind the Soviet armies' western front lay considerable reserves and enormous resources that Stalin would succeed in mobilising for the 'Great Patriotic War', while the German Eastern Army was, as it were, eating into its capital.

A tremendous bombardment at three in the morning surprised most of the Soviet border troops in their sleep. The first attack was carried out by Göring's Luftwaffe. In the battle for aerial superiority, the crucial prerequisite for the strategy of blitzkrieg, the Luftwaffe deployed 3,904 aircraft, around half the number available to the Soviet Air Force. These, however, were taken entirely unawares on the airfields close to the front. On the first day of the war, 1,811 Soviet aircraft were destroyed; by the end of the battles around the border, on 12 July, the figure stood at 6,857. Göring's 'eagles' initially dominated the air, bombing the roads open for the army's spearheads, preventing the Red Army's encircled units from breaking out, and frustrating counter-attacks.

These tasks, and mounting losses, meant that all aircraft were committed, limiting the extent to which a strategic aerial war could be waged against the Soviet hinterland and Russian armaments production.

The strongest German formation was Army Group Centre, whose vanguard was formed by the two armoured groups in conjunction with elite units. By attacking with surprising concentrations of force and working with the Luftwaffe, they broke though the Soviet lines time and again and penetrated deep into the hinterland. Centres of resistance such as Brest Fortress were passed by and left to the infantry. The pincers then met behind the Soviets' main forces, creating pockets which the infantry destroyed or compelled to surrender in bitter and bloody fighting, while the armoured units were already making the next audacious advances to create another encirclement.

In the first weeks, the Red Army was unable to halt the German onslaught. Both sides suffered heavy losses in the battles to clear the pockets. Stalin, who, contrary to German expectations, managed to rally the strength of his enormous empire, was able to conjure up ever more new divisions and plug the holes in the front. He used brutal methods to prevent the reeling Red Army from disintegrating and set up both hefty counter-attacks and extremely dogged defensive positions. Hitler, on the other hand, kept back the Reich's reserves for the planned campaigns against the Anglo-Saxon powers and, in mid July, had the army's armaments programme slowed down to again give priority to the navy and the Luftwaffe.

The German General Staff hoped to destroy the bulk of the Soviet Union's western armies before the line of the Dnieper, in order to open the way for an advance deep into enemy territory. Halder assumed that the Red Army would give battle close to the border, because its doctrine was to resist an enemy attack and then immediately launch a massive counter-offensive to carry the war onto the enemy's territory and annihilate him there. But Halder was evidently not certain about this, because he insisted that the first great encirclement be extended as far back as possible in order to encompass any attempt by the Russians to withdraw. At the Battle of Białystok–Minsk, however, the advancing armoured units were unable to achieve a complete encirclement, and nor were the infantry able to entirely clear the pockets. Large sections of the Red Army escaped and went into hiding in the forests and marshes. This is where the partisan war began, sporadic at first, but giving the SS and the police the pretext for extermination programmes they had already planned.

When the battle ended on 9 July 1941, four Soviet armies had been beaten. The Germans managed to destroy or capture 1,809 artillery pieces and 3,332 tanks, as well as take 323,898 prisoners. Halder presumed that this meant the eastern campaign had essentially been decided. In two weeks, the army had advanced as much as 250 miles into enemy territory. Eastern Poland had been reconquered. In line with the original plans made in June 1940, the Wehrmacht now had in its possession the collateral that Halder had originally wanted as leverage for dictating the peace from this line. The task of destroying the bulk of the Red Army to the west of the Dvina and the Dnieper seemed to have been carried out. Halder turned his and General Paulus's attention to studies for an offensive from North Africa through Turkey and from the Caucasus into Iran.

Halder on how the war in the east was progressing, 3 July 1941:
I consider to be correct the statement by a captured Russian commanding general that we will have to deal with only fragmentary forces east of the Dvina and the Dnieper, none of which will be strong enough to decisively hinder German operations. It is not saying too much to assert that the campaign against Russia was won within 14 days. Naturally, that does not mean it is finished. The size of the territory and the stubbornness of the resistance being put up with all means at the Russians' disposal will occupy us for several more weeks.[175]

In the armaments sector, too, plans for the post-Barbarossa period began to take shape. The OKW had Hitler sign an order focusing production on submarines and aeroplanes at the expense of the army. But the armoured groups were already late in reaching Smolensk. They were supposed to prevent the formation of a new enemy front in the path of Army Group Centre. They did not succeed in doing so. The enemy had gained time and brought up fresh troops. Heavy storms delayed the Germans' advance for days and they had to become accustomed to ever heavier losses. From out of the Pripet Marshes, which had been consciously ignored during the planning process, the Red Army mounted intense counter-attacks.[176] So Guderian's Armoured Group 2 kept being held up on its right flank and being diverted from its proper direction of attack, the Moscow highway. Although they managed to cross the northern Dnieper, the Yelnya salient, which was the starting point for an attack on Moscow, could only just be held in the teeth of ferocious Soviet counter-attacks. There developed weeks of positional warfare – a heavy setback for Barbarossa.

22. On the edge of Operation Barbarossa: a Russian child near Smolensk, summer 1941.

Armoured Group 3 (Hoth), which had been deployed to the north of the highway, was able to seal off the Smolensk pocket on 24 July 1941. Although here, too, large numbers of enemy forces were able to escape, the Germans had nonetheless beaten three Soviet armies, taking 310,000 prisoners and destroying or capturing 3,205 tanks and 3,120 guns. The commanders of the western powers now also believed that Russia was on the brink of collapse. But the enemy again dug into positions in front of Army Group Centre and continued to fight fiercely. The German troops were exhausted and the other army groups were still far behind. Army Group South was stuck in front of the fortifications around Kiev, and Army Group North was struggling to push forward towards Leningrad.

The Wehrmacht's first blow had inflicted heavy defeats on the Red Army, but had not destroyed its 'active forces'. Carrying out an operational blitzkrieg after the element of surprise had dissipated proved to be riskier and more complicated than had been believed. The advance slowed down, the losses mounted. In the first five weeks, the German Eastern Army lost nearly a quarter (850) of its invaluable tanks. The Wehrmacht was experienced in war and very well led, but it was weakened by the resistance of the Red Army, which was not slacking off. The Germans were very confident in their eventual victory, but the mood in the Army High Command was tetchy and nervous.

On 16 July 1941, the presentation of the most important orders and appointments relating to occupation of the conquered areas prompted Hitler to plainly express his reading of events to his closest circle of advisers. Bormann's notorious minutes show that Hitler wanted to employ the most extreme of measures to control, exploit and settle conquered Russian territory.[177] In the belief, supported by Halder, that, despite the mounting difficulties, the military campaign was practically over and the only thing left was to make a push for Moscow, Hitler turned his attention to his secondary objectives. This led to weeks of increasingly heated dispute with the army's leaders about how the campaign was to be continued.[178]

Hitler in conversation with Army Adjutant Gerhard Engel while out walking on 28 July 1941:

He says he is not sleeping at night because there are a number of things he isn't yet clear on. There are two souls wrangling in his breast, one political-ideological and the other economic. Politically, he would say that the main abscesses have to go: Leningrad and Moscow. That would be the heaviest blow to the Russian people and the Communist Party. Göring has promised that he can do it just with his Luftwaffe, but he has become rather sceptical since Dunkirk. Economically, the objectives are quite different. Although Moscow is also a large centre of industry, the south is even more important, because there is oil, grain, absolutely everything needed to secure our Lebensraum. A land of milk and honey. One thing is clear in any case, that the forces are to be fundamentally restructured. Frittering away tanks to take cities is an offence against the intellect. They have to go into the open spaces to the south. He can already hear the complaints of those who are going to have to give them up; but that doesn't matter.[179]

Halder exerted himself to dissuade Hitler from this idea. The paralysis of the centre, which he so feared, could be tolerated only for a brief time. 'This solution frees every thinking solder from the terrible nightmare of the past few days, in which the Führer's intransigent attitude seemed to presage all too tangibly the complete petering out of the eastern operations.'[180] A week later, Hitler was still dissatisfied and seeking a different solution.

Engel's notes on the mood in the Wolf's Lair, 8 August 1941:

One notices at once how undecided F. [the Führer] is about how to continue the operations. His thoughts and objectives fluctuate constantly. You leave the situation

> meetings no smarter than you went in. This evening, the situation at the end of the day seems to have led to the following: Leningrad certainly must [be taken]; that has to be the case, for political and ideological reasons, and all the more so because Field Marshal von Leeb has said that he can manage it with a lot of artillery and Luftwaffe. In the centre: transition to defence. All mobile troops to go south: Ukraine, Donets Basin and Rostov. At the moment, F. sees the economic subjugation of the Russians as more important, especially as he is being informed from the front and by the OKH that the enemy is so badly beaten that there is no need to take an offensive force into account for the foreseeable future, and certainly not in this year.[181]

The zigzagging of Hitler's instructions led Halder to the verge of a nervous breakdown.[182] Hitler eventually rejected an army proposal that envisaged continuing the assault on Moscow as soon as possible. It was very unusual for the dictator – this was only the second time since his memo on the four-year plan in 1936 – to give a comprehensive written explanation for what he had decided. On 21 August, the army again presented its objective: to take Moscow, because in order to defend the capital and its centre of armaments production, the Red Army would fight a decisive battle. Hitler was of precisely the opposite opinion. Taking the capital would not end the war; Napoleon's example had shown that. 'He needs the Russians' lifelines: oil, grain, coal.'[183] Adjutant Engel had the impression that Brauchitsch and Halder were shying away from the confrontation. 'A black day for the army.'

A day later, Hitler presented his own study, which unambiguously showed that he had a different strategic and operational concept in mind.[184] Halder considered it impracticable. He even had Guderian, whose armoured group was at the heart of it, fly in and try to persuade the Führer that attacking Moscow would make more sense. In vain. In the face of Hitler, the blustering tank general was like a 'rubber lion', in the words of the commander-in-chief of Army Group Centre, General Field Marshal Fedor von Bock.[185] Guderian now even took Hitler's side. Halder toyed with the idea that he and Brauchitsch should offer their resignations. Adolf Heusinger, the head of the army's operations staff, was also ready to do so. They feared their forces would be overstretched and frittered away while the time factor was ignored. But Brauchitsch eschewed conflict with the dictator and asked his colleagues to stay in their posts.[186] When Halder finally resigned, he began the process of ascribing all the blame for embarking on Barbarossa, and for all the subsequent mistakes, to Hitler. In the pamphlet he published in 1949, *Hitler as a Field Commander*, he mercilessly settled the score. In line with his general leniency when it came to his own behaviour, he largely omitted the plenary preparations for Barbarossa, for which he had been responsible. He claimed the catastrophe had been inaugurated with Hitler's decision on 21 August 1941.

So in August 1941, the Wehrmacht had already passed the date on which the attack was scheduled to end, without having attained its objectives. The blitzkrieg had practically broken down. The consequence was a profound leadership crisis. While the Eastern Army rested briefly and prepared to try to push the battered Red Army ever further back, the prospect of a rapid end to the war evaporated. Hitler sought solutions on the strategic level, in so far as he understood it. So the SS stepped up the genocide of the Jews, which in the German dictator's anti-Semitic delusions was supposed, *inter alia*, to be a means of threatening US President Roosevelt, whom Hitler assumed was a stooge of the 'Jewish plutocracy'. The Atlantic Charter about joint postwar policy that Roosevelt and Churchill signed on 14 August (an end to territorial expansion; equality of access to world trade and raw materials; an end to the use of force; the right to self-determination; liberalisation of trade; freedom of the seas) demonstrated that Washington would no longer tolerate the expansion of the fascist power blocs and that the Allies were resolved to go to Stalin's aid with massive provision of supplies.

Now Hitler suddenly discovered the significance of Japan as a means of enmeshing the USSR in a war on two fronts, as had already been discussed in the 1930s. In the meantime, however, the Imperial Navy had won the upper hand in Tokyo and directed Japanese expansion south, against the British – which was what Hitler had wanted a year earlier. Now the Japanese again gave him the cold shoulder. Two years previously, he had left them in the lurch in Mongolia and, now that the Wehrmacht's advance on Moscow had become bogged down, the Japanese saw less reason than ever to change their course. The consequence was that Stalin, in total secrecy, moved his Far Eastern army into the western part of Russia as a strategic reserve and used it at the start of December 1941 to mount a counter-offensive outside Moscow, which took the Wehrmacht completely unawares and dealt it a tremendous blow, knocking it almost off its feet and costing two dozen generals their commands.

The inadequacy of the strategic preparations for the war in the east was shown also in the far north. With meagre German support, the Finns had taken on an enormous and difficult section of the front. As the Red Army retreated from the Baltic countries under intense German pressure and found its rear threatened by the Finns, there came a shocking about-face. The Finns made it clear that they were interested only in reconquering the regions lost in the Winter War of 1939–40 and were not willing to cross the previous borders. They were happy to leave Leningrad to the Germans. Hitler commanded that the metropolis be snuffed out by bombardment and starvation. The German troops were not to accept a surrender. He announced that he would later have the city flooded. Any survivors were to be sent east. But at the northernmost point of the eastern front, Murmansk, there was a shortage of the troops needed to take the crucial port and break the supply route used by the Allies. Outside Leningrad, Army Group North did not have the armoured forces required to rapidly occupy the city because Halder, contrary to the original plan, had refused to detach Armoured Group 3 from the mass of forces moving towards Moscow, and because the northern armies had even had to relinquish their own Armoured Group 4, which was sent to support the centre.

This decision was related to Hitler's intervention in operational leadership, which detached the Guderian group from the centre and ordered it south to conquer the Ukraine.[187] Outside Kiev, the German forces completed the greatest encirclement of all time, defeating five Soviet armies. The Germans took 665,000 prisoners and captured or destroyed 3,128 guns and 884 tanks. German propaganda announced that the end of the eastern war was at hand. But the war went on and on, moving ever further east until the pendulum began to swing back the way it had come.

From the Ukraine, the Italian writer Curzio Malaparte reported his impressions to the newspaper *Corriere della Sera* until German pressure led to his being ordered home and silenced by the Fascist regime.

From Curzio Malaparte's report, September 1941:

And dust and rain, dust and mud, tomorrow the roads will be dry, the huge sunflower fields will creak in the warm dry wind, then the mud will come again, and this is Russia, this is the Russia of the tsars, the holy Russia of the tsars, and this is also the USSR, dust and rain, dust and mud, this is the Russian war, the endless Russian war, the war in Russia in 1941. Nothing to be done, nothing to be done. Tomorrow the roads will be dry, then the mud will come again, and always corpses, burned-out houses, throngs of tattered prisoners with eyes like sick dogs, and again and again the carcasses of horses and machines, carcasses of tanks, of aeroplanes, of trucks, of cannon, of officers, NCOs and soldiers, of women, of old people, of children, of dogs, carcasses of houses, of villages, of towns, of rivers, of forests, nothing to be done, nothing to be done, into the distance, ever further, deep into the 'Russian continent', to the Bug, to the Dnieper, to the Donets, to the Don, to the Volga, to the Caspian Sea. Yes, yes, indeed. 'We are fighting for our bare lives.' And then winter will come. Lovely winter. And then again dust and rain, dust and mud, until it is winter again, the lovely winter of holy Russia, the Soviet Union's winter of steel and cement, this is the war against Russia in 1941. '*Da, da, da.*' We're conquering ourselves to death.[188]

Conclusion

'Danzig is not the objective that this is about': so said Hitler on 23 May 1939 when he met the leaders of his military to prepare them for the imminent war. It was, as so often, only half true. Controlling the port of Danzig and the so-called Corridor between Pomerania and East Prussia was indispensable to securing the Wehrmacht a northern avenue of advance against the Soviet Union. Without this supply route, an attack on the Baltic countries and a struggle with the Red Army could not have been contemplated. By proposing the occupation of Danzig, the dictator was following the logic of military necessity. Humiliating his Polish neighbour was only a side effect of the strategy with which Hitler aimed to get closer to his actual goal: unleashing a war for eastern Lebensraum against Russia. Since 1934, he had been making efforts to draw Poland onto his side, because the Poles had at their disposal the strongest military force on the USSR's western borders and had, under the regime of old Marshal Piłsudski, taken a strictly anti-Bolshevik line. With Poland as an ally or benevolently neutral, the Nazi government would have been able to realise its plans of aggression against the Soviet Union sooner rather than later.

Only in March 1939 did Warsaw ask for support from Great Britain and in doing so definitely reject Hitler's advances. That meant Poland ceased for the moment to be a potential 'anti-Russian trench'. Hitler's preparations for war against the country he had wanted as an ally might themselves have turned the tables again, if Poland had conceded to German pressure over Danzig or been left in the lurch by its new partners and sought an eleventh-hour agreement with the Reich. Then Hitler would finally have had a 'free hand in the east'. The Wehrmacht could have advanced along the northern avenue and through the Memel Territory onto the springboard of the Baltic states, as well as, in the south, via Vienna and Prague onto the springboard of the Transcarpathian Ukraine, which would take them towards Kiev. The USSR's armies would be caught in a pincer movement. Japan was ready to set up an additional front in the Far East. In view of the derisory condition of the Red

, the Wehrmacht could consider itself to have a good chance of dealing ussian troops a devastating blow and initiating the collapse of the USSR.

s we have seen, these ideas were by no means unrealistic in 1938–9. In the Wehrmacht's war games and among its plenary staffs, these thoughts were evidently at the top of the agenda – in contrast with war against the western powers, which Hitler would not rule out as a last resort but which was feared by his officers in a way that war against the Red Army was not. To prevent war in the west, the dictator was even willing, in August 1939, to conclude a formal pact with his arch-enemy. If his gamble had come off, the attack on Poland could also have been the start of war against the Soviet Union, just one of a number of possibilities in 1939.

The struggle against Bolshevism was Hitler's most popular idea, and not only among the German populace. It was on this that he based his foreign and military policy after 1933. By breaking off the secret cooperation with the USSR that had been maintained by the Reichswehr and the governments of the Weimar Republic, Hitler opened up new options for finding allies. These were supposed to allow him to soon wage war against Russia. Of course, he did not have a definite military concept. During the 1930s, he left that to his generals. After all, they had defeated the Russian Army in 1917. To this they added their studies of the wars on Russian soil between 1918 and 1920.

Hitler's 'ideological' ideas, as they are usually parsed from his political manifesto, *Mein Kampf*, are themselves derived from a confused agglomeration of the slogans popular among the right-wing extremists of the time. This was the provenance of his 'orientation on the east' – a volatile, contradictory concept, a utopia that was interpreted many very different ways within the Nazi movement, but did not imply any definite political programme. Hitler himself believed World War I had shown that Germany's most promising road to global power ran through the east. He wanted to take up where the German armies had left off in their victory over the tsar in 1917.

But the origins of Barbarossa, Hitler's eastern war of 1941, lie further in the past. As discussed above, the idea of a German war against Russia emerged at the end of the nineteenth century. The initiative came from fear of having to fight a war on two fronts. This strategic situation was then given a political-ideological dimension. But neither racist, culturally hostile stereotypes nor imperialist economic interests provided a compelling motive for military engagement. The General Staff, moreover, was in the business of sober analysis. And the Russian Army, despite its numerical strength, would present a serious threat to Germany only if the Reich found itself fighting a war on two fronts. In the German Army's operational thinking, the key was to decisively defeat the Russian Army close to the border, to take control of 'collateral' as well as, in favourable circumstances, the tsarist empire's 'sources of life' in the Baltic countries and the Ukraine, and then dictate the peace. Marching on Moscow – that is, into the depths of Russia – would have been dangerous and counter-productive. Napoleon's catastrophe in 1812 was not the only deterrent. Since a war on two fronts would actually be won or lost in the west, in the struggle against France, the Germans could not afford to have their forces committed to the Russian expanses.

With the Schlieffen plan, Imperial Germany finally settled on first deploying the bulk of its troops in the west in order to win a decisive battle there and then turn east afterwards. But the war took a different course than what had been planned. The western offensive became bogged down in the trenches, while the defensive war waged with meagre forces against the Russians turned into an unexpected success. In the east, too, however, there had first been a bloody war of attrition, this time on Polish soil, which continued until the Germans' political measures succeeded in accelerating the disintegration of the tsarist state. Despite the anti-Slavic propaganda and the pan-German ideology of 'racial struggle', the military's leaders had been able to employ a level-headed strategy for undermining the enemy. The support given to Lenin's revolution and the alliances with non-Russian independence movements helped them achieve the long-awaited breakthrough in 1917–18. The collapse of the Russian front and the treaty with the new, weak government even enabled the Germans to undertake operations reaching as far as the oilfields of the Caucasus. A march on Moscow would have been superfluous, because the Bolsheviks' Civil War was already sapping the strength of the Russian heartland.

But the German victory in the east came too late for the tide to be turned in the west. In the meantime, the USA had joined the war. The final German offensive failed. The Reich was forced to give up its fight to become a global power – a bitter experience for its elites and one necessary for understanding both the second attempt to seize global power, under Hitler, and the German General Staff's plans for war in the east.

After the German defeat, Poland was created as a new power in eastern Central Europe. The resurrection of the Polish state proved to be a stroke of luck for Europe, because this still-unstable country succeeded under the leadership of national hero Józef Piłsudski in fending off Lenin's Red Army. This created a situation in which the Baltic states, too, could assert their independence. Piłsudski, a former revolutionary, had used German help to fashion the core of the future Polish Army. However, he soon disengaged himself from this brotherhood-in-arms and, by making contact with victorious France, laid the foundation for Polish strength partly at the expense of the Reich.

The German military, newly re-formed as the Reichswehr, saw France as the chief obstacle to their country's renewal and, in order to cover themselves against a conflict with Poland, sought close cooperation with the Red Army. Anti-Bolshevism and other ideological considerations did not keep the military's leaders from the political conviction that Germany would be able to rise again only with Russian support. This Rapallo policy had the backing of a broad political consensus in the Weimar Republic, including its industrialists, who for a time planned to build economic bridgeheads in Soviet Russia capable of surviving a change of system. It was considered certain that Soviet communism would not last. At the same time, Germany tried to pressure Poland into agreeing to revisions of Germany's eastern border.

The consolidation of Stalinism and the global economic crisis put paid to this phase of German revisionist politics. The establishment of the Third Reich led to a reorientation of Germany's foreign and military policy. It was solely Hitler's decision to break off secret cooperation with Moscow in 1933 and instead to try to find a settlement with Poland. The Reichswehr and the Foreign Ministry, however, continued to favour maintaining good relations with the USSR. Hitler's spectacular pact with Piłsudski in 1934 made it seem possible to reinstitute the German–Polish anti-Russian partnership of 1914–15 and mount a joint war of intervention against the USSR. His most important political adviser on the east, Alfred Rosenberg, was given the task of preparing the concomitant political strategy. Like Hitler, Rosenberg hoped that Great Britain would provide backing for a German–Polish war of intervention. Their expectations centred on the Ukraine, whose independence struggle might herald the fragmentation of the USSR.

With the Anti-Comintern Pact, which Britain and Poland were supposed to join alongside Japan and Italy, Hitler wanted to create a political coalition that would allow him to act against his arch-enemy as soon as possible. But the British and the Poles refused to commit themselves, which did not stop Hitler from continuing to assume that an agreement would eventually be reached.

He was, however, not to succeed in realising his strategic plan, and this was his first failure in foreign politics. The claim made by historians that he had a step-by-step plan in which the attempts to woo Poland were mere chicanery has secured him a reputation as a successful strategist. But his supposed anti-Polish sentiment is largely a myth and the Rauschning conversations are unreliable reconstructions. The German–Polish alliance talks and the other moments of cooperation, including those on a military level, have been left largely uninvestigated in the Polish sources. The same applies to the internal disputes and foreign policies of the colonels' regime, which after Piłsudski's death steered the wavering course between two powerful neighbours that led to Poland's downfall.

Hermann Göring, who in the 1930s was the second most influential politician in the Third Reich after Hitler, made repeated efforts until 1939 to deepen German–Polish relations and lay the foundations for a war of intervention against the USSR. Hitler gave him the task of implementing the four-year plan to expand the economic basis for a war in the east. If Poland ultimately shied away from taking an active part in that, benevolent Polish neutrality would have sufficed for the German plans. The Wehrmacht had fixed its sights on the Soviet Union as early as 1935–6. Now that secret relations with the Red Army had been broken off, the General Staff again had to worry about the possibility of a war on two fronts. But this targeting of the USSR was not a question of territorial defence; after all, there was no German–Soviet border. It was no secret to the military that Hitler wanted to wage a war of intervention in the east, and to do so as soon as possible. The Wehrmacht had to make itself ready to exploit a favourable situation whenever one arose. It did not baulk at the thought. The first plenary work was undertaken in the navy, because a direct confrontation with the strong Soviet fleet was possible in the Baltic. Finland and the Baltic states would not be able to remain neutral; they would be extraordinarily useful as partners. That explains Berlin's intensive efforts to enhance its relations with these already pro-German states, which owed to the Reich the independence they had won in World War I.

The navy's leaders concluded that the only means of securing German dominance of the Baltic zone and its important supply routes would be a preventive war against Leningrad with overland support. This concept of a northern avenue of attack against the USSR fitted with the experiences of World War I and the older ideas of eastern policy that the Baltic German Rosenberg conveyed to his Führer. And any German advance into the east would have been highly jeopardised if there were no secure supply route via Danzig. So it was about Danzig after all, which was why Hitler exerted himself in the 1930s to soothe the simmering conflict with Polish interests over access to the Baltic. But the governments on both sides were not always able to suppress the passions of 'national struggle'. In Danzig, the National Socialists were pushing to rejoin the Reich; in Poland, the nationalist opposition stoked up anti-German feeling. The government in Warsaw, however, seemed open to giving Germany Danzig and an extraterritorial corridor connecting it to the Reich in exchange for receiving large parts of the Ukraine. But they could not allow the Germans to extort things from them or surprise them with a putsch in Danzig and insisted on being treated as an equal partner. So Danzig developed ever more into a matter of prestige that blocked the Germans' northern avenue against the USSR.

The southern avenue was blocked by Czechoslovakia, which had, moreover, concluded a mutual assistance pact with the Soviet Union. When Hitler, at the start of 1938, began his policy of aggressive expansion and gained his first victory in the south-east with the annexation of Austria, he found he had Poland's support for forcing Czechoslovakia to relinquish border provinces with German or Polish populations. After the Munich Conference, he could also assume that the western powers would ultimately tolerate further German advances in the east. If he managed to maintain and deepen this solidarity with Poland, it would open up new opportunities in the north, especially through pressure on Lithuania, and in the south-east, by controlling the Transcarpathian Ukraine. The Ukrainian nationalists, however, with whom German military intelligence was already intensifying its contacts, did not want to make any concessions to Polish interests. An uprising in the Soviet Ukraine could have been supported only via Polish-controlled Lviv. Warsaw feared that the Germans would use the support of the pro-German Slovaks and Transcarpathian Ukrainians to secure their southern avenue in the dismemberment of Czechoslovakia. But a Ukrainian uprising would necessarily have included Polish Galicia. And like Danzig, Lviv occupied a key position in Hitler's planned war of intervention against the USSR. If Poland had declared itself willing to join the Anti-Comintern Pact, it would probably have been easy to come to some understanding with Berlin. But Warsaw hesitated to demand the annexation of the Transcarpathian Ukraine and ultimately lobbied for giving the turbulent region to the Hungarians. This gave Poland a border with Hungary and the hope of extending its influence in South-East Europe, not least in order to counter-balance the ever-stronger German presence in the region.

This power-political rivalry, encouraged by the USA, put obstacles in the way of Hitler's eastern expansion, but could not set it any effective limits. Hungary and Slovakia both sought close cooperation with the Reich. In the Wehrmacht's war games and plenary studies for a southern offensive, the problem was not just Polish-Ukrainian Lviv but also the increasing Polish influence on Romania in spring 1939. Attempts by Germany's alliance partners, Japan and Italy, to mediate with Warsaw were in vain. But in the meantime, the prospects for a war of intervention against the USSR had dramatically improved. From its high point in 1935–6, the Red Army had been practically lamed by the murder of Tukhachevsky and a large part of its officer corps. The extensive 'purges' that Stalin used to stabilise his rule led to a lasting reduction of the USSR's strength. Berlin had been waiting for years for just such a moment of internal unrest. It also seems that Hitler had a hand in Tukhachevsky's downfall in 1937.

In spring 1939, everything was in favour of finally starting the war of intervention against the Soviet Union. Japan, after a test in the previous year, started things off in Mongolia. But Hitler was again unable to weave all his various threads together. The mutual distrust and rivalries of his potential partners in a fascist coalition were almost insurmountable. Italy annexed Albania and so became a competitor in the Balkans, and Poland sought protection from Britain as a bulwark against Hitler's pressure. The German dictator began to consider Poland a troublesome, even a dangerous obstacle to his eastern war. His policy of military extortion led the Wehrmacht into Prague in March 1939. Poland was left out and would now be exposed to a geographically extended German threat in the event of war. The Polish government trusted entirely in the assurances of the western powers and proved unwilling either to accommodate the German demands over Danzig or to consider military cooperation with the USSR. But the British–French efforts to conclude an anti-German alliance with Stalin were militarily meaningless in the east. Poland and Russia would never fight side by side on the Vistula, that much was certain, and Stalin had declared that he was not willing to pull anyone else's chestnuts out of the fire. So the Wehrmacht assumed in summer 1939 that the imminent attack on Poland would also lead on to a collision with the Red Army. Chief of Staff Franz Halder, who was later very keen to disguise his involvement in preparing a war of aggression against Poland, attempted after the end of the war to agree a version of events with his former adjutants, something that was recorded by the Americans.[1] No wonder almost all documents relating to the war games have been lost.

Halder was not worried about the eastern front in 1939, but he was about the prospect of Germany being drawn into another war on two fronts. Hitler found a novel strategic solution. His arch-enemy's hints that, in the right circumstances, he would be willing to make an agreement not with the west but with the Reich seemed to present a sensational way out – ideology or no ideology. A pact with Stalin seemed well suited to demoralising the western powers and isolating Poland. If Warsaw gave in to the German demands at the last minute, it would still be possible to set up a joint front against the USSR. Otherwise, it might be possible to defeat Poland with a sudden, overwhelming attack, prompting the western powers to consider their guarantees meaningless and give Hitler a free hand in the east, perhaps in partnership with a drastically reduced Polish satellite state on the 1916 model.

Hitler played an extremely risky game in August 1939 – and lost. The western powers could not be bluffed, but they did leave Poland in the lurch and take on trust that this unnatural alliance between the two dictators would not last long. They planned for a long war of attrition, of which there was a particular fear in Germany. Although the western powers accepted Stalin's annexations after the defeat of Poland, they accepted neither Hitler's territorial gains nor his 'offer of peace'. It was only now that Hitler was forced, if he wanted to retain the initiative, to develop a plan of attack for the west. His General Staff did not, as in 1914, have a Schlieffen plan on file. The long and dogged wrangling that now ensued between Hitler's determination to strike at the west and the extreme worry of the army's leaders is indispensable as a point of comparison for evaluating the switch to the east and the preparations for Operation Barbarossa that began a few months later. For Hitler, it was a case of postponing the war in the east until after victory had been won in the west. The timing of this switch to the east and the circumstances in which it could take place were still indistinct. Everything depended on forcing Britain to back down. The conflict with Stalin could wait, for years if necessary. Whether Hitler really imagined waiting for Stalin to die and the Soviet Union to be destabilised as a result, as he said to Goebbels, is anyone's guess. He was evidently not in a hurry.

Until the surprisingly swift victory in France, war in the east remained a future ambition for Hitler, not an urgent desire necessitating discussion with his intimates. What does it mean that Hitler, on 31 July 1940, announced his 'definite decision' to attack the Soviet Union in the spring? The period from that crucial moment in the history of World War II to the failure of Operation Barbarossa has been the subject of this investigation and the area where it has questioned the prevailing interpretation. Its conclusions are:

1. Purported statements made by Hitler in which he supposedly declared his intention to attack the Soviet Union at the end of June 1940 do not stand up to examination. Rather, one gets the impression that these quotations, printed mainly in postwar memoirs, were born of a desire to ascribe all blame for the German–Soviet war to Hitler. The statements and autobiographies of leading officers have connected these claims with the thesis that the Reich was in a strategic crisis situation as a result of Stalin's aggressive foreign policy and the westward advance of the Red Army.

2. Until now, little attention has been paid to the fact that the German plans for war were developed as a matter of routine, so to speak, by the German General Staff. The army's chief of staff, Franz Halder, used the deployment of AOK 18 for reasons of greater border security in the east as a means of again taking up the considerations and preparations of the previous year. The plan was to risk a rapid exchange of blows with the Red Army without any large-scale mobilisation, that is, from a standing start. With the Guderian group as a spearhead on either the northern or southern avenue and with a gradual reinforcement by other troops, whose unloading areas were already determined, it would be possible – Halder believed – in late summer 1940 to conquer 'collateral', especially areas of economic surplus in the Baltic states and the Ukraine, in order to then dictate the peace as in 1918. It could have been the war of intervention often considered in the preceding years, only without the Polish contribution.

3. By limiting himself to traditional operational thinking that aimed at fighting decisive battles close to the border, Halder ignored the political and strategic levels of a campaign that was to exceed all the previous dimensions of war. He relied on a static assessment of the enemy, which was not free of prejudices and clichés, but was not wholly unrealistic, either. This was not the pivotal point. As Stalin gathered in the last fruits of his pact with Hitler, occupying the Baltic states and Bessarabia, he extended his frontier zone in precisely the areas that the Wehrmacht considered its most important avenues of attack against the USSR. Compared with summer 1939, the Red Army now had a far more extensive forward buffer on which to give battle. Even if

the Wehrmacht managed to defeat significant parts of the Red Army on this terrain, the Soviet leadership would have time to form a new front along the fortifications of the older border, bring up reserves and newly mobilised units, and transport important industries deeper into the Russian hinterland. In this way, the aggressor's war of movement would become weaker from phase to phase, especially because the front would become broader and broader while the defenders reaped the benefits of operating on interior lines.

4. The basic concept of a decisive battle close to the border was originally to be complemented by a favourable political situation. In the 1938–9 model, the collision with the Red Army was not only supposed to take place 180 miles further east, but also be supported in the Baltic states by local military forces equivalent to around 20 divisions (they fell into the hands of the Red Army in 1940) and in the Ukraine by an uprising of anti-Soviet forces that would tie up the bulk of Stalin's armies. Moreover, a Japanese attack in the Far East would prevent Stalin from moving up strategic reserves and allow the German attack to concentrate on the northern and southern avenues – all elements that no longer appeared in the Halder plan in summer 1940.

5. What older history-writing described as the 'lesser solution' by no means aimed, and this must be emphasised, at the total destruction of the USSR. When, in July 1940, Hitler was briefed on the plans for an offensive approach to securing the eastern border, that evidently prompted him to again engage with his long-term goal of waging war in the east. In discussions of how to mount the conflict with Stalin after the expected agreement was reached with Britain and the war ended in the west, Hitler decided to wait for the victory over the British before the attack on the Soviet Union, but decided also that this would then consist not of individual thrusts from a standing start, but of an attack along the whole length of the front from the Baltic to the Black Sea. As to his motive, he was not primarily concerned – and nor was Halder – with defeating Bolshevism, but with improving his power-political situation. He would have waged his eastern war even if Russia had still been ruled by a tsar! In the German struggle for global power, the switch to the east after victory over Britain was to provide a Lebensraum invulnerable to any blockade. For Hitler, it was about territory and resources.

6. From Hitler's 'definite decision', Halder drew the conclusion that the operational plans should be centred on making a rapid assault on the enemy capital. In the following months, he subordinated everything to this traditional concept, while Hitler remained attached to the Baltic/Ukrainian idea.

Moreover, Halder had the concept drawn up with only half the Wehrmacht's plenary strength and – to prevent any friction – in closed circles. Priority was still being given to the war against Britain. There were numerous operations, such as attacks on Gibraltar and North Africa, as well as Operation Sea Lion, which were meticulously planned but not all of which were carried out. Halder was not convinced by Hitler's idea but did nothing to dissuade the dictator, nor even to improve the conditions for an attack. Of course he did not want, as in the previous year, to get involved in a test of strength with Hitler, especially as he must have had the impression that the dictator was in no way committed to his 'irrevocable decision'.

7. It was of the greatest significance for the course and outcome of Barbarossa that Halder was perfunctory and afraid of conflict when it came to the question of armaments and the development of a political strategy. The intervention model of the 1930s had generally been conceived as taking on the characteristics of a war of liberation. Even Rosenberg thought of the minorities in terms of freeing them from Russian dominance and the Bolshevik 'yoke'. Halder and the whole nationalist conservative elite could have taken this up in continuation of their experiences in World War I. Hitler, however, was not thinking in those terms, and Halder remained tight-lipped. So he considered it a personal success when he managed, against Hitler's will, to secure the Hungarians as partners for the eastern campaign, but did not say a word about how important it was to involve the Japanese. In this, Halder was striving to become a kind of imperial-era chief of staff and so assert the primacy of the army both over the rival branches of the Wehrmacht and in running the war as a whole.

8. Not only did the German Army in July 1940 already have the blueprint of an earlier plan – which was taken up by Hitler and was in March 1941 altered to become a plan for a racially ideological war of annihilation – but there are also clear indications that, after the war failed, Halder concealed his involvement in switching the Wehrmacht to the east and in planning Operation Barbarossa. Franz Halder, as an adviser to the US Army, his former adjutant and Barbarossa-planner Reinhard Gehlen, now head of the West German intelligence service, and Adolf Heusinger, the former head of Halder's operations staff, now the first inspector general of the Bundeswehr, all had good reasons for positioning Hitler as solely responsible for the war in the east and for the failure of a supposedly brilliant operational plan. Just like the other generals who needed an excuse for their participation, they

painted Stalin as the real offender. Members of the younger war generation, who shaped West Germany's idea of the Nazi period in their writing, cherished Halder and, to varying degrees, interpreted Hitler's motivation in deciding on Barbarossa as deriving not chiefly from the strategic situation, but from his racially ideological programme of Lebensraum and his concomitant step-by-step plan of expansion, which in July 1940 envisaged a breakthrough in the east.

It is time to finally shelve the idea of Hitler as a brilliant commander and Halder as the last chief of the General Staff to embody Prussian–German tradition. The conduct of Operation Barbarossa displays not only moral, but also professional failure on the part of a bygone military elite, of whom too few reached the insight that Staff Lieutenant Colonel Graf von Stauffenberg formulated thus in 1942: '[T]his war, from the moment when we made the mistake of attacking Russia, has not been possible for Germany to withstand, neither in men nor materiel and not even with the best of leadership.' And Staff Colonel Helmuth Stieff, Stauffenberg's boss in the organisation department, wrote to his wife on 10 January 1942: 'We have all burdened ourselves with so much guilt – because we are after all co-responsible – that I can only see this coming punishment as just atonement for all the shameful acts that we Germans have committed or tolerated in the past years.'[2]

Abbreviations

ADAP Akten zur deutschen auswärtigen Politik (Documents on German Foreign Policy)

BA Bundesarchiv (Federal Archives)

BA-MA Bundesarchiv-Militärarchiv (Federal Military Archives)

GB Generalbevollmächtigter für die Kriegswirtschaft (General Plenipotentiary for the War Economy)

GenStdH Generalstab des Heeres (Army General Staff)

GPU Gossudarstwennoje Polititscheskoje Uprawlenije (The Soviet Union's secret police)

HGr Heeresgruppe (Army Group)

NKVD Narodnyy Komissariat Vnutrennikh Del (People's Commissariat for Internal Affairs; Soviet secret police)

OB Oberbefehlshaber (Commander-in-Chief)

OKH Oberkommando des Heeres (Army High Command)

OKW Oberkommando der Wehrmacht (Wehrmacht Supreme Command)

Op.Abt. Operationsabteilung (Operations Staff)

PAAA Politisches Archiv des Auswärtigen Amtes (Foreign Ministry Political Archives)

PzGr Panzergruppe (Armoured group)

SA Sturmabteilung (Assault division, brownshirts)

SS Schutzstaffel (Protection squadron)

VfZG Vierteljahrshefte für Zeitgeschichte (Contemporary History Quarterly)

WFStab Wehrmachtführungsstab (Wehrmacht operations staff)

Notes

Introduction

1 An overview of the current state of research is provided by Rolf-Dieter Müller and Gerd R. Ueberschär, *Hitlers Krieg im Osten* (Darmstadt, 2000).

2 Hitler's address to soldiers on the eastern front, 22 June 1941, printed in Gerd R. Ueberschär and Wolfram Wette, *'Unternehmen Barbarossa'. Der deutsche Überfall auf die Sowjetunion 1941* (Paderborn, 1984), pp. 319–23.

3 For a discussion of the preventive war thesis, see: Bianka Pietrow-Ennker (ed.), *Präventivkrieg? Der deutsche Angriff auf die Sowjetunion* (Frankfurt, 2000); Rainer F. Schmidt, '"Appeasement oder Angriff"? Eine kritische Bestandsaufnahme der sog. "Präventivkriegsdebatte" über den 22. Juni 1941', in Jürgen Elvert and Michael Salewski (eds), *Historische Debatten und Kontroversen im 20. Jahrhundert. Jubiläumstagung der Ranke Gesellschaft in Essen, 2001* (Stuttgart, 2003), pp. 220–33; Dirk W. Oetting, *Kein Krieg wie im Westen. Wehrmacht und Sowjetarmee im Russlandkrieg 1941–1945* (Bielefeld and Bonn, 2009).

4 See Gerhard Schreiber, a colleague of Klink's, in *Das Deutsche Reich und der Zweite Weltkrieg*, 10 vols (Stuttgart and Munich, 1979–2008), vol. 3, p. 354, n. 273.

5 Andreas Hillgruber, 'Das Russland-Bild der führenden deutschen Militärs vor Beginn des Angriffs auf die Sowjetunion', in Hans-Erich Volkmann (ed.), *Das Russlandbild im Dritten Reich* (Cologne, 1994), p. 128.

6 See references in Christian Hartmann and Sergej Slutsch, 'Franz Halder und die Kriegsvorbereitungen im Frühjahr 1939. Eine Ansprache des Generalstabschefs des Heeres', *VfZG* 45 (1997), p. 467.

Germany and Its Neighbours to the East

1 See Konrad Canis, *Bismarcks Außenpolitik 1870–1890* (Paderborn, 2004).

2 See Klaus Hildebrand, *Bismarck und Russland: Aspekte der deutsch-russischen Beziehungen 1871–1890* (Friedrichsruh, 2003).

3 See comprehensively Mechthild Keller (ed.), *Russen und Russland aus deutscher Sicht. 19. Jahrhundert: Von der Jahrhundertwende bis zur Reichsgründung (1800–1871)* (Munich, 1991).

4 *Neue Rheinische Zeitung*, 15 February 1849; see generally Helmut Krause, *Marx und Engels und das zeitgenössische Russland* (Gießen, 1958).

5 See Keller, *Russen und Russland.*

6 Quoted in Fritz T. Epstein, 'Der Komplex "Die russische Gefahr" und sein Einfluss auf die deutsch-russischen Beziehungen im 19. Jahrhundert', in Immanuel Geiss and Bernd Jürgen Wendt (eds), *Deutschland in der Weltpolitik des 19. und 20. Jahrhunderts* (Düsseldorf, 1973), p. 149.

7 On 13 January 1887, quoted in ibid., p. 153; see also Michael Schmid, *Der 'Eiserne Kanzler' und die Generäle* (Paderborn, 2003).

8 See Epstein, 'Der Komplex', p. 149.

9 Ibid., p. 153.

10 Here in agreement with Andreas Hillgruber's *Bismarcks Außenpolitik* (Freiburg, 1972) against the contentious theses of Fritz Fischer's *Griff nach der Weltmacht. Die Kriegszielpolitik des kaiserlichen Deutschland 1914/1918* (Düsseldorf, 1964).

11 See Wolfgang Wippermann, *Die Deutschen und der Osten. Feindbild und Traumland* (Darmstadt, 2007).

12 See Piotr Szlanta, 'Der Erste Weltkrieg von 1914 bis 1915 als identitätsstiftender Faktor für die modern polnische Nation', in Gerhard P. Groß (ed.), *Die vergessene Front. Der Osten 1914/15* (Paderborn, 2006), pp. 153–64.

13 Norman Davies, *White Eagle, Red Star: The Polish–Soviet War, 1919–20* (London, 2003); Gerhard Wagner, *Der polnisch-sowjetische Krieg* (Wiesbaden, 1979).

14 *Der polnisch-sowjetrussische Krieg 1918–1920* (Berlin, 1940), vol. I. The planned second volume was never produced.

15 See *Das Deutsche Reich und der Zweite Weltkrieg*, 10 vols (Stuttgart and Munich, 1979–2008), vol. 8, pp. 608–12.

16 Agricola (pseud.), *Das Wunder an der Weichsel* (Berlin, 1937), p. 146.

17 See below, p. 229.

18 On his life, see Hans Meier-Welcker, *Seeckt* (Frankfurt am Main, 1967).

19 On Niedermayer's life, see Ulrich Seidt, *Berlin, Kabul, Moskau. Oskar Ritter von Niedermayer und Deutschlands Geopolitik* (Munich, 2003).

20 On the role of the Reichswehr, see, inter alia, Jun Nakata, *Der Grenz- und Landesschutz in der Weimarer Republik 1918–1933. Die geheime Aufrüstung und die deutsche Gesellschaft* (Freiburg, 2002).

21 See Rolf-Dieter Müller, *Das Tor zur Weltmacht. Die Bedeutung der Sowjetunion für die deutsche Wirtschafts- und Rüstungspolitik zwischen den Weltkriegen* (Boppard, 1984).

22 Erich von Manstein, *Verlorene Siege* (Bonn, 1955), p. 14.

23 Memorandum of Seeckt's on 11 June 1922, reproduced in Hans-Adolf Jacobsen (ed.), *Misstrauische Nachbarn. Deutsche Ostpolitik 1919/70. Dokumentation und Analyse* (Düsseldorf, 1970), pp. 33 f.

24 See overview in Włodzimierz Borodziej and Klaus Ziemer (ed.), *Deutsch-polnische Beziehungen 1939–1945–1949. Eine Einführung* (Osnabrück, 2000).

25 Norbert Krekeler, *Revisionsanspruch und geheime Ostpolitik der Weimarer Republik. Die Subventionierung der deutschen Minderheit in Polen 1919–1933* (Stuttgart, 1973); Rudolf Jaworski and Marian Wojciechowski (eds), *Deutsche und Polen zwischen den Kriegen. Minderheitenstatus und 'Volkstumskampf' im*

Grenzgebiet. Amtliche Berichterstattung aus beiden Ländern 1920–1939 (Munich, 1997).

26 Memorandum by Colonel Joachim von Stülpnagel on 6 March 1926, ADAP, B, vol. 1, pp. 341 ff.

27 The Polish civil-rights campaigner Adam Michnik in 1973, quoted in an essay by Gerhard Gnauck, 'Sperriger Nationalheld. Marschall Piłsudski – eine nicht unumstrittene Vaterfigur', *Neue Zürcher Zeitung*, 12 March 2005.

28 Ladislaus Sikorski, *La Campagne Polono-Russe de 1920: Préface de M. le Maréchal Foch* (Paris, 1928).

29 Reichswehrministerium (Heer), 'Die polnische Armee', 8 August 1927, BA-MA, RH 12–2/59.

30 Ibid., p. 30.

31 See the Troop Office's illustrated study 'Heeresmechanisierung und motorisierung in Polen', March 1931, BA-MA, RH 12–2/59.

32 Here and in the following: Heeresleitung, 'Die Sowjetrussische Armee', 10 June 1926, BA-MA, RH 12–2/59.

33 Müller, *Tor zur Weltmacht*, p. 147.

34 Note of Mittelberger's on 7 May 1928, PAAA Handakten Dirksen. On the annual inspection tours, see Mittelberger's memoirs contained in his estate, BA-MA, N 40/11.

35 State Secretary Carl von Schubert, quoted in Kirstin A. Schäfer, *Werner von Blomberg – Hitlers erster Feldmarschall* (Paderborn, 2006), p. 77.

36 Troop Office, No. 213/28, 17 November 1928, PAAA, Handakten Dirksen, Russische Militärangelegenheiten.

37 Schäfer, *Blomberg*, p. 70.

38 In his memoirs, written during World War II, quoted in ibid., p. 71.

39 Manfred Zeidler, *Reichswehr und Rote Armee 1920–1933. Wege und Stationen einer ungewöhnlichen Zusammenarbeit* (Munich, 1994), pp. 295, 298.

40 Schäfer, *Blomberg*, p. 78.

41 After various accounts, there is now also a record of the speech as presented to the Soviet secret service, see Andreas Wirsching, '"Man kann nur Boden germanisieren". Eine neue Quelle zu Hitlers Rede vor den Spitzen der Reichswehr am 3. Februar 1933', *VfZG* 49 (2001), pp. 517–50. On the problems with the speech and its interpretation, see Klaus-Jürgen Müller, *Generaloberst Ludwig Beck. Eine Biographie* (Paderborn, 2008), pp. 100–2.

42 Note of Fischer's on 13 September 1932, BA-MA, RH 1/79.

43 Hans von Seeckt, *Deutschland zwischen Ost und West* (Hamburg, 1933). Parallel considerations can be found in the oft-cited work of a German expert on Russia, Otto Hoetzsch, *Die weltpolitische Krafteverteilung seit den Pariser Friedensschlüsse*, 6th ed. (Leipzig and Berlin, 1933).

44 Note by General Curt Liebmann, reproduced at Thilo Vogelsang, 'Neue Dokumente zur Geschichte der Reichswehr 1930–1933', *VfZG* 2 (1954), pp. 397–436.

45 Friedrich Immanuel, *Der große Zukunftskrieg – keine Phantasie!* (Berlin, 1932), pp. 5, 54–60, 128. The author was a retired colonel whose work was published

by Offene Worte in Berlin's Bendlerstraße, where all the military's regulations were published.

46 Adolf Caspary, *Wirtschafts-Strategie und Kriegsführung. Wirtschaftliche Vorbereitung, Führung und Auswirkung des Krieges in geschichtlichem Aufriss* (Berlin, 1932), p. 224.

47 Paul Hilland, 'Autarkiemöglichkeiten der deutschen Metallwirtschaft. Zur Tagung der Gesellschaft Deutscher Metallhütten- und Bergleute in Berlin', *Die Deutsche Volkswirtschaft* 1/9 (1932), pp. 267–71. The author was executive president of the German Trade and Industry Congress.

48 The numerous verbatim quotations of Hitler's supposed statements are not authentic, but were constructed by Rauschning after the fact. He was evidently at pains to explain the recent attack on Poland through Hitler's state of mind, as he assessed it in 1939. Rauschning and Hitler met only a few brief times. The supposed 'conversations' are thus largely fiction. See Fritz Tobias, 'Auch Fälschungen haben lange Beine. Des Senatspräsidenten Rauschnings "Gespräche mit Hitler"', in Karl Corino (ed.), *Gefälscht! Betrug in Politik, Literatur, Wissenschaft, Kunst und Musik* (Nördlingen, 1988), pp. 91–105.

49 Hermann Rauschning, *Gespräche mit Hitler* (Zürich, 2005). Marcus Pyka's introduction examines its provenance and reception. See Jürgen Hensel and Pia Nordblom (eds), *Hermann Rauschning. Materialien und Beiträge zu einer politischen Biographie* (Osnabrück, 2003).

50 Martin Broszat, *Nationalsozialistische Polenpolitik 1939–1945* (Stuttgart, 1961), pp. 182 f.

51 Ian Kershaw, *Hitler. 1936–1945* (Stuttgart, 2000), p. 330.

52 Speeches on 28 July 1922 and 13 April 1923, reproduced in Ernst Boepple (ed.), *Adolf Hitlers Reden*, 3rd ed. (Munich, 1933).

53 See his article 'Ostorientierung?', *Völkischer Beobachter*, 18–19 April 1926.

54 Elke Fröhlich (ed.), *Joseph Goebbels. Die Tagebücher, Teil I: Aufzeichnungen 1923–1941*, 14 vols (Munich, 1997–2005), vol. 1, pp. 161 f. Goebbels's diaries are available in various partial English translations.

55 Adolf Hitler, *Mein Kampf* (Munich, 1927), vol. 2, p. 301.

56 Ibid., p. 316.

57 Marian Wojciechowski, *Die polnisch-deutschen Beziehungen 1933–1938* (Leiden, 1971), p. 7.

58 Thilo Vogelsang, 'Hitlers Brief an Reichenau vom 4. Dezember 1932', *VfZG* 7 (1959), pp. 429–57.

59 Werner Daitz, 'Außenhandelspolitik und Ostraumpolitik', Nationalsozialistischer *Wirtschaftsdienst* 23, 3 October 1932.

60 Bernd-Jürgen Wendt, 'Danzig – Ein Bauer auf dem Schachbrett nationalsozialistischer Außenpolitik', in Manfred Funke (ed.), *Hitler, Deutschland und die Mächte* (Düsseldorf, 1976), pp. 774–94.

61 Henryk Bułhak, *Polska-Francja: Z dziejów sojuszu 1933–1936* (Warsaw, 2000).

62 Quoted in Bernd-Jürgen Wendt, *Großdeutschland. Außenpolitik und Kriegsvorbereitung des Hitler-Regimes* (Munich, 1987), p. 78.

63 Günter Wollstein, *Vom Weimarer Revisionismus zu Hitler* (Bonn, 1973), p. 42.

64 Klaus Hildebrand, *Das vergangene Reich. Deutsche Außenpolitik von Bismarck bis Hitler* (Stuttgart, 1995).

65 H.Dv.g 26, 'Die russische Armee', 1 November 1933, BA-MA, RHD 5/26; see also Müller, *Tor zur Weltmacht*, pp. 254 f.

66 Quoted in ADAP, C, I/2, p. 463.

67 Speech by the head of the OKH on 1 July 1933, BA-MA, RH 1/v.79.

68 Schäfer, *Blomberg*, p. 71.

69 Note by Bülow, PAAA, Büro des Reichsministers, Az. 9, 'Russland', vol. 29.

70 Wolfgang Ramonat, *Der Völkerbund und die Freie Stadt Danzig 1920–1934* (Osnabruck, 1979).

71 Herbert von Dirksen, *Moskau, Tokio, London* (Stuttgart, 1949), p. 122.

72 Wacław Jedrzejewicz (ed.), *Papers and Memoirs of Józef Lipski, Ambassador of Poland* (New York, 1968), pp. 78–80.

73 Rainer F. Schmidt, *Die Außenpolitik des Dritten Reiches 1933–1939* (Stuttgart, 2002).

74 Karina Pryt, *Befohlene Freundschaft. Die deutsch-polnischen Kulturbeziehungen 1934–1939* (Osnabrück, 2010).

75 Heidi Hein (ed.), 'Documents and material on East Central European history – Modul Zweite Polnische Republik', [online], <http://quellen.herderinstitut.de/M01/texte/Abt04/Dok06.doc/TextQuelle_view> (accessed 16 August 2010).

76 On this largely unknown episode, see Verena Moritz, 'Information und Desinformation. Anmerkungen zur Rolle der "Österreichischen Legion" im Verhältnis zwischen Wien und Berlin 1933–1935', *Zeitgeschichte* 36 (2009), pp. 217–39.

77 Schmidt, *Außenpolitik*, p. 157.

78 Hildebrand, *Das vergangene Reich*, p. 590.

79 Rauschning, *Gespräche mit Hitler*, pp. 112 f. There are some doubts about its authenticity in Gottfried Schramm, 'Der Kurswechsel der deutschen Polenpolitik nach Hitlers Machtergreifung', in Roland G. Foerster (ed.), *'Unternehmen Barbarossa'. Zum historischen Ort der deutschsowjetischen Beziehungen von 1933 bis Herbst 1941* (Munich, 1993), p. 34. Theodor Schieder, in his *Hermann Rauschnings 'Gespräche mit Hitler' als Geschichtsquelle* (Opladen, 1972), made some criticisms, but still described it as a very valuable source. In any case, there is no record in other sources that Hitler made anti-Polish declarations in the early 1930s.

80 Max Domarus (ed.), *Hitler. Reden und Proklamationen 1932–1945. Kommentiert von einem deutschen Zeitgenossen*, 2 vols (Munich, 1965).

81 Hitler's statements taken from the account of the later Field Marshal Freiherr Maximilian von Weich, quoted in Hildebrand, *Das vergangene Reich*, p. 589. See also *Das Deutsche Reich und der Zweite Weltkrieg*, vol. 1, p. 582.

82 Fred W. Winterbotham, *The Ultra Secret* (London, 1974), pp. 4 f. During World War II, Winterbotham was head of 'Ultra', the top-secret operation that succeeded in breaking the German Enigma code.

83 See, for example, Gottfried Niedhart, 'Appeasement: Die britische Antwort auf die Krise des Weltreichs und des internationalen Systems vor dem Zweiten Weltkrieg', *Historische Zeitschrift* 226 (1978), pp. 67–88; Frank McDonough, *Hitler, Chamberlain and Appeasement* (Cambridge, 2002). From a Russian perspective, *Geschichte des zweiten Weltkrieges 1939–1945* (Berlin, 1975), vol. 2, p. 339.

84 Schmidt, *Außenpolitik*, p. 159.

85 Schramm, *Kurswechsel*, p. 34.

86 Marian Wojciechowski's work on German–Polish relations has still not been surpassed to this day, even though it appeared in 1965 in Poznań, then in German in Leiden in 1971. Her studies, too, are based largely on the early work by Hans Roos, that is, on German sources and the writings of Poles in exile. A comprehensive, source-based investigation of Polish reactions to German offers of alliance has yet to be produced.

87 Hans Roos, *Polen und Europa* (Tubingen, 1957), pp. 138 f.; Wojciechowski, *Die polnisch-deutschen Beziehungen*, p. 88.

88 Alexander Motyl, 'Ukrainian nationalist political violence in inter-war Poland, 1921–1939', *East European Quarterly* 19 (1985), pp. 45–55.

89 See comprehensively Frank Golczewski, *Deutsche und Ukrainer 1914–1939* (Paderborn, 2010).

90 Friedrich-Christian, Prince of Schaumburg-Lippe, *Ein Porträt des Propagandaministers* (Wiesbaden, 1963), p. 75. The author was Goebbels's adjutant.

91 Frank Grelka, *Die ukrainische Nationalbewegung unter deutscher Besatzungsherrschaft 1918 und 1941/42* (Wiesbaden, 2005), p. 142.

92 For more detail on the visit, see Schaumburg-Lippe, pp. 72–6.

93 Fröhlich (ed.), *Goebbels*, vol. 3, p. 63 (entry for 16 June 1934).

94 Title page of the reports on the Eastern Zone, March 1935.

95 Walter Geisler, 'Die deutsch-polnische Raumgemeinschaft im Gesamt-Ostraum', *Ostraum-Berichte* 1 (1935), pp. 9–20.

96 Roos, *Polen*, p. 140.

97 German embassy in Moscow, No. A/90, 'Die Gestaltung der deutsch-russischen Beziehungen', 9 January 1934, ADAP, C, II/1, No. 171.

98 Quoted by Nadolny, ibid.

99 Note: 'Unser Verhältnis zu Sowjetrussland', ibid.

100 According to the account of Major-General Eugen Ott, the former German military attaché in Tokyo, Hitler thought deeply in January 1934 about the possibility of attacking the Soviet Union and dismissed Ott's misgivings by saying: 'I disagree. I'm judging instinctually here. The future will show which of us is right.' Message of Ott's on 16 March 1955, quoted in Roos, *Polen*, p. 144.

101 The head of the Troop Office, T3 Ia No. 137/34g., 'Military-political Study Far East 1934', 29 April 1934, BA-MA, RH 2/v.1877.

102 Hans-Günther Seraphim (ed.), *Das politische Tagebuch Alfred Rosenbergs 1934/35 und 1939/40* (Munich, 1964), Appendix, pp. 163–7 (entry for 12 May 1934).

103 Ibid., p. 16 (entry for 29 May 1934).
104 Ibid., p. 41 (entry for 11 June 1934).
105 Speech by the head of the Eastern department, Georg Leibbrandt, at the start of 1934, PAAA, 'Geheimakten 1920–1936, Az. Russland, Pol. 2, Politische Beziehungen Russland zu Deutschland', vol. 12. In 1941, Leibbrandt became head of the main political department in the Reich Ministry for the Occupied Eastern Territories.
106 Thus according to unverifiable information from Litvinov published in 1955; see Roos, *Polen*, p. 145.
107 Josef Piłsudski, *Erinnerungen und Dokumente* (Essen, 1935), p. 5. There were numerous other publications in Germany that bolstered a positive image of the marshal; see, for example: Heinrich Koitz, *Männer um Pilsudski* (Breslau, 1934); A. Loessner, *Josef Piłsudski. Eine Lebensbeschreibung auf Grund seiner eigenen Schriften* (Leipzig, 1935); Friedrich Wilhelm von Oertzen, *Marschall Pilsudski* (Berlin, 1935); Josef Piłsudski, *Gesetz und Ehre* (Jena, 1935).
108 The German Armed Forces Military History Research Office library has copy No. 179.
109 Seraphim, *Tagebuch Rosenbergs*, p. 66 (entry for 21 January 1935).
110 Roos, *Polen*, p. 209.
111 Wojciechowski, Die deutsch-polnischen Beziehungen, p. 107.
112 Report by the German ambassador on Göring's visit to Warsaw, 1 February 1935, in ADAP, C, III, No. 474, pp. 877 f.
113 Seraphim, *Tagebuch Rosenbergs*, p. 68 (entry for 2 February 1935).
114 Message from General Schindler to Beck about the conversation with Blomberg on 22 February 1935, BA-MA, N 28/1. The Polish account, which is based on documents later published in exile, claims that the proposals for a military alliance were made by Göring; see Roos, *Polen*, pp. 210 f.
115 Reports from the ambassador on 22 January 1935 and the military attaché on 23 January 1935, quoted in Roos, *Polen*, p. 210.
116 Szembek's diary, published in 1942 (entry for 1 February 1935), quoted in Golczewski, *Deutsche und Ukrainer*, p. 680.
117 According to Golczewski, the Polish politicians were 'not uninterested', ibid.
118 That was what the French ambassador had been told; see J. Laroche, *La Pologne de Pilsudski. Souvenirs d'une ambassade 1926–1935* (Paris, 1953). The most important Polish sources are Szembek's diary and the Polish government's White Papers on Polish–German and Polish–Soviet relations between 1933 and 1939.
119 Roos, *Polen*, p. 211, n. 15.
120 Golczewski, *Deutsche und Ukrainer*, p. 681. There do not seem to be any reliable sources for this meeting. The Polish generals are said to have asked Göring to be a little more reticent with the marshal; see Roos, *Polen*, p. 211.
121 Here contrary to the interpretation in Roos, *Polen*, p. 211.
122 Lew Sozkow, *Sekrety Polskoi Politiki* (Moscow, 2009), pp. 17–20.
123 See Wojciechowski, *Die deutsch-polnischen Beziehungen*, p. 264.

124 Archiwum Akt Nowych (Warsaw), Ministerstwo Spraw Zagranicznych 108. I thank Prof. Marek Kornat for the information.

125 See Schmidt, *Außenpolitik*, p. 165.

126 Fröhlich (ed.), *Goebbels*, vol. 2, p. 504.

127 See Rudolf A. Mark (ed.), *Vernichtung durch Hunger. Der Holodomor in der Ukraine und der UdSSR* (Berlin, 2004).

128 See Müller, *Tor zur Weltmacht*, p. 281.

129 On this, see Gerhard Groß, *Von Moltke bis Heusinger. Operatives Denken im deutschen Heer* (Paderborn, 2012).

130 'War games' on the level of the General Staff rest on assumptions and posited situations, which provide the material for training leadership processes, just as, on the troop level, on 'manoeuvres', they are used to train the equivalent skills. Usually, two groups are formed, 'red' and 'blue'. The referees' situational information should be as accurate as possible. See Lieutenant General Halder, 'Warum Manöver?', *Die Wehrmacht*, 28 September 1937, p. 1. In 1937, Halder was in charge of the only large-scale Wehrmacht manoeuvre, which his biographer, Christian Hartmann, calls 'an enormous run-through for the imminent war'; see Christian Hartmann, *Halder. Generalstabschef Hitlers 1938–1942*, 2nd ed. (Paderborn, 2010), p. 421. The extant documents for these war games do not necessarily indicate definite intentions on the part of the military's leaders. Plenary studies and directives for feasible scenarios are produced in preparation for making possible 'decisions', but they do not mean that they will be enacted. The same goes for mobilisation and alarm plans for individual units; they do not come into force until issued as orders.

131 Müller, *Beck*, pp. 232 f.

132 Navy War Academy, 'Strategisches Kriegsspiel No. 2', F.A. 1933/35, vol. 1, BA-MA, RM 20/965.

133 Reichswehrministerium/Ausl. I, No. 1744/35, re the Russian air force's options for deployment against Germany, 23 May 1935, PAAA, estate of Renthe-Fink, Pk. 3, No. 19.

134 Inspector of the communications troops to the chief of the army's General Staff, 'Sondereinsatz Estland', 21 May 1937, BA-MA, RH 2/3007.

135 Documents for Fritsch for notification of Finnish officers, 27 September 1935, BA-MA, RH 1/v.79.

136 Psychological research department of the defence ministry, No. 241/35g, 'Investigations into national psychologies', No. 5 of 2 November 1935 and No. 6 of 2 December 1935, BA-MA, RH 2/v.981.

137 General Max Hoffmann, *Der Krieg der versäumten Gelegenheiten* (Munich, 1923).

138 Piłsudski, *Erinnerungen und Dokumente*, vol. 2, pp. xiii f.

139 Agricola, *Wunder an der Weichsel.*

140 See Bogdan Musial, *Kampfplatz Deutschland. Stalins Kriegspläne gegen den Westen* (Berlin, 2008).

A War of Intervention against the Soviet Union?

1 Situation report, Army General Staff, Operations Department, 7 August 1939, BA-MA, RH 2/724.

2 Marek Jabłonski, *Wobec zagrożenia wojna. Wojsko a gospodarka Drugiej Rzeczypospolitej w latach 1935–1939* (Warsaw, 2001).

3 Rolf-Dieter Müller, *Das Tor zur Weltmacht. Die Bedeutung der Sowjetunion für die deutsche Wirtschafts- und Rüstungspolitik zwischen den Weltkriegen* (Boppard, 1984), pp. 282 f.

4 Notes on the speech on 12 November 1935 in the Wehrmacht Academy, BA-MA, RH 8/v.957.

5 Note for Rosenberg on 25 November 1935, BA, NS, 43/49.

6 Message from Göring's chief adjutant to Captain von Friedeburg, 18 February 1936, BA-MA, RW 6/v.102.

7 Quoted in Frank Golczewski, *Deutsche und Ukrainer 1914–1939* (Paderborn, 2010), p. 681, n. 10.

8 Account of a conversation about the general European situation and Hitler's plans between the American ambassador to France, William C. Bullitt, and Foreign Minister von Neurath on 18 May 1936 in Berlin, quoted in *Der Prozeß gegen die Hauptkriegsverbrecher vor dem Internationalen Militärgerichtshof. 14. Nov. 1945 – 1. Okt. 1946*, 42 vols (Nuremberg, 1947 and after), vol. 37, pp. 588–92, doc. 150-L.

9 Wilhelm Treue (ed.), 'Hitlers Denkschrift zum Vierjahresplan', *VfZG* 3 (1955), pp. 184–210; see *Das Deutsche Reich und der Zweite Weltkrieg*, 10 vols (Stuttgart and Munich, 1979–2008), vol. 1, p. 276.

10 Speech made by Hitler at the annual meeting of the Deutsche Arbeitsfront, 12 September 1936, quoted in Max Domarus (ed.), *Hitler. Reden und Proklamationen 1932–1945. Kommentiert von einem deutschen Zeitgenossen*, 2 vols (Munich, 1965), vol. 2, p. 642; see also Manfred Weißbecker, '"Wenn hier Deutsche wohnten..." Beharrung und Veränderung im Rußlandbild Hitlers und der NSDAP', in Hans-Erich Volkmann (ed.), *Das Russlandbild im Dritten Reich* (Cologne, 1994), pp. 9–54.

11 Winston Churchill, *Der zweite Weltkrieg* (Stuttgart, 1954), vol. 1, p. 276.

12 *Der Prozeß*, vol. 36, p. 490, doc. 416-EC.

13 Note on a conversation of high-ranking Luftwaffe officers presided over by Göring, 2 December 1936; see ibid., vol. 32, doc. 416-EC, p. 335.

14 Report from 24 June 1936, quoted in Wilhelm Deist, 'Die deutsche Aufrüstung in amerikanischer Sicht. Berichte des US-Militärattaches in Berlin aus den Jahren 1933–1939', in Alexander Fischer et al. (eds), *Russland-Deutschland-Amerika* (Wiesbaden 1978), pp. 279–95.

15 See Gerhard Krebs, *Japans Deutschlandpolitik 1935–1941*, 2 vols (Hamburg, 1984).

16 Elke Fröhlich (ed.), *Joseph Goebbels. Die Tagebücher, Teil I: Aufzeichnungen 1923–1941*, 14 vols (Munich, 1997–2005), vol. 2, p. 622 (entry for 9 June 1936).

17 Ibid., pp. 726 f. (entry for 15 November 1936).

18 Marian Wojciechowski, *Die polnisch-deutschen Beziehungen 1933–1938* (Leiden, 1971), pp. 329 f. Stalin was given detailed information about this conversation by an agent in the Polish Foreign Ministry; see the report to Stalin dated 25 March 1937 in Lew Sozkow, *Sekrety Polskoi Politiki* (Moscow, 2009), pp. 132–6.

19 Hans Roos, *Polen und Europa* (Tubingen, 1957), pp. 242 f.

20 Ibid., p. 243, with statements from Brauchitsch and Manstein.

21 Wojciechowski, *Die deutsch-polnischen Beziehungen*, pp. 336–8.

22 Ibid., p. 339.

23 Hitler to State Secretary Szembek on 12 August 1936. Germany was said to have no interest in disturbing the Polish–French relationship, 'as long as the loyalty of the German–Polish relationship did not suffer from it'; quoted in Roos, *Polen*, p. 244.

24 Marek Kornat, *Polityka równowagi 1934–1939. Polska między Wschodem a Zachodem* (Krakow, 2007).

25 There has been no comprehensive analysis of Polish–Japanese relations. I refer to the work of Gerhard Krebs, 'Japanische Schlichtungsbemuhungen in der deutsch-polnischen Krise 1938–39', *Japanstudien, Jahrbuch des Deutschen Instituts für Japanstudien* 2 (Munich, 1991), pp. 207–58.

26 See ibid., p. 208.

27 On speculation about a secret Japanese–Polish military pact, see Rolf Ahmann, *Nichtangriffspakte: Entwicklung und operative Nutzung in Europa 1922–1939* (Baden-Baden 1988), pp. 195–203.

28 Speech by Himmler on the Wehrmacht's education in national politics, January 1937, *Der Prozeß*, vol. 29, p. 234, doc. 1992(A)-PS.

29 Speech by government adviser Dr Burandt: 'Principles, implementation and lessons of a war game for the General Plenipotentiary for the War Economy', Institut für Zeitgeschichte, 3 February 1937, MA-468, pp. 5764–74.

30 See Kurt Hesse, 'Rohstoffwirtschaft in ihrer Bedeutung für die Kriegsführung', *Der deutsche Volkswirt* 11 (1937), pp. 961 ff., and the remarks of the former inspector of motor-transport troops Erich von Tschischwitz, 'Der Kriegsplan unter vorwiegender Betrachtung des Landkrieges', *Militärwissenschaftliche Rundschau* 2 (1937), p. 580.

31 Note of Schacht's on 6 February 1937 and message of Neurath's on 11 February 1937 reproduced in Johann Wolfgang Brügel (ed.), *Stalin und Hitler. Pakt gegen Europa* (Vienna, 1973).

32 Patrik von zur Mühlen, *Zwischen Hakenkreuz und Sowjetstern* (Düsseldorf, 1971), p. 37.

33 Sozkow, *Sekrety Polskoi Politiki*, pp. 48–50 (NKVD report of 10 February 1936) and pp. 210 f. (document from the Polish General Staff on intelligence work about the USSR, 31 August 1937).

34 Oscar Reile, *Geheime Front. Die deutsche Abwehr im Osten 1921–1945* (Munich, 1963), p. 254.

35 Rudolf Ströbinger, *Stalin enthauptet die Rote Armee. Der Fall Tuchatschewskij*

(Stuttgart, 1990). In 1939, the Wehrmacht's official publishing house was still selling a novelistically presented biography in which he was described as the cold, merciless and exorbitantly ambitious scion of an old noble family, 'who after his successful career was buried in some Russian field'; see Agricola (pseud.), *Der Rote Marschall. Tuchatschewskis Aufstieg und Fall* (Berlin, 1939).

36 Wojciechowski, *Die deutsch-polnischen Beziehungen*, p. 340.

37 Theo Sommer, *Deutschland und Japan zwischen den Mächten 1935–1940* (Tubingen, 1962), p. 56.

38 Wojciechowski, *Die deutsch-polnischen Beziehungen*, p. 332.

39 BA-MA, RH 2/1054.

40 Klaus-Jürgen Müller, *Generaloberst Ludwig Beck. Eine Biographie* (Paderborn, 2008), p. 183.

41 Ibid., p. 181.

42 See the account of the activities of Dr Taubert (anti-Bolshevism in the Propaganda Ministry) until 31 February 1944, partially reproduced in Friedrich Arnold Krummacher and Helmut Lange, *Krieg und Frieden. Geschichte der deutschsowjetischen Beziehungen* (Munich and Esslingen, 1970). Eberhard Taubert was a departmental head in the ministry; during the war game, he was the head of the blues' propaganda company, i.e. the German side. After 1941, he was head of the 'General Department Eastern Zone'.

43 Golczewski, *Deutsche und Ukrainer*, p. 773.

44 Fröhlich (ed.), *Goebbels*, vol. 3, pp. 348 f. (entry for 28 January 1937).

45 Assignment of tasks for Case Red, March 1937, as well as further documents in BA-MA, RW 13/22 and 23.

46 Müller, *Beck*, p. 240.

47 Directive on 23 June 1937, reproduced in *Der Prozeß*, vol. 34, pp. 732 ff.

48 Memorandum from Fritsch to Blomberg in August 1937, reproduced in Walther Görlitz (ed.), *Generalfeldmarschall Keitel. Verbrecher oder Offizier? Erinnerungen, Briefe, Dokumente des Chefs OKW* (Göttingen, 1961).

49 See Müller, *Beck*, pp. 258–74.

50 Wojciechowski, *Die deutsch-polnischen Beziehungen*, p. 335.

51 On the complicated story of its provenance and the recurring doubts about the authenticity of Hitler's reported statements, see Bradley F. Smith, 'Die Überlieferung der Hoßbach-Niederschrift im Lichte neuer Quellen', *VfZG* 38 (1990), pp. 329–36.

52 See Müller, *Beck*, pp. 271 f.

53 Luftwaffe plenary study, 1938, BA-MA, RL 7/61–64.

54 Tasks assigned to the navy in 1937–8, quoted in Gerhard Schreiber, 'Zur Kontinuität des Groß- und Weltmachtstrebens der deutschen Marineführung (Dokumentation)', *MGM* 26 (1979), pp. 101–71.

55 See particularly the concluding discussion of war game A, BA-MA, RM 20/1100.

56 Ibid., p. 11.

57 Ibid., pp. 118 f.

58 Navy war game 1938, BA-MA, RM 20/1095.

59 Discussion concluding the operational war game of Station O, 1938, BA-MA, RM 20/1102.
60 Ibid., p. 76.
61 Ibid., p. 80.
62 Ibid., p. 81.
63 Speech notes for the commander-in-chief, RM 20/1100, p. 4.
64 Ibid., p. 6.
65 Wojciechowski, *Die deutsch-polnischen Beziehungen*, p. 393.
66 Piotr Łosswoski, *Ultimatum polskie do Litwy 17 marca 1938 roku* (Warsaw, 2010), pp. 305–17.
67 Ibid., p. 399.
68 Report by the German ambassador to Warsaw, Moltke, 22 March 1938, ADAP, D, V, doc. 33.
69 Wojciechowski, *Die deutsch-polnischen Beziehungen*, pp. 404 f.
70 See, for example, Rainer F. Schmidt, *Die Außenpolitik des Dritten Reiches 1933–1939* (Stuttgart, 2002), p. 318.
71 Müller, *Beck*, pp. 313–19.
72 Ibid., p. 319.
73 Thus according to the report of his personal adjutant, Fritz Wiedemann, quoted in ibid., p. 322. Müller doubts the verbatim reproduction of Hitler's statements, but not their gist.
74 Galeazzo Ciano, *Tagebücher 1937/38* (Hamburg, 1949), p. 157.
75 On the Polish position and military preparations against Czechoslovakia, see Marian Zgorniak, *Europa am Abgrund 1938* (Berlin, 2002), and Marek Piotr Deszczyński, *Obstatni Egzamin. Wojsko Polskie wobec kryzysu czechosłowackiego 1938–1939* (Warsaw, 2003).
76 See Detlef Brandes, *Die Sudetendeutschen im Krisenjahr 1938* (Munich, 2008).
77 Müller, *Beck*, pp. 323 f.
78 See report on the war games for leading officers 'Thüringen 115 – 22.05.38', BA-MA, RL 7/155.
79 Müller, *Beck*, p. 335.
80 Ibid., p. 323.
81 See Hans Ehlert, Michael Epkenhans and Gerhard P. Groß (eds), *Der Schlieffenplan. Analysen und Dokumente* (Paderborn, 2006).
82 On his life, see Christian Hartmann, *Halder. Generalstabschef Hitlers 1938–1942*, 2nd ed. (Paderborn, 2010).
83 Still in February 1945, quoted in Sebastian Haffner, *Anmerkungen zu Hitler*, 26th ed. (Frankfurt am Main, 2006), p. 51.

The Turning Point in German–Polish Relations

1 Beck's instructions to Lipski on 19 September 1938, reproduced in Marian Wojciechowski, *Die polnisch-deutschen Beziehungen 1933–1938* (Leiden, 1971), pp. 468 f.

2 In this case, Ribbentrop was speaking about the Reich adopting a benevolent position; see ibid., p. 508.

3 Oscar Reile, *Geheime Front. Die deutsche Abwehr im Osten 1921–1945* (Munich, 1963), p. 245.

4 Message from the OKW on 5 October 1938, ADAP, D, IV, doc. 39; note by Undersecretary of State Ernst Woermann, 7 November 1938, ibid., doc. 46.

5 Conversation on 14 October 1938, ibid., doc. 62.

6 Wojciechowski, *Die deutsch-polnischen Beziehungen*, p. 540.

7 For a Polish perspective, see Stanisław Żerko, *Stosunki polsko-niemieckie 1938–1939* (Poznan, 1998).

8 Andreas Hillgruber, 'Deutschland und Polen in der internationalen Politik 1933–1939', in Ernst Hinrichs (ed.), *Deutschland und Polen von der nationalsozialistischen Machtergreifung bis zum Ende des Zweiten Weltkrieges* (Braunschweig, 1986), p. 52.

9 Wojciechowski, *Die deutsch-polnischen Beziehungen*, pp. 539–51.

10 Quoted in Frank Golczewski, *Deutsche und Ukrainer 1914–1939* (Paderborn, 2010), p. 816.

11 Galeazzo Ciano, *Tagebücher 1937/38* (Hamburg, 1949), p. 40 (entry for 9 November 1937). In this sketch of the Anti-Comintern Pact's future, Ciano considered the cooperation of three countries to be especially important: Spain as a bridge to the Atlantic, Brazil to dominate South America and, in the east, Poland as a bulwark against the USSR.

12 BA-MA, RHD 18/623, *Taschenbuch Polnisches Heer*, p. 7.

13 Gerhard Krebs, *Japans Deutschlandpolitik 1935–1941*, 2 vols (Hamburg, 1984), p. 215.

14 Affidavit from 28 August 1945, quoted in *Der Prozeß gegen die Hauptkriegsverbrecher vor dem Internationalen Militärgerichtshof. 14. Nov. 1945 – 1. Okt. 1946*, 42 vols (Nuremberg, 1947 and after), vol. 28, pp. 238 f., doc. 1759-PS.

15 Ciano, *Tagebücher*, pp. 296 f. (entry for 15 December 1938).

16 Note of Beck's in the Polish government White Papers, doc. 48.

17 Here and in the following as recorded by the diplomat Schmidt, 5 January 1939, ADAP, D, IV, No. 119, p. 128.

18 Note of Ribbentrop's on 9 January 1939, ibid., No. 120, p. 133. The Polish sources and particularly Beck's memoirs indicate that Warsaw believed, despite Hitler's declarations, that Germany had serious ambitions in the Ukraine, which made settling the Danzig question seem impossible. See critically Hans Roos, *Polen und Europa* (Tubingen, 1957), p. 392, especially n. 107.

19 Ibid., pp. 133 f.

20 Dirksen on 4 January 1939, ADAP, D, IV, pp. 316 f.

21 Oshima's report on 27 December 1938 about his talks with Hitler was handed over to the Polish government by the Japanese ambassador to Warsaw; see Roos, *Polen*, p. 392.

22 Ibid., p. 395.

23 Frank Grelka, *Die ukrainische Nationalbewegung unter deutscher Besatzungsherrschaft 1918 und 1941/42* (Wiesbaden, 2005), p. 179.

24 Jürgen Pagel, *Polen und die Sowjetunion 1938–1939* (Stuttgart, 1992).
25 See Grelka, *Die ukrainische Nationalbewegung*, p. 179.
26 According to Kornat's interpretation in 'Sehenden Auges. Polens Außenpolitik vor dem Hitler-Stalin-Pakt', *Osteuropa* 59/7–8 (2009), pp. 47–74.
27 Note of Ribbentrop's on 1 February 1939, ADAP, D, V, No. 126.
28 Roos, *Polen*, pp. 396 f., with reference to the Polish sources.
29 Krebs, *Japanische Schlichtungsbemühungen*, p. 222.
30 Quoted in Golczewski, *Deutsche und Ukrainer*, p. 872; the author remarks on the uncertain provenance of the source.
31 Roos, *Polen*, p. 397.
32 Paul Leverkuehn, *Der Geheime Nachrichtendienst der deutschen Wehrmacht im Kriege* (Frankfurt, 1957), p. 131.
33 Galeazzo Ciano, *Tagebücher 1939–1943* (Bern, 1946), p. 46 (entry for 28 February 1939). On the conversations, see ibid., pp. 44 f. (entries for 25–7 February 1939).
34 Kornat, 'Sehenden Auges', p. 49.
35 *Das Deutsche Reich und der Zweite Weltkrieg*, 10 vols (Stuttgart and Munich, 1979–2008), vol. 1, p. 662.
36 Rainer F. Schmidt, *Die Außenpolitik des Dritten Reiches 1933–1939* (Stuttgart, 2002), p. 307.
37 Max Domarus (ed.), *Hitler. Reden und Proklamationen 1932–1945. Kommentiert von einem deutschen Zeitgenossen*, 2 vols (Munich, 1965), vol. 2, p. 1075.
38 Hitler's directive of 21 October 1938, ADAP, D, IV, No. 152.
39 Walther Görlitz (ed.), *Generalfeldmarschall Keitel. Verbrecher oder Offizier? Erinnerungen, Briefe, Dokumente des Chefs OKW* (Göttingen, 1961), p. 196.
40 The commander-in-chief of the army, deployment order 'Case East', 30 January 1939, BA-MA, RH 2/830.
41 See *Das Deutsche Reich und der Zweite Weltkrieg*, vol. 1, p. 525.
42 The commander-in-chief of the army, directive for 3rd Army High Command in the event of war, 8 December 1938, BA-MA, RH 2/830.
43 The commander-in-chief of the army, deployment order 'Case East', 30 January 1939, BA-MA, RH 2/830.
44 Army Group Command 3, directive for first deployment, 4 February 1939, BA-MA, RH 24–14/3.
45 Roman Knoll, *Uwagi o polskiej polityce 1939* (Warsaw, 1939), pp. 9 ff.; see Roos, *Polen*, p. 145.
46 Hans Roos, 'Die militärpolitische Lage und Planung Polens gegenüber Deutschland 1939', *Wehrwissenschaftliche Rundschau* 7 (1957), pp. 181–202.
47 State Secretary von Weizsäcker to Ambassador von Mackensen in Rome, 5 March 1939, ADAP, D, IV, No. 456, p. 509.
48 ADAP, D, VI, No. 61.
49 Polish government White Papers, doc. 61.
50 Quoted in Johannes Kalisch, 'Von der "Globallösung" zum "Fall Weiß". Die deutsch-polnischen Beziehungen 1938–39', in Dietrich Eichholtz and Kurt Pätzold (eds), *Der Weg in den Krieg* (Berlin, 1989), p. 395. Kleist was the 'eastern consultant'

in the 'Ribbentrop bureau', a parallel organisation to the Foreign Ministry; after 1941, he was responsible for the Baltic zone in the political department of the Reich Ministry for the Occupied Eastern Territories.

51 Elke Fröhlich (ed.), *Joseph Goebbels. Die Tagebücher, Teil I: Aufzeichnungen 1923–1941*, 14 vols (Munich, 1997–2005), vol. 6, p. 300 (entry for 25 March 1939).

52 Ian Kershaw, *Hitler. 1936–1945* (Stuttgart, 2000), p. 241.

53 ADAP, D, VI, No. 99, p. 98.

54 ADAP, D, VI, No. 149, p. 154.

Preparations for the War in the East

1 Günter Wollstein, 'Hitlers gescheitertes Projekt einer Juniorpartnerschaft Polens', *Universitas* 38 (1983), pp. 525–32.

2 David Dilks (ed.), *The Diary of Sir Alexander Cadogan, 1938–1945* (London, 1971), p. 166.

3 BA-MA, RM 20/1096.

4 Note of Raeder's on the change of fleet commander, October 1939, BA-MA RM 7/177.

5 Plenary study 1939, BA-MA, RM 20/1033.

6 1/Skl. Ia 109, Top secret study for war in the Baltic Sea, BA-MA, RM 20/1134, pp. 7 f.

7 On the possibility of using gas in 1939, see the compilation of requirements arising from the study for war in the Baltic, BA-MA, RM 20/1136, p. 199. On the deliberations of 1941, see quartermaster general's/army supply department list of materials needed for battle around Leningrad, 22 February 1941, reproduced in Günther W. Gellermann, *Der Krieg, der nicht stattfand* (Koblenz, 1986).

8 BA-MA, RM 20/1134.

9 BA-MA, RM 20/1136, p. 192.

10 Note of Naval Command, Ia in Group East, draft from 26 April 1939, comment on it from 26 April 1939, BA-MA, RM 20/1133. See on the background the study 'The North Sea theatre in a German–British naval war', 13 April 1939, RA-MA, RM 20/1117.

11 Whether this is equivalent to deciding to declare war on Poland has been variously evaluated by historians; see, for example: Klaus-Jürgen Müller, *Das Heer und Hitler. Armee und nationalsozialistisches Regime 1933–1940* (Stuttgart, 1969), p. 391; Ian Kershaw, *Hitler. 1936–1945* (Stuttgart, 2000), p. 1141, n. 44.

12 See account of his speech on 22 August 1939, ADAP, D, vol. VII, No. 192, in which he explained that everything was dependent on him, but that some criminal might neutralise him at any time.

13 Staff Colonel Edgar Röhricht devotes just two lines of his memoirs to this war game; see Edgar Röhricht, *Pflicht und Gewissen* (Stuttgart, 1965), p. 143. See also Christian Hartmann, *Halder. Generalstabschef Hitlers 1938–1942*, 2nd ed.

(Paderborn, 2010), p. 133, where the author remarks only briefly that Halder had had Russian intervention played through.

14 Report on the Army General Staff exercise 1939, 17 May 1939, BA-MA, RL 7/158.

15 Helmut Krausnick and Harold C. Deutsch (eds), *Helmuth Groscurth. Tagebücher eines Abwehroffiziers 1938–1940. Mit weiteren Dokumenten zur Militäropposition gegen Hitler* (Stuttgart, 1970), p. 492.

16 BA-MA, RHD 18/371. The first edition is from 1936.

17 Ibid., p. 117.

18 *Der Prozeß gegen die Hauptkriegsverbrecher vor dem Internationalen Militärgerichtshof. 14. Nov. 1945 – 1. Okt. 1946*, 42 vols (Nuremberg, 1947 and after), vol. 37, pp. 546–56, doc. 079-L; ADAP, D, vol. 6, pp. 477–83.

19 See, for example: *Das Deutsche Reich und der Zweite Weltkrieg*, 10 vols (Stuttgart and Munich, 1979–2008), vol. 1, p. 689; Josef Henke, *England in Hitlers politischem Kalkül, 1935–1939* (Boppard, 1973).

20 ADAP, D, VI, doc. 433, pp. 478 f.

21 Corresponding statements that Hitler supposedly made on 8 March 1939 in a speech to officers, industry representatives and party functionaries should be handled with care. These come from an account leaked to the American ambassador to Paris in September 1939; see *Das Deutsche Reich und der Zweite Weltkrieg*, vol. 1, p. 669.

22 OKW/WStb Nr. 1010/39g.K., 'Germany's oil supplies in a war', April 1939, BA-MA, Wi/I.37.

23 Report by Krauch to the General Council, 20–1 April 1939, BA, R 25/14.

24 Reich Department for Economic Development, 'Possibilities for a greater economic zone under German war leadership', August 1939, BA, R 25/53; Reich Department for the War Economy, 'German foreign trade in the event of war', July 1939, BA, R 24/83.

25 OKW/WStb, Major Petri, 'Foreign war economy', May 1939, BA-MA, Wi/I.216; memorandum for the Office for Research into the War Economy, 'The economic zone of a war between Germany–Italy and Britain–France–Russia', 4 May 1939, BA-MA, Wi/IF5.3150.

26 Lecture by Lieutenant Colonel Fach (OKW/War Economy Staff), 'Russia and the four northern European states and their military and economic significance', 10 June 1939, BA-MA, Wi/I.29.

27 Quoted in Marek Kornat, 'Sehenden Auges. Polens Außenpolitik vor dem Hitler-Stalin-Pakt', *Osteuropa* 59/7–8 (2009), p. 53.

28 Memorandum from Mussolini on 30 May 1939, ADAP, D, VI, No. 459, Appendix. Four weeks previously, Göring had visited Rome and indicated the possibility of a rapprochement with Russia in order to allay Il Duce's fears about the outbreak of a general European war. There was no lie he was not willing to tell. In response to Mussolini's questioning, Göring claimed that the Führer had no intentions in the Ukraine and that he himself, as a member of the cabinet, had never seen any document relating to that country. Hitler had confirmed to him only recently

that he had no ambitions in the Ukraine. Account of the conversation between Göring, Mussolini and Ciano on 16 and 18 April 1939 in ADAP, D, VI, doc. 211, pp. 215–19.

29 Speech by Hitler on 23 May 1939 to the leaders of the Wehrmacht, *Der Prozeß*, vol. 37, pp. 546–56, doc. 079-L.

30 See Alvin D. Coox, *Nomonhan: Japan against Russia, 1939* (Stanford, 1990).

31 See Bogdan Musial, *Kampfplatz Deutschland. Stalins Kriegspläne gegen den Westen* (Berlin, 2008), p. 402.

32 Quoted in Kershaw, *Hitler*, p. 1141, n. 50.

33 BA-MA, RH 10/1. See Torsten Diedrich, *Paulus. Das Trauma von Stalingrad. Eine Biographie* (Paderborn, 2008), p. 131.

34 OKH/GenStdH, 12. Abt. (III), 25 June 1939, BA-MA, RH 2/2324.

35 Reproduced by Rolf Elble, *Die Schlacht an der Bzura im September 1939 aus deutscher und polnischer Sicht* (Freiburg, 1975), pp. 236 f.

36 All that has survived are the appendices to the war diary from 22 August 1939 onwards. These are copies that were damaged in the fire in the War Studies Department on the 27–8 February 1942.

37 BA-MA, RH 10/1.

38 Hans-Günther Seraphim (ed.), *Das politische Tagebuch Alfred Rosenbergs 1934/35 und 1939/40* (Munich, 1964), p. 173 (entry for 15 June 1939).

39 Cover note for the eastern memorandum from Arno Schickedanz to the head of the Chancellery, Hans Heinrich Lammers, 15 June 1939, ibid., p. 168.

40 *Der Prozeß*, vol. 12, p. 390, doc. D-811.

41 BA-MA, RHD 18/346.

42 See Klaus Mayer, 'Eine authentische Halder-Ansprache? Textkritische Anmerkungen zu einem Dokumentenfund im früheren Moskauer Sonderarchiv (Dokumentation)', *Militärgeschichtliche Mitteilungen* 58 (1999), pp. 471–528.

43 Christian Hartmann and Sergej Slutsch, 'Franz Halder und die Kriegsvorbereitungen im Frühjahr 1939. Eine Ansprache des Generalstabschefs des Heeres', *VfZG* 45 (1997), p. 495. The two authors comment on their shock that Halder made statements of this kind with helpless criticism of his 'blitheness' and 'incompetence': how could a military professional in 1939 have wanted to implement Hitler's ideological programme with such 'irresponsible war games' (ibid., p. 475)?

From the Hitler–Stalin Pact to Operation Barbarossa

1 On the trade aspect of negotiations, see Ingeborg Fleischhauer, *Der Pakt. Hitler, Stalin und die Initiative der deutschen Diplomatie 1938–1939* (Berlin and Frankfurt, 1990), also on the following.

2 See Baumgart, who is comprehensive and discusses the sources; Winfried Baumgart, 'Zur Ansprache Hitlers vor den Führern der Wehrmacht am 22. August 1939', *VfZG* 16 (1968), pp. 120–49. Although Hitler forbade anyone to take notes, three separate accounts exist, two of them unsigned.

3 Account of the speech on 22 August 1939, ADAP, D, vol. VII, No. 192.

4 Carl J. Burckhardt, *Meine Danziger Mission 1937–1939* (Munich, 1960), pp. 341 ff.

5 According to Manfred Messerschmidt, 'no clarity' can be gained on whether Hitler wanted to carry on into the USSR immediately after subjugating Poland. A policy of that kind would have been unrealistic, but not unthinkable; see *Das Deutsche Reich und der Zweite Weltkrieg*, 10 vols (Stuttgart and Munich, 1979–2008), vol. 1, p. 696.

6 ADAP, D, VII, doc. 193, p. 172, quoted from a dubious British document.

7 Unsigned account, ibid., doc. 192, p. 170.

8 Hans-Günther Seraphim (ed.), *Das politische Tagebuch Alfred Rosenbergs 1934/35 und 1939/40* (Munich, 1964), p. 87 (entry for 21 May 1939).

9 Ibid., p. 90 (entry for 22 August 1939).

10 Ibid., pp. 92 f. (entry for 25 August 1939, evening). The reference is to Russian Foreign Minister Aleksandr Izvolsky, who on the eve of World War I was a driving force behind a British–Russian alliance.

11 Elisabeth Wagner (ed.), *Der Generalquartiermeister. Briefe und Tagebuchaufzeichnungen des Generalquartiermeisters des Heeres General der Artillerie Eduard Wagner* (Munich and Vienna, 1963), p. 105 (entry for 29 August 1939).

12 Extract from the war diary of Admiral Albrecht, quoted in Baumgart, 'Zur Ansprache', p. 148.

13 Paul Otto Schmidt, *Statist auf diplomatischer Bühne 1923–1945. Erlebnisse des Chefdolmetschers im Auswärtigen Amt mit den Staatsmännern Europas. Von Stresemann und Briand bis Hitler, Chamberlain und Molotow* (Bonn 1949; new ed. Munich, 2005), p. 463.

14 See Wagner, *Generalquartiermeister*, p. 135 (entry for 21 September 1939).

15 Since the 3rd Army High Command files from this period do not survive, the details of this change are obscure.

16 See more comprehensively, *Das Deutsche Reich und der Zweite Weltkrieg*, vol. 1, pp. 111–35.

17 Wagner, *Generalquartiermeister*, p. 135.

18 See XIII.AK/Ic Nr. 176/39g, 'Encounter with Russian troops and aeroplanes', 19 September 1939, BA-MA, RH 24–13/144.

19 Message from Army Group North to AOK 3, 23 September 1939, BA-MA, RH 20–3/2.

20 Walther Hubatsch (ed.), *Hitlers Weisungen für die Kriegführung, 1939–1945* (Munich, 1965), p. 32.

21 Wagner, *Generalquartiermeister*, p. 134 (entry for 18 September 1939).

22 Hitler's speech in Danzig, reproduced in Max Domarus (ed.), *Hitler. Reden und Proklamationen 1932–1945. Kommentiert von einem deutschen Zeitgenossen*, 2 vols (Munich, 1965), vol. 2, pp. 1354–66.

23 Seraphim (ed.), *Tagebuch Rosenbergs*, pp. 98 f. (entry for 29 September 1939).

24 Elke Fröhlich (ed.), *Joseph Goebbels. Die Tagebücher, Teil I: Aufzeichnungen 1923–1941*, 14 vols (Munich, 1997–2005), vol. 7, p. 130 (entry for 30 September 1939).

25 Wagner, *Generalquartiermeister*, p. 137 (entry for 29 September 1939).

26 On Hitler's decision about subjugating the western powers, see *Das Deutsche Reich und der Zweite Weltkrieg*, vol. 1, pp. 238 ff.

27 Franz Halder, *Kriegstagebuch. Tägliche Aufzeichnungen des Chefs des Generalstabes des Heeres 1939–1942*, ed. Hans-Adolf Jacobsen, 3 vols (Stuttgart, 1962–64), vol. 1, pp. 86–90 (entry for 27 September 1939). Halder himself noted when his diaries were being edited that the notes he made on 27 September 1939 were only rediscovered in 1950 and did not purport to be a full account of Hitler's declarations; see ibid., n. 1.

28 Memorandum and guidelines for war in the west, 9 October 1939, reproduced in Hans-Adolf Jacobsen, *Dokumente zur Vorgeschichte des Westfeldzuges 1939–1940* (Göttingen, 1956), pp. 5 ff.

29 Reproduced in Wagner, *Generalquartiermeister*, p. 145.

30 Ibid., p. 139 (entry for 6 October 1939).

31 Max Ludwig, 'Deutsch-russische Zusammenarbeit', *Wehrtechnische Monatshefte* (September 1939), pp. 386 f.

32 Oskar Ritter von Niedermayer, 'Sowjetrussland. Ein wehrpolitisches Bild', *Militärwissenschaftliche Rundschau* 4 (1939), pp. 704–23.

33 Seraphim (ed.), *Tagebuch Rosenbergs*, pp. 104 f. (entry for 1 November 1939); see also Ulrich Seidt, *Berlin, Kabul, Moskau. Oskar Ritter von Niedermayer und Deutschlands Geopolitik* (Munich, 2003).

34 'Thoughts on the outbreak of war 1939', BA, NS 10/37. See also generally Wolfgang Michalka, 'Vom Antikominternpakt zum euro-asiatischen Kontinentalblock: Ribbentrops Alternativkonzeption zu Hitlers außenpolitischem "Programm"', in Wolfgang Michalka (ed.), *Nationalsozialistische Außenpolitik* (Darmstadt, 1978), pp. 471–92.

35 See Heinrich Schwendemann, *Die wirtschaftliche Zusammenarbeit zwischen dem Deutschen Reich und der Sowjetunion von 1939 bis 1941: Alternative zu Hitlers Ostprogramm?* (Berlin, 1993), pp. 73–149.

36 Dietrich A. Loeber (ed.), *Diktierte Option. Die Umsiedlung der Deutsch-Balten aus Estland und Lettland 1939–1941. Dokumentation* (Neumünster, 1972).

37 Ulrich von Hassell, *Vom andern Deutschland. Aus den nachgelassenen Tagebüchern 1938–1944* (Zürich and Freiburg, 1946), pp. 86 f. (entry for 11 October 1939).

38 'On the military situation at the end of the Polish campaign, late September 1939', reproduced in Helmut Krausnick and Harold C. Deutsch (eds), *Helmuth Groscurth. Tagebücher eines Abwehroffiziers 1938–1940. Mit weiteren Dokumenten zur Militäropposition gegen Hitler* (Stuttgart, 1970), p. 474. Similar in a further special study of 'The Russian question for Germany', ibid., pp. 490–2.

39 Wagner, *Generalquartiermeister*, pp. 147 f. (entry for 3 November 1939).

40 Hildegard von Kotze (ed.), *Heeresadjutant bei Hitler 1938–1943. Aufzeichnungen des Majors Engel* (Stuttgart, 1974), pp. 66–8.

41 OKH/GenStdH/OQu I/Ausb.Abt. (Ia), 'Tactical experiences in the Polish campaign', BA-MA, RH 27-7/2.

42 Gerhard Groß, 'Das Dogma der Beweglichkeit. Überlegungen zur Genese der deutschen Heerestaktik im Zeitalter der Weltkriege', in Bruno Thoß and

Hans-Erich Volkmann (eds), *Erster Weltkrieg Zweiter Weltkrieg. Ein Vergleich* (Paderborn, 2002), p. 160. Williamson Murray, 'The German response to victory in Poland: A case study in professionalism', *Armed Forces and Society* 7 (1981), pp. 285–98.

43 Karl-Heinz Frieser, *Die Blitzkrieg-Legende* (München, 1995), p. 29.

44 On the 'munitions crisis' in German armaments production, see *Das Deutsche Reich und der Zweite Weltkrieg*, vol. 5/1, pp. 406 ff.

45 Bogdan Musial, *Kampfplatz Deutschland. Stalins Kriegspläne gegen den Westen* (Berlin, 2008), p. 411.

46 *Das Deutsche Reich und der Zweite Weltkrieg*, vol. 4, p. 57.

47 Kotze (ed.), *Heeresadjutant*, p. 69 (entry for 23 November 1939).

48 Bernd Martin, 'Das "Dritte Reich" und die "Friedens"-Frage im Zweiten Weltkrieg', in Wolfgang Michalka (ed.), *Nationalsozialistische Außenpolitik* (Darmstadt, 1978), pp. 526–49.

49 Hitler quoted in Fröhlich (ed.), *Goebbels*, vol. 7, p. 228 (entry for 12 December 1939).

50 Sergej Slutsch, 'Stalins "Kriegsszenario 1939": Eine Rede, die es nie gab', *VfZG* 52 (2004), pp. 597–635. The faked report was first disseminated by a news agency on 28 November 1939 and has drifted in various forms through the press and the literature.

51 Fröhlich (ed.), *Goebbels*, vol. 7, p. 187 (entry for 9 November 1939), p. 249 (entry for 29 December 1939).

52 Ibid., p. 166 (entry for 24 October 1939).

53 Ibid., p. 190 (entry for 11 November 1939).

54 Ibid., p. 194 (entry for 14 November 1939).

55 Nicolaus von Below, *Als Hitlers Adjutant 1937–45* (Mainz, 1980), p. 217.

56 The reference is to Oswald Spengler, *The Decline of the West* (Munich, 1922).

57 ADAP, D, vol. 8, p. 475; reproduces letter dated 3 January.

58 Letter from Hitler to Mussolini, 8 March 1940, ibid., p. 690.

59 Domarus (ed.), *Hitler*, vol. 2, pp. 1448 f. (entry for 24 January 1940).

60 Fröhlich (ed.), *Goebbels*, vol. 7, p. 283 (entry for 25 January 1940).

61 Report by Frank during the first meeting of the Reich Defence Committee for Poland, 2 March 1940, BA-MA, RH 53–23/22.

62 Message from Keitel to the heads of the Wehrmacht's branches, 27 January 1939, quoted in Domarus (ed.), *Hitler*, vol. 2, p. 1449.

63 For example, by Ernst Klink in *Das Deutsche Reich und der Zweite Weltkrieg*, vol. 4, p. 192, n. 10. In the text itself, the author says that this was no normal military routine, but was prompted by mistrust of Stalin.

64 Halder, *Kriegstagebuch*, vol. 1, p. 107 (entry for 18 October 1939).

65 *Das Deutsche Reich und der Zweite Weltkrieg*, vol. 4, p. 192.

66 'Regulations for the Movement and Combat Exercise for Motorised Units 1939', (Berlin, 1939), BA-MA, RH 10/1.

67 Manstein, unpublished diary, German Armed Forces Military History Research Office (entry for 24 October 1939).

68 Hans-Adolf Jacobsen, *Dokumente zur Vorgeschichte*, p. 17.
69 Study on 11 January 1940, BA-MA, RH 2/390; *Das Deutsche Reich und der Zweite Weltkrieg*, vol. 4, p. 194.
70 On the details, see Rolf-Dieter Müller, *Hitlers Ostkrieg und die deutsche Siedlungspolitik* (Frankfurt, 1991), pp. 14 ff.
71 Account of the discussion on 16–17 January 1939 in Łódź, reproduced ibid., p. 129.
72 Opinions of 19 February 1940 and 14 April 1940, BA-MA, RH 53–23/56.
73 Klaus-Jürgen Müller, 'Zu Vorgeschichte und Inhalt der Rede Himmlers vor der höheren Generalität am 13. Marz 1940 in Koblenz', *VfZG* 18 (1970), pp. 95–120.
74 Müller, *Hitler's Ostkrieg*, p. 22.
75 See Frieser's groundbreaking work, *Die Blitzkrieg-Legende*.
76 *Das Deutsche Reich und der Zweite Weltkrieg*, vol. 5/1, pp. 406 ff.
77 Ibid., vol. 4, p. 203.
78 On the current state of research, see Rolf-Dieter Müller and Gerd R. Ueberschär, *Hitlers Krieg im Osten 1941–1945. Ein Forschungsbericht* (Darmstadt, 2000), p. 30.
79 Fröhlich (ed.), *Goebbels*, vol. 4, pp. 205, 216 (entries for 5 and 11 July 1940).
80 See *Das Deutsche Reich und der Zweite Weltkrieg*, vol. 5/1, pp. 486 ff.
81 Halder, *Kriegstagebuch*, vol. 1, p. 357 (entry for 15 June 1940).
82 Halder, *Kriegstagebuch*, vol. 1, p. 362 (entry for 18 June 1940).
83 Galeazzo Ciano, *Tagebücher 1939–1943* (Bern, 1946), entry for 18–19 June 1940.
84 Note by Loßberg, 24 June 1940, BA-MA, RW 4/581.
85 Halder, *Kriegstagebuch*, vol. 1, p. 372 (entry for 25 June 1940), n. 1.
86 *Das Deutsche Reich und der Zweite Weltkrieg*, vol. 4, p. 206.
87 Provisional instructions to Army Group B from the army's commander-in-chief, as well as the formal orders from OKH/GenStdH Op.Abt. (Ia), No. 375/40g.Kdos., 26.06.1940, BA-MA, RH 20–18/40b. New divisions were formed in so-called waves, each with the same kind of equipment. The 'white year groups' were those who had not received any regular training during peacetime. Since the Treaty of Versailles did not allow Germany to have national service from 1920 onwards, there were fifteen year groups missing between then and its reintroduction in 1935. They had to receive catch-up training after being conscripted and were not seen as fully capable.
88 Minutes, 28 June 1940, BA-MA, RH 20–18/40b.
89 Army commander-in-chief, No. 377/40g.Kdos., 29 June 1940, BA-MA, RH 20–18/40b.
90 Halder, *Kriegstagebuch*, vol. 1, p. 375 (entry for 30 June 1940).
91 In Ernst Klink's account, the chronology of events is breached various times, because the author believed Stalin's actions to be the real reason for the start of the plenary work; see *Das Deutsche Reich und der Zweite Weltkrieg*, vol. 4, pp. 210 f.
92 See, for example, Andreas Hillgruber, *Hitlers Strategie. Politik und Kriegfuhrung 1940–1941*, 2nd ed. (Munich, 1982).

93 Franz Halder, *Hitler als Feldherr* (Munich, 1949).

94 Bernd Wegner, 'Erschriebene Siege. Franz Halder, die "Historical Division" und die Rekonstruktion des Zweiten Weltkrieges im Geiste des deutschen Generalstabes', in Ernst Willi Hansen, Gerhard Schreiber and Bernd Wegner (eds), *Politischer Wandel, organisierte Gewalt und nationale Sicherheit. Beiträge zur neueren Geschichte Deutschlands und Frankreichs* (Munich, 1995), pp. 287–302.

95 Ibid., p. 37.

96 Ian Kershaw, *Hitler. 1936–1945* (Stuttgart, 2000), p. 415, with corresponding reference to sources.

97 Below, *Als Hitlers Adjutant*, p. 262.

98 David Irving, *Hitlers Krieg. Die Siege 1939–1942* (Munich and Berlin, 1983), pp. 191–5. Here in contradiction of Ueberschär's interpretation, which is based on Below; see Gerd R. Ueberschär, 'Hitlers Entschluss zum "Lebensraum"-Krieg im Osten', in Gerd R. Ueberschär and Wolfram Wette, *'Unternehmen Barbarossa'. Der deutsche Überfall auf die Sowjetunion 1941* (Paderborn, 1984), pp. 83–110.

99 Bernhard von Loßberg, *Im Wehrmachtführungsstab. Bericht eines Generalstabsoffiziers*, 2nd ed. (Hamburg, 1950), pp. 105–7.

100 Irving, *Hitlers Krieg*, p. 514, n. 195.

101 Hillgruber, *Hitlers Strategie*, p. 219.

102 Walter Warlimont, *Im Hauptquartier der deutschen Wehrmacht 1939–1945. Grundlagen, Formen, Gestalten* (Frankfurt am Main and Bonn, 1962), pp. 150 f.

103 Karl Klee, *Das Unternehmen 'Seelöwe'. Die geplante deutsche Landung in England 1940* (Göttingen, 1958), p. 189.

104 Hermann Böhme, *Entstehung und Grundlagen des Waffenstillstandes von 1940* (Stuttgart, 1966), p. 79.

105 Here in agreement with Klink; see *Das Deutsche Reich und der Zweite Weltkrieg*, vol. 4, p. 210.

106 Ulrich Ringsdorf, 'Organisatorische Entwicklung und Aufgaben der Abteilung Fremde Heere Ost im Generalstab des Heeres', in Friedrich Kahlenberg (ed.), *Beiträge zum Archivwesen, zur Quellenkunde und zur Geschichte. Festschrift für Hans Booms* (Boppard, 1989), pp. 800–10; David Thomas, 'Foreign armies east and German Military Intelligence in Russia, 1941–45', *Journal of Contemporary History* 22/2 (1987), pp. 261–301.

107 Erich Helmdach, *Überfall? Der sowjetisch-deutsche Aufmarsch 1941* (Neckargemünd, 1976).

108 Heinz Höhne, *Canaris. Patriot im Zwielicht* (Munich, 1976), p. 430.

109 Report about the behaviour of the Soviets in occupied eastern Poland, 28 October 1939, reproduced in Norbert Müller (ed.), *Das Amt Ausland / Abwehr im Oberkommando der Wehrmacht. Eine Dokumentation* (Koblenz, 2007), p. 143.

110 Andreas Hillgruber, 'Das Russland-Bild der führenden deutschen Militärs vor Beginn des Angriffs auf die Sowjetunion', in Hans-Erich Volkmann (ed.), *Das Russlandbild im Dritten Reich* (Cologne, 1994), pp. 125–40.

111 Evaluation of captured Polish archives on 25 July 1940, BA-MA, RH 2/2732.

112 On his life and his role in the eastern war, see Johannes Hürter, *Hitlers Heerführer. Die deutschen Oberbefehlshaber im Krieg gegen die Sowjetunion, 1941/42* (Munich, 2006).

113 Halder, *Kriegstagebuch*, vol. 2, p. 4 (entry for 1 July 1940).

114 Note by Marcks, quoted in *Das Deutsche Reich und der Zweite Weltkrieg*, vol. 4, p. 207 (emphasis in the original).

115 AOK 18, Ia, 'Deployment of the 18th Army', 9 July 1940, BA-MA, RH 20–18/40b.

116 The directive was signed by Küchler on 22 July 1940, BA-MA, RH 20–18/40b (emphasis in the original).

117 See sketch in *Das Deutsche Reich und der Zweite Weltkrieg*, vol. 4, p. 208.

118 Halder, *Kriegstagebuch*, vol. 2, p. 21 (entry for 13 July 1940).

119 Quoted in Domarus (ed.), *Hitler*, vol. 2, p. 1556.

120 Halder, *Kriegstagebuch*, vol. 2, p. 31 (entry for 22 July 1940). Brauchitsch informed his chief of staff about the conversation a day later.

121 Ibid., pp. 32 f.

122 Klink pointed this out in 1983; see *Das Deutsche Reich und der Zweite Weltkrieg*, vol. 4, p. 213, n. 66. Halder's interpretation can be found again in a letter to Jacobsen, the editor of the diary, on 10 December 1962, reproduced in Halder, *Kriegstagebuch*, vol. 2, p. 41, n. 2. Even the most recent Hitler biography contains this mistaken interpretation; see Kershaw, *Hitler*, pp. 412 f.

123 Message from AOK 18 on 23 July 1940 saying that Marcks will arrive on the evening of 29 July 1940, BA-MA, RH 20–18/41b.

124 *Das Deutsche Reich und der Zweite Weltkrieg*, vol. 4, pp. 211 f.

125 Halder, *Kriegstagebuch*, vol. 2, p. 37 (entry for 26 July 1940).

126 Ibid., p. 39 (entry for 27 July 1940).

127 Kershaw, *Hitler*, p. 415.

128 Halder, *Kriegstagebuch*, vol. 2, p. 46 (entry for 30 July 1940).

129 'Observations on Russia', 28 July 1940; see *Das Deutsche Reich und der Zweite Weltkrieg*, vol. 4, p. 320.

130 Warlimont, *Im Hauptquartier*, p. 127.

131 Hillgruber, *Hitlers Strategie*, p. 127.

132 On his biography, see Kirstin A. Schäfer, *Werner von Blomberg – Hitlers erster Feldmarschall* (Paderborn, 2006).

133 Domarus (ed.), *Hitler*, vol. 2, p. 1556.

134 Postwar study by Heusinger and Heinrici, *The Campaign in Russia*, quoted in *Das Deutsche Reich und der Zweite Weltkrieg*, vol. 4, p. 206.

135 Based on statements and documents from the Nuremberg trials as well as on the then still-unpublished Halder diaries, the German-American historian Gerhard L. Weinberg produced a first overall interpretation in 1953, which was put on broader foundation by Andreas Hillgruber several years later. Bernd Stegemann's scepticism about the sources was harshly rejected by Hillgruber. The overview by Gerd R. Ueberschär portrays the unchanged state of research. See Gerhard L. Weinberg, 'Der deutsche Entschluß zum Angriff auf die Sowjetunion', *VfZG* 1 (1953), pp. 301–18; Hillgruber, *Hitlers Strategie*; Andreas Hillgruber, 'Noch

einmal: Hitlers Wendung gegen die Sowjetunion 1940. Nicht (Militar-) "Strategie oder Ideologie", sondern "Programm" und "Weltkriegsstrategie"', *Geschichte in Wissenschaft und Unterricht* 33 (1982), pp. 214–26; Bernd Stegemann, 'Hitler's Ziele im ersten Kriegsjahr 1939–40', *Militärgeschichtliche Mitteilungen* 27 (1980), pp. 93–105; Gerd R. Ueberschär, 'Hitlers Entschluss'.

136 Halder, *Kriegstagebuch*, vol. 2, pp. 46–50 (entry for 31 July 1940); note of Raeder's about the meeting with Hitler on 31 July 1940, BA-MA, RM 7/177.

137 Halder, *Kriegstagebuch*, vol. 2, pp. 49 f. (entry for 31 July 1940).

138 Karl-Heinz Frieser, 'Die deutschen Blitzkriege: Operativer Triumph – strategische Tragödie', in Rolf-Dieter Müller and Hans-Erich Volkmann (eds), *Die Wehrmacht. Mythos und Realität* (Munich, 1999), pp. 182–96.

139 See Hillgruber's discussion with Weinberg: Hans-Günther Seraphim and Andreas Hillgruber, 'Hitlers Entschluss zum Angriff auf Russland (eine Entgegnung)', *VfZG* 2 (1954), pp. 240–9, with a conclusion by Gerhard L. Weinberg, pp. 249–54.

140 Major-General Marcks, 'Draft Operation East', 5 August 1940, BA-MA, RH 20–18/45.

141 See map of roads in the east, provisional edition because of outdated sources, July 1940, Appendix 2 to AOK 18 Ia/OQu No. 420/40gKdos, 5 August 1940, BA-MA, RH 20–18/41(b).

142 See, for example, Hillgruber, 'Russland-Bild'.

143 See *Das Deutsche Reich und der Zweite Weltkrieg*, vol. 4, p. 222.

144 Chief of Foreign Armies East, assessment of Situation Red, 10 September 1940, BA-MA, RH 20–18/46.

145 See *Das Deutsche Reich und der Zweite Weltkrieg*, vol. 4, p. 244.

146 Halder, *Kriegstagebuch*, vol. 2, pp. 103 f. (entry for 16 September 1940).

147 Heinz Guderian, *Erinnerungen eines Soldaten* (Heidelberg, 1951).

148 Kotze (ed.), *Heeresadjutant*, p. 86 (entry for 10 August 1940).

149 Ibid., pp. 87 f. (entry for 15 September 1940).

150 RM 7/177, p. 15 (entry for 26 September 1940).

151 See comprehensively Torsten Diedrich, *Paulus. Das Trauma von Stalingrad. Eine Biographie* (Paderborn, 2008), pp. 179–93.

152 *Das Deutsche Reich und der Zweite Weltkrieg*, vol. 4, p. 210.

153 Ibid., vol. 5/1, pp. 113–89.

154 Ibid., vol. 4, pp. 230–3.

155 Ibid., pp. 234 f.

156 Operational study of 7 December 1940, BA-MA, ZA 1/1732.

157 Halder, *Kriegstagebuch*, vol. 2, pp. 211–14 (entry for 5 December 1940).

158 Hubatsch (ed.), Hitler's Directives, pp. 96–101.

159 Kotze (ed.), *Heeresadjutant*, p. 92 (entry for 18 December 1940).

160 Ibid., pp. 92 f. (entry for 17 January 1941). Halder was on holiday and had Paulus informed after his return; see Halder, *Kriegstagebuch*, vol. 2, pp. 243 f. (entry for 16 January 1941).

161 Walther Hubatsch (ed.), *Hitlers Weisungen für die Kriegführung, 1939–1945* (Munich, 1965), pp. 121–4 (Directive No. 24, 5 March 1941).

162 Halder, *Kriegstagebuch*, vol. 2, pp. 257–61 (entry for 28 January 1941).

163 Record of the discussion with the quartermaster general on 20 January 1941, BA-MA, RW 4/v.715.

164 Halder, *Kriegstagebuch*, vol. 2, p. 261 (entry for 28 January 1941).

165 'Regulations on military authority, security and administration in the rearward areas and prisoner-of-war camps', February 1941, BA-MA, RH 3/v.132. These are the war-game documents for Army Group South.

166 Percy Ernst Schramm (ed.), *Kriegstagebuch des Oberkommandos der Wehrmacht (Wehrmachtführungsstab) 1940–1945. Geführt von Helmuth Greiner u. Percy Ernst Schramm. Bd. I: 1. August 1940 - 31. Dezember 1941. Zusammengestellt und erlautert von Hans-Adolf Jacobsen* (Frankfurt, 1965), vol. 1, pp. 340 f. (entry for 3 March 1941).

167 Kotze (ed.), *Heeresadjutant*, pp. 96 f. (entry for 16 March 1941). In the background, Himmler was evidently massively opposed to the military administration. He complained to Hitler that his 'pacification initiatives' were being sabotaged by 'old generals'. He thought it would be best to replace the field commanders with SS men; see ibid., p. 100 (entry for 7 April 1941).

168 The best description and analysis is in Johannes Hürter, *Hitlers Heerführer. Die deutschen Oberbefehlshaber im Krieg gegen die Sowjetunion, 1941/42* (Munich, 2006), pp. 1–3.

169 Halder, *Kriegstagebuch*, vol. 2, pp. 336 f. (entry for 30 March 1941).

170 See Kotze (ed.), *Heeresadjutant*, p. 102 (entry for 10 May 1941, with Tresckow's contradiction of the commissar order) and Rolf-Dieter Müller, 'Kriegsrecht oder Willkür? Helmuth James Graf v. Moltke und die Auffassungen im Generalstab des Heeres über die Aufgaben der Militärverwaltung vor Beginn des Russlandkrieges', *Militärgeschichtliche Mitteilungen* 2 (1987), pp. 125–51.

171 Quoted in *Das Deutsche Reich und der Zweite Weltkrieg*, vol. 5/1, p. 857.

172 Rolf-Dieter Müller, *An der Seite der Wehrmacht. Hitlers ausländische Helfer beim Kreuzzug gegen den Bolschewismus 1941–1945* (Berlin, 2007).

173 Fröhlich (ed.), *Goebbels*, vol. 4, p. 696 (entry for 16 June 1941).

174 Sven Felix Kellerhoff, 'War der Angriff auf die Sowjetunion ein Präventivschlag?', in Lars-Broder Keil and Sven Felix Kellerhoff, *Deutsche Legenden. Vom "Dolchstoß" und anderen Mythen der Geschichte*, 2nd ed. (Berlin, 2003), pp. 68–91.

175 Halder, *Kriegstagebuch*, vol. 3, p. 38 (entry for 3 July 1941).

176 During a rapid advance, the Germans had neither the time nor the manpower lastingly to mine or guard the barriers on their flanks. The decisive question had been whether not only infantry, but also tanks and heavy guns could be moved around this region, thus creating a force that would need to be countered with larger German formations.

177 Note of Bormann's on 16 July 1941, reproduced in *Der Prozeß gegen die Hauptkriegsverbrecher vor dem Internationalen Militärgerichtshof. 14. Nov. 1945 - 1. Okt. 1946*, 42 vols (Nuremberg, 1947 and after), vol. 38, doc. 221-L, pp. 86 ff.

178 See *Das Deutsche Reich und der Zweite Weltkrieg*, vol. 4, pp. 489–96. On the situation for Army Group Centre, see also the study by the New Zealand military

historian David Stahel, *Operation Barbarossa and Germany's Defeat in the East* (Cambridge, 2009).

179 Kotze (ed.), *Heeresadjutant*, p. 107 (entry for 28 July 1941).

180 Halder, *Kriegstagebuch*, vol. 3, p. 134 (entry for 30 July 1941).

181 Kotze (ed.), *Heeresadjutant*, p. 108 (entry for 8 August 1941).

182 Christian Hartmann, *Halder. Generalstabschef Hitlers 1938–1942*, 2nd ed. (Paderborn, 2010), p. 281.

183 Kotze (ed.), *Heeresadjutant*, p. 110 (entry for 21 August 1941).

184 Hitler's study reproduced in Schramm (ed.), *Kriegstagebuch des Oberkommandos der Wehrmacht*, vol. 1, p. 1063.

185 Quoted in Hartmann, Halder, p. 284.

186 Georg Meyer, *Adolf Heusinger. Dienst eines deutschen Soldaten 1915 bis 1964* (Hamburg, 2001), pp. 156 f.

187 See the new account by David Stahel, *Kiev 1941: Hitler's Battle for Supremacy in the East* (Cambridge, 2013).

188 Curzio Malaparte, *Die Wolga entspringt in Europa. Vorwort von Heiner Müller* (Cologne, 1989), p. 130.

Conclusion

1 Christian Hartmann, *Halder. Generalstabschef Hitlers 1938–1942*, 2nd ed. (Paderborn, 2010), p. 128.

2 Quoted in *Das Deutsche Reich und der Zweite Weltkrieg*, 10 vols (Stuttgart and Munich, 1979–2008), vol. 9/1, pp. 773, 784.

Bibliography

Agricola (pseud.), *Das Wunder an der Weichsel* (Berlin, 1937).

——— *Der Rote Marschall. Tuchatschewskis Aufstieg und Fall* (Berlin, 1939).

Ahmann, Rolf, *Nichtangriffspakte: Entwicklung und operative Nutzung in Europa 1922–1939* (Baden-Baden, 1988).

Akten zur deutschen auswartigen Politik (ADAP) 1918–45 [German Foreign Policy Records]

Series B: 1925–33 (Göttingen, 1966–78),

Series C: 1933–7 (Göttingen, 1971–5),

Series D: 1937–45 (Baden-Baden, 1950 ff).

Alexander, Manfred, *Kleine Geschichte Polens* (Stuttgart, 2008).

Baumgart, Winfried, 'Zur Ansprache Hitlers vor den Führern der Wehrmacht am 22. August 1939', *VfZG* 16 (1968), pp. 120–49.

Below, Nicolaus von, *Als Hitlers Adjutant 1937–45* (Mainz, 1980), published in English as *At Hitler's Side: Memoirs of Hitler's Luftwaffe Adjutant 1937-1945* (Barnsley, 2001).

Besymenski, Lew, *Stalin und Hitler. Das Pokerspiel der Diktatoren* (Berlin, 2002).

Boepple, Ernst (ed.), *Adolf Hitlers Reden*, 3rd ed. (Munich, 1933).

Böhme, Hermann, *Entstehung und Grundlagen des Waffenstillstandes von 1940* (Stuttgart, 1966).

Borodziej, Włodzimierz, and Klaus Ziemer (ed.), *Deutsch-polnische Beziehungen 1939–1945–1949. Eine Einführung* (Osnabrück, 2000).

Boysen, Jens, 'Nationale Minderheiten (Polen und Elsass-Lothringer) im preusisch-deutschen Heer während des Ersten Weltkriegs 1914–1918', *Nordost-Archiv* (2008), pp. 108–36.

Brandes, Detlef, *Die Sudetendeutschen im Krisenjahr 1938* (Munich, 2008).

Broszat, Martin, *Nationalsozialistische Polenpolitik 1939–1945* (Stuttgart, 1961).

Brügel, Johann Wolfgang (ed.), *Stalin und Hitler. Pakt gegen Europa* (Vienna, 1973).

Bułhak, Henryk, *Polska-Francja: Z dziejów sojuszu 1933–1936* (Warsaw, 2000).

Burckhardt, Carl J., *Meine Danziger Mission 1937–1939* (Munich, 1960).

Canis, Konrad, *Bismarcks Außenpolitik 1870–1890* (Paderborn, 2004).

Caspary, Adolf, *Wirtschafts-Strategie und Kriegsführung. Wirtschaftliche Vorbereitung, Führung und Auswirkung des Krieges in geschichtlichem Aufriss* (Berlin, 1932).

Churchill, Winston, *The Second World War, Volume 1: The Gathering Storm* (London, 1948), published in German as *Der zweite Weltkrieg* (Stuttgart, 1954).

Ciano, Galeazzo, *Tagebücher 1939–1943* (Bern, 1946).

—— *Tagebücher 1937/38* (Hamburg, 1949).

Coox, Alvin D., *Nomonhan: Japan against Russia, 1939* (Stanford, 1990).

Craig, Gordon A., *Germany 1866–1945* (Oxford, 1978).

Das Deutsche Reich und der Zweite Weltkrieg, 10 vols (Stuttgart and Munich, 1979–2008), published in English as *Germany and the Second World War*, 10 vols (Oxford, 1990–2014).

Davies, Norman, *Heart of Europe: A Short History of Poland* (Oxford, 1984).

—— *White Eagle, Red Star: The Polish–Soviet War, 1919–20* (London, 2003).

Deist, Wilhelm, 'Die deutsche Aufrüstung in amerikanischer Sicht. Berichte des US-Militärattaches in Berlin aus den Jahren 1933–1939', in Alexander Fischer et al. (eds), *Russland-Deutschland-Amerika* (Wiesbaden, 1978), pp. 279–95.

Der polnisch-sowjetrussische Krieg 1918–1920, vol. 1 (Berlin, 1940).

Der Prozeß gegen die Hauptkriegsverbrecher vor dem Internationalen Militärgerichtshof. 14. Nov. 1945 - 1. Okt. 1946, 42 vols (Nuremberg, 1947 and after).

Deszczyński, Marek Piotr, *Obstatni Egzamin. Wojsko Polskie wobec kryzysu czechosłowackiego 1938–1939* (Warsaw, 2003).

Diedrich, Torsten, *Paulus. Das Trauma von Stalingrad. Eine Biographie* (Paderborn, 2008).

Dilks, David (ed.), *The Diary of Sir Alexander Cadogan, 1938–1945* (London, 1971).

Dirksen, Herbert von, *Moskau, Tokio, London* (Stuttgart, 1949), published in English as *Moscow, Tokyo, London: Twenty Years of German Foreign Policy* (London, 1951).

Domarus, Max (ed.), *Hitler. Reden und Proklamationen 1932–1945. Kommentiert von einem deutschen Zeitgenossen*, 2 vols (Munich, 1965), published in English as *Hitler: Speeches and Proclamations 1932–1945*, 4 vols (London, 1990–2005).

Ehlert, Hans, Michael Epkenhans and Gerhard P. Groß (eds), *Der Schlieffenplan. Analysen und Dokumente* (Paderborn, 2006).

Elble, Rolf, *Die Schlacht an der Bzura im September 1939 aus deutscher und polnischer Sicht* (Freiburg, 1975).

Epstein, Fritz T., 'Der Komplex "Die russische Gefahr" und sein Einfluss auf die deutsch-russischen Beziehungen im 19. Jahrhundert', in Immanuel Geiss and Bernd Jürgen Wendt (eds), *Deutschland in der Weltpolitik des 19. und 20. Jahrhunderts* (Düsseldorf, 1973), pp. 143–59.

Fischer, Fritz, *Germany's Aims in the First World War* (London, 1967).

Fleischhauer, Ingeborg, *Der Pakt. Hitler, Stalin und die Initiative der deutschen Diplomatie 1938–1939* (Berlin and Frankfurt, 1990).

Frieser, Karl-Heinz, 'Die deutschen Blitzkriege: Operativer Triumph – strategische Tragödie', in Rolf-Dieter Müller and Hans-Erich Volkmann (eds), *Die Wehrmacht. Mythos und Realität* (Munich, 1999), pp. 182–96.

——*Die Blitzkrieg-Legende* (München, 1995), published in English as *The Blitzkrieg Legend* (Annapolis, MD, 2012).

Fröhlich, Elke (ed.), *Joseph Goebbels. Die Tagebücher, Teil I: Aufzeichnungen 1923–1941*, 14 vols (Munich, 1997–2005).

Geisler, Walter, 'Die deutsch-polnische Raumgemeinschaft im Gesamt-Ostraum', *Ostraum-Berichte* 1 (1935), pp. 9–20.

Gellermann, Günther W., *Der Krieg, der nicht stattfand* (Koblenz, 1986).

Geschichte des zweiten Weltkrieges 1939–1945, vol. 2 (Berlin, 1975).

Gnauck, Gerhard, 'Sperriger Nationalheld. Marschall Piłsudski – eine nicht unumstrittene Vaterfigur', *Neue Zürcher Zeitung*, 12 March 2005.

Golczewski, Frank, *Deutsche und Ukrainer 1914–1939* (Paderborn, 2010).

Görlitz, Walther (ed.), *Generalfeldmarschall Keitel. Verbrecher oder Offizier? Erinnerungen, Briefe, Dokumente des Chefs OKW* (Göttingen, 1961).

Grelka, Frank, *Die ukrainische Nationalbewegung unter deutscher Besatzungsherrschaft 1918 und 1941/42* (Wiesbaden, 2005).

Groß, Gerhard, 'Das Dogma der Beweglichkeit. Überlegungen zur Genese der deutschen Heerestaktik im Zeitalter der Weltkriege', in Bruno Thoß and Hans-Erich Volkmann (eds), *Erster Weltkrieg Zweiter Weltkrieg. Ein Vergleich* (Paderborn, 2002), pp. 143–166.

——*Mythos und Wirklichkeit. Geschichte des operativen Denkens im deutschen Heer von Moltke d. Ä. bis Heusinger* (Paderborn, 2012)

——*Von Moltke bis Heusinger. Operatives Denken im deutschen Heer* (Paderborn, 2012).

Guderian, Heinz, *Erinnerungen eines Soldaten* (Heidelberg, 1951), published in English as *Panzer Leader* (New York, 1952).

Haffner, Sebastian, *Anmerkungen zu Hitler*, 26th ed. (Frankfurt am Main, 2006), published in English as *The Meaning of Hitler* (London, 1979).

Halder, Franz, *Hitler als Feldherr* (Munich, 1949), published in English as *Hitler as War Lord* (Putnam, 1950).

——*Kriegstagebuch. Tägliche Aufzeichnungen des Chefs des Generalstabes des Heeres 1939–1942*, ed. Hans-Adolf Jacobsen, 3 vols (Stuttgart, 1962–4), published in English as *War Diary 1939–1942* (Barnsley, 1989).

Hartmann, Christian, *Halder. Generalstabschef Hitlers 1938–1942*, 2nd ed. (Paderborn, 2010).

——and Sergej Slutsch, 'Franz Halder und die Kriegsvorbereitungen im Frühjahr 1939. Eine Ansprache des Generalstabschefs des Heeres', *VfZG* 45 (1997), pp. 467–95.

Hassell, Ulrich von, *Vom andern Deutschland. Aus den nachgelassenen Tagebüchern 1938–1944* (Zürich and Freiburg, 1946), published in English as *The Ulrich von Hassell Diaries, 1938–1944: The Story of the Forces against Hitler inside Germany* (Barnsley, 2010).

Helmdach, Erich, *Überfall? Der sowjetisch-deutsche Aufmarsch 1941* (Neckargemünd, 1976).

Henke, Josef, *England in Hitlers politischem Kalkül, 1935–1939* (Boppard, 1973).

Hensel, Jürgen, and Pia Nordblom (eds), *Hermann Rauschning. Materialien und Beiträge zu einer politischen Biographie* (Osnabrück, 2003).

Hesse, Kurt, 'Rohstoffwirtschaft in ihrer Bedeutung für die Kriegsführung', *Der deutsche Volkswirt* 11 (1937).

Hildebrand, Klaus, *Das vergangene Reich. Deutsche Außenpolitik von Bismarck bis Hitler* (Stuttgart, 1995).

——*Deutsche Außenpolitik 1933–1945. Kalkül oder Dogma?* (Stuttgart, 1971).

——*Bismarck und Russland: Aspekte der deutsch-russischen Beziehungen 1871–1890* (Friedrichsruh, 2003).

Hill, Leonidas E. (ed.), *Die Weizsacker-Papiere, 1933–1950* (Frankfurt, 1974).

Hilland, Paul, 'Autarkiemöglichkeiten der deutschen Metallwirtschaft. Zur Tagung der Gesellschaft Deutscher Metallhütten- und Bergleute in Berlin', *Die Deutsche Volkswirtschaft* 1/9 (1932), pp. 267–71.

Hillgruber, Andreas, *Bismarcks Außenpolitik* (Freiburg, 1972).

—— 'Die "Endlösung" und das deutsche Ostimperium als Kernstück des rassenideologischen Programms des Nationalsozialismus', *VfZG* 20 (1972), pp. 133–53.

——*Hitlers Strategie. Politik und Kriegfuhrung 1940–1941*, 2nd ed. (Munich, 1982).

——'Noch einmal: Hitlers Wendung gegen die Sowjetunion 1940. Nicht (Militar-) "Strategie oder Ideologie", sondern "Programm" und "Weltkriegsstrategie"', *Geschichte in Wissenschaft und Unterricht* 33 (1982), pp. 214–26.

—— 'Deutschland und Polen in der internationalen Politik 1933–1939', in Ernst Hinrichs (ed.), *Deutschland und Polen von der nationalsozialistischen Machtergreifung bis zum Ende des Zweiten Weltkrieges* (Braunschweig, 1986).

——'Das Russland-Bild der führenden deutschen Militärs vor Beginn des Angriffs auf die Sowjetunion', in Hans-Erich Volkmann (ed.), *Das Russlandbild im Dritten Reich* (Cologne, 1994), pp. 125–40.

Hoetzsch, Otto, *Die weltpolitische Krafteverteilung seit den Pariser Friedensschlüsse*, 6th ed. (Leipzig and Berlin, 1933).

Hoffmann, General Max, *Der Krieg der versäumten Gelegenheiten* (Munich, 1923), published in English as *The War of Lost Opportunities* (London, 1999).

Höhne, Heinz, *Canaris. Patriot im Zwielicht* (Munich, 1976), published in English as *Canaris: Hitler's Master Spy* (London, 1979).

Hubatsch, Walther (ed.), *Hitlers Weisungen für die Kriegführung, 1939–1945* (Munich, 1965), published in English as *Hitler's War Directives, 1939–1945* (Edinburgh, 2004).

Hürter, Johannes, *Hitlers Heerführer. Die deutschen Oberbefehlshaber im Krieg gegen die Sowjetunion, 1941/42* (Munich, 2006).

Immanuel, Friedrich, *Der große Zukunftskrieg – keine Phantasie!* (Berlin, 1932).

Irving, David, *Hitler's War* (London, 1977), published in German as *Hitlers Krieg. Die Siege 1939–1942* (Munich and Berlin, 1983).

Jabłonski, Marek, *Wobec zagrożenia wojna. Wojsko a gospodarka Drugiej Rzeczypospolitej w latach 1935–1939* (Warsaw, 2001).

Jackel, Eberhard, *Hitler's World View: A Blueprint for Power* (Cambridge, MA, 1972).

Jacobsen, Hans-Adolf, *Dokumente zur Vorgeschichte des Westfeldzuges 1939–1940* (Göttingen, 1956).

—— *Der Weg zur Teilung der Welt. Politik und Strategie 1939–1945* (Koblenz and Bonn, 1977).

——— (ed.), *Misstrauische Nachbarn. Deutsche Ostpolitik 1919/70. Dokumentation und Analyse* (Düsseldorf, 1970).

Jaworski, Rudolf, and Marian Wojciechowski (eds), *Deutsche und Polen zwischen den Kriegen. Minderheitenstatus und 'Volkstumskampf' im Grenzgebiet. Amtliche Berichterstattung aus beiden Ländern 1920–1939* (Munich, 1997).

Jedrzejewicz, Wacław (ed.), *Papers and Memoirs of Józef Lipski, Ambassador of Poland* (New York, 1968).

Kalisch, Johannes, 'Von der "Globallösung" zum "Fall Weiß". Die deutsch-polnischen Beziehungen 1938–39', in Dietrich Eichholtz and Kurt Pätzold (eds), *Der Weg in den Krieg* (Berlin, 1989), pp. 381–402.

Keller, Mechthild (ed.), *Russen und Russland aus deutscher Sicht. 19. Jahrhundert: Von der Jahrhundertwende bis zur Reichsgründung (1800–1871)* (Munich, 1991).

——— (ed.), *Russen und Russland aus deutscher Sicht. 19. / 20. Jahrhundert: Von der Bismarckzeit bis zum Ersten Weltkrieg* (Munich, 2000).

Kellerhoff, Sven Felix, 'War der Angriff auf die Sowjetunion ein Präventivschlag?', in Lars-Broder Keil and Sven Felix Kellerhoff, *Deutsche Legenden. Vom "Dolchstoß" und anderen Mythen der Geschichte*, 2nd ed. (Berlin, 2003), pp. 68–91.

Kershaw, Ian, *Hitler 1936–1945: Nemesis* (London, 2000), published in German as *Hitler. 1936–1945* (Stuttgart, 2000).

Klee, Karl, *Das Unternehmen 'Seelöwe'. Die geplante deutsche Landung in England 1940* (Göttingen, 1958).

Knoll, Roman, *Uwagi o polskiej polityce 1939* (Warsaw, 1939).

Koitz, Heinrich, *Männer um Pilsudski* (Breslau, 1934).

Kornat, Marek, *Polityka równowagi 1934–1939. Polska między Wschodem a Zachodem* (Krakow, 2007).

——— 'Sehenden Auges. Polens Außenpolitik vor dem Hitler-Stalin-Pakt', *Osteuropa* 59/7–8 (2009), pp. 47–74.

Kotze, Hildegard von (ed.), *Heeresadjutant bei Hitler 1938–1943. Aufzeichnungen des Majors Engel* (Stuttgart, 1974), published in English as *At the Heart of the Reich: The Secret Diary of Hitler's Army Adjutant* (London, 2005).

Krause, Helmut, *Marx und Engels und das zeitgenössische Russland* (Gießen, 1958).

Krausnick, Helmut, and Harold C. Deutsch (eds), *Helmuth Groscurth. Tagebücher eines Abwehroffiziers 1938–1940. Mit weiteren Dokumenten zur Militäropposition gegen Hitler* (Stuttgart, 1970).

Krebs, Gerhard, 'Japanische Schlichtungsbemuhungen in der deutsch-polnischen Krise 1938–39', *Japanstudien, Jahrbuch des Deutschen Instituts für Japanstudien* 2 (Munich, 1991), pp. 207–58.

——— *Japans Deutschlandpolitik 1935–1941*, 2 vols (Hamburg, 1984).

Krekeler, Norbert, *Revisionsanspruch und geheime Ostpolitik der Weimarer Republik. Die Subventionierung der deutschen Minderheit in Polen 1919–1933* (Stuttgart, 1973).

Krummacher, Friedrich Arnold, and Helmut Lange, *Krieg und Frieden. Geschichte der deutschsowjetischen Beziehungen* (Munich and Esslingen, 1970).

Laroche, J., *La Pologne de Pilsudski. Souvenirs d'une ambassade 1926–1935* (Paris, 1953).

Leverkuehn, Paul, *Der Geheime Nachrichtendienst der deutschen Wehrmacht im*

Kriege (Frankfurt, 1957), published in English as *German Military Intelligence* (London, 1954).

Loeber, Dietrich A. (ed.), *Diktierte Option. Die Umsiedlung der Deutsch-Balten aus Estland und Lettland 1939–1941. Dokumentation* (Neumünster, 1972).

Loessner, A., *Josef Piłsudski. Eine Lebensbeschreibung auf Grund seiner eigenen Schriften* (Leipzig, 1935).

Loßberg, Bernhard von, *Im Wehrmachtführungsstab. Bericht eines Generalstabsoffiziers*, 2nd ed. (Hamburg, 1950).

Łosswoski, Piotr, *Ultimatum polskie do Litwy 17 marca 1938 roku* (Warsaw, 2010).

Ludwig, Max, 'Deutsch-russische Zusammenarbeit', *Wehrtechnische Monatshefte* (September 1939), pp. 386 f.

Malaparte, Curzio, *Die Wolga entspringt in Europa* (Cologne, 1989), published in English as *The Volga Rises in Europe* (Edinburgh, 2000).

Manstein, Erich von, *Verlorene Siege* (Bonn, 1955), published in English as *Lost Victories: War Memoirs of Hitler's Most Brilliant General* (London, 1958).

Mark, Rudolf A. (ed.), *Vernichtung durch Hunger. Der Holodomor in der Ukraine und der UdSSR* (Berlin, 2004).

Martin, Bernd, 'Das "Dritte Reich" und die "Friedens"-Frage im Zweiten Weltkrieg', in Wolfgang Michalka (ed.), *Nationalsozialistische Außenpolitik* (Darmstadt, 1978), pp. 526–49.

Mayer, Klaus, 'Eine authentische Halder-Ansprache? Textkritische Anmerkungen zu einem Dokumentenfund im früheren Moskauer Sonderarchiv (Dokumentation)', *Militärgeschichtliche Mitteilungen* 58 (1999), pp. 471–528.

McDonough, Frank, *Hitler, Chamberlain and Appeasement* (Cambridge, 2002).

Meier-Welcker, Hans, *Seeckt* (Frankfurt am Main, 1967).

Meyer, Georg, *Adolf Heusinger. Dienst eines deutschen Soldaten 1915 bis 1964* (Hamburg, 2001).

Michalka, Wolfgang, 'Vom Antikominternpakt zum euro-asiatischen Kontinentalblock: Ribbentrops Alternativkonzeption zu Hitlers außenpolitischem "Programm"', in Michalka, Wolfgang (ed.), *Nationalsozialistische Außenpolitik* (Darmstadt, 1978), pp. 471–92.

Moritz, Verena, 'Information und Desinformation. Anmerkungen zur Rolle der "Österreichischen Legion" im Verhältnis zwischen Wien und Berlin 1933–1935', *Zeitgeschichte* 36 (2009), pp. 217–39.

Motyl, Alexander, 'Ukrainian nationalist political violence in inter-war Poland, 1921–1939', *East European Quarterly* 19 (1985), pp. 45–55.

Mühlen, Patrik von zur, *Zwischen Hakenkreuz und Sowjetstern* (Düsseldorf, 1971).

Müller, Klaus-Jürgen, *Das Heer und Hitler. Armee und nationalsozialistisches Regime 1933–1940* (Stuttgart, 1969).

——'Zu Vorgeschichte und Inhalt der Rede Himmlers vor der höheren Generalität am 13. Marz 1940 in Koblenz', *VfZG* 18 (1970), pp. 95–120.

——*Generaloberst Ludwig Beck. Eine Biographie* (Paderborn, 2008).

Müller, Norbert, *Das Amt Ausland / Abwehr im Oberkommando der Wehrmacht. Eine Dokumentation* (Koblenz, 2007).

Müller, Rolf-Dieter, *Das Tor zur Weltmacht. Die Bedeutung der Sowjetunion für die deutsche Wirtschafts- und Rüstungspolitik zwischen den Weltkriegen* (Boppard, 1984).

——'Kriegsrecht oder Willkür? Helmuth James Graf v. Moltke und die Auffassungen im Generalstab des Heeres über die Aufgaben der Militärverwaltung vor Beginn des Russlandkrieges', *Militärgeschichtliche Mitteilungen* 2 (1987), pp. 125–51.

——*Hitlers Ostkrieg und die deutsche Siedlungspolitik* (Frankfurt, 1991).

——*An der Seite der Wehrmacht. Hitlers ausländische Helfer beim Kreuzzug gegen den Bolschewismus 1941–1945* (Berlin, 2007), published in English as *The Unknown Eastern Front: The Wehrmacht and Hitler's Foreign Soldiers* (London, 2012).

——and Gerd R. Ueberschär, *Hitlers Krieg im Osten 1941–1945. Ein Forschungsbericht* (Darmstadt, 2000), published in English as *Hitler's War in the East 1941–1945: A Critical Reassessment* (Oxford, 1997).

Murray, Williamson, 'The German response to victory in Poland: A case study in professionalism', *Armed Forces and Society* 7 (1981), pp. 285–98.

Musial, Bogdan, *Kampfplatz Deutschland. Stalins Kriegspläne gegen den Westen* (Berlin, 2008).

Nakata, Jun, *Der Grenz- und Landesschutz in der Weimarer Republik 1918–1933. Die geheime Aufrüstung und die deutsche Gesellschaft* (Freiburg, 2002).

Niedermayer, Oskar Ritter von, 'Sowjetrussland. Ein wehrpolitisches Bild', *Militärwissenschaftliche Rundschau* 4 (1939), pp. 704–23.

Niedhart, Gottfried, 'Appeasement: Die britische Antwort auf die Krise des Weltreichs und des internationalen Systems vor dem Zweiten Weltkrieg', *Historische Zeitschrift* 226 (1978), pp. 67–88.

Oertzen, Friedrich Wilhelm von, *Marschall Pilsudski* (Berlin, 1935).

Oetting, Dirk W., *Kein Krieg wie im Westen. Wehrmacht und Sowjetarmee im Russlandkrieg 1941–1945* (Bielefeld and Bonn, 2009).

Pagel, Jürgen, *Polen und die Sowjetunion 1938–1939* (Stuttgart, 1992).

Pietrow-Ennker, Bianka (ed.), *Präventivkrieg? Der deutsche Angriff auf die Sowjetunion* (Frankfurt, 2000).

Piłsudski, Josef, *Erinnerungen und Dokumente* (Essen, 1935).

——*Gesetz und Ehre* (Jena, 1935).

Pryt, Karina, *Befohlene Freundschaft. Die deutsch-polnischen Kulturbeziehungen 1934–1939* (Osnabrück, 2010).

Ramonat, Wolfgang, *Der Völkerbund und die Freie Stadt Danzig 1920–1934* (Osnabrück, 1979).

Rauschning, Hermann, *Gespräche mit Hitler* (Zürich, 2005).

Reile, Oscar, *Geheime Front. Die deutsche Abwehr im Osten 1921–1945* (Munich, 1963).

Ringsdorf, Ulrich, 'Organisatorische Entwicklung und Aufgaben der Abteilung Fremde Heere Ost im Generalstab des Heeres', in Friedrich Kahlenberg (ed.), *Beiträge zum Archivwesen, zur Quellenkunde und zur Geschichte. Festschrift für Hans Booms* (Boppard, 1989), pp. 800–10.

Röhricht, Edgar, *Pflicht und Gewissen* (Stuttgart, 1965).

Roos, Hans, '"Präventivkriegspläne" Piłsudskis von 1933', *VfZG* 3 (1955), pp. 344–63.

——'Die militärpolitische Lage und Planung Polens gegenüber Deutschland 1939', *Wehrwissenschaftliche Rundschau* 7 (1957), pp. 181–202.

——*Polen und Europa* (Tubingen, 1957).

——*A History of Modern Poland* (London, 1966).

Schäfer, Kirstin A., *Werner von Blomberg – Hitlers erster Feldmarschall* (Paderborn, 2006).

Schaumburg-Lippe, Friedrich-Christian, Prince of, *Ein Porträt des Propagandaministers* (Wiesbaden, 1963).

Scheil, Stefan, *1940/41. Die Eskalation des Zweiten Weltkriegs* (Munich, 2005).

Schieder, Theodor, *Hermann Rauschnings 'Gespräche mit Hitler' als Geschichtsquelle* (Opladen, 1972).

Schmid, Michael, *Der 'Eiserne Kanzler' und die Generäle* (Paderborn, 2003).

Schmidt, Paul Otto, *Statist auf diplomatischer Bühne 1923–1945. Erlebnisse des Chefdolmetschers im Auswärtigen Amt mit den Staatsmännern Europas. Von Stresemann und Briand bis Hitler, Chamberlain und Molotow* (Bonn, 1949; new ed. Munich, 2005).

Schmidt, Rainer F., '"Appeasement oder Angriff"? Eine kritische Bestandsaufnahme der sog. "Präventivkriegsdebatte" über den 22. Juni 1941', in Jürgen Elvert and Michael Salewski (eds), *Historische Debatten und Kontroversen im 20. Jahrhundert. Jubiläumstagung der Ranke Gesellschaft in Essen, 2001* (Stuttgart, 2003), pp. 220–33.

Schmidt, Rainer F., *Die Außenpolitik des Dritten Reiches 1933–1939* (Stuttgart, 2002).

Schramm, Gottfried, 'Der Kurswechsel der deutschen Polenpolitik nach Hitlers Machtergreifung', in Roland G. Foerster (ed.), *'Unternehmen Barbarossa'. Zum historischen Ort der deutschsowjetischen Beziehungen von 1933 bis Herbst 1941* (Munich, 1993), pp. 23–34.

Schramm, Percy Ernst (ed.), *Kriegstagebuch des Oberkommandos der Wehrmacht (Wehrmachtführungsstab) 1940–1945. Geführt von Helmuth Greiner u. Percy Ernst Schramm. Bd. I: 1. August 1940 – 31. Dezember 1941. Zusammengestellt und erlautert von Hans-Adolf Jacobsen* (Frankfurt, 1965).

Schreiber, Gerhard, 'Zur Kontinuität des Groß- und Weltmachtstrebens der deutschen Marineführung (Dokumentation)', *MGM* 26 (1979), pp. 101–71.

Schwendemann, Heinrich, *Die wirtschaftliche Zusammenarbeit zwischen dem Deutschen Reich und der Sowjetunion von 1939 bis 1941: Alternative zu Hitlers Ostprogramm?* (Berlin, 1993).

Seeckt, Hans von, *Deutschland zwischen Ost und West* (Hamburg, 1933).

Seidt, Ulrich, *Berlin, Kabul, Moskau. Oskar Ritter von Niedermayer und Deutschlands Geopolitik* (Munich, 2003).

Seraphim, Hans-Günther (ed.), *Das politische Tagebuch Alfred Rosenbergs 1934/35 und 1939/40* (Munich, 1964).

——and Andreas Hillgruber, 'Hitlers Entschluss zum Angriff auf Russland (eine Entgegnung)', *VfZG* 2 (1954), pp. 240–9, with a conclusion by Gerhard L. Weinberg, pp. 249–54.

Sikorski, Ladislaus, *La Campagne Polono-Russe de 1920: Préface de M. le Maréchal Foch* (Paris, 1928).

Slutsch, Sergej, 'Stalins "Kriegsszenario 1939": Eine Rede, die es nie gab', *VfZG* 52 (2004), pp. 597–635.

Smith, Bradley F., 'Die Überlieferung der Hoßbach-Niederschrift im Lichte neuer Quellen', *VfZG* 38 (1990), pp. 329–36.

Sommer, Theo, *Deutschland und Japan zwischen den Mächten 1935–1940* (Tubingen, 1962).

Sozkow, Lew, *Sekrety Polskoi Politiki* (Moscow, 2009).

Stahel, David, *Operation Barbarossa and Germany's Defeat in the East* (Cambridge, 2009).

——*Kiev 1941: Hitler's Battle for Supremacy in the East* (Cambridge, 2013).

Stegemann, Bernd, 'Hitler's Ziele im ersten Kriegsjahr 1939–40', *Militärgeschichtliche Mitteilungen* 27 (1980), pp. 93–105.

Ströbinger, Rudolf, *Stalin enthauptet die Rote Armee. Der Fall Tuchatschewskij* (Stuttgart, 1990).

Szlanta, Piotr, 'Der Erste Weltkrieg von 1914 bis 1915 als identitätsstiftender Faktor für die modern polnische Nation', in Gerhard P. Groß (ed.), *Die vergessene Front. Der Osten 1914/15* (Paderborn, 2006), pp. 153–64.

Thomas, David, 'Foreign armies east and German Military Intelligence in Russia, 1941–45', *Journal of Contemporary History* 22/2 (1987), pp. 261–301.

Tobias, Fritz, 'Auch Fälschungen haben lange Beine. Des Senatspräsidenten Rauschnings "Gespräche mit Hitler"', in Karl Corino (ed.), *Gefälscht! Betrug in Politik, Literatur, Wissenschaft, Kunst und Musik* (Nördlingen, 1988), pp. 91–105.

Treue, Wilhelm (ed.), 'Hitlers Denkschrift zum Vierjahresplan', *VfZG* 3 (1955), pp. 184–210.

Trotha, Thilo von (ed.), *Alfred Rosenberg. Kampf um die Macht. Aufsätze von 1921-1932* (Munich, 1937).

Tschischwitz, Erich von, 'Der Kriegsplan unter vorwiegender Betrachtung des Landkrieges', *Militärwissenschaftliche Rundschau* 2 (1937).

Ueberschär, Gerd R., 'Hitlers Entschluss zum "Lebensraum"-Krieg im Osten', in Gerd R. Ueberschär and Wolfram Wette, *'Unternehmen Barbarossa'. Der deutsche Überfall auf die Sowjetunion 1941* (Paderborn, 1984), pp. 83–110.

Vogelsang, Thilo, 'Neue Dokumente zur Geschichte der Reichswehr 1930–1933', *VfZG* 2 (1954), pp. 397–436.

——'Hitlers Brief an Reichenau vom 4. Dezember 1932', *VfZG* 7 (1959), pp. 429–57.

Volkmann, Hans-Erich (ed.), *Das Russlandbild im Dritten Reich* (Cologne, 1994).

Wagner, Elisabeth (ed.), *Der Generalquartiermeister. Briefe und Tagebuchaufzeichnungen des Generalquartiermeisters des Heeres General der Artillerie Eduard Wagner* (Munich and Vienna, 1963).

Wagner, Gerhard, *Der polnisch-sowjetische Krieg* (Wiesbaden, 1979).

Warlimont, Walter, *Im Hauptquartier der deutschen Wehrmacht 1939–1945. Grundlagen, Formen, Gestalten* (Frankfurt am Main and Bonn, 1962), published in English as *Inside Hitler's Headquarters* (London, 1962).

Wegner, Bernd, 'Erschriebene Siege. Franz Halder, die "Historical Division" und die Rekonstruktion des Zweiten Weltkrieges im Geiste des deutschen Generalstabes', in Ernst Willi Hansen, Gerhard Schreiber and Bernd Wegner (eds), *Politischer Wandel, organisierte Gewalt und nationale Sicherheit. Beiträge zur neueren Geschichte Deutschlands und Frankreichs* (Munich, 1995), pp. 287–302.

Weinberg, Gerhard L., 'Der deutsche Entschluß zum Angriff auf die Sowjetunion', *VfZG* 1 (1953), pp. 301–18.

Weißbecker, Manfred, '"Wenn hier Deutsche wohnten…" Beharrung und Veränderung im Rußlandbild Hitlers und der NSDAP', in Hans-Erich Volkmann (ed.), *Das Russlandbild im Dritten Reich* (Cologne, 1994), pp. 9–54.

Weißbuch der polnischen Regierung, Die polnisch-deutschen und die polnisch-sowjetischen Beziehungen im Zeitraum von 1933 bis 1939 (Basel, 1940).

Wendt, Bernd-Jürgen, 'Danzig – Ein Bauer auf dem Schachbrett nationalsozialistischer Außenpolitik', in Manfred Funke (ed.), *Hitler, Deutschland und die Mächte* (Düsseldorf, 1976), pp. 774–94.

—— *Großdeutschland. Außenpolitik und Kriegsvorbereitung des Hitler-Regimes* (Munich, 1987).

Wette, Wolfram, *Die Wehrmacht. Feindbilder, Vernichtungskrieg, Legenden* (Frankfurt, 2002).

Winterbotham, Fred W., *The Ultra Secret* (London, 1974).

Wippermann, Wolfgang, *Die Deutschen und der Osten. Feindbild und Traumland* (Darmstadt, 2007).

Wirsching, Andreas, '"Man kann nur Boden germanisieren". Eine neue Quelle zu Hitlers Rede vor den Spitzen der Reichswehr am 3. Februar 1933', *VfZG* 49 (2001), pp. 517–50.

Wojciechowski, Marian, *Die polnisch-deutschen Beziehungen 1933–1938* (Leiden, 1971).

Wollstein, Günter, *Vom Weimarer Revisionismus zu Hitler* (Bonn, 1973).

—— 'Hitlers gescheitertes Projekt einer Juniorpartnerschaft Polens', *Universitas* 38 (1983), pp. 525–32.

Zeidler, Manfred, *Reichswehr und Rote Armee 1920–1933. Wege und Stationen einer ungewöhnlichen Zusammenarbeit* (Munich, 1994).

Żerko, Stanisław, *Stosunki polsko-niemieckie 1938–1939* (Poznan, 1998).

Zgorniak, Marian, *Europa am Abgrund 1938* (Berlin, 2002).

Index

Because of the frequency of occurrence, the terms 'Germany', 'Soviet Union', 'USSR', 'Russia' and 'Adolf Hitler' have not been included in the index. Bold page ranges signify a full discussion on the relevant subject. Italic page references signify illustrations.

The principal German lines of attack on the Eastern Front, 1941–2
Viipuri (Vyborg)
Leningrad
LENINGRAD F
HELSINKI
VOLKHOV FR
Volkhov
Narva
Tallinn
STOCKHOLM
NORTHWESTE
Demyansk
Pärnu
ARMY GROUP NORTH
Pskov
KALININ F
Riga
Front line 17 November 1942
Daugava
Nevel
BALTIC SEA
Klaipėda (Memel)
Front line 22 June 1941
Vitebsk
Dnieper
Kaunas
Vilnius
Königsburg (Kaliningrad)
18th Army
16th Army
4th Panzer Group
Mogilev
Danzig (Gdańsk)
9th Army
Neman (Memel)
Minsk
3rd Panzer Group
Berezina
ARMY GROUP NORTH
Szczecin
Białystok
Gomel
4th Army
2nd Panzer Group
Brest-Litovsk
Pripyat
BERLIN
Poznań
WARSAW
Western Bug
ARMY GROUP CENTRE
Lublin
Kiev
Wrocław
6th Army
Oder
1st Panzer Group
Zhytomyr
Vistula
Lviv
PRAGUE
17th Army
ARMY GROUP SOUTH
Vinnytsia
Uman
Dniester
Front line 22 June 1941
Hungarian Brigades
Southern Bug
Prut
Romanian Corps
Danube
Bratislava
VIENNA
11th Army
BUDAPEST
Iaşi (Jassy)
Drava
Romanian 3rd Army
ZAGREB
Romanian 4th Army
Ploieşti
Map source: MGFA (Militärgeschichtliche Forschungsamt) 04833-13; MGFA 4849-01; MGFA 04851-01.